Dear Self:
A Year in the Life of a Welfare Mother

by
Richelene Mitchell

Foreword by
Imam Zaid Shakir

Introduction by
Melanie Mitchell

Copyright © 2007 NID Publishers.

NID Publishers Books may be purchased for educational, business, or sales promotional use. For information please write: Special Markets Department, NID Publishers, P.O. Box 657, Hayward, CA 94543-0657

Manufacturing by BookMasters, Inc.

Book design by Susanah I. Pittam

Production management by Monteil S. Shakir

Library of Congress Cataloging-in-Publication Data

Mitchell, Richelene, 1933–1975

Dear Self: A Year in the Life of a Welfare Mother: sheds an informing and penetrating light on race relations, poverty, mothering, gender relations, and many other pertinent issues.

ISBN: 978-0-9792281-0-0

1. Sociology: family and relationships   2. African American Studies: race relations   3. Gender Studies: marriage and divorce

LCCN: 2007920385

NID Publishers, P.O. Box 657, Hayward, CA 94543-0657
www.nidpublishers.com

852-8322

Dedicated to
The Eternal Black Mother

I would hurl words into this darkness and wait for an echo, and if an echo sounded, no matter how faintly, I would send other words to tell, to march, to fight, to create a sense of the hunger for life that gnaws in us all, to keep alive in our hearts a sense of the inexpressibly human.

Richard Wright
Black Boy

TABLE OF CONTENTS

FOREWORD

Much has been written about the "underclass" of this country, from the pious yet irreverent pontification of pundits who decry the insolence, sloth, and general lack of initiative working to create that underclass, in their view, to the well-meaning but generally misguided opinions of an array of voices ranging from white liberals to black nationalists and leftist revolutionaries. The remarkable nature of the pages you are about to read lies in the fact that they are written by a member of that underclass, articulated by a voice uniquely qualified to speak on the subject. This is noteworthy, for rarely do we read anything intelligible and deep about the poor by the poor.

The fact that Richelene Mitchell, who penned these powerful letters, was a member of the underclass is not unique. Many share what would be viewed by some as that dubious distinction. However, her broad reading, keen intellect, and poetic sensitivity gave her the ability to write about the life of the urban poor in a way that reveals sociological, psychological, cultural, political, and religious insights rarely revealed by even the most informed outside observers. She is able to combine the deep insight of an insider with the intellectual acumen of a highly educated outsider. Herein lies the source of the power and depth of these pages.

From a life that was shaped by the full array of forces providing the context for the African American Diaspora, she was able to convey the joy, pain, hope, and despair that has characterized the black experience in America. Born to a Georgia sharecropper and having grown up in the heart of the Cotton Belt, she would journey to Philadelphia to attend high school while living under the care of relatives who were beginning to experience the upward mobility witnessed by some members of a nascent black urban middle class. Denied by poverty what surely would have been a stellar college career, she married and, through a series of unhappy circumstances, ended up in a sprawling public housing project in New Britian, Connecticut, on welfare, with seven children to prepare for adulthood. It was there that she decided to exercise her deep literary yearning by writing a series of letters to herself. Entitled *Dear Self,* those letters would eventually chronicle an entire year of her life, hence, the title we have chosen for this publication, *Dear Self: A Year in the Life of a Welfare Mother.*

As I read through these letters, articles, essays, and poems, I was struck by her struggle to maintain her humanity in the face of crushing realities that begged the pessimistic cynicism she frequently exhibits. Sometimes the passages she pens are lively and lengthy. Sometimes they are cold, short, and blunt. As yet another hard year of struggling with the humiliation of welfare unfolds, as the burden of another year of shattered dreams and unfulfilled promises grinds on, the tone of her writings gradually becomes increasingly dominated by doubt, one could even say by despair. The letters finally come to an abrupt end. The exhaustion of the writer is reflected in the drying up of the pen's once prolific yield. The descent is swift, the ending is not happy.

One of the most salient features of these letters is the deep insight they shed on the nature of race relations in America. Our mother was no racist. However, she knew what oppression was, and she identified the source of her oppression, to a large extent, as an insidious form of racism buttressed on the reality of white supremacy. For many, her insights in this regard will prove difficult to bear. However, she is not writing in a vacuum; she is writing on the basis of her experience living in what Malcolm X referred to as the "armpit" of America. As opposed to shrinking from what she has to say in that regard, the reader should acknowledge it for what it is. For only by acknowledging the racism that has plagued and continues to plague our society will we begin to be able to transcend it.

One would hope that this journal of a poor woman's year of struggle would end on a happy note. One would hope that the public housing projects would bring forth the positive social benefits envisioned by their architects. However, such an ending would be unfitting. It would be unfitting because the ravages of the Vietnam War, the initial salvos in the war on drugs in the black community, and a wide array of other factors make the devastating hopelessness chronicled in the closing page of this journal a harbinger of things to come for the black urban poor in America.

The male-headed domiciles that once formed a majority of all households found in the black community would become a staggering minority. The waves of drugs—heroin, angel dust, and finally crack—that would wreak havoc on the poorest communities was just beginning. The chains, knives, and clubs that were the weapons of choice in intensifying cycles of gang violence would be replaced by handguns and assault rifles.

Perhaps the most devastating loss in the African American community would be that of the strong black mother, what our mother termed the "Eternal Black Mother." In that sense, she was part of what was possibly the beginning of the end of a long line of great, strong, selfless African American mothers. Regardless of her personal struggles, she would find the energy, love, and devotion to sacrifice for her children. She did not smoke, she used no drugs, she never brought alcohol into the home, and on only rare occasions did she take what she called a social drink. What little money she could muster up she would spend on us before indulging herself. She was content with finding her joy in little things that required little or no expenditure.

As our country moves deeper into this new century, the prospects are not good for the urban poor. Drugs and violence ravage our poorer neighborhoods. Gentrification presents another source of dislocation, destruction, and dysfunction in those communities. The schools are failing, political disenfranchisement by various means is a menacing reality, and the prisons are filling up with unprecedented numbers of largely young men, drawn primarily from the ranks of the underclass.

The pages before you offer no concrete solutions to these problems. They do, however, offer something that is integral to beginning to think meaningfully about a solution, namely, understanding. I am absolutely confident that no one will read our mother's words and go away without a greatly enhanced understanding of the lives and struggles of the urban poor. If that is indeed the case, she did not pen these words in vain, and a new reality for poor folks in America has shined its dawning rays on a better world.

Imam Zaid Shakir
November 16, 2006

INTRODUCTION

I was raised in a loving household, the middle child of seven wide-eyed, carefree children. I shared with my siblings the unflinching devotion of a beautiful woman we would know in our formative years as "Ma." Ma was all we had, forced into single parenthood after ten years of a migratory, turbulent marriage. We occasionally visited our father, however disconsolate in his long-distanced separation from his family, yet our mother was the ever-present force who would pray to her God that we grow up to be productive human beings.

We lost our mother just a few months into her forty-first year of existence. While other parents would soon enjoy the freedom of an empty nest, our mother, after years of dejection and inexorable struggle, would never experience the liberating autonomy found in being responsible for only her own life. Likewise, we, as thriving adults, would never have with her a mutual camaraderie or share with her in the jubilant laughter of a repeated joke or tall tale. Surely Ma recognized that she would soon meet her Lord, for only a year before she died, perhaps by way of a premonition, she willed to us in *Dear Self* a revealing glimpse into her dynamic life. Through *Dear Self* and other writings, we are better able to understand our mother's personal battles with epilepsy and depression, as well as racism and the exclusionary tactics hidden within the social welfare systems that deceptively coerced her and other men and women of color into its shameful embrace during the tumult of the midsixties, seventies, and beyond.

Conversely, we can take great pride in our mother's numerous triumphs over discrimination and gender inequalities, as noted in her inclusion in the Daughters of the Revolution and Friends of the Library, along with her

selfless involvement with the NAACP, EOC, and numerous black-owned small businesses within the community.
The beloved poet and lecturer Nikki Giovanni believed, "I
really don't think life is only about the I-could-have-beens.
Life is only about the I-tried-to-dos. I don't mind the failures but I can't imagine that I'd forgive myself if I didn't
try." As revealed in *Dear Self*, Richelene Mitchell believed
you could escape the clutches of poverty, if but for a moment, to be one that tried to do.

Like many women of her generation, Ma delighted in
her womanliness, though she wasn't engendered only to
tasks that would define her femininity. She could lift a bed
with one hand, and spank the hiding child beneath it with
the other. She could pound a hammer and nail as well as
strike a resolute accord between irate police officers and
the few wayward teens in our midst that "the pigs" were
hell-bent on imprisoning. She stood tall for justice, cow-
ering to no man, woman, or situation; however, she would
often reflect on her own cynicisms and biases with prayers
to God for forgiveness for her imperfections. She was often
overheard crying out to God to give her strength.

She loved sports, as exhibited by her flair for softball,
often slugging away with the neighborhood children in
the dusty field behind our housing unit. Our mother was
an avid walker, holding her head high and proud as she
gracefully sauntered up and down the city walkways. Ever
conscious of her waistline, she walked not only out of necessity but also to control her weight.

A gifted seamstress, she was envied by many a woman
and was relentlessly sought out for the stylish designs she
created and wore daily. I know now that she sewed not
because she enjoyed it (though she did for a while), but because she could not otherwise afford to dress as fashion-
ably as she did if she had to buy the same outfits.

Some of my fondest memories are of the Thanksgiving and Christmas feasts Ma would so lovingly prepare, where the menu would consist in part of pans of golden cornbread, dressing, turkey and gravy, and sweet potato pie. All meals in Richelene's kitchen were memorable, albeit routine, beginning with a daily breakfast of grits and eggs, old-fashioned oatmeal or generous bowls of corn flakes, bananas, and powdered milk. Meals, no matter how scant, were all gratefully eaten by her hungry brood over our wobbly, cracking, yellow Formica kitchen table.

I am confident in my declaration and speak for my siblings when I lament, "Oh how we loved our mother." Not only was she our caretaker and exemplar, but other children of our close-knit community also revered Mrs. Mitchell. Not a day went by that someone from another family was not welcomed into our home. Like many of the other households in our housing project, ours had an open-door policy. If you came by, you came in. If you hadn't eaten, you'd be fed. There were always enough chicken necks, biscuits, and gravy. I recall Mom, unbeknownst to the recipient and many times to us, readily giving up her portion so another could eat. Perhaps those were the nights she'd suffer grand mal seizures, waking in the morning with an unshakeable lethargy that she would matter-of-factly blame on insomnia for fear we would learn of her affliction. Rarely did our mother give us any indication that she was anything other than a little tired or a little bothered.

We came of age in an era when you didn't question adults. Certainly, we were too young or too naive to ask the purpose of the prescription medications kept stored in the kitchen cabinet. We knew only of her bad nerves. Left only to his or her devices, when does a child see a parent as anything other than a nurturing beacon of health and vitality? Alice Childress, the early nineteenth-century essayist, wrote, "Like snowflakes, the human pattern is never cast twice. We are uncommonly and marvelously intricate in thought and action, our problems are most complex and, too often, silently borne." Our mother, like many before her, while afflicted by illness, poverty, and despair, bore the weight of a generation enslaved to injustices, imperceptible to many, but to the Almighty, revealed and made perfect in a pan of buttermilk biscuits.

Personally, memories of my mother's uncompromising character and tireless spirit are framed in my mind like a valuable Charles Bibb pen and ink drawing. Her adamant prayer that her children become productive members of society compels me to strive to do more than I think I am capable of. Her fervor is in my spirit; her convictions, at home in my soul. The hymns sung in honor of her Lord are the same melodies I now hum with hands flung to the heavens in praise. Be it revealed that my evocative ramblings are often confused with those of an unsuspecting fifteen-year-old who never dreamt that she would one day become a motherless woman raising grandmotherless children. My offspring have only my oft-guarded recollections of their Grandma, bridging them to a little-known woman revealed only in spirit, albeit well enough for them to be forever influenced by her very essence that serves as the template of every helix in their DNA. We are irrefutably linked, they to me, me to my siblings, and generations yet revealed to the woman who is and will forever live between the lines in her numerous editorials and essays. In *Dear Self*, she delivers unapologetic social commentary and offers bold reminders that civic responsibility, community involvement, and family allegiance are ongoing challenges for all, especially in today's egoistic environment. As Marian Wright Edelman articulated, "We must serve consciously as caring role models, emphasizing the ethic of service, not consumption."

Consequently, our collective purpose, as my mother espoused in *Dear Self*, is to become productive human beings contributing to society in a way that pays homage to those who came before us, leaving for those that follow a better world to inhabit. George Washington Carver supported the ideal that no individual should come into the world and then exit without leaving behind him distinct and legitimate reasons for having passed through it.

Will we pass through this life unblemished due to our inaction, or will we bear that mighty crown of victory, however imposing, our scars signifying our participation in the struggle for justice and equality? Will we distinguish ourselves with contributions that are good and just, however small, and serve as an instrument for change? Whatever the charge, be forever blessed. Our mother was not unblemished as she worked in her small ways to fight for justice. In those small ways and through the children she sacrificed so selflessly to raise, she has made a change in the world. May she and the change she wrought be forever blessed.

Melanie Mitchell Calloway
September 3, 2006

12–19–72

Dear Self,

For years I've been writing letters, letters, and letters. I, of the itchy fingers, remember the ones I wrote to old boyfriends when I couldn't find the right words or courage to tell them in person that I no longer wanted to date them. And I remember the ones I wrote when I changed my mind and decided I wanted to date them after all. I remember the one I wrote when a love affair was over and I was left hurting, and the ones I wrote to relatives and friends spouting "profound" thoughts and insights that bubbled from my overflowing well of wisdom. And, agonies of agonies, I remember all the outpourings to the editors of the *Hartford Courant* and the *New Britain Herald* and how I prayed they wouldn't publish them, but most of the time they did, and I was embarrassed for days. Letters, letters, letters! I am always striving to enlighten, and to make people a little more understanding and loving. Trying to save the world! Suddenly it dawned on me that the world would most definitely remain the same, and I, least of all, would never be the one to change it. After all, who am I but a poor miserable welfare recipient who can't even pay my own way through life? Just a weary little traveler who is groping in darkness but who sometimes feels I see small glimpses of truth and light that I am compelled to share with others. Who gave me a mandate to tell people how to live, how to love?

So, self, in December of 1972, after a letter to the editor pleading for mankind to "strengthen the ties that bind us all instead at further dividing ourselves," I vowed that henceforth when my fingers began itching to write a letter, I would simply sit down and write a letter to myself, and this is it. This is my first letter to you, self. I had hoped the writer's itch wouldn't afflict me before the first of the year. New Year's Day seems an appropriate time to begin any new thing. But a chronic case of "letter-writis" like mine is hard to arrest, and so I must write.

Self, the year 1972 was pretty rocky, yet on second thought it was no rockier than most of the preceding years. I feel it was even better than some previous years, in some respects.

SUMMARY OF 1972

I'm still on welfare, I'm still struggling to stretch a few dollars that are screaming for mercy; I'm still calling forth every bit of ingenuity I possess to feed and clothe and cope with six growing children, and more and more beginning to indulge myself in self-pity. In 1972 I exchanged chicken-pox, measles, and mumps for broken ankles, broken feet, broken teeth, lacerated eyes—if I have to look at one more cast or crutch, I will scream, and scream, and scream. I'm still hoping to meet that big, beautiful black man, a tower of strength I can lean on; sometimes meeting everything but . . .

So many truths and realities were brought into clear focus this year that it almost frightens me. So many years I thought I had faith in God, faith in tomorrow. Now, so suddenly, tomorrow is here. And the truth seems to be that my faith in God is gone, or fast deteriorating, like grains of sand ebbing into the sea. Like doubting Thomas, my heart cries, "Show me a miracle, Lord!"

One truth that was painfully brought home to me this year is the transience of life. My good and gentle little brother, Ba Boo, fell victim to life's transience this year. The circle is broken. Did I say little brother, self? Actually he was ten years older than me. But I feel justified calling him my "little" brother. For in certain points of experience and fights with life, I feel that I, my parent's youngest daughter, am older than any of my eleven brothers and sisters. I'm the seventh daughter. I wonder if seventh daughters really are witches, as I read somewhere. If so, I like to think I'm a good witch. Anyway, Ba Boo is gone.

Why is it so often that those who are good and pure and loving die in the flowering of their days, while cantankerous old "meanies" seem to just keep right on rolling, year after year, like Old Man River? It still hurts when I think of gentle little Ba Boo lying there in his casket. He wore a blue suit, and the hint of a smile seemed to play about his mouth, but he was dead. He was so still, so cold, so very, very dead. And why couldn't I stop the tears from flowing and the hurt from hurting as I gazed on that body that was so recently alive, warm, vital, and mobile? Wouldn't it have made more sense for me to weep for him while he was still trapped in this vale of tears? Shouldn't I be rejoicing that now he is free? And I, I'm still bound by life, by welfare, by my struggles to survive—by the right to deliver six little lives safely to the shores of adulthood. Perhaps, unconsciously, the tears shed were for me and for the legions of others who are not free.

Dear God, how I wish I still had the faith of my childhood! How I wish I could once more run through freshly ploughed fields, free and unbound, reveling in the feel of the good earth, moist and fresh under my feet. How I wish I could roam again through the woods of Georgia, smelling sweet bubbles, just budding, and honeysuckle. Then it seemed the God my parents believed in so steadfastly was so close I could almost reach out and touch him. I could almost feel his hand holding mine as I raced over green grass, through the pasture, trying to outrun and catch a rabbit with my bare hands. But I never caught the rabbit. It was always just one step ahead of me.

We were poor, self. God, we were poor! But we were so well-insulated in our little cocoon of innocence and ignorance of the cruel realities of life that we were happy. Just to chase butterflies on a sun-splashed day; to splash in the creek in "Captain Terrell's" pasture, to sit on the porch in the twilight hours and listen to Ma and Dad sing, this was the stuff that happiness was made of.

> Savior! Savior! Hear my humble cry,
> While on others thou art calling,
> Do not pass me by!

Ma and Dad sang and sang, and as we jumped off the porch to catch the bugs that were beginning to decorate the darkness with brief flickers of light, we didn't stop to wonder why Ma and Dad sang so fervently or why there were tears in their voices. How could we know that they knew the Savior seemed to be calling only on the white folks and passing out blessings to them while he was passing us by? And yet they trusted Him. One day he would hear their humble cry and deliver them. Yes, self, life was pure and uncontaminated then. We were close to nature; close to God.

Now I find myself a little lost and envying those who still hold dear and honestly cherish the belief that the dead are merely sleeping and the soul is alive and well with God. It saddens me that life has conditioned me to be a freethinker and brought me almost to the brink of agnosticism. Dear God, help my unbelief! I do so want to believe my dear brother's soul or spirit is happy somewhere, free from all the cares and burdens he bore so gently here. Oh well, he is gone. "Dust thou art to dust returneth," so said the sage. Good fruit is harvested in the Fall. Ba Boo went home at harvest time.

I know I've rambled in this letter, self. But that's the way I feel today—like rambling among the joys and pains of yesterday, but in a few minutes I'm going for a job interview. I have no real hopes of getting it, but after seven years on welfare, I'm moving on to something better in 1973-someway, somehow. It sounds terribly pessimistic to say I have no real hopes of landing this job, doesn't it? That's a defeatist attitude, you say? Well that's what I am now, a defeatist and a pessimist. But this is a contradiction, isn't it? I just said I'm moving on to something better in 1973, but that's what I am, a bundle of contradictions.

My thirty-ninth birthday overtook me in November. As I said before, tomorrow is here. Forty is grabbing at me greedily, and when forty gets a hold of you, you're heading for the incline. But somebody said life begins at forty. So I think I'll make it a beginning instead of an ending. How's that for optimism, self'?

Until later,
Richelene

7:30 P.M.

LATER: Interview accomplished. Mr. X, who interviewed me, was the usual smiling polished personnel manager. He was very courteous, efficient, and charming. No, he didn't say the job was already promised to one of the four other applicants who interviewed yesterday. He said, "I'll call the two or three applicants who impressed me most favorably within a week or so and give them a typing test." This is the first time I ever applied for a job and the interviewer filled out my application for me.

Sometimes the incongruities of life are just too much, self. After suffering what I know was a gracious rebuff in my job-hunting efforts, on reaching home, I called a doctor's office for an appointment. I've been plagued by an excruciating backache and swollen feet for several weeks. The doctor's receptionist sweetly informed me they don't take welfare patients. What are you going to do? Those doctors who refuse state patients just might have a good point: Maybe we should all just drop dead and solve a multitude of problems.

Truth and realities! I suppose it was only fitting that the year should bow out by bringing home a few more to me. I'm going to bed now. I will write again when the spirit moves me. Maybe the old hand will begin to itch again on New Year's Day and I'll present you with a conglomeration of resolutions.

Good night self,
Richelene

12–23–72

Dear Self,

I was reflecting on the struggle to raise seven children. Childbearing is a fate that usually befalls the hapless female. However, due to the female being put out of action or feigning such a state in order to escape to the hospital to rest up for the next attack, this sorry lot may befall the usually exempt male for short periods of time (Oh happy day)!

Thus, he too would find this guide to survival informative. It might save his life, his sanity, or both. First on the agenda is a strong defense. The best being to self-hypnotize so that the continuous din does not really penetrate the brain but crashes against the skull and bounces back, hopefully to knock one of the wilds out temporarily. Since this is highly unlikely due to the toughness of their hides and the hardness of their heads, simply pray that you will be able to withstand it.

Did you ever slide down the hallway on a skateboard at 2 A.M. as you sleepily groped your way to the baby's room? It may give you a scare, but it sure gets you there a lot faster. Since the end justifies the means (however unintentionally), don't beat the war drums. But be on your guard at all times, from the time you search every nook and cranny of the house looking for lost shoes in the morning and finally shove them out the door until they converge back on you in the afternoon.

You may slip into a feeling of false security after the departure of the school-age wilds. But never underestimate the innocent-eyed preschoolers. They too are capable of dastardly deeds. For instance, I often hear my four-year-old cheerily and tunefully singing his version of the Jackson Five's hit song "I'll Be There." He says, "I'll be bare, I'll be bare." He sings with gusto, "Just call my name, I'll be bare!"

Two out of three times, he is too bare, that is. Having mastered the art of dressing and undressing, but preferring the art of undress, very often I find him parading around in his little brown birthday suit. Encountering this bare situation many times a day and gradually growing more disoriented, I find myself walking around singing happily, "I'll be bare, I'll be bare . . ." Anybody like to ogle at midriff bulge and stretch marks???

If you should have a little wild of this persuasion, tune him out, tune him out! Those preschoolers can really work on your mental processes, it's literally psychological warfare. Between alternating periods of howling for the sheer pleasure of seeing you disintegrate before their eyes and fighting because they like the way you referee, they look at you with wide-eyed innocence.

So even though you may hate yourself for applying a few well-placed wallops on the end of their anatomy for best effect, by all means do it! This tranquilizes them enough to send them off to the Land of Nod. Thus, you can regroup your nerves enough to withstand the onslaught from the school-age wilds, who always come back much too soon.

The wise old sage said, "Spare the rod and spoil the child." I spare the rod, not to spoil the child, but because the minute I reach for the rod, that's the last I see of the child. I only see legs flying in all directions. By this time, their nefarious warfare has weakened me to the point that I don't have the strength to drag little wilds from underneath beds or out of the oven or any other opening large enough for a small body to squirm into and hide. If you should ever find yourself in this humiliating predicament, instead of going on a wild hunt or child hunt, your best strategy is to start laughing—however hysterically. And don't ever try to rest among the wilds. The littlest ones will swoop down on you and try to drown you in "drooly" kisses and smother you with hugs. This is under the pretext of loving you.

When this happens to me, I start ironing. Trying to rest among the wilds is a fate worse than ironing. You may try this also. As all things do eventually pass, the weary, wary day finally ends. Then we go into the Battle of the Baths. "But, Ma, I bathed yesterday! Make her go first! I'm not even dirty, etc. etc." Since No.7 has usually bared his all anyway, he usually does the honor of going first.

After the Battle of the Baths has been fought and won, I venture into the bathroom. A soothing bath should calm my jangled nerves. As I'm about to open the door, I notice a trickle of water beneath it. Aha! Another trap! They have covered the floor with nice, soapy water, hoping I would slip and be done in! Reaching just inside the door into the dirty clothes hamper, I spread a "gory" pathway of clothes, and thus I thwart their last effort of the day to destroy me.

I trust my methods of doing battle with the wilds will prove helpful to others so beleaguered, regardless of race, creed, or color. Thus far, I have survived. If the wilds don't get me, I pray that the ecologists won't. Admittedly, I may have caused the population explosion.

Nevertheless, each night as they lie sleeping, peacefully and angelic, I kiss each surprisingly human face.

They just might turn out to be civilized human beings after all. Who knows, but that one or more might grow up to enrich humanity in some way. Perhaps there is a scientist here or a doctor there. Barring that, No.7 would make a wonderful artist's model. For he has no compunction about being "bare."

At any rate, I've learned to be thankful for small blessings (though I do sometimes wish I hadn't got so many of them). So at night, I retreat to my room and thank God for the simple joy they've taught me to appreciate so well, blessed quietness. Another day's journey, and I'm so glad!

STILL LATER: A very touching and inspiring thing happened last night. Donna's little Kenny was sick with a temperature of 105. So she took him to the emergency room To her surprise thcy have a black resident doctor there now, and he took care of Kenny. She was quite taken with his manner. She said I should meet him. Ha! Ha! Ha!

Anyway later last night he called, because Donna brought Kenny home before they could check to see if his temperature was down, and he was concerned. Now, I ask you, self, isn't that beautiful? Considering all the coldness and indifference we experience at the hands of the medical profession, except for rare cases, what a refreshing change!

I can't help but think how much the emotional quality of our health, if nothing else, could be improved if we had more caring concerned black and minority doctors to turn to. Oh sure, for years we blacks have said: "I don't want nobody's black doctor. They don't know what they are doing." God forgive me, I've said it in the past myself.

Now that growth, maturity, and awareness have encompassed me, like many other blacks, I'd much prefer a black or minority doctor. Since many of our ills are psychological in origin anyway, we minorities would probably get more psychological uplift from "our own." And just that uplift would be conducive to better health and well-being. My pediatrician is Puerto Rican, and I love that man. Not just because my family was turned down by a Jewish doctor, because of personality clashes, he said. I say it was because he didn't want this big hunk of welfare junk. He already had as much as he could stomach. I just like Dr. Enriquez's unhurried, quiet, gentle, and friendly way. He makes you feel like people.

Jeffrey says he's going to be a doctor. I hope and pray this is a real calling, and not just something I've planted in his mind selfishly. But I admit I'm encouraging him in that direction. I hope he'll be a neurologist (for obvious reasons) or a neurosurgeon, but whatever branch of medicine he chooses, if he is committed, humanity will be the better off.

Here is another interesting tidbit from today's paper:

> Scorpio can be sensuous and these persons often have strong appetites for food and love. Scorpio is secretive and, in 1973, will break from past patterns and emerge in a role featuring unique self-expression. Scorpio can build from past ruins, these individuals are possessive but proud when protégés succeed on their own. Natives of this Zodiacal sign are filled with contradictions but there is something basically warm, and loving in their natures.

Very interesting indeed . . .

Until later,
Richelene

P.S. I had a little chat with _____ this morning. Her daughter was falsely arrested for shoplifting a couple of months ago. They found the girls who really committed the act, but were giving _____ a hard time as she tried to clear her daughter's name and get a retraction published in the paper. Memorial Day, two Caucasian boys were wrongly arrested for some minor incident and two or three days later, a retraction was published in the paper. This is another double standard of justice. Why do I even bother to get upset and continue to harp on these transgressions against us? I know, and everyone else knows, this is routine treatment for us, but my sense of justice and fairness is outraged anew over each fresh incident, and I get angry. Why, why, why does one's racial label accord one people one standard of justice and another people a different one? Why, why, why? Is it ever to be so?

_____ 's son wrote a letter to the editor, which she let me read to see if it sounded all right. It did, indeed, sound all right, especially for the oppressor's ears. It sounded all right for a black person who wishes to express indignation or anger in a subdued manner that will not offend "delicate white ears" or arouse hostility in the "peaceful" hearts of good white folks. To each his own, as in all things. But, self, if I were in her place, this is the letter I would have written:

Dear Editor,
Once again it has been proven that America has two standards of justice: one for whites, one for blacks. One hundred and nine years after black people were set free by proclamation, white America still seeks to keep them in bondage—not with physical chains, but with chains of indifference and injustice. Now, instead of the slave masters wielding whips, we have the police wielding guns

and the powers-that-be wielding unfair and unjust
authority over the masses of blacks. We are still not free.

Recently my teenage daughter was subjected to 1973's
version of liberty and justice . . .

Why continue? Of course _____ can't speak up this
way. Her husband has a good job, and it wouldn't be good
for him to arouse hostility in his boss. I dare to speak out
as the spirit moves me because I have nothing, thus nothing to lose. When one has no world and no ties that bind
one to tradition or conformity, one is freer. So what if I
make some folks angry? If I lose my welfare benefits, I'll
either make it somehow or I won't. If I lose my life, I'll
have only true freedom to gain. So any way you look at it
I have nothing to lose. I've never striven for popularity or
friendship in this world. If I have a few real friends, I'm
grateful. And the others can't really hurt me no matter
how they try. I truly believe that all things work for good,
for those that are right in their hearts.

Good night,
Richelene

1–1–73

Dear Self,

Here I am again. January 1, 1973. It's a new year, a new
beginning. A grand new chance for all of us to slough off
all the old prides and prejudices that made us less than
what we ought to be or would like to be and make at least
small beginnings toward being better human beings.

Would you believe that, since I wrote you last, I never
thought I'd see this day? I was so terribly sick all weekend
that I was sure that 1972 was determined to make its own

last dying gasps one with mine. No kidding! I was almost afraid to go to sleep, even if the pain in my body had permitted sleep, before 12 last night—so certain was I that I would never awake. And so I saw the New Year in. Miracle of miracles, I feel much better today. Throat still sore; glands in the neck and groin still swollen and painful; a few dull pains still in my back; but the excruciating pain is gone. This is a good beginning for the New Year. One thing is for certain, though, I'll never go through such agony again without seeing somebody's doctor. One reason that I always hesitate to go to the emergency room at the hospital is that they always treat you so "pooh pooh" when they finally get around to seeing you until you end up feeling foolish for coming and wish you'd just stayed at home and fought it out.

In a way it was probably just as well that I was too physically ill to be depressed over spending New Year's Eve alone. Holidays are always so lonely when you have no one special to spend them with. Of course, the children always keep things from being unbearable—still it's not the same as being with someone of the opposite sex that really means something to you. (Male and female created He them), and that's a fact—Women's Lib to the contrary.

_____ called, as usual, and asked to spend the evening with me. For that matter I had several choices, had I felt up to going out. But it's just as lonely to be with someone with whom you have no real rapport on special occasions as it is to be completely ignored. I much prefer the latter. _____ is a terribly nice man, as far as I know; but he's not someone I'd care to get romantically involved with. Perhaps I'm still bound up in the unliberated woman's bag. My idea of the right man for me is still someone I can look up to, respect, and depend on, if necessary. And as much as I've waited to be and tried to be completely independent, perhaps I have to finally admit that I am a dependent woman. At any rate, _____ certainly does not fill the bill in that respect. How can you look up to, respect, and depend on a forty-four-year-old bachelor who still lives at home with his parents and is evidently somewhat dependent himself? And it's pain enough that a platonic relationship is not what he has in mind, even though I've told him repeatedly that's all there can be between us. Gotta go now and drag myself into the kitchen and prepare some semblance of a meal for the kids.

1–2–73
8:30 A.M.

Back again. Would you believe that _____ stopped by shortly after I wrote my last sentence yesterday? Listen to this. Often when I feel unwell or unsociable or overly busy, I'll tell the children to say I'm not in if someone I don't especially care to see at the time drops by unexpectedly (wrong I know, I resolved to stop this practice this year). Well, when _____ knocked at the door, Jeffrey (four years old) ran into the living room yelling at the top of his voice, "If it's _____ mom says don't let him in!" Groan-n-n. I was almost paralyzed with embarrassment when Alan opened the door and that's exactly who it was. Surely he must have heard. Oh well, I've told him that I prefer people to call before dropping in. To me, it's very poor manners for anyone to visit before calling ahead to see if it's convenient. I do love people and like to have company, but a little advance notice is not asking too much.

    I'm not really superstitious, but there's an old superstition among black folk of the South that if a man enters your home first in the New Year, it will bring you good luck. So maybe _____ brought me good luck. Here's to hoping! Also, I sincerely hope that _____ has a good year also. I feel that he is terribly lonely, so my prayer for him is that he will find the right someone for him this year. Come to think of it, if I spent as much time hoping and praying for my own happiness as I do for others', perhaps something spectacular would happen.

While I was feeling too bad to do much of anything, I finished reading Barbara Seaman's *Free and Female.* I read a very penetrating book full of many true facts and observations. However I do take issue with much of what she writes. Of course, I know no one writes to be agreed with; they write to present ideas, opinions, and truths as they see them as individuals. Her supposition that an inherent masochism leads waifs and losers to find each other rang false to me. Granted I've attracted more than my share of the losers of this world, but masochistic I am not. How else could I have found the courage to oust a punitive husband and set sail with six children on my own? Then again, maybe she's right. How else could I have endured his inhuman treatment long enough to begat six children? Perhaps that really was masochism. Well, so much for that. Let the past bury the past. I'm resolved to live the NOW at it's best and truly hope for the future!

Yesterday's *Parade* had a beautiful set of resolutions for 1973, Max Erlichman's, *Desiderata.* I had already clipped it from a previous article and put it away in a treasured place for future rereading, but seeing it set forth on the cover of *Parade* as a set of resolutions for the New Year really got it together for me. What a beautiful, beautiful philosophy to live by. It's almost as good as the Ten Commandments. "Go placidly amid the noise and haste, and remember what peace there may be in silence. . . ." "Speak your truth quietly and clearly. . . ." "Be yourself. . . ." "Nurture strength of spirit to shield you in sudden misfortune. . . ." "Be at peace with God. . . ." "Keep peace with your soul. . . ."

"Strive to be happy. . . ." Now that I think of it, this has always been my philosophy of life, it just seems clearer and more sensible to me now. This is where it's at!

So instead of trying to put together what surely would amount to a humbling set of resolutions of my own, I shall imprint in my mind the above—just as the Ten Commandments and the Sermon on the Mount are imprinted in my mind. Together, these creeds to live by should complete the process of my becoming a human being.

Most definitely, I will strive to be happy this year whether my circumstances change appreciably for the better or not. No doubt the ruler of the Universe had a purpose for relegating me to the position in life that I occupy. It's an ongoing position that I've railed against with tears, curses, and many abortive attempts at self-sufficiency. It will not be easy to live with the damnable fact that I am on welfare, a burden on society, but I'll try harder to say, "Thy will be done," sincerely and accept the things that I cannot presently change more gracefully. Let it be, dear Lord, please! I will strive to be happy, and to make others happy as far as I can.

I must go now. I have to hang out the wash and put another load in.

> HAPPY NEW YEAR SELF!
> Richelene

1–3–73

Greetings Self!

Old itchy fingers are here again. I had the urge to write a letter to the editor; as a matter of fact I was inclined to write two. So since I've promised myself faithfully not to commit that act again, I'd better unload to you.

Several issues have been in the news the last few days that agitated my "letter-writis" unmercifully, but I did not give in. On Christmas night a young Puerto Rican boy was shot to death here while attempting to burglarize a package store. Quite a lot of controversy has raged since then, pro and con. Yours truly can't quite decide if she's aligned with the pros or the cons. Most likely I'm somewhere in the middle. Of course, my deepest sympathy is with Miguel's family, and it does seem that the officer could have aimed at the boy's lower extremities to stop him rather than shooting him in the head. Yet an even greater sadness and tragedy is that such a young boy, fifteen years old, should have been out indulging in criminal activity on Christmas night. Where does one place the blame, on the parents, on the society? Who really can say where the blame lies?

I dare not advance my own private theories on the root causes of juvenile delinquent behavior. After all, who am I? What great school of higher learning do have I a diploma from? What gives me the gall to think that I have even a little knowledge of behavior motivation? Me, a mere statistic on the welfare rolls. Yet I do feel that I have some insight into why people behave as they do, especially those on the same level as myself—those like Miguel and his family. If the "book-learned" people could only accept the fact that living itself educates you beyond belief, perhaps all of us could join forces and work toward solutions to many of society's problems. And, baby, when life has brought you and taught you like I have been brought and taught, do you ever get an education! The school of hard knocks is a hard taskmaster indeed.

You know where I think problems like Miguel's begin? They begin in the womb. I honestly think that what we will become is predetermined. Fatalistic? Yes. Some of us have a stacked deck before we even have a chance. I've experienced it in my own life, and in my family's life. I see it all around me in families I know.

But back to Miguel! His sister publicly stated that her parents had never been able to handle him. Why? Was he just bad? No, but in the sense that he evidently could not control his behavior. How easy it is to say that his parents failed him by not loving or disciplining him properly or that society failed him by closing him in an unsuitable environment, etc. If this is the case, what about all the youngsters in wealthy white families that go wrong? Oh, to heck with theories. Who am I to think that I can figure it out when so many much smarter people have failed? Miguel is dead, as dead as my poor brother Ba Boo, and no one can bring him back. What can we do but keep groping in the darkness of ignorance, hoping to find the flicker of light that will illumine our pathway and show us how to prevent such tragedies?

The other letter to the editor that tried to escape from these itching fingers was the law that forces children to support a parent or parents on welfare. It seems such a callous, unfeeling law, definitely designed to keep the poor groveling in the dirt from generation to generation.

We poor mortals who must sop from the public trough live only in the hope that our children will move on to a better life than we have. What irony that just as soon as they are of an age to support themselves they are immediately hounded to chip in and take care of dear old Mom or Dad as the case may be. Naturally, if children feel a certain amount of love and concern for their parents' welfare, they want to help as much as possible. But once they take on the responsibility of their own care or get married, it is wrong for the state to put further financial straits on them unless they are truly able to contribute.

I would be the first to agree that they do owe a debt of gratitude to society, but if they turn out to be decent, self-sustaining citizens and human beings, doesn't the debt automatically obliterate itself? God knows if my seven all grow up to be able to take care of themselves, and not end up on welfare, I'll be the most grateful and happy mother alive, but so much for that.

Sometimes I wish that I had the time to really sort out all these random thoughts and make something of value out of them. But how can I when there is so much to do and so many diversions? For instance, Jeffrey is whining at me right this minute to pick clay out of his hair, clay from the Headstart program. They really must be molding his brain down there! Besides that, I've got to do the upstairs floor and sew a dress I cut out yesterday. Woman's work, bah!

I have a real goodie for you as soon as I have time to write again.

So long for now,
Richelene

1–6–73

Dear Self,

Me again, suffering from acute "letter-writis." There are so many subjects that I want to explore with you today that I hardly know where to start. Besides, there's so much to be done here in the house that I feel guilty for even taking out a few minutes to write.

I'm thoroughly disgusted and depressed. It seems that I'll never in this world be able to live in the nice, clean, neat place I've always so yearned for. It's just so unfair. It isn't as if I've yearned for a big mansion, fine cars, or mink coats—all I've ever asked of life is just ordinary, neat, and livable surroundings, not the best, not the worst.

Yet everywhere I've lived there have been wall problems and mud holes in the yard. In Atlanta, in the projects where we lived, the floor was even concrete! Nigger proof, they called it. Do you really want to know what my fondest dream has always been? I just want simply to have a nice, velvety green lawn. That's hard to believe, isn't it? Of all the grand and wonderful things in this big world, the only thing I've ever desired beyond all else is a nice green lawn. Everywhere I've moved to, nice mud holes and dirt, dirt, dirt has greeted me. Oh, the unfairness of it all! Perhaps I'll realize my dream when I'm under the green, green grass.

The thing that sent me reeling into my present state of depression is my kitchen ceiling. Listen to this. Last summer I labored hard and painted the ceilings in the living room and kitchen. Ah-h-h, how nice and clean it looked, but, alas, no sooner had the kitchen ceiling dried than it began to peel (fate against me, as usual). By fall it was a total mess. So I called the housing authority and explained the problem. Under the circumstances, they said, they'd have someone repaint it.

Day before yesterday, the man arrived to paint. So happy was I that I almost grabbed him and kissed him. By the time he had finished, my urge to kiss was replaced by an urge to kick him in the behind. Such a job he did! Just slapped more paint over the old paint—so the ceiling looks like a solid white jigsaw puzzle with many of the pieces missing. I called the Housing Authority, but Mr. Scricca was not in. Why should they pay someone for such a sloppy job? Wonder if he'd have messed over it the way he did if he had been doing a private house? Most definitely not! What the heck, I might as well just forget it. Nothing ever turns out right for me. I am talking about born to lose. Well I told you already that pessimism is my name now. I also told you I was going to strive to be happy, didn't I? Contradictions, Contradictions! It sure is powerfully hard to be happy when you're black, poor, and walled in all around.

It's a funny thing. A few short years ago, I was so full of hope and optimism. I was the original happy little moron. Reality hadn't set in. I honestly and truly thought that I could get out there and lick the world with one hand and raise my six children alone with the other. Then I had planned to sit back on my laurels and say, "See what I did all by myself, world?" How soon the world got its licks in on me. Knocked me down, but I'm not out yet. So here I am one of those old lazy welfare freeloaders.

It almost scares me now that the children are growing up. I almost resent being under this tremendous burden of raising them. Sometimes I actually wish I had never had a child. Yet I know that I do love them and got an awful lot of joy from them when they were smaller. Sometimes the total responsibility of all this just overwhelms me. They say the last mile of any journey is always the hardest. How I hope and pray that none of them will ever have to travel this road I've traveled. And if they must, God forbid, may they never sink into the abyss of self-pity that I seem to be fast sinking into.

So, as the working people would say, "If I'm so tired and disgusted with my life as it is why don't I get my behind out there and get a job?" I'm very afraid that I'm psychologically unfit for the workaday rat race now. It's tough out there with all those liberated females. I was the square peg that never fit in even when I was out there. The cats really dug their claws into yours truly. I'm just not tough enough to survive out there. Besides, unless the work is stimulating or I'm kept so busy that I haven't the time to think and get bored, it's almost more than I can bear, and how many typing jobs are truly stimulating?

1–7–73
Sunday afternoon

I went to Black Magic with my girlfriend, Gwen, last night. Black Magic is a bowling game, minor gambling, I suppose, where you pay $3.75 for three games of bowling and you can win money depending on how well you bowl, or how lucky you are. Red and green pins are inserted along with the white pins. For instance, if the head pin comes up Red and you get a strike, you win $1.00. If it comes up green and you get a strike, you win 50 cents. There are other variations up to a hundred dollars for a strike. You may have guessed that the hundred-dollar variation rarely comes up. Anyway I managed to pick up $4.50 in money shots, which wasn't bad. Even so, I shot what started out as a good game. I had 105 in the fifth frame, then proceeded to blow it, ending up with a 166 game. Another lady had a 171 game, so she collected the $7.50 pot for the ladies.

Earlier this fall, I got angry at the way they're running the Black Magic game and wrote a letter of complaint to the Brunswick Bowling Corporation in Skokie, Illinois. Surprisingly, I got a positive response. They got in touch with the biggies at Stadium Lanes and the biggies called me in for a conference about the complaints. Mr. _____ promised me most pseudo-sincerely that everything would be straightened out and we would no longer get the runaround when we go there to play Black Magic on Saturday night. In light of the history of black people's lives being so finely interwoven with false promises from whites, I knew that this was just one more.

This was borne out last night. It so happened that five of us women of darker hue showed up to bowl Black Magic. Things were proceeding as usual. The paler ones had all the lanes reserved and filled, as they do from week to week. We all got very disturbed at having to wait around while they figured out a way to "squeeze us in." So my letter accomplished as much as, in my heart, I knew it would—nothing. If it wasn't for the fact that I enjoy the game so much and the fact that I knew they'd like it so much if we darker ones did not show up again, I'd never go back. But since it will hurt them—it's better for us to keep coming than if we stayed away—I shall return. So what do I mean when I say it is hard to be happy when you're black, poor, and walled in? Or should I say walled out? Baby, it's a white man's world, and don't let anyone try to tell you otherwise. Liberty and justice, for who?

Upon leaving Stadium Lanes, we decided to drop by the Elks Club for a drink. There, injury was added to insult. The minute we walked in, some drink-sodden specimen of black mankind started in blabbing a stream of stinky-breathed inanities in my face. I figured if I ignored him, he'd go away. Eventually he did. No sooner had we fought our way through the smoke and weaving bodies and found a table, than a fresh youngster plopped down at our table and proceeded to "flatter" me by telling me, are you ready for this, "You're not getting older, you're getting better!" You can imagine the boost this gave my morale as I looked upon the swarming hordes of young maggots squirming and squiggling on the dance floor. Among all those babes who just turned eighteen along with my oldest daughter, we few oldsters must have stood out as ancient oaks in a forest of saplings. I'm sure I won't make that scene again.

Last night convinced me more than ever that I'll never be a drinker—one whiskey sour and my head was spinning. Guess I'll digress back to ginger ale. Another thing I was convinced of is that I'll never be able to comfortably walk into a night club without a male escort. My discomfort must have been written on my face as plain as my nose. Steve's cousin Barbara and her husband were there. She immediately remarked that I looked as if I were someplace that I shouldn't be. I was. I should have taken my $4.50 from Black Magic and headed straight home. No doubt, I would feel better about everything today. Is there such a thing as a hangover from one drink? I sure have a headache today.

Must stop and cook dinner now. Incidentally, I'm still going to strive to be happy.

We'll see how it goes as the year rolls on.

So long,
Richelene

1–8–73

Hi Self,

Today is Monday, the beginning of the second week of this brand new year. I think I'll try to make this a year of continual new beginnings. Each week I will resolve anew to make fresh starts to live by the creed that I elected for 1973. I just received in the mail this little note from the YMCA:

> Dear Applicant,
>
> We have filled our position for a Clerk-Typist, receptionist. Thank you for applying and we wish you good luck in your job hunting.
>
> Sincerely,
> New Britain, YMCA

So that's that. I have nothing more to add.

I feel much better today. Most of the pain in my upper back is gone and the glands are back to normal. Wow! What a siege this was! It could have been nothing more than the London Flu that's making the rounds. Now I must knock on wood. Since October, every time I was sure a cold was over, the old throat got sore and I was right back where I started. Must be that my resistance is low.

Heaven knows it should be. A mother can never afford the luxury of giving in and really pampering herself long enough to completely get well from any illness, at least a poor mother can't.

I have a confession to make. This morning I went back to bed and stayed there until 11:30. How good it felt. There was a time when I couldn't do that. It would have made me feel so guilty. Today I felt not the slightest twinge of guilt. I just couldn't get going and suddenly it dawned on me that after eighteen years of mothering, with all that entails, I deserved to rest in peace one morning.

Usually these "out-of-it" mornings occur after I've suffered a seizure or a series of seizures during the night. It's almost too good to be true, but I haven't had a seizure in about three months. The last two episodes scared the heck out of me. There was a series of seizures that made me so afraid I feared I wouldn't come out of it. Can you imagine being caught in the throes of some invisible thing that has you weighted down so you can't move? And the blood is pounding in your brain, and you feel as if your head is going to explode any moment. You try to move a toe, a finger, anything, but you can't. And your heart starts to pound and gallop like a wild thing trying to escape from your chest. And the harder you fight to escape the thing that has a hold on you, the tighter it clutches you. Either you snap out of it or pass out. I am talking about someone being grateful to wake up alive the next day. Grateful to jump out of bed and look out the window and say hello to a new day—whatever it brings! Being alive under the most trying circumstances is probably a lot better than being dead. Frankly, it is not an especially comforting thought to know that my children may wake up and find me dead from a nocturnal seizure one morning.

I know I should tell the children about my affliction but just can't get up the courage to do so. The doctor told me that I should, and common sense tells me I should. I will get up the courage soon. Those last, very severe episodes occurred while I was working at a coat factory operating a power sewing machine. Being an epileptic and very sensitive to noise, and having suffered from head noises all my life, the loud humming of the machines was almost unbearable. This must have contributed to the severity of the last two seizures. Yet while working in that factory, with my hands constantly busy, and the noise blotting out the thoughts of helplessness that sometimes plague me, I was content to a certain extent, much more so than when doing routine office work. Had I not become so terribly tired and the seizures had not become so much worse, I could have continued to work there. It doesn't contribute to your peace of mind to know that people think you're just a big, healthy, lazy thing that could work like anyone else when you have an invisible affliction that's not evident to the casual observer. In truth I could work full time if I was responsible only for myself. As it is, everything is just too much.

At the time that the last seizures occurred, the doctor had increased my medication. I was taking Dilantin four times a day, two at bedtime. Evidently the Dilantin has no effect when countered by undue physical and emotional stress. Once I delicately approached the doctor at the clinic about trying a drug that I read about on me. He really lit into me. Of course, I was not trying to be smarter than he was or to treat myself, but if a person is willing to volunteer to have a newer drug tested on himself, it seems the medical profession would welcome a chance to research something that might prove beneficial to a lot of people. Oh well, guess I'm just an eccentric; that sounds much nicer and more eloquent than saying, "I guess I'm just a nut."

I had an EEG in September, but haven't been back to the clinic since, so I don't know whether the old nervous machinery is better or deteriorating. The buses in Hartford are still on strike, and I can't afford to take a taxi. Perhaps when, or should I say if, the buses start to run again I'll call and see if they'll let me come back.

1–9–73

I went for groceries this morning. I had to wait for a solid hour for the taxi to come to bring me home. I'm so sick of having to depend on the cabs to get groceries home. I wonder if we'll ever have our own transportation? Being without transportation in New Britain is such a hardship! Life could be so much more livable if we had any kind of old jalopy to get around in. As it is, we can't even go to church, much less to many other affairs that could contribute to a fuller life for all of us. Better days are bound to come someday. They must!

Br-r-r! Was it frigid this morning! If walking in cold weather is good for you, I received a double dose of good health this morning, walking to the store. The children have been walking to school every day to cut down on expenses. The Welfare Department used to include bus fare for the children in the budget, but no more. It's a very long walk to Washington Jr. High School and a shame that bus fare is not supplied for them. My friend Evelyn called and offered a ride for the children if they wait for her on Slater Road. I relayed the message to them. Just as I knew, they said they would continue to walk. They're truly chips off the old block, crazy. I had planned to start giving them car fare, now that the weather is so cold, but since they claim to like the walk so well that they would turn down a ride, I won't press it on them. I don't know whether to classify their attitude as independence or stupidity. Most likely it's a mixture of both, as in my case.

Miriam called and we talked for quite a while. Somehow we got into a discussion of racial attitudes. We both admitted to a certain amount of racial prejudice, which has more or less been thrust upon us by whites themselves. But we have both resolved to try to overcome it, if white folks will let us. It seems so hard for them to resist the temptation to remind us of our racial differences whenever relationships of work or recreation bring us together. I, personally, could so easily go on feeling that I'm just relating to another human being whenever I have occasion to interact with them. But sooner or later, subtly or not so subtly, they will inject some racial comment into the conversation thus reminding you that you're not just two human beings, but one is black and the other is white. Why? Is their sense of whiteness so much a part of their sense of personhood that they unconsciously do this or is it that they sense that some of us blacks see them as nothing but people like ourselves and they consciously seek to convey to us that this is not so?

To be fair, I must admit that I do feel that many times, some whites are sincerely trying to put you at your ease by making certain comments that are racially oriented. What they don't know is that their efforts are wasted on me. I really don't see any reason to feel ill at ease with them, under normal circumstances, unless they make it so. And they almost always succeed in doing so. Will we mortals ever learn to accept each other as just that, mere mortals?

Later
Richelene

1–10–73

Hi Self,

Back again. It is another day. A day to be happy to live to learn to drink in the joys of being alive, to sing, to give, to love to live!

Now I've decided that instead of writing to appease my letter-writing instincts, I shall begin keeping a diary of sorts for the year 1973. I will chronicle one year in the life of a poor black woman and see how things progress, regress, or stand still. I think I'll cast off my cloak of pessimism and dare to predict things will progress. Whether they do or not, it will be interesting to see what subtle nuances of meaning or insights I can glean in a year's time.

One thing I've already found out since I began writing to you, self, and that is it's very hard to write every day. Not only because of the time element, but also the mere effort involved in sitting down and writing. It seems that the things that I should write about come to me most lucidly in the wee morning hours when I'm unable to sleep. I inherited the curse of insomnia from my father. I can remember hearing him talk of how he often lay awake all night and then got up at five o'clock and worked all day. My own experience has documented his statements. Often, I'm tempted to get out of bed and take pen in hand at two or three in the morning and pour out my thoughts, but so far, I've resisted the urge. The time might be better spent that way than tossing and turning and praying for blessed sleep to come. Eventually, I might find myself utilizing my sleepless hours by writing.

Right now it's 7:45 A.M. I got up at six and prepared breakfast for the brood. Afterward, I prepared four lunches and washed the dishes. Then I ran upstairs and got Jeffrey up and dressed him for "Headstart." While Candace and Melanie are fighting it out in the bathroom, I've decided to scribble a few notes. Once they're out, I must go in, take a bath and get dressed to go bowling. I bowl in a league every Thursday morning. Bowling is my lifeline. I like throwing a strike and scattering all the pins; I strike a blow at all the accumulated frustrations and hurts and disappointments that life has lined up in a neat little row inside me, and as the pins scatter, and that place is left gloriously free for a little while, so the cluttered place inside me is swept clear and free for a little while. Bowling almost fills the place that religion used to occupy inside me. This is a distortion, one that I must correct. Somehow I must once again put religion back into its proper perspective in my life. Maybe that's the clue to better days for us. I will try.

Have to go now. I will get back to you later.

Sincerely,
Richelene

1–12–73
7:50 A.M.

Just went through the daily morning routine again. I must take a few minutes out to jot down some happening of the last two days and my thoughts and feelings about them.

A black man just opened up the dry cleaners across the street. I sure hope it turns out to be a successful venture for him. I took two loads of cleaning for the machines over to him. He is most intelligent and articulate. Another truth was brought home to me even in this. No matter what the black man does, the white man is trying to kick him in the behind and keep him down. The new owner of the cleaners was telling me now that the man he bought the business from sees that he is pulling in a nice volume of business, the man is trying to force him to pay back taxes that he should have paid. He feels that he has no choice other than to pay them, since he is using this man's pressing equipment until he can purchase his own, and the man surely would deny him further use of the equipment if he balks at paying these taxes, thus forcing him to give up the business. It really kills you when you think of how the white man has and continues to exploit and manipulate the black man, and how terribly dependent we remain. They say you're shiftless and lazy if you're content to accept the status quo and take life as it comes; yet, when you try to lift yourself up by those proverbial "bootstraps," they're trying to cut the straps off and stomp you back down. "Damned if you do and damned if you don't" must have been coined for the black race.

I feel so sorry for the little man at the cleaners, trying to do all his work himself to keep down expenses. He has a bad hip and is limping. One has to admire his gumption.

I would gladly go over and help him out a few hours a week for no pay, but dare not suggest such a thing. The world is so full of evil, meanness, and treachery that those of us who desire to be loved and giving feel frustrated and thwarted. How can you express your true self when the vultures are forever swarming around watching and waiting to swoop down on you? And how can you be sure who the vultures are before they descend upon you? Yet if it's true that good always overcomes evil in the end, perhaps we have to throw off our protective armor and be brave enough to live life according to the dictates of our hearts.

V.W. called last night asking about the situation at Black Magic. It appeared to me that he felt that our seeing a subtle racism or elitism at Stadium Lanes may have been hallucinations—perhaps so. I always allow room for doubt. But what, really, can you say to someone like V.W. about a situation like this? He happens to be one of those "colored boys" that white folk enjoy having around. By his buffoonery, he elevates and substantiates the white man's preconceived notions of himself as a superior being. With a black person like V.W. around, there is no threat to this notion of superiority; nor are they made to look at their deficiencies.

Good old fun V.W. is synonymous with the grinning, clowning, darkie that the white man of the South loved as he would a pet monkey. And so he ends up feeling these whites that he associates with are without racial prejudice because they accept him so well. The pity is that he cannot perceive their basis of acceptance.

But, put a well-educated, highly intelligent, superior black man on their team! The attitude would be completely different. They might respect him and grudgingly admire him, but the warm acceptance would not be there, for their superiority would be annihilated. That is, unless he happened to be with a team of well-educated highly intelligent, superior white men.

Yet, I refuse to call men like V.W. "Uncle Toms." I read *Uncle Tom's Cabin* and found Uncle Tom to be admirable, by my standards. Why he became a symbol of the "butt-kissing" black is beyond me. I thought him good and noble. If he was so groveling, why did he choose to be beat to death rather than reveal where the two black women were hiding? If he is symbolic of Uncle "Tomism," then I say we could use a few Uncle Toms today. It's people like V.W. who get my goat. But let me depart from this subject before I really get upset.

I have an appointment for a job interview at Channel 30 today at three o'clock. But I am not going to keep it. In my heart I know I'd be wasting my time and theirs by going. How, by any stretch of the imagination, could anyone think that the people at Channel 30 would take a high school graduate, out of the labor force for eight years, and hand him or her a plum like a $10,000–per-year position? And this when hordes of young college graduates are begging for work? Never happen!

Mrs. Willis, the secretary of the local NAACP, referred me for the job. By virtue of my many letters to the editors and several published articles in local newspapers, it seems that some people think I have quite a bit of un-explored and unused potential. Frankly, I think so too. But I am, above all, realistic. Too realistic to think that those white people at Channel 30 would pay $10,000 per year for raw undeveloped talent and potential. I like to think that if they were truly caring human beings, they would care enough to want to help lift one person off the welfare rolls and put him in a position to support a family of seven. But I cannot stretch my credulity far enough to even suppose that such people are in charge at Channel 30. People, as a whole, just don't care that much, except to damn us for being on welfare. So I will not go.

Call it pessimism (perhaps it is), lack of confidence (it is not), or whatever you wish.

I call it realism. You can't live in this hard world for thirty-nine years without beginning to become aware of human nature.

Sure, as the TV commercial says, "There are people born every day who can create art, make peace, abolish in-justice, etc., but if they don't get the education, they may never get the chance." I believe I am one of those people who could contribute something toward making things a little better in some way, but I don't have the education. Not the piece of paper that's required anyway. Let me make one thing clear, though, I sincerely believe that, given a for-mat to work from and minimal training, I could do the job at Channel 30 as well as anyone, regardless of formal edu-cation. Incidentally, the position is Coordinator of Mi-nority Affairs. It requires a person who can serve as a liaison between Channel 30 and the minority community.

In spite of everything, I still have a gut feeling that there is a place for me somewhere in this world. That place is not on welfare forever and it is not pounding a typewriter forty hours a week for $95.00. It is a place where I can contribute to love, peace, and understanding between people. It's a place where I can help and serve humanity in some way, as I've always felt the ruler of the universe intended me to. Someday, someway, before I depart this earth, I will find my place!

Until later,
Richelene

1–14–73

Dear Self,

I went to Black Magic again last night. Gwen called ahead and made a reservation for five. Perhaps they are opening the game up to a certain extent. And, I had a good relaxed time even though I only won 75 cents. The thing that counts in Black Magic is picking up your money shots, unless you get a tremendously high game or series. In that case you can win for high game or high series. My games were better than last week, but I missed most of my money shots. I ended up with a 499 series, which is good. Instead of releasing the ball straight down the center, I am shooting from the second arrow on the right again. It seems to be working. I will stick with it for as long as it works.

The group we bowled with last night was quite congenial, much friendlier than the "cold fish" we bowled with last week. Not that it matters to me. I simply enjoy the game and the challenge. Even though one has to admit that it is more pleasant when people are pleasant, whether they are or not, I enjoy Black Magic.

I was surprised to find the kids up and watching TV when I got home at 12:45 A.M. They were watching wrestling. I sat down and joined them. It was quite thrilling to see our "own" Bobo Brazil licking the heck out of that big blob of white meat. That's a terrible thing to say, isn't it? Well, I'm sure they feel the same way when their "own" is beating ours. I wonder if I'll really be able to erase the prejudices that the years and life have conditioned me to? I'm still resolved to try.

_____ called again last night. I was sincerely hoping that he had found someone that would erase his loneliness and bring him some measure of the happiness that all of us are seeking in man-woman relationships. Evidently he hasn't or he wouldn't be calling me again. Hope he won't be as persistent as before. How do you get across to a man that you just aren't interested in a romantic relationship with him, even though you do like him well enough not to want to hurt his feelings or be downright mean? After all these years, I still try to be gentle with such men, and they always end up mistaking kindness for weakness. With some of them, you do have to be blunt, even if you end up feeling a little sorry later.

It's about five o'clock now. It is a quiet, rather melancholy Sunday afternoon. No matter how one's belief in a static, sitting-on-a-throne God might waver and wane, if one ever was truly believing, as I was, Sunday remains a day of distinction, of reverence. This is a day that calls forth a somber, wondering spirit and still seems incomplete without formal worship in a house of God.

While I cannot say that my concept of God is the same as in my youth, there is no denying that in the deep recesses of my being, I know that there is a power larger than man. It's a power that transcends our insignificant little selves and unites us with the universe. We are children of the universe. Thus we can be larger than we are and move beyond our limited sphere if we would only open up to receive the power that waits to be tapped. Call it God, Omnipotent One, Supreme Being, Ruler of the Universe, or whatever you perceive it to be it is there. There is a spiritual side of life that supports and reinforces our physical life. Just as St. Paul said, "His strength is made perfect in weakness." How else have so many of us weaker mortals managed to survive? I must get back to church soon.

Sincerely,
Richelene

1–15–73

Dear Self,

Here, half the month is gone already, and I've made such a puny start at keeping my resolutions. My prejudices are still almost intact and I don't know if I'm appreciably happier or if I've made anyone else happier. As a matter of fact, I greatly fear that someone was made unhappier by me last night, inadvertently.

Guess who called last night? It was Don, my former husband. This is the first time he's called in over a year, and it was quite a surprise. He was coming to New Britain quite frequently over a year ago, until I notified the authorities of his whereabouts and they served a warrant on him for support. He then did his usual vanishing act.

Talking to him, it was quite evident that he has not changed. The few times I've talked to him before since we separated, always on the phone, I dare not encounter him personally, his conversation has been very limited, with him doing all the talking.

Last night I decided to feel him out, try to discuss a few points of interest with him and assess his present state of mind. He immediately got angry when I questioned him about his adamant stance in regard to helping to support the children. Same old Don! As long as things are going his way and he is not crossed, he is the most amicable of men, but the slightest disagreement or displeasure sends him on a wild tangent.

And after eight years of being apart and knowing all that contributed to our being divorced, he dared to infer that he would not be averse to our getting back together. The man is sick, sick, sick. Dear God, continue to keep our paths from crossing and protect me from this obsessive child of yours. Comfort him, love him, help him, and keep him. Above all, please keep him away from me.

I do not say that to be mean, only because he cannot accept reality. Reality being that there can never be other than a friendly relationship between us again. This he will not have, even at the expense of discontinuing all contact and relationship with his children.

How sad it is that two supposedly mature adults cannot be friends. When, together, they have contributed to the world's overpopulation by six. If only he could see in the light of reason and accept the fact that there can never be a marriage between us. There never was. Of course, we had a legal contract, but a marriage it was not. It was just a terrible mismatch between two people of completely diverse temperaments who never should have gotten together.

Nena and George O'Neill very accurately spelled out the insurmountable obstacles that we confronted in our "closed marriage" in their book *Open Marriage*. Don imposed on me all the pitfalls—jealousness, possessiveness, domination, manipulation, subjugation of my selfhood, the works. Like the "keep them pregnant and barefoot" adage. To be fair to myself, I tried to submerge my own individuality and uniqueness in order to "ride it out." But the ride was too rough, and I had to break out. I had to be free. I had to be myself, which he would not allow me to be. I know now that I can never be an appendage of another human being. I've got to be me, no more, no less. Unless the fates are kind enough to send me someone who will grant me that right, in an open marriage, I shall remain alone for the duration.

The children know that their father has never helped to support them since we parted, but I have never tried to turn them against him. So they still feel good when he gets up the nerve to call or appear. This is their right, and I shall never try to make it otherwise. But how warped a man must be that he can go from day to day, year after year, without doing anything for his own. How did he get that way? Where do you place the blame? On the father that deserted him as a child? Or on a sick mind? Or on the society that thought it good to psychologically castrate and disenfranchise the black man? Who can say?

That I should have been one of those singled out to reap the harvest of such conditioning has been a bitter pill to swallow. At the same time, who am I to feel that I should have been spared the suffering I've endured when thousands of my sisters have endured and are enduring the same thing? When I talk to other welfare mothers, both black and white, it is amazing how similar is the fabric of which our lives are woven. Seemingly, the problems we share are no respecter of colors, which causes me to accept yet another truth: I cannot place the blame for my present status on race alone; there are so many contributing factors.

Donna just brought little Kenny, my second grand-child, so I must stop for now.

Later,
Richelene

P.S. *Lady Sings the Blues* is at the drive-in. I would dearly love to see it, but if either of my "suitors" ask me to go I will refuse. Though I don't think it's too likely any of them will call. I seem to have successfully cooled their ardor. The phone has been very silent for the past two weeks, and that's fine with me. Not only does it get terribly tiresome telling people the same thing over and over, but it provides more time, peace, and quiet to jot down the daily happenings and type them up. Maybe I'll suggest going to see the movie with several of my girlfriends. Though I must admit the thought of sitting in a drive-in movie with a group of women is almost as unappealing as sitting there with a male that I have no romantic feelings for. How lovely it would be if that "special" man would appear, but from where? I'm beginning to feel that I'll have to draw up a blueprint and make him myself! Now that's an idea!

BLUEPRINT FOR A MAN FOR ME

1. Start working from the inside out. Begin with generous portions of love. By love, I mean a big heart overflowing with desires to do well and help one's fellow man.
2. Interlace those desires with threads of intelligence, kindness, sincerity, and a magnanimous spirit. Add a quiet strength and sense of purpose.
3. Sprinkle with tolerance and a good sense of humor, mix well with maturity.
4. Put it all together with a healthy libido.
5. Pour all this into 190 pounds of solid black or brown flesh and blood, mold securely onto a 6'2" frame. If material obtainable does not equal 190 pounds or a 6'2" frame, lesser proportions of the outside structure may be substituted. After all, it's what's inside that counts—facial features are negligible.
6. Lastly, breathe into him the breath of life and put him into a good-paying, satisfying job of any kind. Then love, cherish and keep him forever—cause, baby, you've got yourself something worth keeping.

Note: At no time have I stated that I possess comparable qualities of my ideal man, but in all fairness to myself, I think I do have some qualities that could complement his. And with him being the man that he would be, he would understand and forgive my shortcomings and love me anyway.

1–16–73

Dear Self,

It's "check day." As usual all the welfare recipients waited with bated breath and empty stomachs for the check to come, hoping that the mailman would not be too late for them to get to the bank before it closed and hoping that the check itself would not be late, as is sometimes the case.

_____ called and asked to borrow car fare so she could get downtown to the bank to cash her check. Wonder whatever made her assume that I, a welfare recipient like her, had money when she didn't? Luckily, I did have a couple of dollars left over this time. Of course, this was no mere coincidence. I made sure I'd have a couple left. God knows how many times "check day" has rolled around and I didn't have one red cent, and then the check was late. How hard it is to stretch the small amount we get from one check to the next. But I've learned to do it pretty well now, unless some unforeseen emergency comes up—which was happening with alarming regularity for a while. Hope I'm being given a breathing spell now. Anyway I was happy that I could loan _____ car fare today.

While waiting for the mailman, I caught the end of *Let's Make a Deal* on TV. In the back of my mind, I was dreading the long wait for the taxi to get the groceries home. So when the Big Deal turned out to be a car, among other things, I found myself wiping away an involuntary wetness from my cheeks. It's so unfair. This world is so full of things that people are giving them away, yet it seems so impossible for me to get anything beyond the bare "older" gentlemen who have offered me cars and other goodies if I'd enter a liaison with them. Unfortunately, they were not to my liking and through the years I've refused to compromise my sense of values. Now I begin to wonder if I was prudent, or stupid? Life certainly could have been a lot easier for me in material ways. The incongruity is that the couple of men that I have had close relationships with have been as poor and as without worldly goods as me. It doesn't make much sense, does it?

Right now I would so love to replace the junk in the house with furniture, especially the living room. I just took one chair out that finally gave up the fight to survive. The other chair and the sofa are trying with all their might to resist the temptation to collapse, but I fear that they too may soon see the futility of their existence and give up. Then what? I'm sorely tempted to throw the whole shebang in the cellar and leave the living room completely bare until such time as I can refurnish it. Now every time I'm downtown, I find myself gazing longingly at beautiful living room suites in store windows. Funny, but my lack of nice things never bothered me until recently. Maybe it's just the thought that I'll soon be forty with nothing to show for it but a houseful of children and grandchildren that's getting me down.

The mailman finally arrived just in time for _____ and me to get to the bank before it closed. The different varieties of welfare recipients were lined up to cash the "check." They all are different, yet all the same—dependent. The mixture is a curious lot that runs the gamut from neatly dressed, head held high, seeking to hide their dependency and hopelessness behind a facade of "presentability" and pride to the frankly hopeless and bedraggled, despair covering their faces like a well-fitted mask, all pride, all hope gone.

Will I perhaps enter the latter category someday? No, some-how, someway I will move on to a better life!

Behind me, in the Food Stamp line, a wizened little old white lady fidgets, worry veiling her eyes. She taps me delicately on the shoulder and asks in a quavering voice if she may go ahead of me since she has a doctor's appoint-ment which she fears she may be late for if she has to wait her turn. I let her get in front of me in the face of dark stares from other recipients behind me. She smiles grate-fully, but continues to watch the clock and fidget. The line is long ahead of us. "Wonder if someone up front would let me in," she queries, half to me, half to herself. "Why don't you ask," I venture. "They just might."

She timidly moves forward and mercy of mercies, taps _____ on the shoulder and states her case. _____ turns on her like Hell's fury broke loose and fires a stream of invectives at her. The little old lady, tears blurring her eyes, makes her way back to her place in front of me. I feel ashamed. _____ is a big, mean black woman of my acquaintance who would not hesitate to vent her frustrations on the devil himself. Had I known that she would be the one the lit-tle old lady would approach I could have spared her by warn-ing her not to approach her. And so the circus, as the smug, secure "haves" say of the "have-nots," goes on check day.

Upon leaving the bank, I went to the Newbrite Plaza material store. I found a lovely black plaid remnant for $2.00. I will make a pair of pants to go with my black vest. Whenever I find such a tremendous buy as this, I always attribute my luck to the finger of fate pointing the way to it. I wish the finger of fate would point the way to some-thing a little bigger soon. Not that I'm ungrateful for small blessings, it's just that some larger blessings would do very nicely at this stage of my life.

I bought the usual supply of groceries. By now I could zip through Shop-Rite blindfolded. It gets pretty monotonous eating the same thing week after week, but how much can you vary a menu without a varying increase in food money. And with everything going up a few cents each week, it's almost hopeless. One has to be a magician to feed seven people on $43.00 a week. Unfortunately, I'm not a magician and end up spending $10 to $15 over. This being money that is supposed to cover other needs. On the other hand, perhaps I am a miracle worker of sorts, or else we could never survive on what we manage to survive on. How good it will be when at least one or two get out of school and are able to pay their own way.

Can you understand why I take advantage of every possible opportunity to advise youngsters coming along now to never have more than one or two children? If one can responsibly raise one or two children now, he's doing well. I'm Planned Parenthood's greatest advocate. "Do as I say," I tell the youngsters, not "do as I did!" Experience is such a hard and thorough teacher.

Above everything, I hope my own children will take what they are experiencing to heart and limit their families to what they can assume responsibility for. Then my living and suffering and preaching shall not have been in vain. For the record, I did try to limit my family, but my husband threw away every contraceptive the doctor prescribed for me. And so, through my fear of him, I became a baby producing factory. Jeffrey, number seven, is a whole different story, which I will elaborate on when the spirit moves me. I think I'll stop now and go upstairs and cut out my pants so I can begin sewing early tomorrow morning.

Guess what I'm reading now? It is entitled *A History of the Occult*, by Colin Wilson. It was previously offered by the Doubleday Book-of-the-Month Club. So they sent me an irresistible offer, five books for a dime, to rejoin. The five books I selected are *The Occult, Free and Female, Open Marriage, The Passions of the Mind*, and *The*

Peaceable Kingdom. What does that say about me, that I'm unduly interested in the inner life, that I am a Free Soul, or what? I think that it merely says that I like to read and am interested in all facets of life. *The Occult* is very interesting, but strains the credulity considerably. Why is it that feats of mysticism such as St. Joseph of Cupertino, the Flying Monk, flying through the air, and the miraculous healings of Cagliostro are not in evidence today? *The Occult* makes for interesting reading, but I am skeptical of its contents. At any rate, it is not a good book to go to sleep by. I read about three pages of *Wild Goose, Brother Goose* today, so think I'll read that tonight.

On this note, I must close.
Richelene

P.S. Would you believe that I took a vow of poverty long before I knew that poverty had taken a vow on me? I would now like to be released from that vow!

1–17–73

Dear Self,

The mud-dirt-mess syndrome just sent me into another depression. I knew the nice feelings of the past couple of days were too good to last. They never do last very long.

So what set this one off? Donna, my oldest, eighteen years old and mother of two, married of course, just tracked in a nice trail of mud on my newly scrubbed kitchen floor. The mud in itself is depressing enough, as I told you before, but a "so-called" grown woman walking through the mud? It's just too much. I guess it just points out more poignantly than ever that she is still just a child who, over-anxious to be an adult, is masquerading as a woman.

How I hope her marriage works out and she grows and matures enough to handle the responsibility she brought on herself much too soon. God knows I'm unable to do it for her. I'm still completely submerged myself. She is headstrong, restless, domineering, and unreasonable, so like her father. Perhaps the years and life will mellow her; I hope so. I do hope she'll be spared much pain in the process.

If I were wealthy, I'd take the two little angel boys she has brought into the world and raise them myself. As a matter of fact, if I were wealthy, I wouldn't be constantly complaining to you about my own lot in life, self. Money can do so much to make life more livable. If I were wealthy, released from the constant grind of just trying to survive, I could thoroughly enjoy raising my own children, every one of them. They're really pretty nice people, all things considered. Sometimes I think I must be an awful mother for complaining so about the hardships encountered in trying to raise my family alone. Oh well, tomorrow is bowling day again. It's time to scatter the frustrations again.

Dear God, please, you said, "Ask and ye shall receive." Someday grant me a yard where mud and dirt won't be tracked in every time someone enters; grant me a nice, clean place and the type of situation that is conducive to keeping it nice and clean as I so love to live in a nice clean place; and grant that when my other children move out and have children of their own, they will live far enough away so that I'll be happy to see them come for a visit; and grant that by then I'll have a nice, comfortable, loving companion to share what life I have left with; and grant me a reasonable time to enjoy these blessings; then

I promise I shall not complain or wheedle or beg any more favors of you—and when my time comes, I will go willingly, peacefully. Amen.

1–18–73
8:40 A.M.

After a good night's sleep and upon awakening to a gorgeous January morning clothed prematurely in Spring's bright, warm clothing, I am thoroughly ashamed of last night's depression. In reality, I am really grateful that Donna lives only four doors away—so that I can watch over her and the babies to a certain extent. And she does need watching over, although she doesn't know it.

How good it would have been if my mother or someone had been close enough to lend me a helping hand during the early struggles of motherhood. One thing seems certain, Donna and Steve are happy in their young marriage and seem to be making a good adjustment. They are far happier and better adjusted than her father and I ever were. I just hope they don't grow away from each other over the years.

7:45 P.M.

Back from bowling. I am more depressed than ever. We lost all three games, one by only four pins.

1–19–73

Hi Self,

After running up and down stairs all morning, cleaning, changing beds, etc., I relaxed and watched *Password* while eating lunch. I enjoy trying to guess the word and wish I could go on the show. The thought for the day at the end of the show was: "Whatever your lot in life, build on it!" Just beautiful! Worth pondering and following through on. I shall try to do that as it ties in with my resolutions for 1973. It will be interesting to see just how this year turns out. I shall certainly continue keeping a journal of it.

How strange life is. During the years when things were really "hopping"; the years when babies were coming every year; when Don was terrorizing me with his fits of anger, threatening me with guns and knives; when we were roaming the country from California to New England in cars that threatened to breathe their last breath at any moment; when there were days when we could not be certain of where the next meal or rent was coming from; when I could not so much as go to the corner store alone without facing an interrogation upon my return; when my nerves were so shattered that they cried out for the release of a complete breakdown, which never quite came; when life was not worth living and I swallowed a bottle of aspirin to end it all, and promptly vomited it back up because of the nausea of pregnancy; when hell on earth was contained within the walls I called home; when I had neither the time nor the inclination to keep a written account of things although a diary would have been really interesting then. Now, those years are locked in memory's room behind the door marked "yesterday." The now, the time that comes from the moment, is the appointed time to live. My now is peaceful and free of the conflicts of yesterday, and so I do not look back except to remind myself I do have so much to be thankful for, and who knows what good things might wait for us behind the door marked "tomorrow."

Frances called and suggested that we go to see *Lady Sings the Blues*. Going to a drive-in movie with another woman is not my idea of an exhilarating evening, as I said before, but the movie itself should be enjoyable. In a sense, it might be better to see it with a woman. That way there will surely to be no diversions, not if you discount the fact that Jeffrey and her two young sons are going. Frankly, I'd prefer to leave the children home, but since she is the driver, her word is the law.

I went to a conference for Candace. Mr. Nolan stated that Candace is progressing very well and is reading much above her grade level. All the Mitchells are avid readers, except Kenneth. He is the least intellectually inclined, but plays guitar in a high school band that seems to be going places. The thing that Mr. Nolan seems to think that we should work on most with Candace is her moods. I informed him that all my children have their fair share of personality quirks, and although I do what I can to try to guide them, I'm very much afraid that I, and others, will more or less have to accept them as they are.

I feel certain that had I not had the strength to dissolve the nightmare that passed as a marriage when I did, the children would have been totally wrecked, not to mention their mother. It was a while after Don was out of the house before the nervousness and trauma subsided. I honestly believe that our breaking up was the salvation of us all.

1–20–73
7:30 P.M.

I watched pro bowling on TV this afternoon. How effortlessly the pros get those marks. I enjoyed the show, as usual. One thing disconcerted me somewhat. During the last and most important part of the match between Barry Asher and Don Johnson, occasionally the camera switched to Don Johnson's wife, who sat there, her eyes closed, her lips moving in prayer. It struck me as somehow obscene or sacrilegious. How presumptuous of her to think that God had time to look in on a bowling match when thousands of people are starving; when man is busily engaged in destroying his own brothers in wars; when people are suffering from unconquerable disease; when black Americans are still fighting for their God-given rights that have been denied them; when brotherhood and justice are words we've only heard, and peace on earth seems an unattainable dream. Yet there she sat praying for her husband to win! Perhaps it's mean of me, but the very fact that she prayed so hard, for such a mundane thing, made me very happy when Barry Asher won.

When I stated that I "prayerfully" buy a lottery ticket each week, I merely meant hopefully. As much as I hope to be better off someday, there are too many things in the world deserving of prayer for me to squander one prayer on money.

Later,
Richelene

Sunday night

I got so engrossed in *The Occult* that I spent all day in bed reading. I finished it too. With all its "incredibilities" and mind-bogging grotesqueries, it is a compelling and interesting book. Perhaps there is something to this Faculty X, by which we could project more meaning into life, but I think it's best that I leave mine dormant. I have enough to cope with just trying to keep track of the little monsters I have already without conjuring up a contingent of demons to complicate matters further. In my opinion, Aleister Crowley, Madame Blavatsky, and all of the witches, etc., were simply suffering from schizophrenia or some other drastic personality abnormality, along with acute sexual aberrations.

I saw *Lady Sings the Blues.* Diana Ross was truly great in the role of Billie Holiday, and Billy Dee Williams was just too much as Claude McKay. He is truly a masterpiece of black architecture. If his true self is as compassionate and loving as the role he portrayed, he could easily be my ideal man. Silly, isn't it, an almost forty-year-old woman fantasizing? That's one of the advantages of being young at heart.

Seriously, before I left, Donna said that she knew I'd find him as "mind-blowing" as she and the rest of the females from fifteen to fifty-five have found him. I, the cool, level-headed one, stated that I doubted that he would impress me. But I promised that after my assessment of him, I would tell her truthfully my reaction. And so today I truthfully reported to her that even I saw all the qualities that make a man—that is, as he portrayed the role. She read my blueprint for my ideal man before I left. She said, "He is all of this." Indeed he was, par excellence.

The pain and sorrow of Billie Holiday's life that led up to her turning to dope was not clearly delineated to me, but one still felt a sense of pity and sympathy for her that she should have become addicted to drugs as a crutch. Yet in a sense, we all have our crutches that we hobble through life on. Welfare is the crutch that I must lean on now. Who is qualified to say whether Billie Holiday was weaker than I because she took dope, or stronger than I because she was paying her own way through life?

There is something that is a little disquieting about Frances, the girl I went with. Nothing seems to evoke much enthusiasm or life in her. Some vital essence seems to be missing. For instance: Apparently she saw nothing much about Billy Dee Williams, Diana Ross, or the movie itself that aroused any sparks of interest or meaning. She stated that if the movie had been much longer, she would have been bored to death. Another friend and I have tried to interest her in bowling, to no effect. This past summer she played one game of tennis with me, and that was the end of that. I plan to play with my children this summer. And at parties or dances it's as if she is wound up in a tight little ball, afraid or unable to unwind and really laugh and be happy. But I suppose this is just her personality, and I must respect it and accept her as she is, just as she must accept me as I am.

Still it does seem that some kind of recreation or activity should evoke a genuinely pleasurable response and lightness. No doubt there are things that I am not aware of that do make her light up with pleasure.

Last night was thoroughly enjoyable to me. The moon was so big and bright and gorgeous that it competed shamelessly with the movie for my attention. By calling on Faculty X (uh uh!), I was able to absorb every last ounce of substance from both; even the children were not too distracting.

To be fair to Frances, I can empathize with her and her lack of vitality. She is, like me, a divorcee. Knowing the hardships and frustrations involved in trying to be breadwinner, mother and father to children, I can well understand the energy can be drained and vitality sapped at times. I also know the depths of despair that life can sometimes plunge even the strongest into. Besides, she is seven years younger than me and perhaps has yet to learn some of the finer points of coping with life's vicissitudes. I am no master of the art, even now, but am learning every day.

One of my "admirers" called. I was eating dinner so saw no reason to let my food get cold. This resulted in an abrupt end to the conversation. I will continue to wait for "Mr. Ideal" to materialize.

Good night,
Richelene

P.S. The children just called me to the window to observe a particularly beautiful sunset. Across the mountains, the sky is emblazoned with different hues of orange and blue. How good that already they are able to see some of the simple beauties that give us glimpses of a larger reality.

1–22–73

Dear Self,

It's another Monday morning. I got off to such a glorious start this damp, cloudy morning that it is too good to be true. The morning began rather "draggily," but I forced myself to keep going—and pretty soon I was going at a pretty normal pace.

I got the kids out and literally tore into my housework. Washed and hung out three loads of clothes in the cellar, ironed a few things, washed my hair, swept the upstairs, and was sweeping the kitchen in preparation for mopping when the *Phil Donahue Show* caught my eye. Today's show was about four exceptional children. I missed the first one, but the other three were as follows: a little girl born without arms and legs, a fifteen-month-old black girl born with sickle cell anemia, and the fourth case was two children in the same family. The first boy was born without eyes, was retarded, and had cerebral palsy and his brother was born without one eye and was "hydroencephalatic." How pitiful. And yet how serenely the families had accepted and loved these children. Love was mirrored on both the parents' and the children's faces. The mother of the two boys, her face animated and alive, explained so beautifully how they had learned to accept, and live with their exceptional children, as they could not change them. Now I feel more ashamed of myself than ever for expending so much self-pity on myself. It's a funny thing, but by writing down these seemingly trivial day-to-day occurrences and examining them in a new light, I am coming to a new awareness and perspective of life. As uneventful and trivial as these things may seem to some, they are teaching me, and life definitely seems to be taking on new meaning.

Now, I will journey into the mystical. In an earlier letter, I stated that I had not had an "episode" or seizure in several months. Early this morning, I had a light one, complete with hallucinations—a big, black demon, no less. Now, although I've never told anyone, for fear of them thinking me some kind of weirdo, I've always had hallucinations along with many of the seizures.

Knowing that I was an epileptic and having read up on it enough to know most of the symptoms that typify the disease, never has it entered my mind that I was having visions, either inspired of God or the Devil. I simply accepted them as manifestations of my affliction. I'm still quite certain of this, but that this particular episode should coincide with my reading *The Occult* is slightly disconcerting. This too was coincidental with the full moon and also the beginning of my monthly cycle, so I know normal monthly nervous tension and stress triggered it.

Here is yet another coincidence again. Just after the *Phil Donahue Show* went off, *Dialing for Dollars* featured a spiritualist minister, Rev. Louise Hagan. It seems somehow uncanny for all these related incidents pertaining to psychic phenomena to occur just now. Rev. Hagan stated the belief that when we die we only shed our bodies as a snake sheds its skin; then we graduate to another planet.

Her belief is that we are the same in our next life as we were in this one, or else how ever would we recognize each other. Also she believes that we are continually reincarnated. She states that she was born with the gift of being a medium between the living and the dead and that she has often been in the other world while in her astral body. In the spirit world, they could not see her, even though certain "sensitivities" knew of her presence. She states that they have streets, hospitals, stores, just as we do here. If the spirit world has one house surrounded by mud, I just know it's reserved for me.

Far from making me happy that there really is another world, if it is as she says, it depresses me. After all, who wants to graduate to the same set of problems that we can't seem to solve here on earth? Sorry, Rev. Hagan, I can't afford to buy your theory, but that there might be another world for departed spirits seems possible.

I spoke earlier of the great faith of my childhood. Nothing delighted or awed me more than reading the Bible. Then I accepted everything literally, just as my parents still do. However, as I grew older and waged the fight to live and cope with my health problems, I often wondered if the visions of the Prophets might not have been manifestations of illness rather than divinely inspired.

My own compulsive letter-writing made me wonder if St. Paul was not just an afflicted saintly letter-writer who hoped to inspire his brethren toward a more charitable life. In fact, his several referrals to his "thorn in the flesh" and his gratefulness for not being scorned for it often made me suppose that he must have suffered from epilepsy.

Now the real conflict: Any work or deed that is directed toward further humanizing mankind has to be from a good source. Since God is good and God is love, one can accept the scriptures as divine inspirations. One incident in my life stands out above all others. The night that I joined the little Baptist church in Georgia, upon beginning my walk to the altar, I was immediately aware of a sensation of being lifted and floating. It was as if I had suddenly been lifted outside my natural body and was soaring on clouds of lightness and joy. This was not brought on by any incantations on my part, or by a spiritualist. It just happened. Nor has it happened since. I believed then and continued to believe, for many years, that it was the spirit of God taking hold of my body. In the deep recesses of my soul, I still believe that, which is why I can never become a true agnostic. The trials of life, since then, have led me to the brink of agnosticism, but that experience keeps me from plunging over.

If this was merely a manifestation of epilepsy, why has it never reoccurred like the other symptoms? Why did it happen only at the time that I was acknowledging my Christian beliefs? And if, as I theorized earlier, all the people who inhabited the pages of *The Occult* were mentally ill, because of the psychic phenomena they experienced, am I not the same? Are all people either sick or well, good or evil? If one is good, does that mean that he has a well brain and if he is evil it follows that his brain is sick; on the other hand, if he is good, does it mean that his actions are dictated by a good spirit from another world, and if he is evil, it must follow that his actions are dictated by a bad spirit from another world? If man operates on his own will, then it must follow that he is accountable for the mean things he does and should be punished. Yet if man is controlled by a destiny beyond himself, how can he be held accountable for the evil or good that he does? If the spiritual life begins and ends in the brain, then all the sick or evil ones will simply die and that is the end of it all. And all the well or good ones will simply die and that is the end of it all. Somehow I believe that there is a place for departed spirits and "Dust thou art, to dust returneth" is not the ultimate end of man. But who can answer my questions with certainty?

And now to descend to earth and to the grocery store before the rain begins.

Until next time,
Richelene

3:00 P.M.

P.S. I just got back from the grocery store. The taxi was there within five minutes. I was thinking how marvelous that was until I saw the driver—the one driver that I have bad vibrations with. Naturally he charged me 20 cents more than the other drivers normally do. Once again it was accentuated that we can't have it all. The good and bad are usually interlaced.

1–23–73
8:45 P.M.

Dear Self,

President Lyndon B. Johnson died late yesterday. It's always sad to hear of anyone's death, great or small. Yet LBJ's death did not give me the same jolt that President Kennedy's did. But the circumstances are worlds apart; thus one's reaction is bound to be different.

No doubt LBJ did render a great service to our country; and no doubt he did much for my people with his Civil Rights legislation. Yet the Great Society that he envisioned did not materialize, and I am still poor, on welfare, and surrounded by mud. And thousands of others share my plight. But at least he tried. And so despite the color of his skin, his power, and his wealth, that great equalizer of all mortals, death, has claimed him. He now belongs to the ages like many before him and still more after him.

Connie called today and asked if I'd make a jumpsuit for her sister. I have declined to sew for other than the family since I've been in Connecticut. Now, with Jeffrey in "Headstart" for half a day, I can perhaps begin to do a little outside sewing from time to time. She is giving me leeway to design the jumpsuit in whatever way I choose to. Great! Don't enjoy sewing by patterns (Jeffrey just rushed in and informed me that he killed a ten-foot-tall spider in the cellar!).

I went with Evelyn to bowl a couple of quick games late this afternoon. The first game I scored 136. The second game, I scored 215! Why can't I come up with a game like that when it counts—in the league or at Black Magic?

Mr. Z, the District Manager, made a point of coming over and saying hello and asking how I was. Gave him a quick hello, and then proceeded to miss my spare. White people, especially white men, can be so charming when not many other whites are around.

After dinner, the children and I had a most interesting conversation. Alan, fourteen, stated that a teacher of his, Mr. T (white of course), has a habit of calling his students pigs, stupid, morons, etc. Ricky, sixteen, recalled that when he had him as a teacher, he called one boy a "destructive nigger"! It makes one wonder who that moron really is. Alan stated that just a day or so ago, this teacher told a girl student that she stank, then proceeded to open the windows and behave in a thoroughly juvenile way. All this is from a supposedly mature man, he must be at least fifty, who is teaching our children.

And yet many adults castigate the youth of today for having no values. No doubt this teacher is an isolated case, but the children often relate similar incidents by other teachers. Am I derelict, as a parent, for not protesting? Or do I have a right to protest since I am not paying their salaries, they are paying mine?

I think I'll escape to my room and go to bed. The noise of a basketball game on TV plus seven enthusiastic viewers does not inspire good writing, if such there be in me.

And so good night self,
Richelene

1–24–73

Dear Self,

What an intriguing sequence of events: Saturday, a new president is sworn in; Monday, an old president dies; and an old heavyweight champion is defeated, ushering a new one in; Tuesday, peace in Vietnam is announced; and so the ever revolving cycle of the old and the new, rejoicing and sorrow goes on. Laughter and tears are always so closely interwoven.

This was one of those unbelievable mornings. I did a few hand washables and hung them out. Then I stood flat-footed and ironed fifteen shirts and blouses, eighteen pairs of pants, and several miscellaneous articles. It has been a long time since I pulled that tour de force of ironing. I love to iron, when the spirit hits me, but it doesn't hit me that often these days.

I then proceeded to type Ricky's term paper on ecology. It was quite interesting, though not developed as well as it should have been, due to his putting it off to the last minute and rushing. I must try harder to motivate my children to do what has to be done without procrastination. I did find the paper informative. For instance, did you know that in Berkeley, California (I used to lived there; in fact, Ricky was born there), each citizen has 28.1 square feet of parks and each automobile has 968 square feet of roads; that London had a smog problem as early as 1285, created by the burning of soft coal; that babies are born with evidence of DDT in their bodies? So we learn from everything we do. Ricky likened the automobile to a denizen of evil polluting the air.

Headstart called at 11:30. Jeffrey was sick and vomiting. They wanted to know if I could pick him up. Since I do not have one of those "denizens of evil," I said, no. They agreed to keep him until 12:30 and send him home at the usual time. He complained of feeling unwell this morning but insisted on going to school when I asked him if he would like to stay home.

His teacher sent the following note home: "Jeff is a wonderful boy. All the time and attention he gets at home is great. He is very bright and very happy. I find it a joy having him at our center. He has good problem-solving skills, carries on a very good conversation, and knows what's happening in the world around him."

This beautifully summarizes my own opinion of Jeff. He is wonderful! Jeffrey is special. Although he was conceived and born in what the world terms illegitimacy, to me he is more legitimate than any of my children; at least he was conceived in love and peace and unity of spirit.

Jeffrey's birth was complicated by placenta previa, and we are both lucky to be alive. I nearly hemorrhaged to death before a quick caesarean operation was performed. Jeffrey's head is slightly larger than normal and slightly malformed, which I attribute to something that happened at the time of his birth. But he has always been such a joy to me that sometimes my cup almost "runneth" over. He is full of life and love and affection. Yet he is not perfect and can be tempestuous and trying at times, and is truly an individual. The other children have also brought me much joy, but, as I said, Jeff is special.

Right now, he is fairly chomping at the bit to learn. He questions everything and is so anxious to learn to read that I'm sure if I had more time or patience, I could begin to teach him already. For instance, as sick as he was when he came in today, he demanded that I read to him the note that his teacher sent. Already he recognizes many of the alphabets and numbers. He should indeed be ready for kindergarten in September.

So far he seems oblivious of the slight malformation of his head and is secure and happy. Sadly, I know that children can be cruel, adults also, and soon he may be made aware of the "differentness" of his head in such a way that his intellectual and emotional growth may be stunted. I just hope that I can help to make him so secure in his own worth that he will be able to continue to thrive and grow into his full potential.

It's bedtime now, self,

Good night,
Richelene

1–25–73

Hi Self,

It's bowling day again. We lost all three games, but I'm not depressed because of losing—this time. Maybe it's because I'm getting used to it, although I did bowl quite well, my highest game being 190. Still, I'm somewhat down. Think it's mostly because I haven't slept well for the last couple of nights. Donna and Steve came down and watched TV until 12 A.M. last night. I then had a little trouble getting to sleep after they left. I requested today that they not come down tonight.

How good it will be when they can get a TV and other furniture. Sure hope they get straightened out financially soon. But such is the lot of the poor. They are born in poverty, raised in poverty, marry in poverty, live in poverty, and die in poverty. And, thus, the beat goes on—except for the lucky ones who are born strong enough to fight life on their terms and break out of the unrelenting cycle.

It hurts me to the depths of my being to be so terribly afraid that most of my children have not been blessed with the necessary ingredients to be able to overcome the odds. How I hope and pray that I will be proved wrong, but the inherent weaknesses are there. I cannot stick my head in the sand and pretend not to see them. This is one reason that it has seemed to me so important that I be as close to them and give them as much of myself as I possibly can. Even when I tried to be a breadwinner, a mother and a father, a social worker, a psychiatrist, and other things, I knew that I was spreading myself far too thin. It was a burden on my spirit to know that I was neglecting the larger needs of my children because of pride. So much pride that I would not accept welfare if there was any way I could get around it. And so the day was hastened that I could not get around it, and here I am. Sometimes I feel that this was the work of some power beyond myself, because someone wiser than I knew that my children needed me at home.

Most of all, I fear for Ricky. He is so tall, so good looking, so bright, so talented, so basically good-natured, but so emotional, so high-strung, so temperamental, so sensitive, so suggestible, so much alone. Yet I know too that if he can just hang in there and make the negative aspects of his personality work for him instead of against him, he could be something of worth. Only time will tell if this welfare family will be the beginning of a cycle of dependency or will snip the cord now. I say this because only I, in my family, have ever been on welfare.

I dislike that word "welfare" as applied to indigent people. The dictionary defines welfare as health and happiness. As the welfare departments of our country are set up, they apparently are not overly interested in the health or happiness of their charges. The main emphasis seems to be on trimming the rolls, using many methods that work against health and happiness. Then again, looking at it from the average taxpayer's point of view, why should anyone who can't pay his own way through life be either healthy or happy? When will man get smart enough to put more of the wealth of this country to work searching for better ways to cure or control disease of all kinds? A healthy person is a self-sustaining person and a happy person. Someone should change the name of the "Welfare Department" to the "Department of Services to Indigent People" or something more appropriate than "Welfare Department."

I must stop now and do some work. I have to walk over to Bradlees and buy a tape measurer and some panty hose, plus the never ending supply of bread and milk. The food stamps are gone already and "check day" is not until next Thursday. Please, Dear God, make it so that I can be healthy, happy, and self-sustaining before this year ends. I don't know how much longer I can bear the embarrassment of cashing the "check" and knowing I'm a burden on society.

1–27–73

Dear Self,

Today's *New Britain Herald* sports the big headline: "PEACE SIGNED." With those simple words, we dare to hope that peace might truly begin on earth—for a season. For how long can a peace that is simply "signed" and is not born of the hearts of men last? That this peace was not arrived at through an in-depth change in the hearts of men seems certain. For man will continue to be a restless mass of greed, envy, hatred, strife, and contention until he finds the peace that passes all understanding, peace within himself. That the pen that signed the peace papers is mightier than the sword that has taken countless lives and inflicted suffering on so many innocents is true. But has man become wise enough to accept and live by this truth? We can only hope that he has. May each of us truly pray, "Let there be peace on earth, beginning with me," then work to make it so.

Now I am reading *The Passions of the Mind*, by Irving Stone. This is a novel about the life of Sigmund Freud. I am about halfway through the book now. I find it as fascinating as I did *The Occult*. *Passions* presents the other side of the coin regarding the world beyond. Much in it sounds reasonable and valid, much does not. Certain psychic illnesses were well drawn out. But it does seem that Freud got carried away with his associations of sexuality with neurological illnesses. *Passions* also documented something else that I've always suspected: many of the "healers" of psychiatric and neurological illnesses have grave problems of their own. Perhaps that is why many of them enter this branch of medicine. I, myself, feel that this would be a fascinating life's work. There are still so many virgin territories in the caverns of the mind yet to be explored. Yet this must be a terribly frustrating work. In the final analysis, it is so much simpler to set a broken bone, remove a gallstone, or even cure a cancer than it is to cure the sickness of the psyche and brain.

I can truly say that I've never yearned to go to bed with my father, even though I have always thought him the gentlest, sweetest man on earth. That there are some sick souls that do have Freud's beloved Oedipal complex, I have no doubt, but could it possibly be as universal as he would have had us believe?

Jeffrey just brought the mail to me: *The Reader's Digest;* an appointment to take Candace to the orthopedic clinic at Newington Children's Hospital (she has a slight curvature of the spine, scoliosis); and a note from Norman, enclosing a belated Christmas gift for me. How like him. Although he sent the money to pay "Santa" for Jeffrey, at the time, he felt that it was not enough to include a gift for me. So now he sends mine. What a pleasant surprise, even though I had not given it a second thought. As I said before, Norman is most definitely a few notches above average in many ways.

I must get a frame and mail the picture I painted for him for Christmas. I have been waiting for it to dry before mailing it. It isn't that I think I'm a good enough artist to paint pictures for others, having never taken a lesson, but he specifically requested that I paint a landscape for him like the one I painted for myself. The one that I did for him is such an improvement over mine that I can now see just how horrible the first one I did really is. But like anything, we learn by doing, by trial and error. I enrolled in an oil painting class at Nathan Hale Junior High School this fall, but when the instructor gave us a list of all the supplies he wanted us to begin with, I knew class was over for me—I couldn't afford the supplies.

I am so engrossed in *Passions of the Mind* now, I will find it hard to break away and read the new *Reader's Digest*. I will also have to break away and do a little visiting. It would be much too easy for me to become a reading fanatic. I can't afford to become too detached from people.

Until Later,
Richelene

1–29–73

Dear Self,

Monday morning life begins again. I do not count Sunday as the beginning of the week. Sunday is a day set apart—a day of reverence, a day of rest. Monday begins the new week, when man goes back to his work, whatever his work may be. My work is trying to maintain a somewhat stable home for my children. That this is a thankless and even maligned job, especially in circumstances like mine. That there are those that count me as nothing, since I am a welfare recipient, I am well aware.

And yet I feel that I am of as much worth, in the total scheme of things, as the man who sends rockets to the moon; the doctor who cures disease; the woman who has secured a high position in the world of business; the teacher who teaches my children; or even the president who rules America and the Queen who rules England. For as long as I give my best to the job that is mine, and if, by God's grace, I can present these young lives to society as decent, stable, self-sustaining, contributing adults, have I not done as monumental and important a job as any human being? And even failing to accomplish this, if I do my best, have I not done all that is required?

And so the new week begins, with winter roaring back onto the scene, chasing away the gentle spring that had crept in during winter's temporary absence and warmed our spirits. Cruel winter, with its snowy blustering ways, has once again proclaimed its sovereignty over the last days of January. And Spring must wait its turn.

For almost a month now, I've chronicled each day's events, and for the most part, it has been a month devoid of excitement. And yet it has been exciting. For by just taking the time each day to look at life as it is unfolding for us, I begin to get fresh insights into everyday occurrences. I begin to see that nothing is trivial and unimportant if we will train ourselves to glean the vital essences from our everyday lives. I am beginning to find life interesting in a quiet, tranquil kind of way. When I first began this journal, I was so depressed, so pessimistic.

Now, taking each day as it comes, neither daring to dream impossible dreams, nor giving up on life as a lost cause, I am more and more at peace. That the turbulent days will come again, I am sure, but I believe that I will cope with them with far more grace. Is the way to live successfully being slowly revealed to me through this self-analysis of sorts, or am I merely becoming mature in the true sense of the word? Perhaps life really does begin at forty. Something good is happening!

There was no school today, due to the snowstorm. Even the children did not unnerve me as much as they normally do under these circumstances. I hate to think that this is probably just the beginning of my "up" cycle and this time next week, I may be sliding back down, but I won't think of that. I will think positive.

I went to Black Magic again Saturday night, and won $5.15. Not bad. That means I bowled free and made a profit of 40 cents. It's a cinch I'll never get rich at Black Magic, but it's so much fun!

Must go now,
Richelene

1–30–73

Dear Self,

It's another day. Two days before the "check" comes. "Old Mother Hubbard went to the cupboard, but when she got there, the cupboard was bare!" The cupboards and refrigerator are as bare as a baby's heinie today. This is the usual state of affairs several days before "the day."

It never fails to pain me to see the children continually peeking in cabinets and the refrigerator when this time of the poverty cycle rolls around every two weeks. By now I should be able to observe their seeming bewilderment that nothing materializes there with an air of detachment. It's almost as if they refuse to accept the fact that there is no food there, and the next peek will reveal a miraculous abundance of good things to eat. But I am not Christ and cannot feed this multitude on two little fish and five loaves of bread.

Norman's gift, plus the few dollars that Ricky gave me from his after school job and two dollars from shoveling snow yesterday will tide us over, but I still will have to go sparingly in order to have a couple of dollars left in case the "check" doesn't come on time. And of course, I must have my bowling money. No doubt there are many who feel that if things are so tough, I should give bowling up. Never! I deserve this much enjoyment from life. After all, I do not smoke, drink, or eat a lot of candy and junk, so why can't I spend a few dollars for myself bowling?

So I will make a list and send a couple of the children to the store when they get home from school. I would go myself but am somewhat fearful of walking the long distance to Shop-Rite over these icy sidewalks. I had a nice fall on the ice before Christmas. This has somewhat dampened my enthusiasm for walking when it's icy outside.

I had a salami sandwich and a cup of coffee for lunch. This was not at all satisfying as I do not like salami. I sent Alan to the store yesterday, and this was his choice for lunch. Since there were no alternatives available in the house, I ate it and tried hard to be thankful.

Ricky is home from school today. It seems he over-extended himself in his efforts to earn money shoveling snow yesterday. Now his foot that was broken is hurting again. I told him it could be a slight case of frostbite since he was out so long in the cold. Poor Ricky, he is forever running into misadventures of the feet. His ankle on the other foot was broken in a football game the year before last.

I finished *Passions of the Mind*. What a magnificent book. Upon really getting into the book and more into Sigmund Freud, the man, I really began to admire him.

His lack of bitterness at the defection of some of his most beloved disciples, Carl Jung and Otto Rank, and his stoicism in the face of cancer of the mouth—how he must have suffered. He was indeed a bold explorer into the netherlands of the unconscious mind, whether we agree with many of his theories or not.

Still the questions raised both by *The Occult* and *Passions of the Mind* remain unanswered. I wonder if there will ever arise on earth a mortal who can give us definite answers? Is God merely the conscious, logical mind that leads us to try to do good and the Devil the unconscious mind, the one that gives rise to delusions, evil, demoniac hallucinations and all the other wretched actions of man? I must stop this train of questioning that leads nowhere but to more confusion. There is a time for questioning the deeper meaning of life, and I will ever use the right to do so, but abuse of any right is an abomination and leads only to distress.

The main thing is to live the life given to me. Life is for the living, and I will make the most of it as it is given to me.

2:00 P.M.

Donna just brought Kenny and Steven for me to baby sit while she goes to the Employment Office. Kenny is walking at nine months. Steven's eczema is bad again. How I hope he outgrows it or it will go away somehow. He has suffered from the moment of his entry into this world— the poor little fella, he is such an unlovable one. By that I do not mean that one cannot love him. I refer to his inability to allow one to love him, to cuddle and be affectionate with him. Even as a tiny baby, he will be two in March, he would squirm out of your grasp when you tried to cuddle him. Whether the eczema caused his unpleasant personality or the two are interlaced, I do not know.

Kenny is the complete opposite. He is so loving, so affectionate, so good-natured and smiling. So much easier
to love and thus he receives more. Yet Steven is the one
that really needs the most love. Will I try harder to give
him that extra measure of love?

Thinking of the opposite poles of my two little grandbabies' personalities, the different personalities of my own
children are brought to mind. Donna, the first one, is always strong-willed and with a mind completely her own
from the beginning. She is always restless, full of emotions, good and bad. Always obstinate, sure that only she
is right about everything, allowing no room for maybes and
compromises. Her pregnancy at fifteen, and subsequent
premature entry into adulthood, cut me to the core, but
perhaps it was for the best. She does seem calmer, a little
more sensible in some ways, now that she is married. Still,
she is only eighteen, just a child. I hope that by the time reality sets in she will be mature enough to cope with it.

Ricky, the second one, is nervous, high-strung, and
talented. For a boy of almost seventeen, he stays much
too close to home. In a way this is good; in a way it is not.
He should get out more, make friends with some of his
peers. And yet, I was also somewhat a loner as a teenager,
I still am, so what can I say? He'll probably do all right.
Certainly, he has much potential in art.

Kenneth, the third one. Contrary to Ricky, he is out
too much. He plays with a band, the guitar. We rarely see
Kenny, except at breakfast and bedtime. He is quiet, un-
communicative, but a morally good boy, I think. He has
always been the most nonintellectual and has always
brought home the lowest grades, but he'll probably be all
right also.

Alan is the fourth one. How do you describe Alan? He
is loud, argumentative, but can make you laugh quicker
than the rest. At fourteen, he is more or less thoroughly

exasperating. I haven't been able yet to get an inkling of where his potential might possibly lie. He is also good at drawing and also seems to have a literary bent. Loves to read and write little stories. He, too, seems morally good. Like the rest, he has his nervous quirks.

Melanie is the fifth one. At thirteen, she is pretty nice. She and Candace keep their room neat, and she is learning to cook very well. She expressed the desire to go to Goodwin Technical School and take up dress designing next year instead of going to regular high school. I expressed the opinion that she would do better to go on to high school and learn shorthand and typing so that she would at least be equipped to get a job, since she expresses no desire to go to college. Where, around here, could she make use of dress designing except at home, as I do? Am I wrong for discouraging her in this desire? For the most part, I try to allow my children to follow their own minds—with guidance.

Candace is the sixth one. Candace is the gentle one, the lady of the family. She is pretty easy-going for the most part, but also moody. I see more of myself in Candace than any of the others. She is iron-willed behind the gentle exterior and will fight back. I hope, with all my heart, that neither she nor any of the others will ever have to wage the battle that I've had to fight. As I see them now, I just don't think they'd survive. But of course, life itself makes one stronger. Candace is quite thin, as I was, and wants to be a model.

Jeffrey is the seventh one. I drew a personality profile of Jeffrey earlier. He is the special one, the extra dividend of happiness. He may turn out to be just a roguish, rakish never-do-well, as so many last children do, especially boys. On the other hand, with love, care, and guidance, he could turn out to be something of value to society.

Only time will tell whether these products of a mixed-up situation will be assets or liabilities to society; I hope for the best and pray that I will live to guide them and see the end results, good or bad.

Sincerely,
Richelene

1–31–73

Dear Self,

Today, January breaths its last frigid breaths; it was an unusual month in many ways. The roaring lion became a gentle lamb. Or should I say that the lion, winter, lay down with the lamb, spring, for a while? But then, winter woke from its sleep, roared, and frightened spring away. So this, the last day of January, is a cold, bright, and sunny day.

January was also an unusual month for me in that it was a month of stillness, a time of contemplation. I was able to quiet the warring factions of my inner self for a little while and take a good look at the chain of events that have shaped my life up until now. I think I now have hold of something good, a more workable philosophy to live by.

That I raised questions for which I found no pat answers is irrelevant. The relevant fact is that I am alive! I am a functioning human being, a part of the universe, an individual with the potential to do good, to be a good mother and a good grandmother; a woman and a child; an ever-growing, ever-evolving person aware of my self-hood, aware of my oneness with other human beings and one with God and nature; a feeling, throbbing element of a united whole, aware of self, submerging the self, coming into my own as a human being. I am alive and living!

And so exits January's scene, and the month of hearts and love, February, waits to make the scene.

Hearts and Love to you, self
Richelene

2–2–73

Dear Self,

What a difference a day makes! Yesterday and today, just a breath away from the joyous and optimistic parting that I gave January, I have had a terrible lower backache, the old girl can't even bend over. Perhaps it's just psycho-somatic; perhaps there's a physical reason. Anyway I think I'll try to ride it out without going to the doctor.

This is the first time in about three years that I've felt so bad that I couldn't get up and prepare breakfast for the family. I got Melanie up and she grumblingly made breakfast for the crew; Candace cleaned up the kitchen very nicely, grumblingly also. I didn't feel like getting Jeffrey dressed so I kept him home. He grumbled also. Grumble, grumble, grumble! Does mother get sympathy when she's out of action? No, all she gets is grumbles.

Winter has returned with a vengeance. The sky is weeping frozen teardrops, giving everything a coat of treacherous ice. Why can't it just send down plain ordinary clean white snow?

I went to a different bank to cash the "check" yesterday. I was received with the usual stony-faced, shove-the-money-at-you attitude. Wonder how many of the people who scorn us would truly care to change places with us? Not many, I'm sure. Oh well, better scorn than pity.

Luckily, I ran into Melanie downtown at the bus stop. I took her to the grocery store with me so she could push the carriage and do the bending. I tried to get a taxi for over thirty minutes; each time the line was busy. Finally, I called Catherine, a neighbor, and asked if she would give us a ride home. How it hurts to have to bother people for something like that, but what else could I do? Why doesn't a car drop down out of the sky for us? One thing about

Catherine; she is one of the few people that I've ever known who, I feel, sincerely renders a favor, neither begrudging to do so, nor expecting anything in return. I hope I can return the favor in some way soon.

My next door neighbor is sick with the flu. I had planned to keep tabs on her and do whatever I could to help, as she too is poor, black, and alone. I can't now, thanks to my belligerent back (BB). I sure hope the pain will be gone by tomorrow, Saturday, so I can do some real cleaning. I had planned to make slipcovers for the living room chairs today. I will have to postpone it.

I think I'll lie down for a while now. Jeffrey filled the washer with clothes for me. Together, we managed to wash two loads. I will save the rest for Melanie to do.

I dreamed last night at that I was in Atlanta with the family. I was wearing a lavender colored dress, my mother's favorite color. In the dream, my mother was holding up and admiring a white blouse and skirt that I had made. I hope this is not an omen, as mother has always said that at her funeral she wants all of us to wear white instead of black. Mother will be seventy-eight this month. She has lived a long fruitful life, having a progeny of twelve children and scores of grandchildren and great grandchildren. How do you best describe my mother? She and all black mothers are one, the Eternal Black Mother— a tower of strength, mother of hope.

Poor, black, and alien in a land that counted her as nothing but a sub-human beast of burden, a sex object, a chattel, she was a spirit of life, and this indomitable spirit persevered. She raised her sons and daughters to persevere, to overcome the obstacles set before them at every hand by a cruel and inhuman world. This world belongs to the white man, he who called himself human, yet blithely set about dehumanizing every darker race that he touched, in the name of civilization. The black mother is beautiful, strong, and proud. She is a high priestess among women, neither asking to be set on a pedestal, nor requesting that a halo be placed above her head, she is light and love.

She sets about her task of nurturing, guiding, and instilling a sense of dignity and worth in her children, preparing them to stand up and be counted, to assert their worth as human beings, their right to be here.

The Eternal Black Mother! If her man was by her side to help her shoulder the load she carried, she counted herself blessed. If, by some vicissitudes of life, he was not, she did not flinch, but carried on with a will born of purpose, the purpose being to win the victory over the society that sought to suppress and destroy the humanity of her children. And through her trials and tribulations; her moans and prayers; her courage and fortitude; her songs of joy and sorrow, she is winning. Her children will no longer grovel at the white man's feet, gratefully grabbing at the crumbs he throws them. They are throwing off their shackles and standing up straight, demanding their rights as children of the universe—asserting their right to be here.

No, the white man did not civilize the black man. Eternal Black Mother did.

Her children rise up and call her blessed.

Blessings to you, self
Richelene

2-6-73

Dear Self,

I haven't felt like writing for several days. The old back really had me in subjection. I finally decided not to fight it and stayed in bed as much as possible, between creeping, and I do mean creeping, about doing a few necessary chores.

One good thing came of it. I finished reading *The Peaceable Kingdom*. When I ordered the book, had no idea what it was about. When I opened it, and saw that it is about the beginning of a Quaker religious sect, I was surprised. What a sequence of books! *The Occult* is about the psychic life; *Passions of the Mind*, about the life of the mind; and now *The Peaceable Kingdom*, about the religious life.

I haven't enjoyed reading a book so much since I drank in all of Richard Wright's books. After reading his works, I was spoiled for anyone else's for a while. Nothing, not even the Bible, seemed interesting to read for quite a while, even though I ploughed through quite a few: Maya Angelou's *I Know Why the Caged Bird Sings*; *Trixie*; *The Dahomean*, by Frank Yerby; and many others. Then I decided to go through James Baldwin's works. I enjoyed them somewhat and I am sure he is a better stylist than Richard Wright, but Richard Wright's works grabbed me where I live and breathe and have my being. His concluding paragraph in *Black Boy* where he expressed a desire for man's finding a redeeming meaning for having lived and suffered on this earth really knocked me out! But then I suppose this is why most writers write; they are searching for that elusive "redeeming meaning." This, I suppose, is what all people of conscience and thinking people search for.

Certainly the quest was evident in *The Peaceable Kingdom*; George Fox's quest for "that of God" in all people; Margaret Fell's compulsion to do good and help the less fortunate; Aunt Gulie's work among the Indians, her healing instincts; Boniface Baker's relinquishing of his land and worldly goods to his freed slaves. In the peaceable kingdom they created in the wilderness, black, white, and red people lived together peacefully for a while. Perhaps they had found a redeeming meaning. What is my redeeming meaning?

The phrase "that of God in everyone" is beautiful. If only we could follow "that of God" in ourselves and look for and respond to "that of God" in others, we too could have a peaceable kingdom here on earth. No way. Man is too selfish, too steeped in his own importance. We have suppressed "that of God" and declared that God is dead. The pervading thought seems to be that man is an end unto himself. I can see questions for which I still have not found answers formulating in my mind, so I will move on to another subject.

My slipcovers just went down the drain. I had to buy sneakers for Alan and shoes for Jeffrey and Melanie, plus a few other unexpected things came up; maybe next month.

I think I'll go soak my back in a tub of hot water now and get dressed. Still will take it easy though and not press my luck just yet.

6:30 P.M.

I received a letter of solicitation from the National Urban League in New York today. It began:

Dear Friend;

Chances are you don't really understand what it means to be poor, black, and American in 1973. The despair that lives behind crumbling tenement walls is unbelievable to those who have never experienced it. Children who run from rats and roaches; the junkie nodding in the doorway; a mother who ekes out the week on welfare . . . they have strength enough only for survival . . .

I wonder where they obtained their mailing list. This "friend" could write a book on what it means to be poor, black, and American in 1973, 1972, 1971, 1970, 1969, etc., and roaches are like members of the family. In fact, it sometimes pains me to have to squash out the lives of my creepy little friends. After all, they're just trying to make it somehow just as I am. I know what it's like to have some giant stepping on you, squashing out your life's substances. Only I'm still trying to fight, while the roaches are exterminated swiftly, mercifully.

Rats I have had no encounters with. Fortunately, or unfortunately, I missed that bit of black Americana. I haven't been completely overlooked in that area though. When Candace was about three weeks old, in Atlanta, a small mouse got in the bed with us, and almost sent me toppling over the brink. I caught the little cuss in a trap a few days later.

And despair? Dear Mr. Jordan, this "friend" has intimately lain with despair; has lain down with despair and rose the next morning with its vile tentacles still wound tightly around me; has sopped up despair and walked with despair; has breathed despair, absorbed despair until I became a nameless blob of despair. Your wife may not remember, but one day in 1963, the proud and independent young woman that was me collapsed in tears at work. Why? The young woman had left a seven-year old-child, her oldest daughter, to care for a sick baby, the youngest of six; and despair had followed her to work that day.

Your wife was then a social worker at the Welfare Department, the young woman a file clerk. And now your wife is the spouse of the Executive Director of the National Urban League. Whatever happened to the proud young lady? She fell flat on her face and is now living on welfare. Does she envy your wife? No. Her heart rejoices that at least some of her black sisters have climbed the mountain. She feels proud that some of them have big, black beautiful men that they can look up to; can say to the world

"Look at this man that stands proud and tall and tells the white man, with authority, I am a man, and will fight for the right of manhood for all my brothers, and he is mine!"

Oh, yes, Mr. Jordan, I do care about voter registration, unfair employment practices, and suburban zoning laws. I care about everything that restricts my freedom and diminishes my humanity, and that of my brothers and sisters. But presently, I can only contribute my feelings and best wishes. Perhaps some psychic force will emanate from my soul and unite with the soul of some wealthy, generous, and compassionate person to whom your letter has been sent, and he will include a portion for me.

Speaking of writing a book, at one time, I planned to do just that one day. Now seeing all the intricacies involved in writing a book, I realize that I'm not a good enough writer. Then too, maybe I don't write black enough. Having always felt that I was a human being, first of all, I've always written as a human being. For black folks writing to go over big with whites, it has to have a definite black flavor. Since white folks are the ones with the money, if a black writer wants to succeed financially, he has to strive to really flavor it black.

Anyway, my writing is too ordinary, too flat. I wish I could flourish my pen and create those lyrical, abstract, hard to understand phrases that the really good writers spin with such ease. But all that comes from these fingers are simple, honest thoughts, and who cares about what I think?

The truth is I'd be afraid to plunge too deeply into myself and pull out all the essential truths and experiences needed for a really good book. I might get lost in the quagmire of broken dreams, heartaches, and memories best left undisturbed. If I were to write an autobiography, it might possibly yield some fresh insights into the forces that shape the lives of individuals, but I could never dissect myself and lay the pieces of my soul before the public for them to either devour like juicy tidbits or toss aside like so much garbage. It would be too painful either way.

7:30 P.M.

AN INTERESTING TIDBIT

Each day, in the *New Britain Herald*, there is a horoscope for each sign of the Zodiac. Saturday there was the following description of Scorpio—I am a Scorpio:

> Scorpio can be powerful but sentimental, intense but willing to make concessions, Scorpio persons will fight to keep a commitment. These natives dig for information, make wonderful detectives, are creative, possess individual styles and seldom leave anything half-finished. The classical Scorpio is fascinated by astrology, psychic phenomena and the occult. Where love is in picture, Scorpio is all or nothing, hot or cold, no in between. Scorpio should exercise caution in dealing with Aquarius and Leo.

That's very interesting, indeed. Sounds very much like me, as I see myself, and to bring it closer to home—my former husband was a Leo!

_____ called today. She is also a welfare recipient, a mother of seven. She is another classic example of the typical welfare recipient with their hidden frailties: We often commiserate with each other over our mutual problems. Now I'm going to make a bold statement. She is an epileptic and does not know it. How do I know? It is simple: so many of her ailments and symptoms are exactly the same as mine, even including the sleep-paralysis (narcolepsy). She states that often, at night, she is caught up into a state of semiconsciousness where she cannot move, even though she is aware of what's going on around her. Our parents and grandparents called it the little "itches riding you" because they did not know what it was.

Today she said that often at night, she wakes up suddenly with a frightened feeling, and feels as if something is crawling all over her; often her hands and feet are numb. Plus she is increasingly having quivering and pain in the stomach, also insomnia. Many times, in talking with her, she will stop right in the middle of a sentence, forgetting what she was talking about. She also spoke of increasing dizzy spells, all symptoms pointing to a form of petit mal epilepsy.

As I said before, in addition to suffering from petit mal epilepsy myself, I've read up on epilepsy. I dare not suggest to her that she should see a neurologist as people recoil from the thought that there might be something sick about their nervous system or brain. To most people, you're automatically labeling them crazy. Even though I don't talk about my affliction to people, I accept it as a chronic disease, just as diabetes or heart trouble. I know I have a loused up nervous system, but I can function within my limitations and cope with life to a workable degree.

_____ is forever going to doctors for alleviation of her symptoms, but not the right doctor, a neurologist. Of course, she will probably live to a ripe old age without getting the proper medical care, but the journey could be a lot more comfortable for her with the right medications.

Oh, how I'd love to be able to go into the field of neurological research! Just yesterday, there was a lady, a PhD in neurological research, in a commercial on TV. She was also the mother of four children. I know it's not too late for me to get going on a new career, but how do I find the way?

Something else interesting: With a few variations, _____ 's husband was an exact replica of mine, and so were so many other recipients that I've talked with. That also tells me a lot about the odds against women like us marrying the stable, well-adjusted men that we feel we deserve. Besides, at this stage of life, all the stable, well-adjusted men are married, and will stay that way until they die. To be sure, they'll dally around with us, if we're willing, but leave their wives? Never! And, I for one would never want a man who would leave his wife. I would still consider him below par, for that very reason. Complicated, isn't it? The men that are available to us, single or divorced, are for the most part variations of the ones we discarded; discarded sounds terribly callous, so I'll change that to the ones we couldn't make it with.

Wow! This has been a long letter, so I'll close, lest I bore you, self.

Sincerely,
Richelene

2–7–73

Dear Self,

_____ called early this morning to see if I was going to the Headstart PTA meeting. I had forgot all about it. I was in bed nursing my tender, still aching back. Also Jeffrey is home today with a cold.

The wind is angrily unleashing its fury on the house today, mercilessly filling the house with its frigid breath. This must surely be the coldest apartment in New Britain. Right now, I have the oven and all the burners on, hoping to dispel some of the chill. After seven winters here, I should be used to it by now, but I'm not. Repeated calls to the Housing Authority yield nothing but a cursory check by the maintenance men. They fiddle around a little, announce that now I'll be getting lots of heat, and leave us still shivering. When the temperature reaches zero or thereabouts, the pipes all freeze, and I get ice in my bathtub! Most people refuse to believe this. But the children are my witnesses. It is true.

I'm so sick and weary of living in this wretched, cold place that I could scream and scream and scream. But where can I move to with six children? Besides, even if I could find a place to move to, which is next to impossible, where would I get the money to finance the move? I'm stuck here. I'm hopelessly, helplessly, despairingly stuck in this dung heap of so-called "charity," welfare, and public housing.

I, and the rest of the wretched of the earth, deserve better. My children deserve a warm place to live and all the other essentials of life just as surely as Ethel Kennedy's or Jackie O'Nassis' children. What, besides the accident of being born white and wealthy, entitles them to comforts that are denied us? They breathe and eat and feel and defecate (defecate, my ass—they shit) with the same apparatus that we do. When they bleed, it comes out red and liquid just as our blood does. And when they die, they're done, just as we are. Did they create the heavens or make the seasons change places from year to year? Can either of them breathe life into a lump of clay? Did Ethel or Jackie ever make one hair on their head black or white, except with the help of Miss Clairol? Ah, foolish, silly woman, you're raving like a mad woman! The cold must be freezing your brain along with your feet. You're black, poor, hurting, cold, and disgusted, and all the raving in the world will not change those facts.

A sensible plan of action would be to:

1. Forget about being black and poor, you'll never change that, and in reality, you do not want to change the former—you've always counted that a privilege.
2. Make an appointment with your beloved Dr. Byer.
3. Call the Health Department and see if there is anything they can do toward prodding the Housing Authority into improving the heating system here.
4. Go back and re-read all your flowery drivel of earlier this year and delude yourself into thinking that you're happy, or turn off the oven and go back to bed.

At least it's warm there.

10:45 P.M.

I solved this morning's dilemma. I went back to bed. Tonight my back is so much better, it's miraculous.

In talking with _____ this morning, somehow we got on the subject of having babies. She, mother of three, stated that she loves to be pregnant. The claim is that she gets an exhilarating joy and feeling of well-being throughout her pregnancies. So much does she enjoy the state of pregnancy, that if it were not for the responsibilities of the finished product, she would happily have a baby every year! Not only that, but if it were possible for fertilized eggs to be implanted in another's womb, she would cheerfully carry babies for other women for pay!

She was knocked off her feet when I told her that I read that there is currently talk of babies being produced in just that way in the future. This would allow women who miscarry to have their babies carried to term by a surrogate womb. It would also serve to eliminate discomfort for liberated women who work, and who want babies but not the bother of having them. She exclaimed that she would do it happily for a living! How about that? Since many people think that all we welfare moms like to do is have babies anyway, a program of this sort could have far-reaching effects. Women like _____ could become self-supporting in a job they enjoyed, and help humanity at the same time.

Too bad _____ is thirty-two already. By the time such a program, if ever, goes into effect, I greatly fear she will have passed her period of usefulness.

I am going to sleep now.

Good night,
Richelene

2–8–73

Hi Self,

I went bowling this morning. By approaching the lanes very gingerly and propping myself up on my left knee and barely bending, was able to bowl, however badly. Would you believe we finally won a game? I still can't believe it. No thanks to me.

The old back feels so much better that I could dance! As a matter of fact, I did dance a little after dinner. James Brown's "I've Got Ants in My Pants and I Want to Dance" was going strong on the radio and Melanie decided to teach me the newest dance, the "Hoppin' Gator." I wonder what they'll come up with next? I didn't progress too far in my lesson. The cricks and screeches of my body told me that I'd best leave the "Hoppin' Gator" to Melanie and her peers.

I got groceries today. Everything is up a few more cents. I am truly beginning to wonder how we're going to manage to survive if things keep spiraling this way. I am sick, sick, sick of ground beef, hot dogs, chicken wings, I can't afford the whole chickens, pretty soon even the wings will take flight from our diet! There is one bright spot, medium eggs were 59 cents per dozen this week and last week. Several weeks ago they were up to 79 cents per dozen, but bacon was up from 99 cents to $1.09, so the bright spot was dimmed.

I bought one lottery ticket. Maybe next week will be the big one for me. Miriam and I gained a new bowling partner today, white, no less. Evelyn, our regular partner is working on Thursday mornings, so we lost her. I hope this integrated venture works out all right. I will certainly suppress my prejudices if she will suppress hers. We shall see what happens. At least she is a good bowler.

Donna was sick with a splitting headache, so I brought Kenny down to the house. I hope the pill isn't affecting her badly. I know I'm just a meddling mother, but when she became pregnant with Kenny, I wrote her doctor a letter, pleading with him to tie her tubes. It just tore my heart out to see her heading so surely up the road I've traveled, and so much earlier. At least I was twenty when I married. Here she is only eighteen and already a mother of two. I can't stand to see her have a baby every year, a husband unable to provide properly for them and the prospect of only deprivation and misery. One day she may awaken and see the futility of it all, and then it will be too late.

The doctor did not tie her tubes but put her on the pill. I hope it works out. With them living from hand to mouth, from week to week, as it is, another baby would be a tragedy. Although Steve is trying, you can't get blood from a turnip. So if you get a turnip, you have to settle for "pot liquor." One of the things that keep parents like me going is the dream and hope that their children will progress beyond the sphere of life that we have had to "make do" with. It's really devastating to have to watch them also settling for "pot liquor."

Now I understand why elderly women used to feel sorry for me and offer all kinds of wild suggestions for contraception, everything from eating a spoonful of sulfur to drinking nutmeg tea, when I was having a baby every year. They knew what I was heading for. Not only was I too young and dumb to know the reason for their distress, but I was such a hopeless blob of despair, caught up in a miserable, God-forsaken marriage, that nothing really penetrated. It was as if I was without will, drifting along under the will of a man who had cowed me into submission. Oh he was an evil, evil man!

The Dr. Jekyll lured me into marriage; then Mr. Hyde came out. I dared not try to break away because he swore that he would kill me, the children, and any of my relatives who tried to shield us, if I left him. Poor, pitiful weakling that I was, I became a perfect foil for his sick, sadistic nature. And, so I drifted along until finally something inside me found the strength to rise up and rebel, refused to be subjugated any longer. By then it was too late to remedy the damage that the years of physical and mental agony caused. How I wish I'd had the courage to break away after the first baby, but better late than never; and we are surviving. I didn't mean to meander back into that backlog of unhappy memories. It makes me too sad. And so I'll stop now and get some work done.

Until later,
Richelene

2–10–73

Dear Self,

It's Saturday night again. Nowhere to go and no good books to read, so guess I'll look at TV tonight. I finished reading a book about Edgar Cayce last night. Somehow I seem to be getting into this "Occult" or "psychic" bag. I can't deny that it's fascinating. I let Donna read *The Occult* and, as soon as she finished it, she promptly went to the library and got Edgar Cayce and a book about the Fox sisters, who started the spiritualist movement.

Until I read this book about Edgar Cayce, I had never even given reincarnation a second thought, it seemed so implausible. They presented such a strong case for it in this book that it sounds plausible indeed. Their arguments about the ultimate end of the soul could well be as acceptable as any. The more I read, the more I find that my "original" thoughts are not original at all. For instance Edgar

Cayce's statement, "For if it is of God, it must be good," or, "if it is good, it must come from the All-Good, or God," almost exactly mirrors what I expressed earlier, after I had read *The Occult*. A couple of years ago, I enrolled in a writer's workshop in Hartford. One of the professional writers there advised me to read the *Family of Man*. Imagine my amazement when I saw the writings about life's stream there. When I was a senior in high school, I wrote a poem about life's stream and got an A plus, and I was so sure that this was an original stroke of my "genius." I guess there's nothing really new under the sun after all. Is it possible that I'm one of those "thinkers" of old reincarnated? Whoever I was, I must have lived a heavenly life, because I've sure caught hell in this one. I was definitely born with a bad Karma, as Edgar Cayce would say. Think I'll come back next time as Howard Hughes.

Mrs. Wallace, the Physical Education teacher at Diloreto school, called this morning to toss me a bouquet about the "wonderful job" I'm doing raising my brood. These little bedevilers must really behave like paragons of virtue outside the home; people are always complimenting them. I can't quite make up my mind which is the lesser of two evils: to have them act up at home and behave good when they're out in society, or to have them behave good at home and show their other face to society. Too bad they can't be good all the time, but since there are no angels at large on earth today, I guess I'll have to content myself to accept them as they are, a combination of good and bad, just as I am.

Truthfully, it really makes me more nervous than proud when people pour on too much praise. Usually, when I begin to feel really good or secure about anything, something inevitably goes wrong. I must keep the faith though. God and me have brought them this far, we'll make it on.

Sunday
1:45 P.M.

Frances called last night. I promised her I'd go to a Black History Program at AME Zion today at four o'clock. It sounds good, several speakers and lots of singing. I like the singing best. But today my back seems to be having a relapse, so don't think I'll be able to go.

It's a beautiful, bright, and sunny day today, but the wind is howling and it's freezing in here. Lord, if I have to spend another winter in this refrigerator, I just don't see how I'll be able to stand it. The very thought gives me a sick feeling in my soul. There's such a difference in the temperature in my next door neighbor's apartment and mine that it's unbelievable that the two apartments are in the same building, much less the same climate. Why me? Why did I have to be the one to inherit this monstrosity? But why question it; it's par for my course. Perhaps some day I'll know the reason why I've had to taste of all the shitty things of life. There must be a redeeming meaning somewhere, somehow.

This inspires a sermon. I shall take my text from Revelation 7–9:

> After this I looked, and behold, a great multitude which no man could number, from every nation, from all tribes and peoples and tongues, standing before the throne and before the Lamb, clothed in white robes, with palm branches in their hands, and crying out with a loud voice, "Salvation belongs to our God who sits upon the throne, and to the Lamb!" Then one of the elders addressed me, saying, "Who are these, clothed in white robes, and whence have they come?" I said to him, "Sir, you know." And he said to me, "These are they who have come out of the great tribulation; they have washed their robes and made them white in the blood of the Lamb." Amen.

May I assume that my trials and tribulations are preparing me to be worthy to partake of the glories of the hereafter? Well and good, but I still say with the psalmist:

"Hear my prayer, O Lord,
    and give ear to my cry;
    hold not thy peace at my tears!
For I am thy passing guest,
    A sojourner, like all my fathers.
Look away from me that I may know
    gladness, before I depart and be no more!"

End of sermon for today.

Sunday
10:30 P.M.

I just saw *Duke Ellington, We Love You Madly*, a tribute to Duke Ellington on TV. It was fantabulous, to put it inadequately. I saw Sarah Vaughan and Billy Eckstine, two of the idols of my teenage years. They held their own magnificently with Roberta Flack and Aretha Franklin. But, oh, how that Aretha Franklin can stir up your natural soul with a song! Umm-unh!

One skit had Peggy Lee, Sarah Vaughan, Aretha Franklin, and Roberta Flack singing a blues song together. Ricky posed the question, "What does that white one, Peggy Lee, know about the blues?" I don't doubt that the blues are no respecter of persons and Peggy Lee may well be qualified to sing the blues, but she sure isn't qualified to sing them on the same stage with Aretha, Roberta, and Sarah. Those three beautiful black women dig down into your soul and make you feel the pains and sorrows from Sojourner Truth, and Frederick Douglass, on up to Martin Luther King, and Angela Davis. They take you on a trip through Watts, Harlem, Decatur Street in Atlanta, and Mt. Pleasant in New Britain. And when you come back home, wherever home may be, you're glad, sad, and hurting, but it's beautiful! No, Miss White Satin Doll didn't know what she was singing about.

But me, Aretha, Sarah, and Roberta, we know what gave birth to the blues. I've got the blues right now, thinking about laying me down to sleep in that cold, cold room upstairs. But as Ray Charles said tonight, "When I wake up tomorrow morning and see another sunrise, I'll know that everything is going to be all right!" If Ray Charles is blind and can see the beauty in every new sunrise, I sure ought to be able to do the same.

And so good night,
Richelene

P.S. The years have plundered Duke's face, but through the ridges and crevices, his genius still shines through, like a light set on a hill. A beacon that reaches out to us and bids us come and drink from his fountain and enjoy. His gait may be slowed, and the pull of the earth is under his feet, but his genius will never die.

2–13–73

Dear Self,

Ricky is home nursing his feet again today. I am beginning to fear that he and his feet will be waging an ongoing battle from now on. I feel very sorry for him as he had such high hopes of excelling in football and making it a career. Even before the misfortunes that befell his feet, I had tried to talk him into directing his dreams in another direction. In past years, the black man's best hope of shining in life was through show business or athletics. Now with the mainstream of American life being forced into more acceptance of black men at all levels, any black boy with brains and talents should strive to use their brains to cut their niche in life, and stop relying on brawn.

Last week, he finally admitted the futility of his fight with algebra. All the Mitchells, including me, have a mathematical mental block, and he has opted for art. Also, I think he has accepted the fact that his dreams of becoming a great athlete seem to have been dashed at his balking and ill-starred feet. How I hope and pray that he will find his niche in life and make it through without too much inner turmoil.

I received four new books in the mail today; they cost 10 cents: *The Word*, by Irving Wallace; *A World Atlas* for the children; and two volumes of the work of *Kahlil Gibran*. I read *The Prophet* by Kahlil Gibran years ago. I should have my self a delicious time reading for the next week or so, as time permits.

Next weekend there will be a change of pace. I am going to a dance that is being given by the West Indian Social Club. Whether I have a good time or not, it might be interesting food for thought and provide a few slices of life to record in my daily jottings.

I wonder if I'll get even a single Valentine card in the mail tomorrow? I bet I won't. Ah-h those years of yore when I was deluged with messages of trite endearments on Valentine's Day. What did the years of attentions from the opposite sex net me? Nothing but the sad knowledge that no man has ever truly loved me for myself, never truly cared about the real me.

All those years I thought of myself as the tender, timid, little lamb lost-in-the-woods type that brought out the protective instincts in men. I thought that I was the sweet little damsel that they would want to love and protect always. What a revelation when I discovered that far from attracting protectors, the "little lost lambs" of the world attract all the wolves out there in the woods, prowling, searching for "little lost lambs" that they can devour. Daily, I see the victims of the wolves of this world, victims of their own innocence, trust, and naiveté. The casualties fill the welfare rolls, the slums, the mental institutions, and the prisons. Some flee to alcohol and deadly narcotics for solace. Some are completely and forever devoured, they inhabit the cemeteries before their time. And unless the little lost lambs either retreat completely or put on wolves' clothing and claw back, they will always be devoured or maimed for life, their carcasses left for the vultures to swoop down on and finish the job. It is indeed a fact: Only the strong survive.

And still a question nags at me. Are the wolves and vultures evil, and the little lost lambs good, or are they all simply pitiful victims of an inner sickness or a predetermined fate?

Had I not had the strength generated by deep religious and moral convictions, who knows where the road might have led me? On the other hand, having had those guideposts, look where the road has led! But I can feel at peace with myself and my maker and I have no demons of moral decay to exorcise. The human errors that I've made have been balanced on the scales of life and we are even. Life owes me nothing but the freedom to be myself, and I owe it nothing but to allow my fellow man the same freedom that I want for myself. And that is all each of us owe each other, our freedom and our humanity.

Until tomorrow,
Richelene

2–14–73

Dear Self,

What did I tell you? The minute people start really bragging, something happens!

Alan just got sent home from school. It seems that he and one of the teachers have a personality conflict, and Alan called the teacher the "shiny skin head." This was not to the teacher's face, but the teacher overheard it and became quite offended. Now you and I know that many students these days are calling their teachers a lot worse, and many teachers are also calling their students a lot worse. Even so, this was disrespectful on Alan's part, and for all I know, this teacher may truly be deserving of respect. Also, since Alan is the student and the teacher the authority, I want him to learn to respect authority, when it deserves respect. In any event, I agree that Alan should be reprimanded.

I called the principal and explained to him that I will counsel Alan on controlling his emotions and impulses. This, I know, will be to his advantage throughout life. He stated that Alan may return to school tomorrow. Perhaps I'm not taking this as seriously as I should, in the proper context. To me, the fact that Alan thought of his teacher as a "shiny skin head," and unfortunately let it slip out, is not as important as the effects it could have.

I tell all my children, they are black and all their teachers are white. And although these teachers would go livid with rage or swear by all that's holy that it is not so, were I to suggest it to them, most of them have ingrained racial prejudices. The black student has three strikes against him from the "git-go": His color, the teacher's preconceived notions of his "cultural deprivation" and intellectual deficiency, and the teacher's own racial hang-ups. So the black student must either be unusually bright or unusually well behaved or both to really get on with these white teachers. If they are average on both counts, they manage to get through school with a minimum of either interest or antagonism from the teachers. God forbid that they should be below average in either "learnability" or "behavability"; then they are anathema to the teachers.

I am not being paranoid. I went to high school in Philadelphia, Pennsylvania, under all white teachers. Sweet, well-mannered, intelligent, well-groomed Richelene was the pet of most of her teachers. She was the typical, acceptable little nigger. At the same time, those of her black classmates who were slower or not quite so nicely mannered or clean looking were treated entirely different. No allowances were made for them.

So I tell my children to try to be these "nice little niggers" that impress the teachers favorably if they want to get through school with a good record. For the least bit of assertion of personality that does not set well with these teachers will be blown all out of proportion and set down on their records, and this begins a vicious cycle: The student resents being reprimanded for petty infractions that are overlooked in white students, and this gives birth to more serious conflicts. Soon, and eagerly, the teachers label the child a troublemaker. This record follows him from grade to grade and each successive teacher is on the ready to "put down" this troublemaker at the least bit of provocation. Thus begins a series of suspensions, and soon the student begins to feel that perhaps he really is no good, especially if his self-image is not too high to begin with, and his behavior steadily deteriorates until he is either expelled from school altogether or he drops out and drifts into trouble.

Much of this could be avoided if the teachers could truly lay aside their prejudices and overlook minor personality defects—and concentrate on trying to reach and teach the students instead of projecting their own personality conflicts into a conflict with individual students. Of course, I, of all people, know that some students, like some adults, are unreachable and "unteachable," but some of the casualties our schools help to turn out could be avoided, with the proper handling of individual students from the beginning.

Alan is no angel. This I know. He has more than a fair share of personality defects, but he is essentially a good boy and is both reachable and teachable. However, his progress could be seriously stunted and his potential arrested unless both he and his teachers put forth more effort to work toward the same goal, that of his getting an education.

End of session.

Happy Valentine's Day,
Richelene

P.S. After reading through the above, I can see that I let quite a bit of anger and hostility toward whites come through. I wish I could deny it. Yet for any thinking, caring black person to deny that he harbors certain misgivings against whites is a delusion. How can any black person look at his own life and the lives of people around him without a certain amount of anger? How can he read the history of his people without absorbing their sufferings from slavery times on? Suffering is like a two-edged sword: it can temper one and make one more compassionate, or it can stir up an abiding anger. If one is lucky, he can expunge the anger and use the compassion. Or, he can use his anger constructively as a catalyst for his compassion. Perhaps by saying what I really feel about the above situation, some of my anger has been expunged and I can continue the business of trying to overcome my prejudices and become a better human being. Can you imagine the wrath that I would bring down on my head were the principal or teachers at Washington Jr. High to read it? Who does she think she is? Etc., etc.

Valentine's Day turned out very nicely after all. Norman called and wished me a happy Valentine's Day and Jeffrey and Candace made very sweet cards and presented them to me with a big kiss. I am loved!

2–15–73

Dear Self,

I got those low-down dirty blues today! I had a seizure last night. It was quite severe, but fortunately there was only one and not a series. These bouts can really give me the blues! At least there were no hallucinations this time. I wonder why I never see Jesus and angels and beautiful heavenly things when I hallucinate, so I could label them "visions" and put on a turban, proclaiming myself a prophetess or "maharishee" (feminine for maharishi—my invention). Then I could get rich, lecturing and interpreting my "visions." But no, all I ever see are nasty little things like ants and bugs and snakes and green, red, and black demons. Damn! (and I use profanity reluctantly). If I had to be crazy, why couldn't I have been born profitably crazy? Talking about no winning! Maybe epileptics really are demon-possessed; I sure feel demoniacally evil today. Bowling in the league this morning didn't help matters any. Losing is getting to be a real drag. I wonder whatever happened to all those high 500 series and 200 games I used to get so often? I must say our new white partner came through admirably. I think we'll be able to tolerate each other quite nicely if she doesn't get disgusted with our bad bowling and quit.

After we left the alley, I went with Miriam to buy new drapes for her living room. She is getting wall to wall carpeting and all new furniture. I am very happy for her, but looking at all those beautiful things didn't help my funky, low-down, dirty blues any. And the fact that it's the day before "check" day isn't helping my disposition either. You know the old " . . . and when she got there, the cupboard was bare" thing.

The fact that it's dark and cloudy and raining and the kids are going to be complaining because they don't want no beans and rice for dinner isn't helping matters either. My telling them that they should be thankful because lots of children in India and some other countries of the world don't even have beans and rice to eat today isn't going to help matters. The fact that I don't even want them is also not helping matters. How can I try to force someone else to want something I don't even want myself? And the fact that when the paper comes in a few minutes and I see that I haven't won the lottery won't help to erase these low-down, dirty blues either.

> Troubled in mind,
> you better believe I'm blue
> but I won't be blue always
> 'cause the sun is going to shine
> in my back door some day!

Ah-h! Now how many years have I been singing that song? Sunshine must be just around the corner.

Later,
Richelene

7:40 P.M.

P.S. Would you believe not one of the kids complained about the beans and rice? I sprinkled mine liberally with hot sauce, and they were delicious! No kidding. Tomorrow is another day, and I'll make those old blues stay away from my door.

And, so good night.

2–16–73

Top of the morning to you self. I woke up this morning feeling fine as wine. No, I felt like champagne. I had a good night's sleep and I am reborn again. Blues stay away from me today! This is one of those good moments that I intend to drain the last bit of juice from. I plan to use this day until I use it up! And if I must cry tomorrow, tomorrow is another day!

It is now nine o'clock in the morning. I've washed the dishes, defrosted the refrigerator, washed the throw rugs for the living room, and have the slip covers ready to go into the washer. After that I plan to mop and wax the living room and kitchen floors and take down the kitchen curtains and wash them. By then the "check" should be here, so I'll go downtown and get the food stamps, then shop for groceries and also material to make Candace a new outfit to wear to her Charms (marching group) dinner-dance tomorrow night. It's so good feeling like doing what you have to do instead of merely going through the motions. And if this is my one really good day this month, I'm going to make good use of it and worry about the bad days when they get here.

I feel ashamed of one thing that I did yesterday while in my "blue mood." So now I must take a little time out to write it down and analyze it, and try to set it straight with you self.

Since my children have been old enough to understand, I've always insisted to them that I do not want any of them to get romantically involved with a white person, and don't present one to me as a daughter-in-law or son-in-law, or I would disown them.

Lately, a white girl has been calling Ricky, and I told him to tell her to get lost. Last night, she called again, and with my prodding, he was very ugly to her and hung up on her. Now I, the sanctimonious one, am always talking about trying to raise my children to be human beings, and I insist that I want no one to restrict my freedom or diminish my humanity. Yet, I'm doing that very thing to my children.

In fairness to myself, I have never taught them to hate, but I am attempting to transfer my own prejudices onto them, as surely as whites have always attempted, and succeeded for the most part, to project their prejudices onto their children. Granted I have perhaps more basis for prejudices toward them than they do toward me, but I am just as guilty of perpetuating needless grief and unhappiness. For all I know, that little girl that Ricky was so rude to, might well be a beautiful, sensitive human being who was hurt by his meanness (mine really). And when we deliberately offend any person or diminish their humanity, we diminish ourselves.

Sure I am angry because of the untold sufferings and anguish that my people, as a whole, have endured and are enduring, but do I have the right to lump all white people together as cruel and inhuman, just as some of them lump all black people together as lazy, ignorant, dirty, and untouchable? Might I not have been put in a position to foster understanding and love between people, and am I not defiling my charge?

In my heart of hearts, I know that people are just people, and that the accidents of color of skin or texture of hair have no bearing on their humaneness or lack of it.

I think one of the things that has helped to shape my attitude toward whites, along with many others, is this: When my children were small, our house was a gathering place for both black and white children. The white children played with them, fought with them, loved them, slept over with them, and ate with them. But as adolescence approached, there was a gradual, then a total weaning away. Many have moved away, but of those who still live in these projects, I would hardly know them if I met them on the street now.

Why? That old "bugaboo" of sex, romance, interracial dating, and marriage has caused the white parents to pull them away from my children. Suddenly my children are unacceptable companions for theirs. I feel that my children are as precious and of as much worth as theirs. If theirs are too good to associate with mine, then mine are too good to associate with theirs. This is a juvenile, simplistic attitude, but one that is forced upon me.

And yet, and this is agonizingly hard to pull out by the roots and examine in the light of day, deep down inside, I've felt for a long time now that it probably would have been easier for me to have found a white man that had all the qualities that I've felt I needed and wanted in a man than to find these things in a black man. Black men have had to struggle too hard just to live, just to fight their way through this society and survive. They have had neither the time nor the conditioning to be able to try to be sensitive to the inner needs of their women. I'm not naïve enough to think that all white men possess a sensitive, protective nature, as far as their women are concerned, but one gathers that it is more prevalent among them. Yet, although I've had many opportunities, as most black women have, I have never allowed myself to so much as date a white man, even though some would have had more than an obscene, "back alley, behind closed doors" interest in me, and I know it.

But knowing the traditional, ugly, "sniggly purery" sexual oriented attitude that white men have had, and still do for the most part, toward black women and knowing that they, for the most part, are responsible for so many of our men being less than men, I could never become romantically involved with one without waging a terrible war with my conscience.

And knowing that black women have always been the drudges of the earth, misused by both their own men and white men, while those lily-white female creatures have been set on a pedestal, I can't bear the thought of one of my sons further enshrining them. On the other hand, I would not want my sons to take advantage of white girls' vulnerability to the mythical superior sexual virility of all black men, and misuse them. Two wrongs have yet to make a right.

I know I must overcome my prejudices. But, how hard it is when reality is beating you over the head every day like an avalanche of bricks raining on your head.

Anyway, this morning at the breakfast table, I recanted my previous stance. I promised the children that I would never again try to inflict my own prejudices on them. If they should want to date or even marry (though I still hope not) one of another race, I will never interfere and will try to accept their choice. How wonderful it would be if all of us could accept the fact that we are all really one race, the human race!

I didn't mean to use this much of my valuable day writing. I got carried away.

I must get going now.

Later self,
Richelene

7:30 P.M.

P.S. I seem to recall that I said something about "crying" tomorrow morning. Abrupt change of plans; I'll cry tonight. As a matter of fact, I'm crying on the inside right now but will try to keep the tears from falling until I go to bed, away from the children; then I'm going to cry me a river, maybe even an ocean.

My champagne day was turned to gall when time to get the groceries home rolled around.

I called a taxi around two o'clock, but somehow it never got there. They know that on "check" day many recipients need rides home with their groceries, and they resent the inconvenience. Three of us were trying to get a taxi, and the line was continuously busy each time we tried to call to see if the taxi was on the way. My next door neighbor finally "bummed" a ride home, but there was not enough room in the car for my three carts of groceries. I called _____, but she had just gotten home after a scare on the icy streets and was afraid to venture back out; I called _____, she wasn't home; I called _____ and they weren't home.

And of all times, I saw no one in the store that I knew well enough to "bum" a ride with. Often I see "friends" in the store who pretend not to see me because they would feel obligated to offer me a ride home. At such times, to make matters easier on them, I also pretend not to see them. This time, all pretenses would have been laid aside, and I would have got on my knees and begged them to give me a ride home. Finally, when I was so desperate that I was getting ready to brave the snow and icy sidewalks and walk home and send the children back to carry one bag at a time home, only three were home, so they would have had to make about three trips each, Steve's cousin came into the store, and I asked her for a ride home. I got home at five o'clock. Perhaps this doesn't sound like such a traumatic experience, but when you add it to the ongoing frustration of getting the groceries home every week and knowing that I'll be faced with the same problem next week, it's getting to be too much. Maybe I'll just start sending the children to the store daily, but you waste so much that way, and there isn't one bit of room for error here. My God! My God!

I'm so weary.

I bought Candace's material and had planned to make her outfit tonight. I'm just too weary to tackle it. I'm just going to bed and cry until my soul is satisfied. I haven't had a good cry in a long time, so I'm going to let the good times roll tonight. Let this be a lesson to me, never to get excited again when the day begins on a promising note.

2–20–73
8:00 A.M.

Dear Self,

Haven't felt like writing for a few days—not since my depressing "grocery store" adventure, and it's almost that

time again. Still, I don't feel like writing. I just went into
the cellar to see if all the clothes were hung out yesterday,
and there hung Melanie's new navy blue sweater, messed
up, full of lint! She completely ruined it. I've told that
lazy girl hundreds of times to hand wash her good things
and stop putting them in with the regular clothes. Oh the
hopelessness of it all! Next week she'll be harping about
having nothing to wear again. Dear God, if I can just hold
on somehow until they're grown and have spread their
wings and flown the coop!

It seems that more and more each day, my resolve to be
happy is evaporating into thin air; I just brushed a roach off
my leg and squashed him, poor little fellow. I must have
brought him up from the cellar. My self-induced happy
state is slowly being clouded over like an early morning fog
shrouding the sunrise. Now I simply will peacefully accept
the fact that I am quietly miserable whereas, in the past, I
was tumultuously, horrendously, hellishly miserable. My
present state of "miserableness" is an improvement, so
there is still cause for thankfulness. My random happy moments will still come at unexpected times, and I will savor
them; but I dare not get carried away again. I will play the
happy notes in low key.

Saturday night brought a wealth of happy moments,
some rays of sunshine after Friday's storm. I got up early
Saturday morning and made Candace's suit. I then decided
to go with her to the affair after listening to her sad refrain, "All the mothers are always there but you." And so
I made her happy; so was I made happy.

I've always loved and felt a close affinity with children. To me, young children are God's most perfect expression of love. They are so honest, so free, and guileless.
The love and joy that emanates from their unspoiled
young souls warms one and dispels the chills of life like
new spring days dispelling the chill of winter. Perhaps

that's why I've always felt freer when surrounded by children rather than by my own peers. I always attracted children like a magnet, that is, until I became so bogged down and weary under the load of trying to rear my own. My patience gradually wore thin, and I found there was not too much room for other children any more. Yet, over the years, I've always managed to squeeze a few "extras" into my home and heart, from time to time.

So Saturday night was a joy. Watching the children, from five to sixteen, black, white, and Puerto Rican, romp and dance, free and joyous, one felt young, refreshed, hopeful. Several of the mothers and me ventured onto the dance floor and did our thing, along with the children. So what if they laughed at us and told us we weren't "saying" anything. We laughed with them, but we knew what we were saying. We were saying, "We love you," and because you're happy and free, we are happy and free. Tomorrow, or even tonight, we might wet our pillows with tears that you will never know about, but now children of our hearts, you have cleansed our minds of the cares that dragged us down all week. And we are as free as you this moment; we are as happy as you this moment; we are as "young in heart" as you this moment. We are poor, all, but tonight we are rich, all. So dance sweet young innocents, dance while your hearts are light and free. Tomorrow you, like us, will be bound by life. Tomorrow your hearts will often be heavy and your days will fly on windblown wings. So dance, dance, dance!

I was inundated with the warmth of children this past weekend. Steve's mother and sister brought their five children to visit (from New Jersey). Four of them slept here Saturday night. Imagine preparing breakfast for twelve people! I made a big pot of grits, fried bacon, and eggs and made a huge pitcher of orange juice. Admittedly it dented my weekly food budget, but we'll survive as always. I truly enjoyed them, for one night anyway. The oil of praise was poured on the squeaky machinery of my life again, by Steve's sister. Why, why, why do people praise me for only doing what I have to do? What else am I supposed to do, under the circumstances, except put my nose to the grindstone and try to keep the ship of my family afloat somehow, the best way I can? Since, through a series of mistakes and weaknesses or by the dictates of fate, I have all these children in my charge, I'm only doing what I have to do. Most mothers do the same. I'm no paragon of virtue, and I'm much less than I'd like to be both as a mother and as a human being. I neither want nor deserve any more praise than any other mother who is doing her best. It is downright embarrassing to listen to such exorbitant praise at times. To paraphrase Alan, "They make me sound too good." This is his opinion of my estimation of him in the letter on his getting sent home last week; I let him read it. On the other hand, perhaps I should be grateful for folks' kind words; this might just be their way of trying to encourage me to hang in there. Encouragement and praise are fine, but how good it would be if there were someone, somewhere who could offer me something a little more tangible!

I had another bout with my "affliction" last night. But I am still alive today, ready to face whatever the day might bring. I heard on the news last night that the bus crisis in Hartford is well on the way to being resolved, so perhaps I'll be able to go back to the clinic soon. Last year I called a neurologist's office here in New Britain. I explained my problems in getting to Hartford for treatment and asked if they would take me as a patient. The nurse asked me if I was a state patient, said she'd check with the doctor and get back to me. She never got back to me, so I assume that they do not treat state patients. So be it. By His amazing grace, I will continue to make it. Life will go on, and this weary, mean old world will keep right on turning on its rusty axles.

I found one of those miracle values Friday. Grants had corduroy remnants on sale for 79 cents per yard. I got almost four yards of that and a yard and a half of a pretty floral print for Candace's blouse, all for $5.53. Out of that material blossomed a pantsuit for Candace, a blouse, a cute little suit for Jeffrey, and enough material left to make a spring jacket for Jeffrey. This is how I made the suits:

My own designs

Later,
Richelene

2–22–73

Dear Self,

Not much worth mentioning is happening, or maybe I'm caught up in the midst of so much confusion that I'm unable to find a few quiet moments in which to write this week. The children are out of school, it's winter vacation. There has been a steady procession of friends visiting each one. Now, it's Thursday, and I'm ready for a vacation, or a relocation. I look forward to next Monday with eager anticipation.

History is repeating itself with Jeffrey. Two charming little blue-eyed blonde urchins, a sister and brother, are the newest additions to our family. Before Jeffrey is out of bed each morning, they're knocking the door down. Alas, in a few years, the friendship will go the way of most innocent young black-white friendships, it will fade into the dark void of bigotry, fear, and ignorance.

_____ just called. I was quite surprised as he hasn't called in quite some time. I had a very enjoyable chat with him. We covered almost everything from religion to his ever-present innuendoes about sex. One thing I have accepted, I can never hold a conversation with the average man for long without him "reading" sex into some trite, inadvertent statement I make. If there is any possible way a double meaning can be found, they'll find it. How I long sometimes to find someone, male or female, that I could truly express myself to on the subjects that really interest me, and feel free to talk without having to guard every other statement that I make. It seems that I'm so easily misunderstood. Maybe it's because I don't express myself clearly verbally. Oh well, I suppose everyone has this need, the need to find a kindred soul. But at least I can express my innermost feelings and thoughts here, on paper, and it's a wonderful catharsis.

I got an appeal letter from the Epilepsy Foundation of America today. I will send a small donation when the "check" comes. Now I'm trying to clarify with myself why I am definitely sending a donation to this cause when I did not sacrifice and send one in response to the letter from the Urban League. I, personally, am affected by both crusades. The Epilepsy Foundation is researching the disease of epilepsy, seeking a cure; the Urban League is searching for a cure to the disease of poverty. I am a victim of both epilepsy and poverty, so how do I decide which cause takes precedence, which is the more curable? Do epilepsy and other diseases help to perpetuate poverty or does poverty help to perpetuate epilepsy and other diseases? In fact, the two interact. Yet in the final analysis, in my opinion, if disease is controlled or eliminated first, it necessarily follows that poverty will be decreased. A healthy person is a productive person.

2–23–73
2:30 P.M.

I got the groceries home without emotional turmoil today. I decided to go early, and the taxi was easier to get. The driver was very nice. Even though he had to wait behind a long line of cars for several minutes, he didn't complain or charge me extra for the wait. God bless him.

With prices spiraling continuously, yesterday's paper stated that food prices rose 2.1 percent in January; the pinch is really being felt by everyone. Throughout the store, the rise in food prices was the favorite topic of conversation today. One older woman said to me absently, "With prices the way they are, I feel sorry for anyone with a couple of kids to feed." I smiled at her and continued on my sad sojourn through the store. Had I told her that I was shopping to try to feed not two but six children, she might either have reviled me for having so many children or "tch-tched" in pity. I needed neither. I have reviled myself enough and pitied myself enough to do without both from others, so silence was the most feasible reply to her statement.

At the check-out counter, the cashier remarked, "If you can feed your family on $28.50, why can't I?" Silence would not suffice this time. I patiently explained that I only bought that amount because I had only that amount of food stamps left. By next Friday, I will have spent at least fifteen dollars more, and this will be for bare necessities like milk, bread, and lunch meat, no frills whatever. Please, Dear God, give me the strength and courage to keep trying until at least some of my children have arrived safely on the shores of adulthood, and please let them be productive, contributing members of society, forever able to pay their own ways through life.

Sincerely,
Richelene

2–24–73

Dear Self,

_____ called today. He's still unsettled, searching for some elusive something— he doesn't even know what it is—that he may never find. He's still unstable, discontented in every job he tries and probably still killing off bottles. Why do these people who prey on your spirit always find their way to me?

Maybe it's because I'm searching also. And do I truly know what I'm searching for? I think I'm searching for the meaning of life. He is too. I think I'm searching for love.

So is he. I think I'm searching for my true self and my true place in life.

This must be what he is also searching for. Yet we cannot join hands and search together. The search for self, for truth, for love, for meaning is a universal one, and yet so very individual. What may be truth for one may well be false for another. What one may arrive at and accept as self may seem a delusion to another. What one may see and feel is love may seem only infatuation and lust to another. What one may see as a meaning to life may well seem triviality, fanaticism, or vanity to another, but the search goes on, from generation to generation. I think the most important thing, for which we search, is peace of mind, peace within ourselves. Basically, I think I've found that. The bad times, troubled times, the lonely times still come, but the peace that passes all understanding is with me.

Each time _____ calls, he jokingly mentions moving to New Britain. I knew what he is insinuating, and in a way I wish I could say, "Come on." I'm still a normal woman and do get lonely for male companionship at times, but the companionship has got to be right for me, or not at all. It just wouldn't work out between _____ and me. He's much too shallow, too incapable of making a genuine commitment to another. I just can't settle for sex and the bodily presence of a man as some women do. How I wish I could; it would make life a lot easier in many ways, but so much harder in others. Why, why, why does everything have to be so complicated for me? Or do I make it so myself?

Respect is the magic word that must be present in a relationship between any man and me to make a relationship workable. That is so very simple, yet so very hard for me to come by. Without respect, I cannot love a man beyond "Christian charity." And I cannot respect a man who is unstable, irresponsible, and weak. Have I set too high a criterion for respect in a man—stability, responsibility, strength of character, kindness, depth, and fidelity? Is this wrong? Should I try to tolerate weaknesses in a man since I am weak in many ways myself? Somehow I just can't shake off that old-fashioned idea that the man should be the stronger in a man-woman relationship. In order for me to respect him, he has got to be the stronger, and this is something that I cannot presently change in myself. If I were to allow myself to become really involved with a man that I had no respect for, I'd soon lose all respect for myself. Everyone owes it to himself to keep his self-respect.

I suppose everyone has regrets. One of my biggest regrets is that I didn't grab _____ when I had the chance. He was stable, responsible, strong, and I respected him. But I thought he was too young for me. Now I realize that chronological years are irrelevant if maturity and love are present. One man might be completely mature at thirty while another might be immature at eighty. My hindsight has always been better than my foresight.

_____ came over today and asked me to keep her little boy for her while she goes to Detroit, Michigan, to pick up her eighteen-year-old daughter next week. I agreed. He is a very nice little boy and will be company for Jeffrey. Everyone has their problems!

Later,
Richelene

2–25–73
10:10 A.M.
Sunday morning

Dear Self,

The big day finally arrived! I went to the dance last night, and what a big bust for yours truly, and I don't mean big bosom. Was I ever a wall flower! There weren't very many men there, but oh the women! The few men that were there were mostly with their wives and girl-friends, so it was a sad state of affairs for us unescorted females; it's at times like this that one feels that maybe it's better to have a man or husband "of sorts" than none at all. Actually, I anticipated just such an evening as I had, so certainly it was no surprise or disappointment, but I had anticipated some valuable observations on life to reflect upon with you, self. For ever so long last night, it seemed that nothing worth even jotting down and examining would happen. Everything was just blah, period.

But the evening turned out to be far from a loss, after all. So here are my observations:

The first one is that I'm convinced without a shadow of a doubt that I can't drink alcoholic beverages now. _____ had a couple of bottles of "misses"—whiskey sour and screw-driver. I took a small glass of each, and my head was reeling. The rest of the night and this morning, I have had a terrible headache. Until approximately five or six years ago, I was a "teetotaler." Then I began to accept a drink or two at social functions in order to try to better fit in with the crowd. I did not do this because of the pressure, although there always is a lot on a non-drinker, but because I always wanted to blend in with the crowd whenever I allowed myself to be with the crowd. Now I know that I will not only never truly fit in with the crowd, but I'll also never be able to drink. Since, I find no real necessity for either "fitting in" with the crowd or drinking, why force the issue? Although I do not intend to become a hermit, henceforth, I will neither try to fit in with the crowd or pass any alcoholic beverages past these lips. More and more each day I am beginning to see that I might as well stop straining against the natural fabric of which I'm made and just be myself. If I am inherently a misfit, a recluse of sorts, an observer of and "commisera-tor" with the failings and foibles of that segment of mankind who, through no fault of their own, just can't blend in, then I will accept that and be content.

Secondly, there was one great surprise. _____ who recommended me for the job at Channel 30, which I men-tioned earlier in the year, was there. The elite descended to mingle with the peasants for a night, for a reason. They were promoting a dance to be given by the elites on March ninth. So in order to induce the common masses to shell out that $4.00 and make the dance a financial success, they came. In all fairness, they are a very charming and inspir-ing couple. The thing that I admire about them is the fact that they seem to really like and enjoy being with each other. This quality about them warms my jaded heart. I must admit that I hadn't felt overly anxious to face the lady after not following through on the job. Last night we passed a few words, but neither of us mentioned it. And so we both have our own rationalizations of why I didn't go for the in-terview. She'll never state hers to me, and I'll never state mine to her.

The last but most important episode that occurred last night was a poignant conversation with _____ when she drove me home. My heart bled with hers as we talked. If I am one of the "bleeding hearts" of this world, I can't help it; and if we don't do an awful lot of good, at least we do no harm, knowingly. Her son, fourteen, has been miss-ing from home since Thursday. She thinks, but is not cer-tain, that he went to New York with friends. The poor, poor lost young child, and the poor, poor lost and hurting mother. How can I know she hurts, and why are tears falling from my eyes even as I write this? My daughter did the same thing at fourteen, just disappeared for a weekend.

No phone call, no nothing. And I wailed like a wounded animal as I imagined her victim of some brutal, depraved criminal. Finally she appeared, none the worse for whatever or wherever she had been, with the simple explanation that she and some girlfriends just stayed away from home to talk. I didn't press her, and to this day I don't know where she was. Someday I might be able to talk about it with her; now I can't. And so my heart weeps and grieves with _____ 's. She is eternal black mother. So am I. If she has taken paths, in her confusion and loneliness, that I have not, I cannot judge her. We are still the same. I have also fallen short of walking the straight and narrow.

_____ is very intelligent and I always enjoy talking with her. Many of our trains of thought seem to run along the same tracks, but we always digress at the point of religious beliefs. When she spoke so poignantly of the sense of the futility and meaninglessness of life, I softly tiptoed in with an interjection of religion as a leverage for these feelings. She just as softly brushed my interjection aside. One cannot force his own beliefs on another and should never try to, so I do not. Her feeling that the only reason that she was placed on this earth was to suffer, die, and be forgotten might well be valid. I've often felt the same; but a little core of faith and hope always lifts me out of that dark maze of futility.

No doubt she has her own leverage for these feelings. Her fondest dreams, like mine, have been to see her children safely to adulthood as decent, contributing citizens. Now to see her firstborn so lost, so seemingly headed in the opposite direction of what she has lived and hoped for, is almost more than she can bear. I know that feeling also. But mine, at eighteen, has seemingly come to a workable truce with life—so well may hers, in time. I pray with all my heart that her son will somehow be helped to get back on the right road.

Dear God, breathe out your tender mercy on all of your struggling children and open our eyes that we may more clearly see the meaning of our struggles, of our existence. Show us that redeeming meaning! Help us to help each other more to comfort each other more; to love each other more; to be the best that we can be. Amen.

5:00 P.M.

Last night, _____, in the dark night of her soul, stated that she cannot think of one thing for which to be thankful. That was an extreme statement for her to make. From my point of view, she has much to be thankful for:

1. Last year she underwent a successful operation for removal of a malignant tumor. Now she is apparently in good health and is holding down a job.
2. Her mother lives with her and watches her children while she works; she must undoubtedly lend a certain stability and moral and emotional support. How often, when I was trying to work, did I ache to have someone reliable and responsible at home to watch over my children.
3. She has a car.
4. Her three other children are healthy and thriving.
5. During these dark hours of emotional stress with her son, she must be able to glean some comfort and support from her mother. I had no one to comfort me during my time of need with my daughter. In retrospect, I can say that the Good Lord must have comforted me—otherwise, I couldn't have borne it.

I tried to comfort her as best I could, but our best efforts at reassurances are puny and inadequate at such times.

Now it seems like a good time for me to make a list of my own blessings:

1. A degree of health and strength that at least enables me to hold my own within the family framework.
2. Children that are at least within the realms of healthy and normal and who are amenable to discipline and guidance.
3. An allotment of money that at least enables us to survive. I hope to repay it all someday, somehow.
4. A mind that is alert enough to grasp the world around me and see glimpses of truth and beauty, and is ever searching, ever wondering.
5. A sense of humor and the ability to laugh at life at appropriate times.
6. The ability to sew, to create attractive clothing out of bits and pieces of material.
7. Donna's apparent adjustment and contentment in marriage.
8. The companionship of others, when needed, to break up the loneliness and monotony of life.
9. The ability and opportunity to be alone, at times, to meditate and contemplate life, or just to read and listen to soft music on the radio.
10. The desire to help, to heal, to grow, to love, to give, to be at peace.
11. H-O-P-E.

If I were so inclined today, no doubt I could rip off a comparable list of things that are anathema to me. But for now I will look on the bright side.

Sincerely,
Richelene

P.S. Parnell, the little boy next door, and Jeffrey just came in. Parnell announced to me, "Jeffrey has these sexy hands." I couldn't quite get out of him how he came to that conclusion. The best he had to offer was, "On TV they said this lady had sexy hair." How this fits in with sexy hands for Jeffrey escapes me. One thing is for certain, television is giving our children an education. If the "little blonde urchin's" mother knew that already Jeffrey's hands are sexy, I'm certain she would keep her away from him now instead of waiting until she's older. Parnell is a joy. One day recently, he, Jeffrey, and the two little white blondes were just outside the door playing. Parnell asked the little boy how old he was and the little boy replied, "Four." "No," said Parnell, "not four—fo!" "No, four," said little blonde. "It's not four," said Parnell, "It's fo!" "Four!" "Fo!" And so it went. If white folks can try to teach us white English, we can try to teach them black English (according to Parnell).

2–27–73

Dear Self,

Another frigid morning! Horror of horrors! I just remembered that today is my mother's birthday—and I forgot to send her a card. How thoughtless of me. I will have to write her a nice letter wishing her a happy seventy-eighth birthday.

_____ called this morning. She is one of the few, among my friends, that is not divorced or separated from their husbands. But then she is ten years younger than I.

Somehow we got on the subject of "our" men (black men). I'm beginning to think that perhaps we black women do come down too hard and heavy on them, but life has made it so. We've wanted to be tender, loving, cherished creatures, just as white women were, but instead life forced us into the role of matriarchs. To survive, and help our men survive, and our children to survive we've had to muster an "Amazonian" strength. Whereas white women could lean on their men, our men had to lean on us, and we became somewhat lopsided under the load. It never fails to rankle me when white women comment to me, "Oh, you women are so strong!"

Many of us are bitter and angry because we've had to be strong in order to swim against the tides of abuses and injustices that threatened to suck us under. We are bitter because we were never allowed to be what we wanted to be, and we take it out on our men, just as they sometimes take out their bitterness at society on us. In turn, our men are increasingly fleeing to the solace and comfort of soft white arms and the caressing words of pink lips that having had the things that we've wanted all their lives—now want and openly pursue that richer, fuller sex life that black men supposedly assure them. We, on the other hand—having had nothing but a rich, full sex life, now want and openly pursue more of the tangibles like home and material comforts and the intangibles like consideration, true caring, kindness, tenderness, stability, protection. However, to what do we flee? We flee to the jobs that offer us only more poverty and deprivation, and to the welfare rolls that offer us demoralization and more despair.

How ironic that now that black women who have always been treated as men, shouldering more than their share of family responsibility, want to be treated like women; the white women are sick of being loved, cherished, protected, sheltered, and are demanding to be treated like men. Yet, we have a meeting ground. For all of us women, black and white, want, first of all, to be treated as human beings of worth instead of objects or second class citizens. The need for liberation—to be free, full-functioning persons in whatever capacity we choose, housewife, career women, mothers or lovers—is a common denominator.

_____ spoke of, after dire years of marriage, still trying to "train" her husband to be the man she wants him to be. I advised her to forget about trying to "train" him, it's too late. She should now concentrate on trying to bring up her son to be the kind of man that we feel "our" world needs. Furthermore, I fail to see an awful lot of basis to her complaints. She has a husband that is not afraid of work, does not beat her, and they are buying a nice home in a suburban neighborhood. She could be doing a lot worse. My advice to her was to try to tolerate the minor faults and failings of her husband more gracefully, like his not picking up his clothes and socks, etc., if she loves him and wants to preserve her marriage. If she thinks there is something better floating around out there, she is so terribly wrong. But there are a lot of women floating around out there who would grab her husband fast and count themselves blessed.

No doubt once we're able to come to grips with and dissolve our hostility toward our men and society, society for its psychological castration of black men, for placing a load on our "delicate" shoulders that we have always resented, though we tried to keep our resentment hidden behind a facade of strength, martyrdom, and pride, then black men and women will be able to come together again on an honest basis of mutual dependability and support. From that foundation, respect, tenderness, and love can grow.

ANOTHER SIDE OF THE COIN

_____, one of my friends, she is single, separated, and a mother of seven, also called. She was very distraught and frightened because a male, I hesitate to say man, that she dated for a while last year, but broke off with for the usual reasons—irresponsibility, instability, drinking, gambling, etc.—has been harassing her unmercifully this past weekend and today also. I just mentioned this to point out that my other friend had better go down on her knees and thank the Lord that she has a husband worth keeping—because the above is what's floating around out there, unless some fool woman lets a man like her husband get away—and that's not likely.

Alan paid me the nicest compliment today. It suddenly occurred to him that I will be forty this year. "You really don't look it," he said. I asked him whether a nickel would suffice or if he wanted a quarter and proceeded to tell him what a nice boy he is. "I want neither money nor praise for the truth," he stated manfully. I often get nice morale boosters of that nature from many people, but I look in the mirror every day, and I am not deceived. Father time is being no kinder to me than to anyone else. The smile doesn't reach the eyes quite as often; the sprinkling of freckles turning into blotches and the tummy begs me to do sit-ups. But for everything I'm losing on the outside, I'm gaining something on the inside—and, for my purpose in life, it's what's inside that counts.

Good night to you self,
Richelene

I'm now going upstairs to take a hot bath and hop into the bed with Kahlil Gibran (dirty old lady)!

2–26–73
8:40 P.M.

Dear Self,

I called _____ to see if her son had come home. He had. It developed that he had been in New Britain all this time, just taking a vacation, as he blithely explained to her. Oh these children! While we're grieving our hearts out over them, they're off having a gay old time. The parents that don't seem to care at all must lead a much more comfortable life. Perhaps they're bright enough to accept something that we refuse to: most of the children of today are going to do what they want to do in spite of our pleas, admonitions, tears, prayers, and even example. They are an entirely different breed. I go with the old saying: "You can't make a silk purse out of a sow's ear." If they are naturally inclined to be guidable, to walk a straight line, you have no overwhelming problems, but if they are naturally inclined to "walk on the wild side," nothing we can say or do will change that. They more or less have to be given free rein to find their own way, while we stand by ready to help if they let us.

I sometimes reflect on the time of my youth. At a comparable age, when Donna was ungovernable, over-eager to venture into adulthood, my mind was on school, learning, playing—doing the normal childhood things, except that, even then, I was unusually interested in searching for the meaning of life and reading the Bible. I liked boys and was very much aware of them—they made sure of that—but boys and love were for some future time, after I had absorbed whatever I could from school. Of course, there has always been and ever will be fast girls and boys, who sip from the cup of life too soon, but had anyone told me that my daughter would be one of them, it would have been utterly unbelievable. I, who literally ran from boys until I finished high school and who, without reservations, determinedly remained chaste until after marriage at twenty, would raise daughters who would be virtuous and trustworthy young ladies. They would finish high school, go on to college, and do great things with their lives. What surprises life stores up for us, then showers upon us at unexpected times, like sudden downpours on sunshiny days.

How amazed we used to be, as children, when heavy raindrops would suddenly deluge us, without warning, while we romped and played under a bright sun. Then just as suddenly as the rain came, it went. And once again we drank in the warm and glorious sunshine.

So is life ever deluging us with unexpected showers of grief, but happy moments—rays of sunshine—always come again. And if the rain seems to drench us far more often than the sun smiles on us, it is only in our way of looking at life, our measurements of time. One moment of pure joy erases days of misery. One day, sunshine warms our hearts enough to overshadow weeks of rain. Could we truly relish the good times if we never knew the bad times? Life really does equalize in the long run—if we open up and look at our experiences with our inner eyes, the eyes of our souls, rather than our physical eyes.

God knows I've had a hard life, nobody knows but Jesus, as the old hymn goes, but in retrospect, the sum total of my heartaches and hardships is something beautiful. The years of struggles have taught me compassion, understanding, love. I truly believe I am a better human being, or am close to becoming a human being because of my experiences. And, because I've been through it all, I can give more to others who are going through it. I certainly feel compelled to try.

And so I told _____ that I felt sure that just as my daughter groped her way through a lost and trying time during adolescence and seems to have come through safely her son will be all right before too long.

2–28–73

Dear Self,

The last day of February has crept up on me softly, coldly. I was thinking that tomorrow would be the last day of February, but tomorrow March enters with its temperamental and blustery ways. How do I summarize the month of February? Like January it brought no world-shaking events into my private little world, but it was good. It brought many of our POWs back to their loved ones, and thus it brought that usual mixture of sadness and happiness, for already, per yesterday's paper, one POW and his wife are filing for divorce. For me, the month gave some happy moments—some of pure joy and some turbulent moments.

This morning Alan wheedled until I wrote a note to the principal, asking him to excuse Alan from school so that he could attend a Black History assembly at New Britain High School, with some misgivings.

I explained to Alan that I, too, am proud of my heritage and interested in it, but as much as we glory in hearing of the courage and good works of Harriet Tubman and the underground railroad, and exult at the spirit with which Frederick Douglass both fought with his master after tiring of whippings and fought to deliver his people to freedom, and as much as we revere the memory of Dr. Martin Luther King and admire Malcolm X, we cannot forever bask in the reflections of past glories. As Frederick Douglass said before his death, "Others will fight on." We are the others, and we must stop dwelling on the past so much and fight on.

I told him that "now" is the time for him to begin the fight, by first getting a good, relevant education, something that he can use as a weapon to fight and slay the dragons that spit out fire at us today on every hand. And he can more sensibly acquire these weapons by attending class than by going off to listen to what someone did in the past. The past gives birth to the future, but the present is to nurture. We cherish our past history, we are aware of our past, we know where we came from, but do we know where we're going? Now is the time to be about the business of charting a utilitarian course of action for continuing the fight to become truly free human beings, responsible American citizens, and responsible world citizens.

We've revealed our plight to America. We've cast off our cloak of pseudo-content and revealed ourselves, naked in our discontent and our desire to be free, so now we must cease so much empty rhetoric and clamor, and clothe ourselves in knowledge and purpose.

The war that our leaders of yesterday fought in is far from won. They won many great victories, but the fight is still on. Where are our true leaders? When will another Martin Luther King come along, another Harriet Tubman? We have Jesse Jackson, but he is no Martin Luther King. We have Shirley Chisolm, but she is no Harriet Tubman. Still we know that as sure as night follows the day, a Moses, a Ghandi, an Abraham Lincoln, a Martin Luther King will always rise up to light our way, to lead us.

Each of us, an Alan, a Kendrick, an Orlick, a Lois, must prepare ourselves to aid our leaders. Perhaps one of us, as insignificant as we think we are, can be a leader. If we cannot all be leaders, we can support our leaders—each in his own way. A leader never won a victory by himself.

So I try to impress upon Alan and all my children, and all the children that I have occasion to talk with, the need to apply themselves and first get a good education, a solid foundation. From that they can build a better world. Ignorance might be bliss, but knowledge is power. And if knowledge is aided and abetted by wisdom, truth, and compassion, there's no way to lose. Am I rambling in the world of the dreamers, the poets, the mystics? Dreaming impossible dreams? I don't think so!

We may well have the makings of leaders in our midst— in Orlick and Kendrick. They are extremely intelligent twin boys who live on this block with their divorced mother. I truly enjoy having them around and talking with them. Orlick is president of his class at school and Kendrick is a budding poet and writer. He wrote a very touching little play for their Black History assembly.

I see no signals of leadership in my own, so far. But if they grow up to be decent, stable, supportive citizens, I'll have no quarrels with life. One thing I believe, leaders are born, not made (I know someone said that before). So I'll not aggravate myself and my children by trying to mold them into something they are not. I tried with Donna and failed dismally.

SOME REFLECTIONS

As a child I was a leader. As my mother said in a recent letter to Candace, I was always "at the top" in everything. The top of the class, the lead in the school play, the soloist in the church choir, the welcome address giver at programs, the winner in a statewide (black) essay contest, always the leader—though painfully shy and somewhat apart even then.

But somewhere along the road I got waylaid. Was it by the disease that afflicted me from the beginning (strangely, even during the early years when I often had seizures during the day, I never once had one in public or at school)? Did I get waylaid by the indifference of white teachers? They liked me, admired me, and were nice to me, but none saw enough potential in me to really give me that extra help, or push, or encouragement in the direction of my potential that I perhaps needed. Or was I waylaid by my own mediocrity? I soon became aware that I was not nearly as smart as I and others thought once I was "up north," competing with white children in an almost completely white school. Was I waylaid by indecision and confusion? I wanted to be an actress, a dress designer, a singer, a social worker, a missionary, a psychiatrist, an artist, a writer, a wife, and a mother. Was I waylaid by simple lack of motivation on my own part? Mother always said that I was lazy—good for nothing but school and books. Was I waylaid by poverty?

My family members were simple, but good, sharecroppers who barely eked out an existence and could not begin to afford to send me to college. Was I waylaid by race? At that time, society made it doubly hard for a black person to succeed as a writer, artist, or dress designer, which I gave the most thought to. Or was I plainly and simply waylaid by fate—and this is the road that my maker meant for me to travel in order to be molded into a vessel fit to be used in His service? I truly believe the latter—though how I will be used is not quite clear yet.

Then again, maybe I have already put the talents that He gave me to good use. For certainly, during these past years, I have been an actress—smiling when I wanted to cry; acting happy when my heart was bleeding; and pretending that everything was fine when everything was falling apart at the seams.

I have been a dress designer—making clothing for my children and keeping them looking presentable, and sometimes downright gorgeous, with a minimum amount of money. And while I haven't looked liked Jacqueline Kennedy, neither have I been dressed like "Moms Mabley."

I've been a singer—crooning lullaby's to my babies; singing little happy songs to cheer up little tots; singing songs and hymns of praises to God both at home and in church; and I've often sung the gut-hurting, funky blues in the dark hours of my soul.

I've been a social worker—groping to understand and motivate my children—and sometimes the children of others; trying to aid and comfort them in the things for which I knew they need comfort and understanding; trying to help them to overcome the inherent weaknesses that they can overcome, and to live with the ones that they cannot.

I've been a missionary. How often have I tried to give spiritual uplift to others in their misery, even though I was probably more miserable than they? I've given much monetary and material aid to others even though I was as poor as they, and I've tried to elevate the minds and thoughts of others in subtle ways. I've even tried to convert a few.

I've been a psychiatrist. My ears have been loaned for hours on end to friends and acquaintances, sometimes even strangers, who felt a need to unload—a sympathetic ear. When I was asked for advice, I gave it to the best of my knowledge; and when no advice was asked, I gave none. And I have wrestled with the confusions and problems of my children. Last, but by no means least, I have analyzed my own problems and am learning to live with them.

I've been an artist. I've brought happiness to my children by drawing paper doll clothes for them. Once when Candace was small, she even had a little business going selling the dolls I drew for 2 cents each. Now I am trying to learn to paint in oils.

And a writer! Need I say more?

As for being a wife and mother: Now my heart compels me to be completely honest. I was never a wife. In fact, I was never married. I blundered into a marriage contract. For a woman to be a wife, and a marriage contract to support a marriage, love must join man and woman together. Love did not draw me into the legal contract I had. Confusion, discontent, and boredom did. And I perpetrated a great wrong, both to the man I married, and to myself. I know that now. I didn't then. But I paid, and paid for my mistake. Since I had given my body to this man, in the name of love, he used and abused it, in the name of love. And so I became a mother. I am a mother. The eternal black mother.

Now I can only hope that the present will vindicate the past and validate the future.

So I say good-bye to the month of hearts and love.

And good night to you, self,
Richelene

3–1–73

Dear Self,

March marched in calm and serene today, but it brought a low-grade depression along to bestow upon me. Last night, I had a light seizure, so I know that explains my low mood today. I sometimes wonder how many people who are found dead in the morning must die from epileptic seizures—and never knew that they were epileptic. One of the Dionne quintuplets died of a nocturnal seizure, but she knew that she had epilepsy. I really believe many of the "natural" cause deaths and those attributed to heart attacks are derived from epilepsy. When I had those really severe attacks, straining to try and pull myself out of them, I could always feel a terrible strain and tightness about my heart—and sometimes pain. No doubt if I didn't have enough common sense to relax and let the "seizure" take its course, I could bring on something disastrous to my heart. Many times, I know I've been in the valley of the shadow of death.

I can still remember, as a child, when having those terrible seizures in the night (those were different from the ones I have now), my mother would often say through her tears, "Just lay her down, Richmond, and let her die easy." But my mother always refrained to stop trying to shake the "thing" off that held me in its grip. Whether it was my refusal to let go, or that little stubborn streak that so agitated my mother at times, I am still here and still too stubborn to give up. I am still determined to win the victory over my "frailty" and over life.

I bowled with the league this morning—lousily. We won all three games. Yippee!

We had a forfeit team, which means we bowled against no one. It seems that's the only way we'll win these days.

Irma, our white partner, was absent today. I can't blame her for not wanting to be on a losing team. It's downright uncanny how terrible we've bowled all season. It's enough to make a person give up bowling. I took Steven with me this morning. Donna had to take Kenny to the Newington Children's Hospital. He was born with an outward turned foot.

E.P. took off for Detroit to pick up her daughter, so I have an extra little boy until Sunday night. Jeffrey is thrilled at having company for three days.

Norman called today. I wrote him a couple of weeks ago and asked him to send money to help buy Jeffrey a bed as he will be five March 15th and is still sleeping with me. He said that he mailed the money, so I will probably receive it tomorrow. I know it won't be enough to get a good bed, so hope I can find one on sale or a used one some place. One day, when I feel like writing or talking about it, I will tell you more about Norman, self.

Tonight I just want to go to bed and blot out everything in blessed sleep.

Good night,
Richelene

3–2–73
7:30 P.M.

Dear Self,

Today has been such a glorious and busy day that I can hardly find time to "squeeze" in these little experiences of the day, and one from last night. But I must. So I am.

The birds were chattering and singing in happy abandon this morning, heralding a spring that already is flirting with us—teasing us. But we're too well acquainted with the wiles of spring to be deceived by today's warm embraces. Winter is peeking over spring's shoulder, waiting to return and chill our hearts and bodies once more before retreating for another year.

I felt so good this morning, after a good night's sleep, and over-sleeping because the alarm didn't go off. This time I was wary. Instead of singing the day's praises before it was spent, I decided to wait and see if the day would live up to its promises before I took pen in hand. It did.

I got to the bank at 9:30 this morning and got the food stamps. Bought a couple of nice remnants to make two blouses for Melanie; thanks to her messing up her new sweater, she really does need a couple of blouses. I will begin sewing first thing in the morning. The taxi came in ten minutes today. I must be doing something right to deserve two weeks of uneventfully getting the groceries home.

A lady in line at the checkout counter gazed at my cart bug-eyed and exclaimed:

"My! You really shopped!" "I have a lot of children to shop for," I answered. "How many?" she asked. I replied that I don't tell it because they shoot people these days for having as many children as I do, unless you're Ethel Kennedy. Had she known I was paying for the groceries with welfare money, she probably would have wanted to shoot me. At the least, she would have shot me some dirty looks.

Next month a woman's group in Connecticut is planning a statewide boycott of meat—to try to force meat prices down. I'll certainly go along with it, although we all know that if they bring meat prices down, they'll raise the price on other goods to balance things. They'll definitely be the ones to come out ahead. Not us. There's just no winning this war to serve nutritious meals when you're poor and have too many children.

Last night, I'm ashamed to admit, I ate some more words. I wrote another letter to the editor. I just couldn't contain the impulse. Last week there was a story about a welfare recipient, white, mother of five who was burned out in a fire in November. Since then, she and her children have been sleeping on the floor—with no furniture except a stove and a TV. The welfare department no longer provides furniture for recipients, even in emergencies. They claim they are adding an extra amount each month, and we are to save for our needs. This is called the flat grant system. Talking with several black recipients, we were of the opinion that this recipient could have somehow managed to get a couple of used beds, if nothing more, if she had truly tried. But the public responded beautifully, and six beds and many other goods were contributed to the recipient. But in last night's paper, an editorial lauded the recipient involved as a strong, brave, self-respecting woman who has been under terrible hardship because she preferred to work and support her children rather than go on welfare. In effect, it subtly threw off on welfare recipients, insinuating the usual innuendoes. Yet, according to the article, this woman is on welfare—working only to supplement her allotment and, according to her, for self-respect. Evidently the editorial writer didn't read the story—and inadvertently his prejudices showed through.

When I told a friend that I felt like writing a letter, but this time would not sign my name, she cautioned, "If you do write under a pen name, please don't use so many big words and sound so sophisticated or everyone will know you wrote it." This is another thing that people misunderstand about me. They think I use big words in my writing to show off. In truth, I merely use the words that come to me most easily in a free flow of thoughts. Instead of searching for big words, as some think I do, I actually have to stop and grope to find a series of small words—when I could use one big one and be off and about my business. But I did try to use as few "big" words as possible although, as I told my friend, it was hard. Usually when I write, I take for granted that the reader will be able to understand the words I use. If not, I assume that they'll reach for their dictionary, as I do when I'm reading and run across words that I do not know the meaning of. I learn a lot this way. Am I selfish for making such an assumption? Anyway, here is the letter as I wrote it:

Dear Editor:

Evidently the writer of the editorial concerning Mrs. _____'s situation did not read the first story about her misfortune. He commends her for going out to work instead of going on welfare. But, according to the initial story, she is on welfare, receiving $404 per month and adding $8 more, by working 20 hours a week, for a total of $412.00 per month.

The writer of the editorial would have us believe that she is earning $412 per month, by working 20 hours per week as a barmaid. If there were more jobs which women of little education could earn $824 per month for a week's (40 hours) work, as a barmaid or anything else, no doubt many more would be off the welfare rolls.

Mrs. _____ is not alone in working part time to supplement her welfare assistance and to maintain a bit of self-respect. Thousands of welfare recipients are doing the same.

I certainly sympathize with her misfortune (both the fire and the fact that she is trying to raise five children alone), and my heart was also warmed by the beautiful public response. But looking at it from the point of view of many welfare recipients, I believe she could have "squeezed" out enough from her $412.00 per month to buy a couple of used beds—just as I am now in the process of trying to "squeeze" out enough to buy a bed for my son.

But then perhaps white women have not learned to "squeeze" as well as black women since they haven't had to "squeeze" as much.

If I am wrong, and Mrs. _____ is not on welfare—but is a brave and strong woman making it on her own, then my apologies.

The letter is honest expression of my feelings about the subject, but I know it would have been worded somewhat differently if I had not received the exhortation to "layoff the big words." It's just that I've had an ongoing romance with big words for as long as I can remember. As children, we used to have contests to see who could either think up or make up the biggest words; if I didn't always win, I always came in a close second. Exotic words intrigue me. I am a wordomaniac. Perhaps it's hard for one not enamored of big words to understand one that is. So in the future, any writing of mine that is done for public consumption, in any form, will be less "sophisticated."

The man who opened the dry-cleaning store across the street called me to come to work for him for a couple of hours this afternoon. A few weeks ago, I told him I'd like to work for him if he should need help. He says that perhaps he'll need me for a few hours every afternoon. I hope he has some real work for me to do; otherwise, I'll probably go back to Manpower. Today I more or less just minded the store for him while he went someplace on business. We'll see what develops. One thing worries me. He has his lock fixed so that the door is locked by inserting a fingernail file and turning it instead of a key. He thinks this is safer. But anyone could take the same kind of object and easily open the door. With all the young burglars and criminals around, I really am keeping my fingers crossed for him. What a sad, sad, mad, mad world when one's property is in constant jeopardy. But let me not get melancholy tonight. I want to end this wonderful day on a high note.

Good night self,
Richelene

3–4–73
Sunday morning

Dear Self,

I just finished preparing breakfast for the brood, Parnell included. His mother should be back from Detroit tonight. He's a nice little boy and hasn't been any extra strain on my nerves. There are little boys that I know would have had me climbing the walls by now and praying for their mother's return.

Yesterday everything was spinning so until now I didn't have time to converse with you, self—so here I am to catch up on a few random thoughts and occurrences.

I got up early yesterday morning, intending to spend the whole day sewing. I was going to make a little two-piece suit, two blouses and a pair of pants, all of this for Melanie, who never has anything to wear. I had completed the suit, except for the hand work and had begun stitching a blouse when my new boss at the cleaners called and asked me if I could come to work at 1:30. This was at 12:45. So I hastily threw down my sewing and hastily threw myself together and went to work.

The work is pleasant and enjoyable—bagging, doing counter work and operating the coin-ops. I'm very happy that I can help him—and help he does need, more than I can give. But I'm so afraid it's going to be another drain on my spirits. I'm beginning to wonder if it's a blessing or a curse to be born with a sensitive, sympathetic nature. Such persons can do good—or try to—in that they feel for people. And they can exult in the beauty of life and get the sweet and meaningful essences from simple or even painful experiences, but they can also bleed too much, feel too much of the pain and sorrows of others, and become dehydrated. I hope my "soul's juices" will continue to be replenished by warm spring days, occasional days of joyous incidents, feelings of health and well-being from time to time, children's smiles and laughter, burnished autumn days (my favorite time of year), good books, soft music, and all the other little things that I call "soul food." To most of my black brothers and sisters, soul food is chitterlings, collard greens, sweet potato pies and fried chicken; to me, the little things that nourish the spirit are soul food. What brought all this on?

I'm feeling a little sad about my little boss, I say little because he is about 5'5" in physical stature, but in my eyes, he's ten feet tall merely because he is trying to do some tangible things, trying to be a man. He is a man. He needs me at the store because he is now trying to work at another job since the business is not yielding enough profit yet for him to make it on. This besides doing all his cleaning and pressing himself, and he is darned good at it. But he is literally constantly running. How long can he keep up such a pace? He must be at least fifty.

There is a sadness within me also because his situation so poignantly points out the obstacles that black people face when trying to run a business—the main obstacles being financial. Naturally, if they have the financial resources they can easily buy the human resources needed to make the business succeed—or run more smoothly. Already I can see things that will contribute to a loss of customers for my boss. Twice, people have come in for clothing that was supposed to be ready on a given day—and was not ready. I saw the disappointment and chagrin on their faces.

Three strikes are against any black person who goes into business:

1. His color. Even black people are leery of patronizing their own color for fear of inferior services, whether it be doctor, lawyer, garage mechanic, grocer, dry cleaners, or whatever.

2. Lack of capital. In most cases, sufficient money to get a business really going is just not there.
3. Lack of business acumen. In many cases, even with superior skills—black people just do not have the expertise to efficiently operate a business, and cannot afford to hire people who have it.

And so I feel deeply for this giant of a man in his struggles to accomplish something tangible in this society—in New Britain. New Britain is woefully lacking in black enterprise. I do so hope that whatever I can contribute to his efforts will help him along the way. I still can't see how he can do everything he is trying to, spreading himself as thin as he is. I know that nothing worth having ever comes easily, but I am first of all a realist. In order for dreams to become reality, one has to have the necessary materials with which to build. My boss has the guts and the spirit and the skills, but only time will tell whether he can successfully build on his dream.

Steve's cousin is partitioning off half of the cleaners for a men's clothing store, which he hopes to be opening in April. Perhaps once his business gets going, the two will offer support to each other. They will share the rent, and hopefully customers. I admire these men, and my prayers are with them.

Now I'm going to go back to bed and read today's paper.

Later,
Richelene

7:00 P.M.

Evelyn came by and we took several of the children bowling. Would you believe that I bowled 218, 171, and 214 for a 603 series, my highest ever? I still can't get over it, a 390 series in the league and now a 603 series when it doesn't count for anything. Life is so full of frustrations.

3–5–73
5:00 A.M.

Dear Self,

Another week begins. And here I am, in the wee hours of the morning, jotting down thoughts that have been whirling around in my sleepless head. Usually on mornings like this, I just lie in bed, praying for blessed sleep. But I usually receive not sleep, but one of my frightening seizures. Since I dread them more and more, I decided this morning to get up and put the time to better use. I'll probably still be out of it for most of the day, no matter. Sleep is the saving grace for me, in order for me to function properly. It's a good thing I don't have to go to work today, since the cleaners is closed on Mondays.

I talked to _____ last night. She says she is going to bring some work over to the cleaners Tuesday afternoon. I'm going to continue to try to impress upon the people of color that I knew the moral necessity for them to bring their work to our brother and try to help him succeed. When I mentioned that I was working part time, she ventured: "You must be glad to get out of the house." When I replied that I don't mind that much being home, she observed: "Oh yes, because then you can read all day."

I was offended. This is the classic opinion of people that work about people who are at home, "They do nothing but lie around the house all day." Of course, the general impression is that "they" lie around and watch TV all day. But since most of the people that know me know that I like to read and watch very little TV, they conclude that

I lie around and read all day. I invariably become offended when a barb of this nature is thrown my way. How, I wonder, do they think I keep a family of this size functioning fairly normally by lying around all the time! Everyone seems to have the notion that I should be some kind of superwoman. It's really too bad that I have to look so disgustingly healthy in spite of all the battles that I fight daily just to survive, just to keep going.

Is there nothing to do? My head is spinning right now as I try to decide whether to try to finish up the sewing I began Saturday or to go out and scout around for a bed for Jeffrey today. This, besides the fact that dirty clothes galore, accumulated from Saturday and yesterday, are waiting to be washed. I never have and never will wash and do normal household chores on Sunday. As a teenager, I lost a job that I desperately needed because my conscience forbade me to work on Sunday. Any reading that I do will definitely be done tonight, as it always is—except on Sundays and the days that I honestly can't get going after a bout with my "thorn in the flesh." Sunday is my day of rest, and if I choose to lie in bed all day Sunday and read, I know I deserve that much.

To be perfectly frank with you, self, now I'd much prefer to do something more exciting than reading with my Sunday afternoons for a change. It's been quite a while now since a gentleman invited me out to dinner. Maybe I wasn't so wise in shooing all my would-be suitors away after all. This man-less existence is getting to be kind of a drag. Must I finally settle for someone who has a few of the qualities I've been hoping for and try to forget the rest?

I know that there are oodles of strong, good black men, but they are in another culture, another world, apart from the one that I inhabit; and never the twain shall meet.

There are three distinct cultures within the black world, and one borderline.

1. The upper middle class: doctors, lawyers, bankers, insurance executives, teachers, and other professionals—and they only marry people on their own educational level, in their own world.
2. The lower middle class: self-made businessmen; hardworking blue collar workers; brick masons, carpenters, etc., and clerical workers.
3. The lower class: The working poor, barely eking out an existence in menial jobs; welfare recipients; and drifters, chronic unemployables, etc.
4. The borderline class: Folk who have good factory jobs, or other stable jobs, but who are not homeowners and live in housing projects or average apartments.

Since I live in the world of the lower classes, it is with these people that I identify and sympathize most, and it is from this vantage point that I write, always seeking to show the larger world that we are human beings with all the feelings, hopes, dreams, and aspirations of all people. The main difference between us and the people of the other cultures is that we have inherited more than a fair share of the human weaknesses and failings. We did not choose to belong to this world any more than the strong ones chose the world that they are in. None of us chose to be born black or white, none of us chose to be born with inherent frailties that limit our sphere of life. Some of us grope and fight until we find our way out; others live and die in this world. If I should ever be one of the lucky ones to find my way out—God keep me ever willing to throw my sisters and brothers a lifeline to help them out, and to comfort the ones for which there is no hope.

Now it's six o'clock—time to start breakfast. I will get back to you, self, whenever time permits.

6:15 P.M.

Another good day! Mission accomplished! I got all of the sewing done. Tomorrow, first thing, I'll tackle the ironing and mending. And, if I don't forget, I will go to the Headstart PTA meeting.

I've decided to postpone scouting for the bed until Wednesday. I have to go to the welfare office Wednesday afternoon for my six month's interview, so to save car fare, I'll look around while I'm downtown. I must also remember to take Jeffrey with me so he can get his booster shot. Hope I can get done at the Welfare Office and get home in time to go to work. I hate to start being absent so soon.

Just took a nice hot bath, and now I'm going to bed and rest my tired bones.

Until tomorrow,

Richelene

P.S. Most of my close relatives live in the upper middle class and lower middle class world. They are successful. Many of them drive Eldorados, Electra 225s, and Continentals. Most of them own lovely homes. Observing them, from my lowly vantage point, I marvel at their race to see which one can accumulates the most—drive the finest car, live in the finest house, wear the finest clothes. We do not speak the same language. Whereas I marvel at spring's new clothing of green grass and flowers, they marvel at each other's new finery. I often think that little Ba Boo died from the stress and frustration of not being able to keep up with the rest of the family. He was there in the midst of all that finery, and no doubt it bothered him that he was not as successful as they, materially. I am far removed from it all, and I can enjoy my "soul food" to my heart's content, away from all the competition for worldly goods.

3–6–73

Dear Self,

I got a real surprise last night after I had gone to bed and settled down with a Sepia magazine and soft music on the radio.

Guess who broke my blissful solitude with a phone call? The ex-husband! I just don't know about that person (I cannot say man). Now, all of a sudden, he's ready, willing, and able to send money for the children's support, with no strings attached; it'll never happen.

He's evangelizing again. I don't think I mentioned before that he was a "supposed" preacher of the gospel, sanctified no less, when we separated. And he says God is really blessing him financially, so now he's ready to share his largesse with his children. He even said, if I am presently working, I can quit my job and get off welfare and he will send enough money to support us. Now how can I fall for something as fantastic as that? He wouldn't reveal the source of all this sudden affluence. I have two ideas on the subject: He either won the lottery for a large amount or he's fleecing poor, hungry Christians—just as preachers have been doing for time immemorial. If his financial windfall is a result of the latter, God forbid that my children and I should prosper at the expense of poor people's naiveté and hope. One thing I know, he's hardly buckling down and working that hard, as he was never overly fond of legitimate work.

I should have told him in no uncertain terms that I want no part of anything he has. If I've struggled through the rain and the storms for eight years with no help from him, now that the children are approaching a stage of life where they can begin to help themselves, he can go to that hot place that he's supposedly delivering others from. The only reason that I didn't tell him the above is because

I knew he isn't going to send anything—not without some hope that the money might lure me back to him. I've always maintained that I was an obsession in his mind that he called love. But love it could not possibly be.

And now a moment of painful truth, if I even thought for a moment that we could go back together and live like human beings, after all these years, I would not hesitate to try it again. I am most definitely getting tired of being alone. A real woman is no more complete without a man than a real man is without a woman. Women's lib to the contrary, we still need each other in many ways. But, barring a genuine miracle, I know that my ex-husband and I cannot live together. We bring out the worst in each other. Besides, Jeffrey would surely complicate matters even more. If he accused me of infidelity with every Dick and Harvey who came within a mile of me when I was as pure as the driven snow, God only knows the abuse he'd heap on me now.

He's always careful to never let me know his whereabouts when he calls; he knows I'll put the authorities on his trail. Looking at it realistically, it really does seem that he'd be tired of running and dodging by now and decide that it's easier to do the right thing. That is, if he's capable of thinking realistically by now.

Oh well, so much for all of that. We'll see what develops.

Later,
Richelene

3–7–73

Dear Self,

I've got oodles of things to do, but I am taking out a few minutes to give you the latest happenings. I'm sure I won't get another chance today.

Yesterday I called the Welfare Department and asked if I could come in this morning instead of this afternoon. The worker, a man, readily agreed to let me come in this morning at nine. It's always so much more pleasant to deal with men. Is it?

I just this minute answered the phone, an obscene phone call. Some nut wanted to know if I'd like to earn $100 by letting him and a photographer come over and take pictures. Whether it was a prank call or genuine degeneracy, it's frightening. Five years ago, I got a similar phone call, asking if I'd like to earn $1300 for two days' work—posing for nude pictures. Both callers were white. I've seen worse bodies than mine, all things considered, but can't you just see an almost forty-year-old grandmother, stretch marks and all, posing for nude pictures? Anyway, as I was saying, before I was so sickeningly interrupted, the interview wasn't bad. I told the worker that I'm working at a job of sorts, but I am not certain about the pay yet. He told me to inform them when the job becomes remunerative.

After I left the Welfare Office, I looked in several furniture stores for a bed for Jeffrey. I finally, settled on a sad looking Hollywood bed for $78, $83.95 with tax. Tears welled in my eyes as I looked at what I was getting for the money. I know that's not much money, but it's just getting more discouraging day by day to have to settle for less all the time.

I left there and went to Adlers and bought material to make slipcovers. Again I had to settle for less. The material that I liked was too much. I settled for about 15 yards of 99–cent-per-yard material. How wonderful it would be if I could just walk into stores and select the things I like, without looking at prices. As Ricky said to me yesterday morning, I am getting terribly materialistic. At least I'd like to be.

Tonight, I'm going to see *Jesus Christ Superstar* with Frances. It's being presented free to the public at a local church. It should prove to be an interesting evening.

Got to run now,
Richelene

P.S. The letter that I wrote to the editor appeared in last night's paper. I was really surprised that they published it. It really wasn't very nice. Whatever got into me?

3–9–73

Dear Self,

I really overdid it today. I knew when I went to bed that sleep wouldn't come easily as I was so terribly overtired.

I bowled with the league yesterday morning—lost two, won one. I came home, ate a quick lunch—then started right in sewing the slipcovers. I must say they're turning out pretty nicely—but, whew! What a job! The job is further complicated for me because my sewing machine is upstairs, and I had to constantly run up and down the stairs to be sure of the fit. Now my back is tender again. Anyway I finished the chair cover and began on the sofa cover—then had to quit, freshen up a bit, and go to work.

Business was slow, but in a way, it was a good thing. I was just pressing the hems when a customer walked in to pick up his order.

I came home and began sewing again after dinner, but had to quit because I ran out of welting. I will go to the store and get five more yards tomorrow. As sick, sick, sick as I am of eternally scrimping, squeezing, scrounging, and scraping to make ends meet and keep everything in some semblance of presentability and livability, I must say I'm pretty proud that by making the slipcovers for less than twenty dollars, I can at least get the living room looking presentable.

It feels kind of weird to be propped up in the bed writing at this hour. Surprisingly, I was able to drift off to sleep around eleven—but woke up at one knowing that I was heading for a seizure if I kept lying there; I figured the time could be put to better use. Those seizures feel a lot weirder than writing at this hour.

Something else also contributed to my sleeplessness tonight. As I was setting my hair, in preparation for going to bed, Steve came in and Jeffrey brought him upstairs to look at his new bed. He remarked lightly, "Now if Donna kicks me out, I can come down here to sleep." I just as lightly responded, "She's not thinking about kicking you out, is she?" And from that, what I thought was a light innocent response, he took offense. He said I was a mean mother-in-law and was being sarcastic, that I'm always making little sarcastic remarks.

It really threw me for a loop and sent me on a soul-searching tour of myself. Am I really mean? Do I really deliberately throw out hurting barbs? I'm merely human, and no doubt I do at times, just as most people do. But certainly there was no venom in that remark that he took offense at tonight. See what I mean by always having to watch everything I say, because people are always reading something I never intended or even thought of into perfectly innocent remarks that I make? It is nothing new. I'm well used to it by now, but it still hurts. It is enough to make me afraid to open my mouth.

But let me analyze this thing with Steve. I think I understand his "chip." In the first place, understandably, I was not thrilled when my fifteen-year-old daughter began dating a twenty-two-year-old man. Understandably, I couldn't have too high an opinion of a man that age that would fool around with a child. But knowing my daughter, and being unable to reach her, I resigned myself to the situation, and I tried to accept Steve.

Naturally every mother, but especially mothers who've traveled a rocky road, wants her daughter to marry someone who can keep them in a style to which they have not been accustomed. Not someone who will perpetuate the status quo, and I was wounded to my soul when Donna became pregnant—not just for myself and my dreams for her, but for her. She is attractive and got good grades, and she could have done so much better with her life.

Am I hateful or abnormal for not being able to truly take into my heart a man that was unstable, always job-hopping, and had taken advantage of my child? A mean woman would have had him arrested. But Donna insisted that this was the man she loved and wanted to marry, so I went along, with many misgivings and a heavy heart.

Now, every day I see her bogged down in a houseful of junk, trying to take care of two babies and a husband. I see her looking like a frump of thirty—braless, breasts sagging, hair uncombed, instead of a young girl of eighteen. It hurts. I don't blame Steve for all of this, this is one more of those situations where the blame can't be squarely placed. Being the ungovernable, headstrong girl that she was, no doubt if it hadn't been Steve, it would have been someone else. But since it was him, I have to admit that I do resent him somewhat for the role he played (and plays) in the situation.

I try to give them credit where credit is due. He has seemingly stabilized and is working steadily, but still no eighteen-year-old girl should be laboring under such a load. Does feeling like this make me some kind of an ogre? I give them credit for getting along with each other, as far as I can see, and I don't go prying and meddling in their affairs. I help them as much as I'm able to. But maybe my resentment of the situation comes through in subtle ways of which I'm not aware.

The truth is, I think Steve has a chip on his shoulder because he feels inadequate to handle the responsibility he has brought on himself, and he knows that my esteem for the black men that inhabit my world is not high, although I have great sympathy for them. So even though I'm honestly trying to accept him and the life that he is providing for my daughter, perhaps he knows that I still have misgivings about the whole thing. Perhaps he knows that I'm judging him for his inadequacy. I'm not, at least I don't think so. Their life is par for the course for our world. If she is content as she seems to be, and he is trying his best, that's all that matters.

It's now a quarter of three in the morning, and I get up to prepare breakfast for the children at six. I guess I'll try to get a little sleep.

Until later,
Richelene

3–9–73
7:00 P.M.

Dear Self,

Somehow I made it through this day. It wasn't easy, but I got a few things accomplished.

I took Jeffrey to City Hall for his tuberculin test at nine o'clock. He needs this in order to be ready for kindergarten. I left there and went to the city welfare office to see if I could get appointments for the kids at the dental clinic. Always begging, always begging! Oh Lord, how

long? How much longer must I go through the embarrassment and frustrations of having to seek charity that is not
charity?

Am I really in this position because of my own lazi-
ness and shiftlessness after all? Have I been rationalizing
and blaming too much of my inadequacy on my affliction? Could I really find the strength again to remove my
family from the welfare rolls if I would just cast off my
fear and lethargy and dig in? Could I, Lord? I'm so gut tired
and bone-weary of not being able to pay my own way.
Have I committed some monstrous sin for which I'm
being punished? Am I guilty of having too much pride or
not enough? Am I really a worthless, evil, mean, wicked
woman, although I've always thought myself decent and
of worth? I just don't know any more. Do I deliberately
hurt people? I've never meant to. I'm so confused about
my true self now. I thought I knew who I was.

Another thing happened that has made me stop and
dig into my soul again. I was expecting it, and know that
I deserve it. A letter to the editor chastised me for the letter I wrote the other day. I know my letter had overtones
of maliciousness, and in my heart of hearts, I squirmed
even as I mailed it, but sometimes life gets to be so hard
and you get so tired of trying that you get mad at the world
and let your bitterness get the best of you. Was it Rousseau
or Voltaire that once said something to the effect that nature made man loving and good, but society corrupts him?
I readily admit that society and life has conditioned me to
be bitter toward whites, as a whole, but I do not hate. I'd
like to love them, but they won't let me. Life has conditioned me to be bitter toward our men, as a whole. I try to
love them in spite of this. But how do I really expunge the
bitterness and cynicism when life is continuously badgering me? I know that it's also badgering everyone else, but
still how do I revert back to being the pure and loving crea-

ture that I once was? How can years of mistreatment, deprivation, and undue struggling be washed away like so much muddy water and be replaced with springs of cool, clear water, unless the climate is right?

I really am thoroughly ashamed of that letter and wish that I had kept my resolve to thresh out the things I feel compelled to write about private. It's easier, and I can be more honest when I write to you, self. But I couldn't be as bad as all that. At least I'm trying to come to grips with the forces that shape my life and distort my vision. Sometimes I wish I could just go somewhere far away from the world—away from society and all its meanness, vice, evil, and all the things that make us less than what we want to be. Perhaps the monks and other recluses know something that we don't after all.

For now, I suppose a good night's sleep would serve to calm the turbulent sea of my emotions. So I will make a try for it.

Good night,
Richelene

3–11–73
Sunday morning

Dear Self,

To paraphrase Richard Wright's book title, "Laud Yesterday!" You wouldn't believe the emotional trauma that I suffered yesterday, and ended up inflicting it on my children.

I had to go to work at ten yesterday, as Joe wouldn't be able to get there by ten. I got up at six, took down some curtains and threw them into the washer, cooked breakfast, then sat down to type up some of my previous jottings. My ancient warrior, a black Underwood, that I bought before

Christmas for $50.00, broke down on me. Now I'll either have to get it fixed or just continue by hand.

But the real action began when I got to work. I opened up the place and immediately customers began coming in. Most of them were there for work that was supposed to be ready and wasn't. What a mess, a genuine mess all day long! Not one person's garments were ready. Then people began bringing loads of clothes in for the coin-op, and not one of those were done when I left at 5:30. Several people came in and angrily took their clothes back and wanted to know what kind of a business we were running. Many came back time after time until finally some of their things were ready. Of course, they won't come back.

One man suggested that Joe should get out of the dry cleaning business if he doesn't have the proper equipment and help, and doesn't know how to run a business. And through all of this—I was caught in the middle. I wanted to be loyal to Joe, yet I was embarrassed and ashamed of the slip-shod way things were going. I also sympathized with the customers, because I know that when you want or need something at a certain time, for a certain reason—that's just it.

How I can I try to induce people to patronize Joe now? How can I proudly say that I work at Joe's Cleaners? I'm really in turmoil. Already I feel like quitting. It's just too much confusion, and too much mess unsettles me terribly. Everything has to go along fairly orderly or I fall apart. It was all I could do to keep from throwing up my hands and walking out. But tremendous will power, and the knowledge that Joe needed me, somehow kept me there until 5:30. I didn't even take time out for lunch. I couldn't possibly stand that kind of rigmarole every day. Now I'm trying to think of a nice way to quit. Why, why, why? I could really have enjoyed working over there under normal circumstances. But those certainly weren't normal circumstances for a business.

As I said before, black people have three strikes against them from the "git-go" when they enter business. Joe presses beautifully, but it takes more than good pressing to run a dry cleaning business, and it's far from a one-man operation. I feel so very, very sorry for him. What more can I say, except that I hope somehow he can get things on a better footing than they are on now, or he is doomed to failure. This points up once again how helpless we sometimes are even when our desire to help is so strong. I felt so impotent, so useless, even though I keep telling him that I'm there to work, to help out in whatever way I can. I did a couple of mending jobs, in addition to minding the counter, but I know now that whatever help I can give is just not enough to make a dent.

Upon leaving the house yesterday morning, I left definite orders for the kids to wash the kitchen and living room windows, as I wanted to go right ahead and iron the curtains and put them up as soon as I got home. When I got home at 5:50, not one window was washed! The excuse was there was no window cleaner. With me right across the street, they could not run over there to get money to buy some?

After all that I had gone through all day, I should come home to a houseful of sorry, lazy children who couldn't get two rooms of windows washed? It was just too much. I tore into them verbally unmercifully. I just couldn't help it. Ricky ended up crying, and that started me crying and being sorry for riding them so hard, even though I still feel that I was justified. How can the children of today be so lazy? They only want to eat and do whatever pleases them. It is hard to understand. I might have been lazy when I was their age, but I sure did the chores that my parents told me to.

I finally forced Melanie to wash the kitchen windows while I ironed curtains. It seemed best to just leave Ricky alone for a while. His emotions get the best of him much too easily.

After ironing, I finished sewing the sofa cover, pressed both chair and sofa cover, and put them on the chairs. They do look nice, if I do say so myself. But what a day! I didn't have time to think about Black Magic last night. I took a tranquilizer and went to bed.

I'm supposed to go to a tea at South Church this afternoon, but I'm still so worn out I might not make it.

Whew! Laud Yesterday!

So long,
Richelene

3–12–73

Dear Self,

I woke up at 3:30 this morning. I laid there and tossed and turned until 5:30, at which time I went into a seizure. These things are coming too often now. Is it because I'm not taking my medication regularly or was this one brought on by the stress of this past weekend? Or is it simply that I'm getting older and my nervous machinery is breaking down more? Whatever the reason, it's getting harder and harder for me to accept these things. One thing about my condition that depresses me is the knowledge that if these things get worse, I may never be able to function within society as a self-supporting person again.

How can I get up behind mornings like these and go out into a job where I have to interact with people all day long? That's one reason I was so hoping that the job across the street would work out. In addition to being of help, where help is really needed, I would be alone, with no co-workers of different temperaments to contend with. The customers I can easily handle. Just a pleasant smile and a few pleasant words, and they're gone (that is, if the work is ready). Even if I could find a job in a one-girl office, I could be reasonably content. But all of the jobs like that, around here, go to whites. And even if there are some that are "equal opportunity employers," they're usually so far out that without transportation I couldn't take the jobs. It all seems so hopeless.

Maybe I'll try to hang in there across the street a little longer. Joe promised that it won't be as mixed up and messy as it was Saturday. Thinking about Saturday, even now, I almost get sick. I went to the tea yesterday after all. It was a lovely affair, and they had a full house. The theme was love. And on the surface of things, indeed love permeated the place. The audience was nicely integrated, and rather than having Afro-American dancers, Russian Folk Dancers performed. A "Miss Every Woman's Club" was crowned, after raising $400.00 in a fund-raising competition, and there were several solos and piano recitals by young, aspiring performers. The tea brought in $1,000.00 for scholarships for deserving students. After it was all over, the loving whites went back to the security of their white world, and the black elite went back to the security of their world, and I and others like me came back to the misery of our world.

I never fail to feel lonely at these affairs. Maybe it's because I know so few people that I really feel at ease with and can find things to talk about with. Oh, to be glib of tongue! Somehow my brain and my pen have always coordinated with each other better than my tongue and my brain. Then again, why talk, if you have nothing to say? That's why usually when the program or whatever action there is ends, I'm ready to scoot out the door. But since I was with a friend, I forced myself to stay and try to "fellowship" for about a half an hour. Even when I go to church, the minute the service ends, I scoot. This is perhaps not good, but it's me, and that's that. Many people mistake this for haughtiness or "stuck-uppitiness," but it's neither. I just don't have the gift of gab and can't fake it. The gift of gab is a great social asset, and perhaps it can be acquired if one works at it, but I just don't feel it's that necessary at this stage of the game. I'm grateful for the people that I can communicate with, and I can take my own company well enough, and the company of Kahlil Gibran, St. Paul, and scores of others who've left treasures for me to explore in books.

I love people, but I'm better at expressing that love by action instead of words, as puny and insignificant as my expressions might seem. I better go hang out my first load of wash and get this show on the road. I have to take Jeffrey downtown to get the results of his tuberculin test this afternoon, then go to work.

Later,
Richelene

3–14–73

Dear Self,

Woe is me! I had another bout with my narcolepsy last night. What's happening? These things are about to get me down. Besides that, my back is hurting again, and I've had pain in my right armpit for several days. I don't feel any lumps, but my mother used to get cysts in her armpit and eventually had a breast removed for tumors. I do know that these things have a tendency to run in families.

Perhaps I'm just a bonafide hypochondriac due to my shaky nervous system. That's why I always hesitate to go to doctors when I feel bad. Another thing, all day Monday, following that early morning seizure, I had pain around the heart and terrible palpitations or whatever. That has let up somewhat now, but no doubt these continuous episodes are straining my heart to a great degree. How I wish I could look inside my body and brain and see what's really going on in there.

I've told the children that if I, or any of them, should die before we're off welfare, I'm donating the bodies to science. That might be a small contribution to society for our upkeep, and help the living in some way. Even though I have some qualms about the religious aspect of it, I think God will understand; funerals are a circus anyway. If there is a spirit world, and one can look back into this world and see what's going on, I'd like to observe the dissection of my body, especially the brain. Maybe I'd finally find out what made me tick. But if I'm as queasy about blood, etc., as I am now, I wouldn't be able to look.

Once, when I was admissions clerk in a VA hospital, during a lull we were taken to the autopsy room to observe an autopsy. One glimpse and I flew back to my desk. How then can I say I'd like to go into neurological research? Maybe it's just a profound desire to alleviate the suffering of people like me in some way.

Oh, well, in a few minutes I'll put on my happy face, throw my head up and walk over to the shopping center for a few groceries to last until Friday—"check" day. And people will look at me and say, "There goes one of the Welfare Queens—a lady of leisure. She oughta get out and go to work. She's as healthy as I am." God in heaven, how I hope and pray that, by some miracle, a more workable amount of health will be restored to me soon—someway, somehow.

Must go now,
Richelene

3–15–73

Dear Self,

My dream of good health seems to be getting more elusive by the day. I really don't know what's happening— another seizure last night, quite severe and frightening. Perhaps I'm becoming immune to Dilantin and Librium. When I lived in Atlanta, the doctor prescribed phenobarbital for me, in small doses. I felt better while taking it, but I was afraid I'd become addicted to it. Now it definitely seems that some other type of medication should be tried on me. When I first went to the clinic in Hartford, they gave me a drug (I don't remember the name) that made me desperately sick for twenty-four hours, one pill. So they took me off that and gave me Dilantin.

It's really beginning to be very discouraging. I'd rather be dead than to spend the rest of my life just dragging along somehow, a burden on society. The boys say they'll take care of me when they grow up and get jobs, but I know how much easier it is to think noble thoughts and dream beautiful dreams than to bring them to fruition— even with the best of intentions. I want to take care of myself! It's got to work out that way, or I hope that God will be merciful and take me.

I wonder if the bus situation in Hartford will ever be solved so I can go to the clinic. This just shows how little the "haves" really care about the "have-nots." Of course the strong have their automobiles and can get to their jobs or wherever they want to go—to heck with us little people who must depend on the buses for transportation. Oh I'm so sick of being poor. But, I see no change in sight. Wouldn't it be great if I could sell this "year's journal" to a publisher and get rich? Dreams! Dreams! I really do think that some of the things that I've observed and experienced might be enlightening to people that want to be enlightened about the human side of poverty. Perhaps these jottings could give a bit of insight into the world of the poor from a different vantage point. Then again, there's nothing new or different under the sun, and not too many fresh ways of exploring the old. After all, I haven't suffered like Job or even as much as many other people living now. So what's so unique about my life that it would teach anyone anything? Everyone thinks his own life and sufferings are unique.

Got to go now,
Richelene

3–16–73

Dear Self,

I am now at work, and it has been pitifully slow today. I had just washed my hair and put it up in curlers. Then Joe called and asked me to come in early as he had to go out and attend to some business. So I took the curlers out, pinned my hair up and put on this ugly, ugly wig. I hate wigs on myself. I feel so unlike me.

Going in early really knocked my day out of whack, my budget too. It sure isn't easy to do good deeds. This is "check" day and nothing, but nothing, was in the house to eat. Now I won't be able to go downtown and get the food stamps until Monday, which means I'll be spending about $20 until then. It wouldn't be so bad if we had taken in enough for me to be paid a little something, but we didn't. So I took $2.40 out of the cash register, I wrote a note to Joe explaining that I had taken that amount, and he can forget about paying me this week, and sent Melanie to the store for something to go with the fish, which was the only thing in the refrigerator.

When I get home at 5:30, I will walk over to the shopping center and get the "check" cashed. They don't sell food stamps there. I'll buy enough food to last until Monday.

There's a package store two doors away, and they're doing a thriving business. Maybe Joe should have invested in a package store since so many people seem bent on self-destruction anyway (was only kidding). I just can't for the life of me see how he's going to make it there. It's so painful to see him striving so hard against such odds, me and my "do-gooding." And since I've always attracted such rumors and speculations, I'm sure black New Britain has me sleeping with Joe by now. I've been amazed on several occasions to learn that I had been sleeping with men that I was not aware that I had been until I heard it from others. People! I wonder if there really is a reward for people like me, or are we really fools who allow ourselves to be used? I still think that the Supreme Being likes us better when we try to help each other, and we definitely like ourselves better.

I had an invitation for an exciting, loving weekend but declined. Upon my declining, the "propositioner" asked me, "Don't you like love?" If, he had simply asked me, "Don't you like sex," which was what he meant, I could have answered simply, yes. But abusing the word love that way, naturally I launched into a sermon about love. Love is a word that has fascinated me for years. The lust, deceit, treachery, jealousy, and other base emotions that masquerade as love are amazing. I respect and think more of a man that seeks and accepts sex in the name of sex, when sex is all he wants, than one who feels compelled to try to gloss it over by injecting the word love.

Speaking of love, I will have to talk about love later. It's five-thirty, and I've got to get home to the kiddies and to the grocery store.

Talk to you later,
Richelene

10:00 A.M.
Saturday morning

Joe called this morning and asked if I could come in at ten again. I was kind of hoping that I wouldn't have to go in before 12:30, as I had some things to do around the house. In the course of the conversation, he was effusively expressing his gratefulness for my "sweetness and humaneness." He said, "I'm one of the few real human beings that he has had the good fortune to come in contact with these days." I was completely embarrassed and dumbfounded at hearing such high-blown opinions of myself and told him to hold it, not to put me on a pedestal, I might fall off.

I'm not nearly as "human" as he's making me out to be, but I'm working at it. I'm still terribly lacking. For instance, as I walked over to the shopping center and lugged a heavy bag of groceries home, Candy lugged one also, I wondered just how truly "human" I really am. In all honesty, I questioned whether I'm really willing to pay the price for trying to love, or am I just like the majority of people, unwilling to love when real sacrifice of valuable time and energy is involved. Perhaps after all, it is far more practical to love and help the easy way, by throwing out flowery lip-service, by donating beds, furniture, or clothing that we can't use anyway; by donating a few dollars that we won't miss too much to some charity, by giving little token gifts to people who have exerted time and energy to help us, and by doing unto others in proportion to what they do unto us. Or better yet by doing unto them before they can do unto us. Oh, life is so frustrating!

And what happened the minute I walked in this morning, before I could even get my coat off? A customer came in for two pairs of trousers that he wanted today. They weren't ready, so he took them to another cleaners, and so my day of "helpful" (helpless?) agony begins.

Joe said I should take my pay out of fifty dollars that he put in the cash register. How can I when the man from the electric company was here yesterday, threatening to cut off the electricity unless payment is made soon? Maybe I'll just take $20 to cover the amount that I lost by not being able to get the food stamps yesterday. It's very easy to see that he could have quite a thriving business if he had the help he needs to turn the work out. As it is, the word is already around that the business isn't being run efficiently. By the time he might be able to get on a better footing, his foundation will have slipped from under him. When attempting to build a dream, just as in attempting to build a house, the foundation must be solid or the whole structure will crumble.

Since I've let myself get involved in this, I suppose I'll try to stick it out and either ride the tide out or go down with the ship. Then I can at least say with Martin Luther King, "I tried to love somebody."

It's now 5:15, almost quitting time. Today hasn't been as hectic as last Saturday, even though not one person's things, that were due today, were ready. I feel so terribly bad because most of the customers are white, and they already have this preconceived notion of our "slip-shoddy" incompetence in business affairs. That their notions are being so blatantly confirmed, in this case, is more than a little disconcerting. It's downright humiliating. Can I really continue here under these circumstances? One man wanted to wear his suit to a dance tonight, and it's nowhere in sight; another wanted his for church tomorrow morning. How can Joe even think that these people will continue to bring their cleaning to him, no matter how pleasantly I try to gloss it over? It goes against my grain anyway to try to B.S. people.

Joe is such a nice man, such a pleasant man, such a hardworking man, such an optimistic man, and, I believe, a Christian, loving man, but he is not a business man. How I feel for him in his struggles to build his dream on so shaky a foundation.

A girl I knew (a drug addict) came in for some clothing. Apparently she felt the need to talk to someone, to unload. So I listened patiently to her for quite some time. She is struggling to come to grips with life and to raise the baby she has brought into this world. I hope she finds her way out of the maze of despair, loneliness, and fear she is in, and salvages what's left of her life and saves her little daughter. The world is so full of quiet desperation.

Finally, I made it home. Just as I was leaving, a young boy came in to pick up the clothes he planned to wear to a party tonight. Of course they weren't ready. He was so disappointed. It's just too much, too much!

I'm going to bed now and console myself with Kahlil Gibran, although Richard Wright is my true love.

Good night,
Richelene

3–18–73
Sunday morning

Dear Self,

My back and sides are hurting with a vengeance this morning. I'm going to have to take myself to a doctor and at least try to find out if something is physically wrong. After a night of agonizing over the problem of my "job," I decided I can't take it. So I just wrote Joe a letter of resignation. I told him all the things that are hurting his business and that my crazy, mixed-up inner self just can't cope with the situation. I wonder if this is why his other counter girl, an older white woman, quit? It well may be.

Let's face it honestly, self, no matter how well-intentioned we may be, no one wants to be associated with a ball of confusion like that over there; it's a reflection on one's own standards and seemingly a condoning of such inefficiency. Poor, poor man! I'm beginning to wonder if his reasoning power is a little defective if he thinks any amount of "glossing" will offset the way he's running his business, and will keep people coming back. Plainly and simply, he has bitten off more than he can chew, and nothing I can do or say will help appreciably.

I told him in the letter that I'll stay until he can find someone else, if he wants me to.

So the angel has lost her halo so quickly. Once again life and circumstances have triumphed over the desire to be loving and good intentions.

So be it,
Richelene

P.S. Joe was there this morning getting some work out, so I sent the letter over by one of the kids. As soon as he read the letter, he called and asked me if I can try to hang in there for another week or so. He promised faithfully that I won't have to work under the same conditions, that he will have things straightened out so that when people come for their cleaning, it will be ready. All I can say is— we shall see. If it's the same old routine next Saturday, that's my last day there.

I had promised a friend that I was going to the High School revue with her this afternoon, but I'm just too washed out and still in terrible pain. Kenneth's band is playing in the revue, and I'd like to see him perform, but I just can't make it.

I'm lying here in bed reading *Khalil the Heretic*. I am reprimanded by him for sometimes getting the notion that

I would like to flee from the world I'm in and go into seclusion in some green and peaceful wilderness—like monks, etc. He upbraided the monks for segregating themselves from the people in need of knowledge, for fleeing from mankind and from God, for killing their souls while pretending to kill their bodies, for living off gold that was wrought from the poor, for not being among their neighbors to sympathize with them, for not being there to give a word of compassion to a criminal or prostitute.

So perhaps, after all, it is better for us to stay and try to brighten the corner where we are rather than fleeing from the world and its demands upon us. For speaking of giving words of compassion to the prostitutes, yesterday as I was talking with the girl (the dope addict) at the cleaners, _____ came in. After she left, he said to me, "That girl is one of the biggest drug addicts and prostitutes in New Britain." I told him that I knew all that, but was I supposed to act holier than thou and turn her off when she so plainly needed to talk? It didn't hurt or contaminate me in any way, and maybe it helped her.

3–19–73

Dear Self,

After a good night of deep, dream-filled sleep—I feel almost human again.

I had planned to be at the bank at 9:30, but the *Phil Donahue Show* caught my eye.

He had a Dr. Albert Ellis on promoting his book, I can't remember the name of it, but the statement that caught my attention was something he said about many women being afraid to have sexual experience because of a fear of failure and rejection, and fear of not being able to live up to that super sexual being that they've read about so much. That may well be true of some women, but from my own personal experience and from talking to many women who don't hop into the hay with every man that asks them, I've drawn different conclusions. Most women don't behave promiscuously because of:

1. High moral and/or religious standards.
2. Refusal to be used by men that care nothing for them beyond their bodies.
3. Their knowledge that many of the men who try to lure them into bed are inept, inefficient, insensitive, and sometimes inert, so why bother?
4. Many men's "humanitarian" feelings that they are doing any fairly personable looking woman a favor by keeping them from "wasting" their lives, but many women prefer to "waste" their lives by abstinence than to "waste" them by bed-hopping with men on ego trips.
5. Their daily observations of the hanky-panky and abuse that many single women are undergoing just to keep a "man" around.

My own personal belief is that most women who abstain from sexual encounters for long periods of time would gladly and passionately enter a relationship that is meaningful and fulfilling, where they are enjoyed and cared for as a total person, and can give the same care and respect to the man.

I got to the bank by 10:30 A.M., to the grocery store, and back home by 12:15 P.M. Much of that time was spent waiting for the taxi. I ate lunch, hung out some clothes, swept the living room and kitchen, dusted, and got to work at two.

Joe was here, going like a pint-sized tornado, as usual. He left at 3:30 P.M. Had quite a few customers—so it has proved to be well worth his while to stay open today; he's usually closed on Mondays. He apparently took everything I said in my letter in the spirit in which it was intended. If he just manages to get all this work out that people want for Saturday, and I don't have to go through the usual anguish, it just might work out after all.

Know what, self? I'm trying something. I bought material for three little girl's dresses today. I'm going to make them real nice and pretty and bring them over here and see if they'll sell. If they do, who knows? If they don't, two are in Candy's size, and I wouldn't have lost anything. Here's hoping.

It's past 5:30 now, so I'm going to wrap things up and go home. It was a good day, and I'm grateful.

Until tomorrow,
Richelene

3–20 73

Hi Self,

I felt draggy, draggy today. Can't seem to get my sleep pattern back on a workable track, and it's "dilapidating" me. The night before last was good. However, last night was bad. It's undeniable now. Every time I try to work regularly, for any amount of time, I get overtired and my crazy nervous machinery begins to go haywire.

I'm trying to pace myself, but I can feel myself running down already. It's a shame that such disgustingly healthy looking outer trappings often house such fragile inner workings. Already Joe is hinting at my working full time and running the place here before long. This would be the answer to my prayers if I could work here full time for a living wage and get off welfare, but how could he pay me a full-time salary even if by some miracle I could cope with everything full time?

I truly believe that he's going to try with every ounce of his being to improve the operations here. He says he wants to prove to me, to himself, and the customers that he can run this business right. With all the competition, that's his only salvation.

I came in at 1:15 P.M. today. It's now 3:45 and not one customer has been in, oops! And here comes one now! Back again, her order wasn't ready. Dear, dear, dear!

I made one of the little dresses that I cut out yesterday. It's very cute—pink with delicate roses, and trimmed with white lace. Naturally, I think somebody's little doll will look adorable in it, but will it sell? I will try to have three or four ready for the trial run by the weekend.

Boy it's cold in here. I guess Joe can't afford to run the heater right now. He said I could go home if it gets too cold, but I will try to stick it out until 5:30. I'm used to it being colder inside than outside (my apartment) by now. Hooray! The sun just came out, so I can stand in front of the window and warm up.

A big tall brother just brought two suits in that he wants back by Friday. He says if they're not ready Saturday, after I talked him into waiting until Saturday, he and I are going to fight! You better believe these two suits will be ready if I have to take them home and wash and iron them myself, or I definitely won't be to work Saturday. I'm decrepit enough as it is—besides, if I had wanted to keep on fighting, I would have kept my husband, or latched onto another "puncher" by now. He was only kidding, of course.

There's some nice jazz on the radio now that's putting "ants in my pants, and I need to dance." I wish someone nice would invite me out dining and dancing instead of "loving" this weekend. No such luck! I seem to have outdone myself in chasing away the ones that did issue such invitations. So I'll probably spend another week-end at home. It is time for a change of pace!

5:00 P.M.!

Another half hour has crept by, and I'm splitting this scene. Thank God for sunshine. And, a little bit of soul food to replenish a little bit of the substance I lost this afternoon—I just disappointed another customer—and to chase away the physical chill. I wonder if I really am a masochist to endure this? Was Freud right when he said that all women are masochists and all men sadists? No!

Later,
Richelene

P.S. This was definitely an abnormal winter. Know how I know? I didn't get ice in the bathtub even once this winter. Here's hoping for more winters like this, since I see no prospects of moving out of this apartment.

3–21–73

Dear Self,

Ah-h, Spring! Today is bright and sunny, and early this morning I heard the birds calling me to get up and be about my business, and so I am.

I slept well and I am renewed. I got the kiddies off with a good breakfast of hot buttered grits, bacon, eggs, and orange juice. Then I gave Jeffrey a good paddling for playing a doctor type game with his little friend yesterday in the front yard. I explained to him that that was not a nice game for little children to play, in my estimation. I knew the "child authorities" would disagree with me. I then washed the dishes, mopped the kitchen and bathroom floors, straightened up my room, did some hand washables, put two loads of wash in, took a hot bath, and was just going out the door to go to the shopping center for zippers and another piece of material, when the *Phil Donahue Show* caught my eye again.

His show today is about self-respect. His guest, I haven't caught his name, is saying some tremendous things about self-respect, self-image, etc. He's great! Wish I could set everything down here that he's saying. Then again maybe I think he's great because I happen to agree with everything he's said so far. For instance, no matter how much mothers give to their children and husbands, they owe it to themselves to take a little time out just for themselves from time to time; success is coming to terms with ourselves, accepting our negative as well as our positive qualities; self-respect is being kind to ourselves as well as others; in order to love others, we must first be able to love ourselves, not with a narcissistic love, but a healthy love; if we feel that we want to create something, whether it's a painting or anything else, we accept it as an expression of our own selves and do not compare it with what Michelangelo or somebody else did—if it expresses us, that's where it's at; if we want to be professional, we practice, practice, practice; many times we can change our negative and depressive feelings by taking a momentary trip back into memory and dwelling on a time that was particularly relaxing, pleasant, etc.; one must have compassion for himself before he can have compassion for others; to be happy, one cannot be responsible for the opinions of others— good or bad, just be and do the best we can. Right on!

The *Phil Donahue Show* just went off; it's ten o'clock. I'm off to the store.

Later,
Richelene

7:39 P.M.

I'm very pooped, but decided to jot down the rest of the day's happenings instead of flopping into bed or sewing.

The walk to Bradlees was glorious. When I walked out the door, I noticed that icicles were formed on the hand wash I hung out, yet the cold did not penetrate as I walked at a brisk pace. There was something different, something new and fresh in the air. And I noticed that spring's magic wand is already painting the grass green. It's spring!

I don't know if the dresses I make will sell or not, but today I got an order to design and make a little girl's long dress. So who knows?

I just found out why the heat is off at the cleaners— the gas is turned off because the bills haven't been paid. I stuck it out til 5:30 anyway, and luckily for Joe too, because several customers came in. One man brought six pairs of pants to be repaired (his wife must be a liberated woman who doesn't stoop to such mundane tasks as mending); a boy also brought a pair of pants to be cuffed Bet I could do a thriving business if I could open my own place and found it at the right time. If it's for me, a way will be found at the right time.

_____ came in for me to help her with some pants she's attempting to make. She wants to learn to sew without patterns and wants me to teach her, but it is hard for me to teach anyone to sew my way as I have no method. I just kind of improvise as I go along. Sometimes it comes out nice, sometimes it doesn't. Anyway, I took a few minutes out and showed her what to do about her pants as best I could.

It's getting to be a thing every day now, Joe calling me to come in at 1:30 P.M. This is putting my household schedule in a slight scramble. When I go at 3:30, I can cook dinner before I go—now I can't. It was seven o'clock before we ate dinner tonight, and the kids were starving.

I must get that ancient relic of a typewriter repaired so I can type up these jottings. They might make the kids rich someday after I depart this world and go home to my reward.

Good night,
Richelene

3–22–73

Dear Self,

Do I recall singing the glories of spring to you just yesterday? Fickle, fickle, spring—with her unpredictability! Today March is roaring like the proverbial lion. There's a chill in the air that cuts to the bones, and my throat was sore and scratchy this morning.

"Greater love hath no man than a man lay down his life for his brother." Unfortunately, I haven't reached that state of perfection yet, so when Joe called a few minutes ago and asked me to come in, I had to refuse. At some point, common sense had to enter into compassion, or one can be foolish in his "do-gooding." I can't afford to catch pneumonia and maybe die from being in that cold place. I'm feeling too much under par as it is.

I dragged myself bowling this morning—and bowled lousily. We won all three games only because we played the last place team, and we all bowled lousily, except Irma.

_____, the girl who asked me to make the long dress for her little girl, said her sister might be interested in buying the little pink dress. I had planned to sew some this afternoon, but the grand babies are here, so there's not too much I can do except enjoy them and try to keep them from demolishing the place.

Last night, a "gentleman" called, and told me frankly that he'd like to have an affair with me, because he's curious to find out what makes me tick. Now I admire that "gentleman's" honesty in stating his case, but I never knew one could find out what makes people tick by just being sexually intimate with them. I was always of the opinion that the thing, or things, that make people tick was in the cranium, not in the genitals. However, I had long suspected that some people's brains were in the lower part of their anatomy rather than the upper part. Since what makes me tick is above the shoulders, and the only way this "gentleman" could find out what makes me tick would be through time consuming observation and conversation, care, tenderness, etc., his curiosity will never be satisfied.

Seriously speaking, self, it's amazing how some men can take women for such fools. Any woman that would allow her body to be used to satisfy somebody else's curiosity, her brains would most definitely have to be in her genitals, if she has any. Now if she is curious also, and wants to satisfy her own curiosity—that's a different matter. It's amazing the ideas men can come up with to try to lure a "not too easy" woman into bed. Many times they'll throw out sly innuendoes that there must be something wrong with you, in order for you to give in and prove that there isn't. And the really fanatic egomaniacs will often spread the word around that they've made it with you, when they haven't, especially if you've been seen with them once or twice. Men! It's impossible to take them, and impossible to leave them alone.

I guess I'll try to get something done now.

Until later,
Richelene

P.S. I'm back. Want to explore a few more things with you, self, while dinner is cooking. One thing that Joe said when he called me today touched a very sore spot. In the course of the talking about how the business is going to improve and stressing my value to him, he committed a terrible faux pas. He said I'm someone he can lean on. That's all he needed to say to really lower my estimation of him. I'm sick of being leaned on by men. When will my day come, when I can lean on someone for a change? Will the only arm I'll ever be able to lean on be the "Everlasting Arm?" I can remember the congregation singing in a little church in Georgia—the women singing mightily:

> Leaning on Jesus
> Leaning on Jesus
> Safe and secure from all alarm
> Leaning on Jesus
> Leaning on Jesus
> Leaning on the Everlasting Arm!

And now after thinking back on this wonderful old hymn, perhaps I have my answer. If I've got Jesus, and can lean on Him, that is enough. As the hit song says: "We all need somebody to lean on." If I must lend my shoulder for someone to lean on, and I, in turn, must lean on the Everlasting Arm, there will be strength enough to keep us both from falling. Besides, I'm leaning on welfare, and perhaps I pay my dues by allowing others to lean on me, weak as I am.

I've just made another resolution. From now on, I'll discuss the cleaner's business with no one in a critical manner. I'll only talk to you, self, about what goes on. Joe is doing his best. At least he's trying, which is more than a lot of the people who are running him down are doing. I've always rooted for the underdog. So as of tomorrow, I'll exert every ounce of my being that I have left over from my obligations to my family toward helping Joe to succeed. Everyone is trying to discourage me from hanging in there because of the way things are going. Now I'm more determined than ever to help the man—or try to. Someone has to.

It is a funny thing, but typical. I was discussing the situation with a member of a certain very strict religious sect today; she advised me to stop trying to help the man since he should have known better than to attempt something over his head. Yet she is going out witnessing for Christ and attempting to sway others to her beliefs. I have always believed that you lift Jesus more by helping your fellow man in tangible ways rather than by lip-service. So now I'll close my ears to all criticism and do my own thing to the best of my ability. True, the man's judgment was faulty in attempting to build before his foundation was laid, but what's done is done, and if I can help him to salvage his enterprise, I will do all that I can, within reason.

Now I'm going to eat, and then go upstairs and sew.

Love,
Richelene

3–23–73

Dear Self,

Woe is me! Today I can't even talk above a whisper. My humanitarian instincts led me astray (in lieu of common sense). Although I refused to go and suffer in that refrigerator yesterday, the two previous days apparently did their damage. I have a temperature and feel lousy.

Joe called for me to come in early and was quite surprised to find that I really did come down with a cold or laryngitis or whatever. He said that he now feels guilty for having me come in those two days without heat. I assured him that he should not feel guilty for it was my own doing.

If it's still cold tomorrow, even if I feel better, I'm not going in. For that matter, I'm got going back until it gets warm, unless he manages to get the gas turned back on.

I decided to catch the *Dating Game*, since I didn't feel up to doing any household chores. Fred Williamson, the black actor, was on. He asked the girls the question: "I always ask three things of my women, beauty, intelligence, and obedience. If I choose you which of these qualities would you present to me first?" Two of the dumb bunnies immediately piped up that they'd present obedience to him first. Now, he is a choice-looking brother (and is overly aware of it) and I'm sure they really wanted to be chosen for the date, but I would have placed obedience last, even if it meant losing the date. Evidently he was seriously looking for obedience because he chose the one that he thought readily put obedience first. It was a mistake. He got his numbers mixed up. The one he chose didn't even answer that question. Good for him. He's probably used to having women obeying just to be near him. If he really values intelligence in a woman, he would know that no intelligent woman obeys; she loves and accepts a man as a human being, just as he should her. And neither should demand obedience, only respect—if they're worthy of it. Obedience—bah! Oops! I forgot. They were very, very young. At their age, I no doubt would have put obedience first also.

I just happened to notice what's written on this pencil, "Think before Acting." I must learn to do that more and more. If I had been thinking properly, I would have split out of the cleaners the minute I found out the heat wasn't on.

Here's hoping for a better day tomorrow.

Until then,
Richelene

3–24–73

Dear Self,

The voice is a little better today, but old "Momsy" is still too decrepit to go to work—even though spring has returned to tease us with her warm sunny smile.

Since I couldn't muster up enough energy to do anything but cook breakfast, I retreated back to bed and finished reading one volume of Kahlil Gibran's works. I love that man! Had I not fallen so eternally in love with Richard Wright, Kahlil would occupy first place in my affections.

Joe called and asked me to send one of the kids over to get my pay. Reluctantly, I did so, trimming off as much as I could. How I wish I were in the financial position to help him without taking any pay at all. But having only six dollars to last until next Monday (over a week), I had to accept something from him for the time I put in. Life is cruel to some of us. It places in our hearts and minds the desire to do well, to be of service to our fellow man, then proceeds to put all kinds of obstacles in our pathways to prevent us from being what we want to be. No wonder the highway to hell is paved with good intentions.

I wonder if the day will ever come when I can be free to follow the dictates of my heart without the forces of my inner self being at war. One part of me saying, "Go on and give of yourself and your time and energy, of your talents. Freely you have received; freely give. Whatever you give will be returned triple fold." Another part saying, "Don't be a fool. You try to be loving and giving, and people will use you until they use you up; then they'll say too bad and go on about their business." Another part saying, "How can you be sure the person you're trying to help is receiving your help in the spirit in which it is intended? Maybe he appreciates your help and is grateful—maybe he's saying to himself that he's got a good thing going." And as long as we have doubts about whether we truly are willing to give or not, is it not perhaps better to shuck it all until our true motive is resolved within ourselves? Or do we just keep trying, in spite of our cynicism and doubts, and everything will eventually fall into place? Questions, and questions!

I feel lonely and melancholy today. What do I do to dispel this feeling? I'm not in the mood for any more reading, sewing, etc.; I'm in the mood for love. I said love, not just sex!

Later,
Richelene

P.S. I just turned the typewriter upside down and fiddled around with it—and what do you know? It's working! Now I can do some typing.

3–25–73

Dear Self,

It's another Sunday afternoon. Spring flirted with us briefly this morning, then coyly hid behind a barricade of rain clouds. As usual, on my day of rest, I've been in and out of bed all day, reading.

My next door neighbor stopped by for a hello, and we chatted for a few minutes.

I looked across the street at 8:30 this morning, and Joe was there getting yesterday's work out. Oh, poor man. I hope I feel much better tomorrow. My voice is almost back to normal.

Last night _____ brought me a bottle of brandy for my cold. Against my better judgment and resolutions,

I took half a glass, and my head began spinning immediately. So I took a hot bath and fell into bed. I slept good. However, I woke up at three and had a seizure. The doctor told me that epileptics should not drink alcoholic beverages, but I figured the small amounts and the infrequent times that I take a drink couldn't do any damage. I'm sure the brandy didn't bring on the seizure. What about all the ones I've been having recently when I haven't even been near any alcohol? Let's face it, my nervous machinery must be deteriorating.

The buses in Hartford will be running again starting tomorrow, so I'll make an appointment to go to the clinic and tell the doctor about the escapades of my whacky brain waves.

I think I'll lie back down and read the new *Reader's Digest*.

Later,
Richelene

3–26–73
Monday morning

Dear Self,

I know you get tired of my constant complaining, but at least I'm sparing others the gory details, which is more than they do for me, although I really don't mind listening to their problems.

Oh, I'm so tired of dragging and going through the motions of trying to keep things in some semblance of order around here. Where do these "experts" that have no children, or a sensible one or two, get the idea that women who stay home have nothing to do? It's just eight-thirty, and already I've dragged through enough chores to tire me out, and there's plenty more to be done—none of it "busy-work." The one thing I definitely agree with the "experts" on: The best defense against a nervous breakdown, in dealing with the boys' rooms, is to keep the doors closed. That I do.

To make matters worse, the "lost shoe" syndrome struck again this morning. I thought I was past that. Jeffrey could only find one shoe—and since I didn't feel like combing the house to find it, I kept him home. I feel draggy, draggy. O, Lord, just to have a couple of really good days so I can give the house a thorough cleaning!

Now my voice is almost normal, but the cold has settled down into an aggravating cough and runny nose, it's raining outside, and I've got to walk over to the shopping center to shop for groceries today. I hope it lets up long enough for me to get there.

I don't know if I'll make it to the cleaners today or not, although I'd like to. Last night, I was reading an article about the healing power of compassion in April's *Readers Digest*. It spoke of how easy it is for us to stick with someone who is a success, but so much harder to stand by a failure. And when we do stand by a seeming failure, that we believe in, that's when we show true compassion. It made me think about Joe. I truly want to stick by him, since he says he really needs me there, but although I believe in him as a good human being, I don't believe in his methods of running his business. Some of the things that make me believe that he is a good human being are these: I've noticed how he treats the little children that come into the place. There is a candy store next door, and they often come in and ask him for change to buy candy. He'll give them the broom and ask them to sweep, or some little chore, and then give them a little change to buy candy. Some men would just shoo them out. Any man that is gentle with little children has much of God in him. And he does not differentiate between them on the basis of race or color. One day, two teenage black boys were talking with him. I heard him patiently admonishing them never to judge people on their race or color alone, but to accept people on their merit, as human beings. These things make me admire him as a human being.

But to what do I give priority, his humaneness or his business ability? If he was treating the customers cloth-ing, and the customers, with the respect that they de-serve, I would have no doubts whatever that I should stick by him although he seems to be failing. But how can I stand by and see him abusing nice things that people have paid a lot of money for? Even if I told him this, what can he do to improve his service without the proper equip-ment to do the job right?

I've "suffered with him," as the article defined com-passion, but I've also "suffered with the customers." I'm just not in a position at this time, to do this much suffer-ing—so perhaps I should just give it up and channel my "compassion" into less hurtful areas for now. Other situ-ations needing compassion will continue to find their way to me. They always do.

I guess I'll drag myself up now and drag through a few more chores while waiting to drag myself to the store.

Talk to you later,
Richelene

P.S. Thank you for being there to share my burdens and thoughts with, self. If you're bored or disinterested—at least you don't let me know. You always listen patiently, and sometimes you even show me the right thing to do to solve my dilemmas. You're compassionate, and I like you very much.

10:10 A.M.

Back again. The *Phil Donahue Show* was a humdinger today. His guest was a Ph.D. in psychology. This man's theory is that we unconsciously condition and set ourselves up for everything that happens to us. I think he's a dingbat. So I set myself up to be on welfare, to be a failure, by society's standards, by being born an epileptic. And people that die from cancer, heart failure, etc., set themselves up for that by their own subconscious conditioning. And, if an airplane crashes and kills 180 persons, they set themselves up for that? And all the children born retarded or with other deformities set themselves up for what happens thereafter? Black people were over in Africa, running around in the jungle, happily conditioning themselves to be brought to America as slaves? Ridiculous! It might seem that we set ourselves up for certain conditions of life because of family patterns, etc. But if certain members of a family do follow a certain pattern, it's because of what they inherited in the genes—predisposition to certain diseases, etc., not because they willed it. Or, since I believe in predestination, things happen because a power beyond ourselves destined certain things to happen to us.

Shit! If I was going to condition myself for a goal in life, the goal sure wouldn't have been to suffer the mental agony of being on welfare. I would have conditioned myself to be rich—so I could enjoy more of life and give to the suffering poor. That man is full of shit! I wonder why none of my brothers or sisters conditioned themselves to be on welfare, if being on welfare is such a desirable mode of life that I should have conditioned myself for it. And, seeing how "beautifully" I'm getting along on welfare, I wonder why some of my brothers or sisters don't leave their beautiful homes and come to Connecticut and get on welfare? He's full of shit! (Now I'm crying, so I'd better stop.)

5:00 P.M.

Guess the cry was a good catharsis. I feel altogether better this afternoon. The walk to the store in a slight drizzle probably didn't help my cold any, but it refreshed my spirits.

I received a letter from my mother this afternoon. Her closing sentence was, "Don't forget to pray." No, mother, I won't forget to pray. Perhaps I don't pray the moving, lyrical prayers that I heard in church during my childhood and perhaps I don't get down on my knees and pray, "Our Father which art in heaven," as often as I used to. I'm not even sure I know how to pray or what to pray for. Yet I believe that the Supreme Being knows I'm here, and he gets my messages. My ears this morning were a prayer, my sighs in the dark hours of my soul are prayers, my suffering with my fellow man is a prayer, the laughter that breaks forth spontaneously at happy moments is a prayer, and my loving thoughts of you, my hopes of good for all mankind, are prayers. I'm far from the perfect mother, but I do pray daily, and I believe He hears my prayers and pities every groan. I can't write these things to you in a letter. You wouldn't understand. You'd say, "Rich must be losing her mind." You'd show the letter to my sisters and brothers, and they would laugh and say, "She is going crazy up there." But would any of them, even seriously thinking that I might be becoming mentally ill, take the time out from their pursuit of worldly goods to come and see about me? Hardly not! You gave birth to me, mother, but you have never known me. And, sadly, you probably never will now. I don't hold it against you or the family that we've never been close. How can those, even of the same flesh and blood, who look at life through conventional eyes, know one who looks at life with different eyes? You didn't make me different, I didn't make myself different, but I am different.

And so I'll write you a little letter saying, "I hope you and dad are well. We are all fine. The children are really growing. . . ."

3–28–73

Dear Self,

I had compassion on you yesterday and spared you my suffering and complaints. Jeffrey comforted me. I realize that the experts say that you shouldn't let your children see you crying or exhibiting other negative emotions, but I just couldn't help it. My back was hurting so badly. So I just lay there on the sofa and let it all hang out. Jeffrey sat there and patted my back and soothed me like a little angel. I can honestly say that I have never felt more truly comforted and loved. As soon as he saw that he had "made it all better," he trotted outside to play, none the worse for witnessing my distress.

All too soon, he'll be past this truly caring and loving stage, and will be as indifferent to my little ups and downs as the rest of the children are. That is until he grows back into an awareness of the feelings and sufferings of others. Most people, myself included, evolve through all these different stages and eventually metamorphose into human beings. So there is still hope that my other children will grow into more sensitivity to the feelings of others.

I called a urologist for an appointment so I can see if my kidneys are bothering me again. Frequent infections of the urinary tract used to dog me—I almost had to be hospitalized once, but I couldn't get an appointment until next Tuesday, a whole week! By then I'll either be dead or better. At least my spirits were spared the, "I'm sorry we don't take state patients" blow. I thought of going to the emergency room at the hospital, but they would only pooh-pooh me and send me home. My own doctor is the sweetest, gentlest, most patient man in the world—if you can ever get to see him. Usually, it's the same story with him, by the time you get to him, you're either well or dead. Several people I know have given him up, in spite of their regard for his bedside manner, because there is always such a long wait to see him. But, Lord, I'm so tired of hurting! Maybe I'll just pray hard, and perhaps the pain will subside. Prayer seems to be the best antidote and medicine for poor people in many ways. At least it's the most readily available.

I remember, just before Jeffrey was born, how I told the doctor at the clinic that I was in great pain, a kind of pain I had not experienced during pregnancy before. They pooh-poohed me and said, "You're doing fine." The very next morning, after a night of agony, I began hemorrhaging. I remember the clinic in Atlanta. They were giving me phenobarbital. Yet when I asked them to give me an electroencephalogram, they said it didn't seem to be indicated. So I somehow paid a private neurologist to have one done, because I knew I was an epileptic. I remember, at that same clinic, while I was waiting, a young intern blithely said to a decrepit looking black man, "Come on in, we are going to give you the best medicine we have, some phenobarbital." Sure, phenoarbital is a treatment for epilepsy, but to prescribe it without doing the proper tests first seems poor medical care to me. I could go on and on about the disinterested medical care that I, as a poor person, have both experienced and observed, but why bother? Who really cares about the poor, but the poor?

As I said before, I'm sure to be feeling better, or dead, by next Tuesday. There is no way I can hurt this badly for a whole week without a change for the better or the worse. Donna went over and helped Joe at the cleaners yesterday afternoon. Ricky kept the babies for her. I will

probably have to ask her to help him out again this afternoon. She seems to be growing into compassion in some
ways. Growth into human beings is slow and painful.
Look at how long it's taking me.

I just answered my mother's letter. I sent her a water
color painting of two orchids, which Ricky did. I think
they're beautiful. The minute he painted it, I knew it was
for mother, especially since orchid is her favorite color. I
told her that we are very poor in worldly goods; we give
such as we have, and this was our way of giving her flowers, orchids, no less, while she can see them. Someday we
might be able to give her orchids that smell.

I am going to lie down now.

Later,
Richelene

9:50 P.M.

I had just finished writing this morning when Joe called
and asked if I could get Donna to go over and open up the
place this morning. I got dressed and went up there. She
refused. Said she was not going back over there again, it
was too humiliating. So-o-o I got myself together somehow and went over this afternoon. As I approached the
place, I was greeted by a loud argument. Not wanting to
intrude on what was no doubt an embarrassing situation
for Joe, I came back home and called him, and asked what
time he wanted me to come in.

Today being warm and sunny, the proprietors of the
liquor store (white) and the candy store (black) were outside listening in on the argument. Joe's door was open. I
found out when I got there that it was open because a
large black bird had flown in, and he left it open so the
bird could fly out. There is some kind of old superstition

about a bird entering your house is a bad omen, but I can't quite remember what it is. I'm glad I can't. It might make me nervous.

Anyway, I kept looking out my window to see if whoever it was arguing with Joe was gone. I saw the man who sold him the machines come out. I can guess what the commotion was about—money.

When I finally got there, Joe's usually smiling, optimistic face was drawn, and the weak smiles he tried to effect never got near his eyes, and the work piled up was unbelievable. The teenage boy who has been pinch-hitting for me wrote a load of coin-op up for a lady. She called for them today, and they were nowhere in sight. Several customers came for clothing that was not ready, etc. My God! What an impossible battle this man is waging. He undoubtedly must agree with British novelist William McFce, "If fate means you to lose, give him a good fight anyhow." I also believe in giving fate a good fight, but it also makes sense to accept your limitations. Once more I ask you to help me to accept mine more gracefully, Dear God.

If ever a man needed a friend, Joe does. He wants me to come to work at twelve tomorrow. Wishy-washy me, what was my last decision on the matter, to quit or keep trying? How did I ever get involved in this thing anyway? Well, my decision for now is to try to be a friend to Joe a little longer. I finished mending the pants I began last Wednesday in addition to minding the counter. I came home at six, ate dinner, Melanie cooked, and dropped into bed at 6:30. I dropped off to sleep, then woke up at 9:30. So here I am writing.

Whatever it was that laid siege to me, it wreaked havoc cosmetically. I looked at myself in the mirror this morning and was horrified. If anyone had told me this morning that I didn't look my age, I would have slapped them for insulting my intelligence. Anyway, whether the pain was psychosomatic or a flare-up of a chronic infection, I feel one hundred percent better tonight. My arm isn't hurting as much either, although there's still a hard swelling on the under side. Maybe prayer took care of things. The truth is I'm feeling so much better that I want to jump up and down and shout Hooray! But think I'd better play it low key. Speaking of how bad I look, the other night, Donna said, "I've never seen you looking like this." She just didn't know how much pain I was in, although I was dragging around trying to keep going.

So-o-o I will grab a book and go back to bed now. Thanks, Lord, for the relief.

Good night self,
Richelene

3–29–73

Dear Self,

I called my sister in Atlanta last night. In her letter, mother said that my sister was in the hospital, so I called to see how she was doing. To my surprise, she was home. She had undergone some tests, which came out negative, and was feeling much better.

We really talked last night. Really communicated! It seems that this is the first time that we've ever really communicated. I lived with her for a year, from 1959 to 1960, when I left Don for a respite from the horror of our lives. Yet, even then, we were strangers. We got along well and went through the surface amenities of being sisters, but we were poles apart. And I was grateful that she and her husband took us in and allowed us to share their small apartment, but I was never comfortable there. I was still a caged bird that longed to be free. To her and the rest of the family, I was just the mixed-up little girl who should have stayed with her husband and was sure to come to no good end. That I was a mixed-up little girl, I agree. That I should have stayed with the man I married, I thoroughly disagree. Being young and considered attractive, they were sure I'd be unable to resist being sucked into some vacuum of immorality and travel the road to perdition, but I have resisted, and it hasn't been easy. Many times when my children needed food or clothing, I've had to fight to resist the temptation of "easy money" dangled before me by men bartering for an evening of "love." To me, it would have been the "hardest money" I could have earned. So although it's been rough, my integrity is still intact, and I like myself for that, but getting back to my conversation with my sister, last night, we actually talked to each other like two people who know each other, are related to each other, and who like each other.

Has the change that enabled us to communicate taken place in me or in her? Or has life taught us both to reach out more, to try to touch each other more? I don't know. She is pushing the heck out of forty-three and I'm on a collision course with forty, so perhaps life has taught us both.

One thing we both agreed on: We are still young, because we feel young inside, and we both feel that life has much more to offer us—if we are willing to see and receive it. So what if the mirror told me yesterday that the chronological years, man's years, are in cahoots with father time to deface the outer scenery? Today I combed my hair into a nice fluffy au natural, powdered my nose and put on lipstick—and I'm going bowling! And I predict a 200 game or a 500 series today. So there!

Later,
Richelene

4:30 ᴘ.ᴍ.

Back again. I didn't quite reach 500 this morning, but I'll settle for the 496 I got.

I was just getting ready to walk out the door and go to work when I decided to look out the window. Saw a lot of cars over there, a lot of men filing out, and a lot of commotion. When I recognized the man who sold Joe the equipment coming out, I knew something was wrong.

I called over. Joe wasn't there. _____, the man who is opening the Stag Shop was there, and I asked him what was happening. He said, they're putting Joe out because he hasn't been paying the rent, and the money that _____ has been giving him toward the rent has been going elsewhere, and now _____ is uncertain as to whether he should take over the cleaners, or to just get out altogether. I told him if he takes over the cleaners and runs the business right, I'll work for him. So-o-o in spite of everything, it seems my little man's dream has crumbled. I feel kind of at peace inside knowing that I tried to help him and shared his suffering. He was suffering, that I know. Even if he did use the money that _____ gave him for purposes other than what it was intended for, I still believe he did it out of desperation and necessity, and not because he is basically dishonest. Sometimes life can lead us into circumstances that make even the strongest less than they want to be. And it can lead us into pathways that we never intended to travel, and we reach a dead-end. Then we can't go backward, and we can't go forward, so we flail about and thrash around until we fall, exhausted. Sometimes we rise again, sometimes we don't. Joe had been flailing about desperately these past months. So he fell. I hope and pray that he will be able to rise again, but with better reasoning ability.

And so his dream has collapsed at his feet like the little pig's house that was made of straw. Fate huffed and puffed and blew his dream down. God help him, comfort him, and strengthen him to go on.

Sincerely,
Richelene

3–30–73

Dear Self,

The third month of 1973 is almost ended. This has been an interesting month for me, a time of true learning, but what did I learn—to stretch myself a little farther in attempting to reach out to others? That fate will win every time, if she has so ordained it, in spite of our efforts to fight it? That reason is the most valuable asset that we can possess in trying to shape our own lives? That to attempt to go beyond the limits of reason and knowledge is folly? That there is little pure altruism in the world of humans; that most of us have selfish motives intermingled with our attempts to do good? That we humans are frail and fragile of ourselves, but with God we can be stronger than we think we are?

Perhaps no new truths were revealed to me, but my puny efforts at trying to evolve into a human being are making me more aware of the things that I already knew. Making me more willing to forget self and reach out to others.

A few random thoughts and observations:

While combing my hair yesterday, I picked up a mirror with LOVE written across the top in big red letters. I bought the mirror, not to gaze on my own reflection and say, "I love you, Richelene," but for a very dear friend about three years ago. Her skin happened to be white, but she was really just a human being, a genuine human being. She moved away before I could give the mirror to her. So now, whenever I look into that mirror, I think of her. She personified love.

I first met this lady while working on a temporary job as a transcriptionist in December of 1965. It was almost Christmas—and seemingly, there would be no Santa for my children that year. Don and I had just separated, and I had just gone on welfare, and had to turn the money I was earning over to them. The job was just an attempt to salvage a tiny bit of self-respect and dignity. One employee said to me, "See that woman in the red dress, she loves the color red? She's a queer duck."

The "queer duck" introduced herself to me, and we talked. Later she asked if she could take my children to Sunday school with her on Sunday. I agreed as I had no transportation and wanted them to go to church. And that Christmas, Santa came after all. The "queer duck" made Christmas beautiful for my children. Another "queer duck" (the same employee that labeled the lady in red, labeled an older man a "queer duck" also) in the office bought Christmas dinner, turkey and all, for us. And every holiday, thereafter, he sent us a monetary gift, until he became ill and went into a convalescent home. I suspected that the employee that labeled the others must have been sort of a "queer duck" also, because she drove me to the grocery store and brought me home, and she was genuinely friendly to me, which eased my slight discomfort at being the only colored spot on that canvas of white. At that time I was more conscious of color. She was a member of a mostly black Methodist church; she seemed much like a human being who happened to be white. How often have I seen the "queer ducks" of this world doing the nicest things for people? Perhaps "queer duck" is just a pseudonym for human being.

But, I desire to get back to my friend. For over five years this beautiful human being with white skin took my children to Sunday school through rain and storm, sleet and snow. Sometimes I joined them. For over five years this lady watched over us, helped us in many tangible and intangible ways, she commiserated with me when I became "illegitimately" pregnant, visited me, with flowers, when I was in the hospital with my "illegitimate" baby, showered him with gifts, invited me into her home for social functions with her "white" friends, invited me to her wedding when she remarried, turned up at Christmas times loaded down with presents for the children and me, brought heart-shaped cakes on Valentine Days, brought cakes and presents for each of us on our birthdays (she never forgot one), and for all of it she asked nothing in return. She did these same things for many others.

Her second husband died, and she moved away. I don't know where she is now, or even if she is alive, but wherever she is, I think of her with love. I feel ashamed of myself for finding it so hard to erase my prejudices based on race or color, but every time I look into that LOVE mirror from now on, I will be reminded to try harder. If only we could all be genuine human beings, prejudice and bigotry would eradicate themselves. They could not stand against true love. Love to you, dear friend, wherever you are, and as I always said in my thank you notes to you, God bless you.

Sincerely,
Richelene

3–31–73

Dear Self,

It's Saturday, the last day of March. The sky is overcast and brooding—ready to weep.

Why is it on the verge of weeping? Because today the death knell sounds for March, and it forever fades into oblivion? Now April is awaiting her cue to enter and set the stage for flowers and green trees and warmth? April is that most enigmatic of all months; for days she weeps, then suddenly she kisses us with her warm smile, then the next moment, she is cold, disdainful. But enigmas have always fascinated man, so April holds more charm than March, and perhaps that is why March is exiting, weeping. Or is she weeping for Joe and the death of his dream?

It's early, and although I have prepared breakfast, I didn't call the children down. Let them sleep a little later today and tomorrow, if that's what they want to do. I'm not sure if I'll have to go across the street to work today or not. It's now under new management, and yesterday, _____ called me to come over and help him try to sort things out. I went. He's my brother. Although my heart is still heavy from sympathy for Joe, I'll try to help _____ out as long as he needs me. The feeling is not the same though—and it's just as well. Joe was small and vulnerable appearing, and the years were weighing him down. Something about his total self reached out to me and appealed to my better instincts. _____ is just the opposite; he is young, big, strong-appearing. He doesn't appear to really need my help. And here one of the paradoxes of life could be manifested. I, like most people, am more willing to help those who look like they need help, judging by surface appearances, than those who appear capable and self-sufficient. In fact, _____ might really need my help more than Joe did. At least Joe had been in this kind of business for a long time; he had gone bankrupt in a similar business venture, was aware of the mechanisms and inner workings of such a business, and was old enough to know better than to attempt what he did, under the circumstances. I, of all people, should not judge anyone on surface appearances. _____ is a complete novice at this. He is very uncertain and a little fearful, but is going to gamble anyway, one of the advantages of youth. If he fails, he can pick himself up and start off in a new direction much more easily than Joe can. Donna said to me yesterday that he is really counting on me, so here I go again.

I wish him every success. But one thing for sure, I won't suffer the same anguish that I did with Joe. If I see it's beginning to prey on my spirit—I'm gone! Here I go back to the boredom of routine office work.

Better go jump in the tub now so I'll be all set if he calls me to come in today.

Later,
Richelene

7:30 P.M.

Back again. Wonder of wonders—a really good day sneaked up on me! I even had the strength and courage to venture into the boys' rooms and give them a good cleaning. Talking about disaster areas! I changed the linen, pulled dirty underwear and socks out of every nook and cranny I've never seen or heard of before, swept a load of dust from under the beds, and recycled clean clothes back to the washer. By Monday, the two rooms will be back in their former states of disarray, and for the good of my mental health, I'll close the doors again until such time as I have the courage and fortitude to assault their rooms again.

4–1–73

Dear Self,

April first. April entered showering the earth, preparing it for the flowers soon to bud and blossom. This is my day of rest. This has truly been a day of rest. My weary spirit rested from its wrestlings with the problems and sorrows of Joe. The people who I know and talk to find it strange that I felt so deeply about all this—I've caught the vibrations. But I don't beg anyone to understand me. I act according to the dictates of my heart and conscience. Sure I'm a little crazy, but I'm not asking anyone to live with it, and I can live with it pretty nicely. I've made it clear to the children that they're free to go as soon as they feel that their wings are strong enough to fly, if I cannot convince them otherwise, in the event that they want to fly before they're ready. So since I am me, I could not stand helplessly by and watch my brother's dream utter its death rattles, and watch his frantic efforts to save it, like a doctor desperately trying to save a terminally ill patient—without feeling his pain. If I march to the beat of my own drummer and allow others to march to the beat of theirs, what else is there? So now the saga of Joe, as he related to me is ended. He is gone. The cleaners is under new management, and the new manager has all my best wishes for success, but I cannot and will not get spiritually or emotionally involved. I'm still working there, as of now. I will give it my best, but I won't bring any of its problems home with me. If I find myself becoming a "whipping-boy" between the manager and the customers, out I go.

Anyway I probably won't be there too long. The new manager has a strong young wife and several teenage children who can help him run the place. I'm sure as soon as they get a firm grasp of things—I won't be needed. That's fine with me for several reasons, which I won't go into now. But, as of tomorrow, I will open the place at 9:00 A.M. and work until two. And so ends one chapter in the life of a crazy mixed-up "do-gooder" and another begins. I'm a little sadder, but a little wiser, I hope.

I will have to talk to the new manager about the "welfare" situation, so he can begin to take out social security and I can report to my keepers. Things are so tight, I have a good mind to ask him to just hand me a few dollars on an unofficial basis every week. Otherwise, how can I ever hope to get some of the things we need around here? I've been honest all my life—and what has it got me but a hard way to go? Yet I'm afraid to be dishonest. Some people just weren't meant to trifle with God's laws, and I firmly believe I'm one of them. On the other hand, the law that forces welfare recipients to turn over the little money that they can earn to help themselves a little is unfair and unjust, so it must be one of man's laws. And one who follows God's law is free to break man's laws that are unjust. I'm not rationalizing, I truly believe this. So I just might keep this money, because we need it, and let them arrest me. And I will go to jail or suffer whatever consequences I have to, rather than pay it back. How can we continuously barely subsist on what we are doled out, and yet have our hands tied when we try to make life a little better financially, without getting bitter and rebellious?

Easter is almost here. Already I feel the vibrations of new life and the resurrection of hope. I feel the need to go to church on Easter, with all my children, and I want to buy them all new outfits. It's been so long since I was able to buy the boys a nice new outfit now that they're in men's sizes, and their clothes cost so much. This Easter I just want to see us all dressed up, and going to church on Easter Sunday, the way we did when they were younger. I even want a new dress and a new hat for myself, even though I don't really need either. But I want to look and feel new, and young, and pretty this Easter. All this I desire, not as a show to the world, but to celebrate the resurrection of Christ, to celebrate the newness and vibrancy of the spring season.

So if my employer goes along with paying me under the table, and I can buy us all new outfits, if they arrest me the Monday after Easter, I'll go happily.

And I believe the resurrected Christ will understand, and I will be straight with Him, regardless of what man thinks.

Here's to April and to Easter!
Richelene

4–2–73

Dear Self,

I'm at work. Just finished cleaning up the place a little and made a couple of signs to go in the window. I really enjoy doodling around with anything artistic or creative—so making the signs was a little bit of a pleasure for me.

So far (11:20) the only customer that came in was one looking for some articles that we couldn't find. Joe returned and brought some things up from the cellar over the weekend, among them was a coat that I brought over in January and couldn't find before. So I'll pay for it and take it home.

A young black man came in to just kind of "smoke over" the merchandise that is selling. He said that he'd heard that everything is real expensive. Then he made the comment, "He isn't doing anything to help the poor people, he's for himself." I nicely reminded him that these "poor people" that live out here happily go downtown, to New York, and everywhere else and buy things as expensive, or more expensive, than these. And they're giving their money to the white man at these places, so why not buy them here?

So I see already the lips have started flapping about _____'s business. I'm discussing these things with you, self, but my involvement is strictly superficial; I can't suffer over this place any more. People are just too much. Joe tried to be a nice guy, charging people what he thought they could afford to pay, so what happened? He wasn't even making enough to pay his expenses. And, sure, he was lovable, but you can't live off love. And love never has been known to pay the rent. People will use you up in the name of love, if you let them. _____ might not have Joe's lovable personality, but he's not going to let people exploit him to gain their favor or their patronage. He may or may not succeed, but he'll get more respect than Joe, if not love. And I'm sure he isn't venturing into this enterprise to gain anyone's love; he is trying to make a buck just like all the white folks who are in business. Treating your customers with courtesy and friendship is essential for the success of any business, but there has got to be a line drawn at a certain point, or you still don't win. So we shall see how "our" people accept and support this one who is of "our own," trying to stand up and be counted on a competitive basis with the white man. It should prove to be interesting.

1:15 P.M.

Home again. I just ate lunch and I am waiting for the "check" so I can go downtown and get the food stamps, pay the rent, etc. Please, Lord, do I have to say it again or should I just try to be patient a little longer?

Joe just called. I'm really glad he did, not only because of my concern for him, but because I wanted to tell him how sorry I am that things turned out this way for him. Besides, I would have been terribly disappointed in him if he just dropped out of sight without even saying "so long" to me, knowing how concerned I was for him and his venture. He sounds optimistic again. He says he is going to get up, dust himself off, and try again. That's the spirit that America admires. But, although it's good to know he's not grieving, I hope and pray that he has learned enough from past experience to accept his limitations and strive for more reachable goals. I'm younger than he, but life has certainly taught me to strive within my limitations. I might still dare to dream impossible dreams from time to time, but I'll certainly try to build on a firm foundation before attempting to build the dreams. If I see that I don't have the required material for the foundation, then I'll give up the dream or place it in abeyance.

I am buying a small money order to send to the Epilepsy Foundation today. It isn't much, but it might help to light one small candle of understanding. This is their slogan on the stamps they sent in their appeal letter, "Light the Candle of understanding."

Until later,
Richelene

4–3–73
3:15 A.M.

Dear Self,

Here I am writing in the wee hours again. I woke up at 12 A.M. I was unable to go back to sleep. I read from about 1 A.M.until now.

While trying to win the battle over insomnia, my unresolved dilemma as to whether I should go along with the meat boycott crossed my mind. I've been kind of tossing it around in my mind trying to decide if I am wholeheartedly committed to this boycott. For a while I felt that I probably would go along with it, although it wasn't truly resolved in my conscience. I somewhat feared the reaction of others with whom I associate if I didn't go

along with it, as most of them say they are going to boycott. Then I said if a few others are at the meat counters,
I will buy my usual quota, but if no one else is there, I will
be ashamed to go and buy meat. Now I know that I would
really be untrue to my own ideals and conscience if I go
along just because of fear of standing on what I truly believe. In fact, I would be a hypocrite.

Ordinarily, I would have shopped today, but the food-
stamp authorization didn't come in the mail. I was quite
upset. So what happened? The mail man left it next door
by mistake, and by the time the children next door got
home from school and brought it to me, it was too late to
get to the bank.

Perhaps this was fate's way of giving me a little extra
time to come to grips with this meat boycott. So now my
decision is made. I'll buy my usual supply of meat. For in
essence, I have been on a meat boycott from necessity for
years. Whether the meat prices stay the same, go higher
or come down, I'll still be buying the same chicken,
chicken wings, chicken gizzards, hot dogs, tuna, and
hamburger. It's the people who have really been able to
eat meat that are upset. By meat, I mean roasts, steak,
pork chops, lamb, veal, ham, etc. It's been years since I've
even been able to look at real meat, much less buy it, except once or twice a year, on a splurge of enough to fill the
cavities of each of us. Most of the people in my category
have subsisted the same way for years.

Okay, so I'm being selfish. I should go along with it
anyway, so at least somebody can eat meat again, even if
it's not my immediate family. It would be noble of me to
be that great-hearted. And I would be, except for one thing:
I can think of so many other things wrong with this world
that takes precedence over the price of meat. Right now
people, especially white middle class America, are thinking about the price they have to pay to put meat into their

bellies, but what about all the peoples of the world who would happily put anything into their bellies to quiet their hunger? Americans are too fat and too well-fed anyway.

Some strikes that I would like to see and would wholeheartedly support:

1. A nationwide strike to lower the price that people who suffer injustices, because of race or color, have to pay in lost talents, motivation, self respect, and dignity.
2. A nationwide strike to lower the price that welfare recipients have to pay in despair, helplessness, and hopelessness, because they are unfortunate enough to have to use welfare as a crutch to limp through life for short or long periods of time.
3. A nationwide strike to lower the price that ignorance, bigotry, and prejudice cause us to pay in lost happiness, peace, and understanding.
4. A nationwide strike to lower the price of peace throughout the world. The price is giving up selfish greed and the thirst for power, and that is much too high.
5. A nationwide strike to lower the price that individuals who stand up for what they believe in have to pay in enduring ridicule, hatred, envy, and often lies.

In short, I would support a nationwide strike for brotherhood and love. If people mobilized and supported a strike for love, who knows what miracles could be wrought? But since such a strike is highly unlikely because the powers that be prefer the status quo, I shall shop tomorrow and buy my usual supply of chicken, chicken wings, chicken gizzards, hot dogs, tuna, and hamburger. If I'm the only one at the meat counter, so be it.

So now at 4 A.M., I'm going back to bed, and will get up at six.

Sweet dream (there'll only be time for one),
Richelene

The heat still isn't on at the cleaners, so _____ didn't have me come in today.

I'm really glad, because I got to use my good day here at home. At twelve I took an hour out to look at *Black Omnibus* with James Earl Jones. I think it is the best show on TV. It presents the positive side of our heritage in such a beautiful way. Today's show was about gospel music. And, I felt as if I were in church. It really got to me. Cicely Tyson did a beautiful reading about a little black girl trying to integrate an all-white school in the South. It was truly moving. This is the shortest hour on TV for me, not that I look at that many "hours" of TV.

I wish I had my typewriter here so I could type this right up. I loaned it to my next door neighbor. She is typing her nephew's term paper. She broadly hinted at my typing it, as I can type faster than she, but I gently explained that I wasn't feeling up to the extra work, and I could loan her the typewriter. I can't let everybody use me up.

Later,
Richelene

P.S. _____ did call me over to help straighten things out and show his wife and daughter some of the mechanisms at the job. There was quite a bit of work to be done, but together we got most of it done.

This has been an uneventful day otherwise. Hope I'll have the inspiration to wash and iron the kitchen curtains and windows tomorrow. Also have to go to school for a conference with Candace's teacher tomorrow afternoon. It's just a routine discussion about her progress. I missed the Lottery by a mile again today. Usually, I prayerfully buy one ticket per week. I guess my prayers lack potency.

So long for now,
Richelene

4–4–73

Dear Self,

I went to work this morning at 9 A.M. The electricity was turned off, because the men were working on it, so there was no heat. After suffering for over an hour, I came home. The minute I came home, the juice was turned back on, so I'll go back in about fifteen minutes.

So far, I'm treading lightly over there. I can see many pitfalls that could cause trouble or distress, but I am not taking them to heart. I can't afford to. I really don't know how long I'll be there. I'm thinking of quitting; the whole situation just doesn't give me good vibrations the way Joe's whacky little setup did. Maybe I really do like to suffer.

One thing that's slightly disconcerting is the new manager's attitude. With Joe, my spirit was aggravated; with _____ my body is aggravated. I'm sure he's a nice enough man, but he's a born flirt, and he is extremely good-looking, and virile looking. The fires have not nearly gone out in "Momsy," they're merely smoldering. And with someone like _____ around overtly and deliberately fanning the flames, it could lead to following regrettable impulses. If temptation can't remove itself from one, the next best thing is for one to remove oneself from temptation. I told him firmly that I'm not for any hanky-panky this morning, and he says he'll cease and desist in his flirtations. If he does and keeps his hands to himself, I'll stay for a while, otherwise I go.

See what I mean when I say life is always serving me raw deals or complicated hands? Now, I ask you self, how can I continuously run into all these different unsettling situations without really trying? Don't tell me I condition myself for these things, I haven't winked an eye, hiked a skirt, given a deliberately inviting glance, or done one thing to invite these advances. Some men just think they have to try them all. One thing's for sure, no one wins them all, and Big Daddy is sure going to lose this one. See why am I so cynical, skeptical, and sometimes bitter? Just how do people like me go about winning? Phooey!

I'm going back. It should be warming up in there by now.

Later,
Richelene

4–5–73
7:15 A.M.

I didn't have a chance to chat with you again yesterday, self. So I'm snatching a few minutes now. I feel very tired and draggy this morning, but I am going bowling anyway. I told _____ at the beginning that Thursday mornings were my mornings.

I was going to the clinic yesterday, but got downtown and discovered that the buses to Hartford only run every hour on the hour now. My appointment at the clinic was for one o'clock and the next bus didn't run until 1:00 and it was cold and pouring rain so I came back home. I will go next Wednesday afternoon. I hope it will be a nice day.

I don't really feel like going into anything with you this morning, self, but I'm waiting for Candace to get through ironing her pants, so I can press mine. She just came upstairs. I'll get back to you later today.

4–6–73

Dear Self,

Another day—whew! I worked pretty hard today, and how sweet it is to be able to serve the customers with dignity. I hemmed and cuffed several pairs of trousers and did some other mending. So, it was good day.

Happily I won't have to work tomorrow, Saturday. There's plenty for me to do here at home. Just working outside the home even part time really throws a kink in one's home operations—that is if you're the type that enjoys trying to keep a house looking like a home.

In addition to having to make the little dress I promised _____, I have a lot of sewing to do for my children for Easter. I think I'll postpone trying this "Little Girl's Dresses" business for awhile. One thing that made me change my mind is the fact that, as usual people think a home sewer should sew for next to nothing. I've nicely told a few that the best thing for them to do is to learn to sew if they really want to save. I was looking at some little dresses that were more or less of the same material and style that I made. These were in a better store and were selling for twelve and fourteen dollars. But people would expect me to sell mine for three or four dollars. No way. So I think I'll place this little brainstorm in abeyance for a while.

I caught the lyrics of the new soul record, "Ain't No Woman Like the One I Love." They incensed me! Male chauvinist pig! He sings that he kisses the ground his woman walks on because she obeys him and makes no demands on him, and it takes very little to make her happy. That's a typical male attitude. I don't think he really loves her though; he's just got a good thing, as he says. The poor little thing is probably a doormat. Just as I once was.

There are several random topics I'd like to discuss with you, self, but I'm too pooped tonight. Maybe I'll have a little more time tomorrow.

Good night,
Richelene

4–7–73
5:30 A.M.

Good Morning Self,

I had meant to sleep late this morning, but _____ called last night and asked me to come in to work for several hours this morning. Besides, I wanted a little time to chat with you, in a little more depth, so here I am.

_____, the friend whose son was AWOL from home earlier this year, came by to show me her new car. A 1973 Impala. It's yellow, the color of my dream car, and it's gorgeous. Since I'm so all-fired tired of being without transportation, I should be green with envy, but upon looking at my face in the mirror this morning, I notice it's the same color as always. Perhaps I'm too happy for her to feel envious. The truth is, I find it hard to envy anyone anything at all. Sometimes I wonder myself how I can continuously go along with so little of this world's goods, and be so absolutely thrilled when someone I know and like, or even not like so well, gets things. Maybe it's because of my crazy mixed-up inner self. Just as each person's sufferings make me suffer, each person's happiness makes me happy, especially my black brothers and sisters. I'm sorry, I just can't help feeling more of an affinity for my "own." Admittedly, I've encountered much more personal abuse from my "own" than from whites, but this is a feeling that is probably native to each segment of the human race, the leaning toward one's "own."

I've told you before, self, I've known whites that I dearly loved as beautiful people, but the mass of them have inflicted too much abuse on the mass of us for me to be as free of prejudices against them as I'd like to be. I'm still working on the problem though.

But getting back to _____ and her car, she has reconciled with her boyfriend, and this was his reconciliation gift to her. Some gift! One day I'll wake up when it's too late and realize that I should have settled for less, and traveled through life in better style. As my cousins said to me when I attended my brother's funeral in Atlanta, "If you can't get what you want, you better start trying to want what you can get." Now that really makes sense, but I'll keep waiting for someone who comes a little closer to being what I want. I'll compromise in unimportant areas, like outward appearances and financial status, but the inner workings have got to jibe with mine.

I must run now. Have to hem a couple pairs of trousers for the shop. That way, if it is unusually busy over there today, these will be done.

Talk to you later,
Richelene

P.S. Oh, I meant to tell you, the only women that I truly envy are those who are strong and healthy enough to work and make it, with their children, without going on welfare. I have a neighbor who fits into this category. I admire her greatly, but I do envy her stamina. Oh, well, what's the use of making myself sad this morning? The sun is shining, the birds are singing, and I am alive and functioning within my limitations. To heck with the rest!

4–8–73
Sunday morning

Dear Self,

I got a good night's sleep last night and feel good this morning. It's very quiet and peaceful at the moment, everyone else is asleep. I still say I enjoy my children best when they're asleep.

Would you believe it's snowing? It's actually snowing! April is outdoing herself in unpredictability. Now she's pretending she's winter and not too coyly. The ground is covered already. Tomorrow she'll probably tantalize us with a bright sunshiny smile.

I'm cooking a good dinner today: Turkey, stuffing, yams, vegetables, the works. I don't know what got into me. I abhor cooking with a vengeance. Everything else around the house, I enjoy doing. Somehow I've never been able to put my creative instincts into effect in the kitchen. In fact, if it wasn't for the children, I doubt if I'd even go near a kitchen except for a drink of water.

Now that I'm here to chat with you self, all the things that were in my mind to talk about seem to have flown away. But one thing that peeved me was a comment that _____ made the other day. He said, "You're too nice. People will rip you off." I sweetly replied, "Not for long." It really aggravates me to have people forever mistaking kindness for weakness. The world is so full of people who are going around trying to "rip each other off" in some way or another until it doesn't know quite how to take the few who try to be kind, just, and good, because they want to be that way. It makes me sick and angry. One thing seems to escape the run-of-the-mill "rip-offs"—the quiet gentle ones might not say that much and might appear to be easy marks, but if you push them too far, they're ready to "rip you off" more so than the loud mouths. People just don't understand that usually quiet, gentle people can tolerate more of the little and insignificant things that their opposites blow up about, because the gentle ones understand more of human nature. You can learn much more by just being quiet and listening than by flapping your lips constantly. And you can learn more by using your eyes to see than to look. And although the quiet ones don't let on to everything they see and understand, don't ever underestimate them. They'll quietly "rip you off" with no regrets when they know you've forced them into it.

The quiet ones usually understand the motivations behind people's ugly actions, and so they try to be kind and compassionate to people who try to "rip them off," or think they're "ripping them off." Inside, they're usually pitying the poor egotistical creatures who think they are on top of everything.

For instance, I know that people who go around yelling the loudest about what they can do can usually do the least, in whatever area they're bragging about. I know that usually people who brag a lot are insecure, unhappy people who try to cover up their deficiencies with an outside show of overconfidence and braggadocio. I know that women (and men) who make a big show of trying to be or look sexy are usually the least truly sexy. If you've got it, flaunt it, but subtly. Really if you've got it, you don't have to flaunt it. It'll show through anyway. I know that a great majority of men who drive Cadillacs and other ostentatious cars are usually lacking either sexually or personality-wise. But some women so love to be seen either riding in or driving a big fine car until they'll settle for whatever the man is putting down. These types deserve and complement each other. So it's fine with me.

I know that people who take offense easily at real or imagined insults, slights, etc., are usually insecure people who don't like themselves too much. If one is secure within himself and knows his own true worth, he can pass over such trivialities without a backward glance. I only get truly angry when I see someone's dignity being trampled, or the strong oppressing the weak.

I know that people who make a career of trying to "rip-off" other people are very lacking themselves in many ways. So they seek to reinforce their own egos at the expense of tearing down another's. These people are usually sick but in the end they themselves get "ripped-off."

Life has taught me most of the human failings and foibles, both through experience and observation. So I try to be compassionate and help those that I can in my own bumbling way. If they choose to think they're "ripping me off," let them. I know where to draw the line. If I chose to, I could "rip" the "rip-offs" to pieces, but I prefer to live and let live. If I can make living a little better for someone that's good. If I can't, I definitely won't deliberately make it harder.

So now I'm going to "rip-off" a little breakfast and read the newspaper.

Happy Sabbath Day to you self,
Richelene

4–10–73

Dear Self,

It's 10:40. I'm at work. It's raining, and somebody's band is wailing "Georgia" low and sweet on the radio. Believe me it's putting Georgia on my mind. April in Georgia the honeysuckles are budding, ready to burst open and sweeten the air, and the dogwood trees will soon be dressed in resplendent clothing of white and pink blossoms. No doubt the grass has already put on its new green coat, and the robins are nestling in fresh green foliage. The sun is warming the earth, and the farmers are plowing, ready to sow their seeds. And I bet the rabbits are prancing about, defying the hunters to end their pleasure with one well-aimed shot. The squirrels are darting about, their long furry tails waving at the birds. Georgia is my home.

So what if the whites once lynched us and oppressed us at their ugly whims? Blacks have always been abused and oppressed by North and South. In the South they lynched our bodies—in the North, they still lynch our souls. So if hearing "Georgia" on the radio is making me long for "home," that's what's happening. There's harmony there now on a much more honest basis than in the North. There's promise there, promise of a better life for all. And there's hope there, hope that black and white can throw off their respective shields and live together in peace. They're doing it already. So maybe the South is, after all, the promised land.

So what am I doing in Connecticut? I'm stuck, baby, stuck. You can't go nowhere with a houseful of children and no money. But Connecticut isn't bad. I'm grateful that they've taken care of my children and me all these years, but believe me, self, I resent the fact that we should have been forced to be supported by our adopted state, and it pains me even more than it does the taxpayers here. But what could I do? Even if I had money to pick up and go back when the final break was made, I couldn't have gone. I was too tired, and too weary to pick up and move again with my brood.

But I insist that life must have something better in store for us. It has to have. Was it in *Lamentations* that I read, "It is good for a man (human) to bear his yoke in his youth?" I've borne mine—so something better must be on its way. The latter half of life has got to be better than the first half.

Business is very slow today. I don't know if it's because of the weather, because Joe's customers that liked him aren't coming back, or if this venture is heading in the direction of the three before it in spite of everything. I hope things pick up.

Talk to you later,
Richelene

4–12–73

Dear Self,

I finally made it to the clinic yesterday. The weather was venomous, windy, bone-chilling cold. But the day, as a whole, was good in a different kind of way.

The trip over on the bus was nice. Drinking in the scenery, the grass dressing in its spring finery, the trees pregnant with the promise of new life, a few shrubs in blossom was soul food. And a friendly old white man, sitting behind me, kept up a steady banter. I never cease to be amazed at how mellow the aged whites are. Now that they are old and more or less rejected both by their "own" and society, they are lonely and afraid, and they reach out to whoever will talk to them, listen to them, and give them a friendly smile. Often when I am walking downtown, the old white men that line the benches will wave and say hello to me. I usually give them my warmest smile, wave hello to them, and keep walking. Why should I judge them? Perhaps many of them had mellow feelings toward blacks when they were young, but fear of ostracism and rejection by their "own" forced them to hide behind their shields. Now that the winds of winter are blowing hard on their backs, propelling them fast toward the Great Equalizer, death, they realize the futility of their shields and feel free to be themselves. Too bad the majority of us, myself included, lacked the courage to be ourselves completely in the spring of our lives. I'm now facing the autumn of life, the best part, and so the winter shouldn't be too hard. I think I'm shedding my shackles.

The doctor at the clinic was delightfully nice. He remarked on how I must find it slightly unsettling to see a different doctor each time. I merely smiled and shrugged. It was no use going into how used to it I am by now, and how beggars can't be choosy. I asked him whether my last EEG showed improvement, regression or what. He said it showed a slight improvement. Whether he said this to make me feel better, or because it is really true, it sounded good. I was tempted to ask him to please let me read what it said. But knowing it's against medical policy and not wanting to spoil a pleasant encounter, I controlled my curiosity. But between you and me, self, since it's my brain, is it so terrible for me to want to know what they found out about it? After all, I'm the one that has to live with it, and not the doctors.

I told the doctor about the frequency of the seizures last month. He says if I run into frequent episodes in the next three months (I go back to the clinic in three months), they'll put me on phenobarbital again. Hope it won't come to that.

It's always interesting to watch the procession of sick and wretched human beings that one encounters at the clinic. Yesterday there were no really sad specimens evident. There was an unusual looking black man and an unusual looking white girl holding hands and cooing. Since they were so obviously happy together, one couldn't feel sad for them. It's good that they found each other. And there was a darling little two-year-old waiting to see the doctor. She had huge dark eyes, an angel smile that played on your heartstrings like a skilled musician playing a Stradivarius violin, and honey-colored skin. Her mother said already she is on phenobarbital, such a wee little thing to begin a life on drugs. But this is all in the game. Disease is no respecter of age, race, creed, or color. Perhaps if other youngsters were diagnosed and treated at an early age, the jails, prisons, hospitals, and streets would not be filled with carcasses of the living dead. Perhaps if my own case had been diagnosed and treated when I was very young, I would have been spared a lot of suffering. I was thirty before I began treatment for my affliction. By then, the damage was done. There is much hope for Desiree, the little girl at the clinic, and others like her. These ailments are recognized and treated earlier now. My parents merely accepted the fact that I had "fits" and what was there to be done about it?

Desiree was such a happy and appealing little girl, and it was obvious that her young mother was really taken with her; love was written all over her face. She remarked that Desiree has a vivid imagination. I told her that perhaps she'll grow up to be a great writer. Dostoyevsky was an epileptic, and who knows how many other creative people are undiagnosed epileptics. Certainly most of the truly great creative people that I've read of had frailties or eccentricities of one kind or another. I do so hope that her mother will understand that her little girl's whims, moods, eccentricities, or whatever are symptomatic of her illness and will continue to be loving and patient with her. At any rate, I don't think anyone will ever have to sing any sad songs for little Miss Angel-Face. With her beauty and personality, she'll probably be all right. This is what my heart wants to tell me, but my mind tells me that because of her sweetness and beauty, the wolves and vultures will be swooping upon her, licking their chops, ready to devour her in the name of love. I hope and pray that she will be strong enough to elude them and find a good life.

From time to time, I rebel at being in the position that I'm in. But, more and more, I'm glad to be where I am, except for welfare. I like being down here with the people who seem real and loving. I encounter a lot of suffering, but I also encounter many little special kinds of joy. I can't imagine finding nearly as many truly rewarding and happy moments if I were in a higher position in life. The black elite have always impressed me as shallow and pretentious. I belong where I am. I communicate with these people. They give me nourishment for the soul, and, just maybe, I give a little something to them.

Must go now—bowling morning.

Later,
Richelene

Back again. I bowled lousy.

I didn't have to go in to work this afternoon, for which I'm very grateful. I'm so tired and it's just about that time of the month, so I'm completely out of it.

I picked up my Cancer Crusade kits. Filled them in and had Candace deliver them to the solicitors' homes. I've been Captain of this vicinity for three years now. I usually end up having to go out and solicit for one or two of my people, for one reason or another.

Alan and Ricky unsettled me at breakfast this morning. After risking arrest for unreported income in order to buy them something to wear on Easter, they adamantly insist that they do not want to go to church. These kids can really hurt you, but I'm not going to force them to go and spoil it for the rest of us. I will proceed with the ones that do want to go, although it won't be quite the same. This, too, is all in the game.

Still, I have a lot of sewing to do and am wondering where I'll find the time or energy to complete it. But who knows? One of these really, really good days might sneak up on me. Sure hope so.

Oh, yes, self, I meant to tell you the thing that really made yesterday a complete success for me was: The minute I walked into the house, Jeffrey presented me with a "bouquet." He had broken several stems of yellow flowers off somebody's shrub. He's too, too sweet, but I will have to tell him not to bring me bouquets from other people's yards, unless he has their permission.

> Good night self,
> Richelene

4–13–73

Dear Self,

I'm home this morning; I didn't go to work. Since they turned the gas back on, the heater hasn't been working properly. I almost froze over there Wednesday morning, and now I have another cold. My resistance must be really low. I'm not going back over there until the heat is better or the weather is warmer. Maybe the owner, his wife, and children will decide to split the hours between themselves and I won't have go back at all. As I said before, the location is ideal, but I know now that it can't develop into anything self-sustaining for me. So if they can handle things between them, it's fine with me.

At least I felt well enough to give the house a good cleaning this morning, even the boy's rooms. In a few minutes, I'll begin sewing. It is really hard for me to get all the things I like to do around the house done when I have to get out first thing in the mornings. It was much better when I was working in the afternoons. Then I could use my first burst of energy, when I get one, here where it is needed most.

I read an article in last Sunday's paper that said the average housewife should earn $8000.00 a year, if she were paid for her work. I quite agree. Oh, well, things always work out. I've seen it happen in my life too many times to doubt it. Look at the situation with Joe. Just when I thought I couldn't bear any more agonizing over the situation, his operation folded. As Ricky said, he was put out of his misery, and I was put out of mine. There's no agony involved in my job situation now, but there are little unresolved feelings that I have about the situation that nag me. It'll work out.

I must get going now.

Talk to you later, self.
Richelene

One thing that life has taught me and taught me good: If I don't look out for myself—ain't nobody else is going to.

4–15–73

Dear Self,

I had my day of rest today. The day was beautiful, the sun chasing the chill of the past few days away like a bright new love chasing away the emptiness of lonely days. My nose is red and sore from wiping the steady drip, drip, drip of a bona fide head cold. This is getting to be too much. One cold after another, then if it is not a cold, it is something else. What I'd give for a few months free of ailments of one kind or another.

Frances dropped by, and we had a nice little visit. Now that I'm up, thought I would take this opportunity to chat with you a few minutes, self.

The day before yesterday there was a news story about a sick little Puerto Rican girl being refused admission at two different hospitals in Hartford, Connecticut. Five hours later, she died. See what I mean when I say I try to thresh out my illnesses without seeking medical care most of the time? They don't give a damn about the indigent poor. Now the coroner is demanding an investigation of hospital admission procedures. Sure, this will rouse the powers that be for a moment; they'll feign indignation and regret for a moment. Then the beat will go on as before.

How sad that the more fortunate among us find it so hard to accept the fact that they should help the less fortunate and dole out such help as we receive so grudgingly. "Blessed are the poor in heart, for they shall see God," so little baby Rivera is with God. Perhaps I should feel happy that she has been taken out of this world of callousness and indifference before the world could really inflict its venom on her. Maybe she is luckier, after all, than sweet Desiree. What really saddens me is the fact that, after all this time on earth, man, as a whole, still has not learned to love. Will we ever?

I managed to get quite a bit of sewing done yesterday in spite of the drip, drip, drip and a general listlessness. I am hoping for a good week. I will attempt to make Kenny a dress suit of navy blue polyester knit. Wish me luck, self.

I think I'll lie down and complete my day of rest now.

Sincerely,
Richelene

4–17–73

Dear Self,

Here I am at work. It's slow, slow, slow this morning. So I've been doing some repairs on some of the clothing. I just made an awful boo-boo, for which I'll offer to pay.

I hemmed a pair of polyester knit pants and pressed the hems. At home I always press through a damp towel, but here I've been pressing through newspaper. I held the iron on a little too long and made an ugly spot on the hem. The customer will certainly complain, so I'll just fess up and bear the consequences of my bad judgment. That'll be $20.00 out of my Easter money, darn it!

Yesterday was gloriously, gorgeously spring! The temperature almost reached 80 and the air was charged with the essence of spring. Bright sun, birds singing, children playing, housewives soaking in sunshine on their stoops, clothes swaying gently on clotheslines, grass glistening, everybody saying "Nice day, isn't it?" But today is cloudy and muggy, hair-napping weather. Mine is really napped up this morning. Yesterday the weather was dry, and my hair was so nice and neat that a customer asked if I was wearing a wig. White people make you sick with their curiosity about "our" hair.

I had a good day yesterday until after shopping for groceries. On the way home the cab driver made a snide remark about "Welfare Day" and the recipients "loading up." That sent me into one of my "why me" syndromes. No doubt, I should have launched into one of my sermons and put him straight, but what's the use? I've got to keep calling them to get my groceries home and no use making bad matters worse.

Guess I'll get started on Kenny's suit this afternoon.

Talk to you later,
Richelene

P.S. My employer forgave the mistake on the pants and will not deduct anything from my pay. Nice.

4–18–73

Dear Self,

I have about fifteen minutes while I'm waiting to get the bus to Hartford, so I must chat with you now as I probably won't have another chance soon.

Yesterday was hectic once I got home. Cutting out Kenny's suit was a job and a half!

But I finally made it and started sewing on it. So far it seems to be turning out pretty nice, but I have to buy another yard of material; I didn't have quite enough.

At work, I was so busy this morning until it was unbelievable. I had scads of pants to hem and cuff and alter. I'm pacing myself. If they all don't get done, they just won't.

One of the customers, a nice "lippy" fifty's white woman, brought me a big batch of fish this morning. She's one of those people who are in perpetual motion, always doing something, always in a hurry. Not many women of her age can wear junior clothing and get away with it, but she can. She keeps five blind girls and does many other nice things for people. No doubt her zest for life and living and giving keeps her young.

I must go now. Talk to you later.
Richelene

4–22–73

Dear Self,

Easter morning is the day we celebrate the resurrection of our Lord. The day he won the victory over death so that we too might win the victory. The day that Christians the world over gain new hope, new life. The day is beautiful. It's not quite cool, or quite hot—just right.

Right now an Easter service from the Marble Collegiate Church in New York is on, and this is the only church service I'll be able to participate in today. After working so hard all week to get my children and scores of other people ready for church, I was too tired to get myself ready this morning.

So Melanie went to church with one of her friends, and Candace and Jeffrey went with one of theirs. The rest of us are home. How did Easter, such a special family day, ever come to this? I don't quite know, but it saddens me. Less than a month ago, I could see us all going to church together, but reality turned out to be this. How can such simple little dreams fail to materialize?

Oh well, I'll try not to get depressed. Candace looked pretty in her yellow flowered dress, Melanie was cute in lavender and white, and Jeffrey was sharp in navy and light blue. So I will lie back down on the sofa and enjoy the TV service.

Happy Easter self,
Richelene

P.S. Kenny's suit jacket turned out too small, so he didn't wear it. But he was pleased with the pants and wore them. I can't win them all. I tried.

4–23–73

Dear Self,

Another week begins. Easter has come and gone, and so we begin again. Would you believe I was up at six this morning washing and ironing? And the kids are home from school this week—It's Spring vacation.

I didn't go to work or do any alterations for the job Saturday. Right now a change back to typing would be glorious, compared to alterations. Anyway I'm going upstairs to take a nice hot bath and get ready for work. If their kids are manning the place, since they're out of school this week—goody, goody.

Yesterday was a perfect Easter, weather wise. Around four o'clock, Jeffrey and I walked over to a friend's house. This was the first real visit I've paid anyone in ages, and I really enjoyed it. Sunday afternoons are always long and lonely, holidays especially so. My friend is alone with her little family in New Britain; I am alone with my big one. We were both admittedly lonely yesterday afternoon, so when she invited me over, I decided why not? Though I was sorely tempted to flop into bed with a book, I'm now reading the *Biography of George F. Kaufman* and *P.S. You're Not Listening*. Melanie and Candace had gone to a fashion show and dance; Kenneth was playing with the band for the fashion show and dance; Alan had disappeared; Ricky was in his room looking at TV. So the house was too quiet.

When I returned home, Ricky said a man called shortly after I left. He didn't get the gentleman's name;

now I'm wondering who it was. Oh well, the Lord does deliver us from temptation when we get too weak to deliver
ourselves, if we sincerely want to be delivered. Because,
frankly speaking, self, if I had been home, I would have
accepted a date with whoever it was, as lonely and alone
as I was feeling. And I probably would have gone along
with whatever was on the agenda. I'm getting awfully
tired of this "loveless" existence. Why, why, why do I
keep running into all kinds of men but the right kind?
Will I soon settle for less out of sheer loneliness? I'm very
much afraid so, and I don't want to.

Well! Let me get going. The beat must go on.

Later,
Richelene

P.S. My employer just called and said I don't have to come
in this week, their offspring will man the place. Beautiful! Now I can get some spring cleaning done while the
children are home to help. Should I go back to bed for a
little while or just stay up and keep going? I will let you
know my decision later.

LATER: I stayed up and did, guess what? Sewed! I'm sick,
sick, sick of sewing, but seemingly I'm trapped in a sewing
bag for some time. I did some alterations for the store and
sewed some for the family. My poor finger looks like a pin
cushion.

4–25–73

Dear Self,

It seems I'll never find time again to do any in-depth
chatting with you these days.

Perhaps it's just as well. You must get bored with my constant complaining and philosophizing. Enjoy your brief respite! The kids will be back in school next week, and I'll probably lay it on you again, as I'll have a little more time and inspiration.

Donna and her little family spent Easter with her in-laws in New Jersey. When she returned she immediately got a little dig in, small but painful. She is quite enthused over astrology. One of her cousins-in-law is an astrology nut. She summarized Scorpio (me) for Donna—Donna enthused that her picture of Scorpio was me exactly.

The first thing she said was Scorpios are "Still waters that run deep and dirty." Perhaps I'm oversensitive, but it seems she could have left the "dirty" part off in recapping her friend's summarization, in consideration of the fact that I'm her mother. I would have. But that's my girl! Things like tact, consideration for others' feelings, etc., she considers being hypocritical. Call them as you see them is her motto.

Anyway the comment sent me into another "soul-search." I can't figure out what I've done to her or to anyone else, for that matter, that's so "dirty." I could list many little things that I do to try to help her and her family (and others) but can't think of anything that I do that's deliberately underhanded or "dirty." I don't let anyone use me for a doormat any more, so maybe that's dirty. Oh, well, that's life. I suppose if I had fallen into the "constant baby-sitting and sewing trap," I'd be a nice sweet mother, mother-in-law, and grandmother. But since I was not nearly ready for grandmotherhood and still I am over-swamped with the demands of the crew right here in the household, I could not and will not over-extend myself. That, I suppose, makes me a "dirty pooler." As I said before, these kids can cut you to the quick, with no qualms. Perhaps they'll learn consideration and tact someday.

Donna and I have never had a meeting of the minds and spirit; perhaps we never will. But I will continue to help, as I can and not expecting any gratitude.

Must get my Cancer Crusade kits together and turn them in. Of six crusaders, only one returned the kit as they were supposed to. So now it's up to me to get out and round them up and get them in late. Next year, I'll let someone else have a go at it.

Talk to you later,
Richelene

4–27–73

Dear Self,

April is almost gone. Four months of self-analysis, introspection, observations, work, Suffering, and droplets of joy and happiness.

Now we are well into 1973. Have any appreciable changes taken place in my life? Has anything, tangible or intangible, happened to solidify the foundation of my dream to get off welfare? I have the materials to build my dream, but somehow I cannot seem to put the pieces together. Time is hard at my heels, so my dreams cannot withstand too many more deferments. Is it imperceptibly drying up like the flesh on the bones of the aged, when life's substances are slowly draining away? How can I keep the materials for my dream nourished and vital when life is slowly draining the juices away?

I must get going towards something more concrete, but where do I begin?

This year I've made little beginnings, but they, seemingly, are leading nowhere. Still hope is not dead. Before this year is over, I'll have it together. That's a promise. A prophecy!

Today, April is nourishing the earth, quenching its thirst for the rain that will prod the budding flowers into an explosion of color and fragrance.

The children are inside, including an extra from out of town, and it's a study in bedlam.

But I'll survive.

It really would be good to get away from it all for a week or two though. I need a vacation, a change of pace and scenery. This summer I just might get lost by myself for a brief respite from the constant responsibilities of my little world. But why should I need a vacation? After all, I'm a "welfare queen" on a joyous carefree sojourn, a free trip through life. As I'm sometimes asked, "What do you do?" So why should I be tired?

Well, well, self, think I'll lie down and read for a while. I haven't had a chance to do more than read the newspaper for quite a few days.

Later,
Richelene

4–29–73

Dear Self,

This is my day of rest. And do I need it! Excitement for you, self, excitement! Where do I begin? How do you describe a weekend that started out so uneventfully and then suddenly became so interesting?

I will start with the latest developments on my job. I've been telling you how sick I am of sewing. Well, by Thursday, I was sick of looking at pants, much less altering and hemming them. In fact I was sick unto death of sewing—period! So when my erstwhile employer came in with eight pairs of pants for me to do, I told him to begin to look for someone else to do his alterations. And, I would do them until he found someone. He said okay very dryly.

As I told you before, the man is extremely attractive and is one of those men who fancy themselves irresistible to all womankind, from fifteen to fifty. And will try to make it with any personable looking woman from fifteen to fifty. No doubt his success rate is high because he is undeniably a sexy looking "bull-shitter." I have always taken pleasure in showing the sexy "bull-shitters" that I am one woman that can resist them, if I put my mind to it. However, it hasn't been easy at times to spurn his overtures. So my quitting the job in addition to resisting his "irresistibility" must have proved to be too big a blow to his ego.

When I went up to Donna's yesterday, I learned that he had not only told Steve a conglomeration of mess about her seeing other men, but had told Steve that I had been trying to get him to take me out, etc. Now self, you know I never had to ask any man to take me out, and when the day comes that I have to, I will permanently retire from the game of romance. I'm usually very reluctant to accept as truth anything I hear secondhand, especially without hearing both sides of the story, but was somewhat inclined to believe some of this since it came at exactly the time that I had not only spurned the latest advance, but had just given notice on the job. They say that hell has no fury like a woman scorned, but I've come to believe that hell hath no fury like a man scorned.

Anyway, all these rumors and mess about Donna caused a big fight between Donna and Steve. Even if it were true that Donna had been seeing someone, I don't see where it was _____ business to tell him. As far as the lies about me were concerned, I'm too used to such maliciousness to get overly upset about myself. Still, each new incident causes me to pause and try to figure out how people can be so evil and ugly, and I never can figure it out, except that people like that must be sick, sick, sick.

Anyway, later, when the daughter sent a pair of trousers over for me to hem, I sent them back with a note that I wasn't working for them any more and would call later to explain why. So then the wife called, yelling at me about some misgivings between Steve and her husband, tearing Steve and Donna down and speaking glowingly of "my husband this and my husband that." The good Lord must have held my tongue, because I didn't tell her just what her husband really is. I just nicely told her that her husband was far from perfect. He earlier told me that she trusts him implicitly and anything that he denies, she believes him. It's hard for me to believe that she could be that big a fool, but apparently it's true. If he is talented enough to keep her happy while he tom-cats around with whoever will tumble into bed with him, it would have been wrong for me to burst her little bubble or dispel her illusions. After all, they do have six children, so I didn't want to hurt her, though I'm sure had our positions been reversed she would have gleefully filled me in.

Anyway he called later. He's so sorry that he told Steve those things about Donna, he's so ashamed of himself. But he never said one word about or against me, blah, blah, blah.

Now here's the real problem: Steve, Donna, and _____ are all big liars, so it's hard for me to believe either one of them. I don't doubt that there were lies told by all three of them, but how or why did I have to get mixed up in it?

4–30–73

Dear Self,

Thirty days has September, April . . . today's the 30th and final day of April, 1973.

Another month is gone forever.

Gone back to school are the children. Gone is my job, and I can sit here for a minute and peacefully assess the events of these last few days of April.

What did April bring me, and what did it carry out with it? It brought me good moments and bad ones, and took the same with it. Probing into the events of the weekend, I may be forced to accept some more truths, of which I was already aware but may have tried to sidetrack or gloss over.

One: Even though I felt my earning those few dollars without reporting them to the Welfare Department was for a good cause, in my heart of hearts I knew it was dishonest and not really me, even if it was on a minor scale. I've never been able to do anything ugly or dishonest without suffering some consequence. There was a minor war going on inside me, so that dilemma is solved.

Two: Even though I had resisted the overtures of _____ up until then, I had not been as firm with him as I should have been, so there was the tiniest bit of room for him to think that I would succumb to his charms sooner or later. Men like him do have a certain roguish attraction about them. You're aware of the fact that they mean you no good, and yet their magnetism is almost overpowering. Had I kept working there, in my present state of vulnerability, I might have had an affair with him, from curiosity, if nothing else. So now that dilemma is solved.

Three: I have always despised doing alterations. But, I was doing them somehow. In addition to earning a little "free" money to apply to the family's coffer, I was helping _____ as I was only getting half of what he charged, while I was doing all the work, but I resented doing all that work, even pressing the things I altered for half price when had I desired to do that kind of work, I could long ago have been doing a thriving business at home and getting the full price. But I went along with it because it was only a little sideline, not as if I was depending on it to feed and clothe my family. Besides, I looked on it as a contribution toward helping _____ establish himself. The more work that was piled on me for the little I was getting out of it, the more resentful I was becoming. So that dilemma is solved for me.

Four: I earlier spoke of my being too nice and "getting ripped off." No doubt he thought he was "ripping me off," when I was doing all that work for what I was getting paid. He probably thought he was "charming" me into continuing to do it, but he wasn't. I was going along with it for a purpose. Although my "purpose" wasn't terribly wrong, it was still dishonest. So now Mr. Charm will have to get someone else to do his alterations, and I'll bet he'll be paying them the full price, if they're done right. That he should try to get revenge on me for not going along with his program by telling lies and trying to hurt me through my daughter shows just how low he really is. But I'm not worrying about it, as I said before; the "rip-offs" usually get theirs in the end.

We usually pay a price for everything, one way or another. It is not causing me any pain. It was just so unexpected and surprising. I have more important things to worry about than a bunch of mess perpetrated by a group of mixed-up people. But it did make me stop and think. No matter how I try to avoid the little "nastiness" and "evil" of life, they seem to seek me out and burrow in. That old song that says: "Satan is just like a snake in the grass, always in some Christian's path" is true. No matter what path those of us who try to live by the Golden Rule take, Satan manages to rear his ugly head and dart at us. I suppose I might as well stop trying to bypass him and just continue to walk softly and carry a big stick. I will pray for _____, and also for Donna and Steve.

Perhaps the sum total of the truths that April reemphasized to me is this: Nothing in life is free.

To cap the day, Steve's sisters, mother, three nieces and nephews spent the night in New Britain with us. I had the five children to put to sleep and prepare breakfast for. So believe me, I need a day of rest. Thank goodness the kids will be back in school tomorrow!

Happy Sabbath self,
Richelene

P.S. Remember when the place was first opened by my "brothers" across the street and how I carried on about admiring them for their efforts to accomplish something in this racist society? And, how I was hoping and praying for their success? And how willing I was to help in whatever way I could? And this is the way it all ends? Life, life, life!

5–1–73

Dear Self,

The month of flowers has arrived. The violets are peeking shyly at the roses, or soon will be, and yesterday the rich pure green of the grass amazed me.

Another month of living and learning unfolds for me; and it will be interesting to see what new lessons will be revealed or old ones reemphasized. I'm ready to learn—even if the lessons turn out to be painful, as they usually are.

Wouldn't it be nice though, self, if I were given a vacation from the school of life for a month or so? It would be a carefree happy time when I could just relax and enjoy life. I personally feel that I deserve such a time. Anyway, I think I will relax, in a sense, until after school closes for the children. I won't look for a job outside the home this month. I will just do some things, like reupholstering the kitchen chairs and making summer playthings for the children. They really need some.

I won't tempt the fates by either predicting that something unsettling will pop up, as usual, or by daring to hope too hard that nothing will pop up.

So we shall begin May on a note of soft optimism. I've had enough rain to water the flowers; now I will enjoy the pretty blossoms.

Happy May to you, self,
Richelene

P.S. It's now approximately one o'clock, and already the flowers are wilting. The "check" didn't come today. The refrigerator is bare, so I'll have to take a walk over to the bank and take a few dollars out of my emergency fund for a few groceries. If the "check" doesn't come tomorrow, I know something is wrong, but I will hold off on my suppositions until I see whether it comes tomorrow or not. There could be a bit of deviousness or treachery at work.

4:10 P.M.

The man next door just brought my mail, the check, and food stamp authorization over. The mailman left them at his house again. This is getting to be a real habit. I will speak to the mailman tomorrow, if I catch him. There is always something to wilt the flowers and send one in to speculations, etc. Lord, will I ever be out from under this welfare yoke? But then another yoke would replace it. Just give me the strength and courage to keep trying, Lord.

5–4–73

Dear Self,

If this keeps up the flowers will all be drowned. The rain has poured steadily since I decided to enjoy a little sunshine and flowers.

Ricky's foot is out of whack again; he's back on crutches. I see right now that he's going to be obstinate, unreasonable, and unable to accept reality, and how sad it makes me. If he gets married, what a life is in store for his wife, and if he stays single, how much agony and unhappiness awaits him just the same, unless, by some miracle, he learns to control his emotions and learns to be logical.

I've tried to tell him that his feet just won't allow him to participate in sports now, but he is determined to overcome the obstacle of his feet. Determination is admirable, but reason and logic are also admirable, in certain circumstances.

After he sprained his foot this time he went to his room and cried. I didn't say anything because I knew he needed the release, but his crying progressed into a howl bordering on hysteria. I then went up and made him stop it before he was completely out of control. Healthy cleansing tears are one thing; sick crying is another. Poor Ricky! It was no use trying to comfort him. Anything I could have said wouldn't have made a dent toward solace. So I left him alone once I had broken the hysterical reaction. How well I remember his father telling me that even if I didn't want him, he was going to give me *plenty* to remember him by, and, God help us all, he did. What an evil and distorted reason for bringing innocent children into this world to suffer. If only God had given me the strength and courage to break away after the first one, all of these other mixed-up little souls wouldn't be here. Sometimes I say awful things to them because they have such unsettling and hurting personalities. I pray to God to hold my tongue because I know they're not responsible. If I were wealthy, I'd take every one of them for an electroencephalograph. But I'm not, so all I can do is try my best to get through to them and hope that time will take care of many of their little personality quirks. I pray that they'll grow into more control as they mature. If they don't, I pity both them and those that will be closest to them. They have a psychotic father and an epileptic mother. That is a bad combination for progeny. Perhaps there's enough good seed to balance it. I hope and pray so.

9:15 P.M.

I just got back from seeing *Sounder*, by God, what a movie! How realistic! How profound, 1933 in the deep south. That is the year that I was born in a little share-cropper's shack in Georgia, and I've seen almost everything that the movie depicted, except the violence. I've seen the poverty, the despair, the dignity, the endurance, and the hope. How did we manage to escape the violence? Was it because my father was so meek, such a good Christian, so firmly ensconced in "his place" that there was no occasion for the white man to "put him in his place?" Was he a better man, after all, for having the strength to bear up under the hardships and indignities and launch his children onto the path to seek a better life? Could more have been gained had he been the type to rise up and get himself lynched? I don't think so. He was a man. Only a man could endure what he and many others endured and still maintain a sense of dignity and worth and instill the same in their children.

Sounder was definitely life as it was. Many blacks are taking offense at the movie.

I saw only beauty and dignity in it. Looking at the young schoolteacher trying to mold and educate the young, I was filled with awe and admiration, and I suddenly felt so useless, so adrift in life, contributing so little, when I might have contributed so much. Doing what I have to do raising my children on welfare; giving bits and pieces of myself to others that amount to nothing; and by virtue of these scraps, I've tried to convince myself that I am of worth, that I'm giving something of value. In reality, I'm just a weak, helpless creature creeping through life when I'd like to run. Making all kinds of bumbling attempts to reach beyond myself and touch others, but finding that I'm still too selfish, too afraid of being trampled by the strong to truly let go and really give.

More and more I find life forcing me to be less than I want to be even though I still sincerely want to live by the dictates of my heart. But my mind and my heart and the forces of life are constantly at war. Now when people hurt me, I strike back and end up being ashamed of myself. I wrote a horrible letter to _____ behind last week's hurt. I'm not proud of myself for sinking to such a level, although everything that I said was true. The thing that makes me ashamed is that my aim in writing the letter was to hurt him as he had hurt me. The only difference was that whereas he had hurt me with lies, I struck at him with the truth. And, so often, the truth hurts much worse. God help me to forgive and to keep trying to rise above life's pettiness.

Good night,
Richelene

5–7–73

Dear Self,

It's Monday morning again. I didn't realize that it's been three days since I chatted with you. Time flies so swiftly and there are so many little things happening to keep me occupied and preoccupied that I just can't seem to find the time to fill you in, dear self.

Today is a beautiful spring day. The sun is beside it-self with bright magic. And the sky is a clear, clear blue, decorated with a few fluffy white clouds. There's so much I'd like to do—sew, wash more windows, iron, paint, etc. I really don't know quite where to begin. Already, I've hung out two loads of laundry and have some blankets to wash. That's enough about drudgery.

Yesterday _____ came by. It was my day of rest, and I was looking such an unholy mess that I was ashamed to come downstairs. If I had tried to make my-self presentable, it would have taken a solid hour, so I pre-sented myself as is—hair standing on end, raggedy flannel pajamas, no makeup, the works. Quite often now I'm get-ting unexpected visitors on Sunday afternoons, so maybe I'll have to start getting dressed on Sundays, especially for the summer months.

_____ had a little load on her mind that she needed to talk about. She is very intelligent and articu-late, so I enjoyed talking with her. It seems that her white next door neighbors, who are moving, told her that her family makes so much noise (they moved in three months ago) until her family is forced to move. What a nasty and dishonest way of trying to justify the fact that, now that the neighborhood is getting predominantly black and Puerto Rican, they don't want to live here among us. Why didn't they just pick up and move, as most of them are doing, without having to throw out nasty barbs to ease their conscience? I'd like to meet just once, before I depart this earth, a northern white who will hon-estly say that they just plain don't like black people in-stead of always falling back on the traditional stereotyped innuendoes.

I would truly admire, respect, and like such a white person. But no, they'll never admit it and get horribly indignant if you suggest such a thing. Some of their best friends were black, they'll quip. As far as morals, etc., are concerned, most of the whites that I've lived among displayed more bad habits and bad morals than any of the black people that I've known, and I'm not just saying that to try to even the score. I've seen how little the whites discipline their children; and I've never heard a black parent swear at their children as much as the whites I've lived among. Furthermore, the noisiest, wildest party I've ever been close to was given by a young white divorcee who lived next door. I could go on and on—about the infidelity, the drunken fights, the dirty houses, but why bother? I'm only bringing these things up to emphasize that people are just people, with the same basic emotions and failings.

When I first moved here eight years ago, my family was the only black family in this unit; now the family that upset _____ is the only white family in this unit it's only natural that they'd soon be moving. I told _____ that I certainly wouldn't lose any sleep over what those racists had said. Good riddance! It'll be nice when all of them move out because they only cause unnecessary conflict. Every little thing a black child or adult does is blown all out of proportion by them, but they neglect the beam in their own eye. This same white family who upset _____, their son is in trouble constantly with the police. Some of ours are too, but it angers me to have them always antagonizing us for the same offenses that they commit, sometimes in greater degree.

I know I sound hostile and bitter, self. I am at times. But there's no hate in my heart for them, I just have hate for their ways, and attitudes, and dishonesty.

Must go now,
Richelene

5–10–73

Dear Self,

Today was the last day of the winter bowling season (league). We ended up in next to last place, but I finished with a flourish, a 521 series, but no trophy. Oh, well, it's all over—the agony, the trying too hard. Summer league begins in two weeks. I'm going to buckle down and get a trophy this summer.

My next door neighbor is moving back south in two weeks. She's had it with welfare, northern inhospitality, etc., and feels that she'll be happier back in the southland. I hope things will be better for her, though in situations like hers and mine, our problems go with us wherever we go. So I'd just as soon stay here and wrestle with mine as lug them anywhere else. When you're black, poor, and afflicted, there is no easy resting place to lay your head.

She suffered a nervous breakdown years ago and hasn't been the same since, she says. But if, God willing, she can find more solace and peace of mind elsewhere, may she go with God. So many black people have found the promises of the North empty and false. They've trudged through the valleys and waded through the rivers of despair and indignity of the South. And they sought a better country, sought to climb the mountain, to reach the pinnacle, the promised land of the North. And always the Promised Land yielded only more despair and indignity for the masses, compounded by the hypocrisy of whites whose rhetoric is at odds with their deeds. In short, the Promised Land promised more than it was prepared to deliver to blacks.

Now, many are trekking back to the South, disillusioned, and sadder, but wise enough to see that honesty in human relations, even if it's honest hate, is preferable to sugar-coated hate that tastes more bitter than gall when it is swallowed by its victims. While I, personally, prefer to live in an all black neighborhood, living among whites has been an education. Whites, like John Griffin, have simulated black skin in order to live among, and supposedly better understand, the black condition. I don't recommend their ploys. They write their books about the experience and make a mint, then return to the safe white world. I used to think that I'd like to be able to pass for white for a while so that I could live among and study the white condition. Seemingly, their condition needs more studying than ours. But now I know I don't need such an experience. I've studied the white condition from where I am, and I've come to the conclusion that if they could dispel their false notions of superiority and accept all human beings as just that, we'd be on our way to harmony.

We are all merely children of the human condition. Why this fact is so hard for whites to accept and live by will forever escape me. Antagonism breeds antagonism, just as hate breeds hate, and so the race problem is perpetuated. Our only salvation is for whites to change their ways and hearts. But I greatly fear that this will never happen to the extent that's needed.

On this note, I'll close for now, self.

Sincerely,
Richelene

5–11–73

Dear Self, I got a phone call this morning at 5 A.M. It was my brother who lives in Philadelphia. Of course, a phone call at that hour made me brace for bad news, but it was good news. They're coming up to New Britain Sunday to spend Mother's Day. This was quite a surprise considering that this will be only the third time they've visited us in the eight years we've been here.

So-o-o now I'll have to try to figure out a menu for about ten additional people. Thank God for one thing: This time I have a small emergency fund that I can use for dinner. I won't have to sink into the desperate depression that I plunged into when my sisters visited last summer, and I was *flat* broke. I vowed then that I would never be down to zero dollars again, whether on welfare or not. This will just about deplete my emergency fund, but I'll sacrifice in the next month or so and build another small one for just such unexpected events.

I'm glad also that I managed to get the kitchen chairs done last week. Although the whole house is still strictly junksville, at least it is presentable enough so that I won't have to feel ashamed. Everything looks clean neat and pleasant. My next door neighbor, who is moving back south, is giving me some furniture that she isn't taking with her. I truly appreciate the gesture, but would just as soon not bring any more furniture of just about the caliber of that I already have into the house. The day might not be too far away when I can get some real furniture. I'd just as soon leave everything "as is" until then. But how could I tell her that? So I'll have the boys go over and bring the things over and put them in the basement until further consideration.

Should I prepare a large ham or a turkey? Which will stretch farther? The thought of trying to prepare enough food depresses me slightly (I hate to cook), but how sweet it is to have a few dollars in reserve! But how tired I am of being poor, poor, poor!

Got to go now.

Later,
Richelene

5–14–73

Dear Self,

Mother's Day has come and gone. It was nice, a success. The relatives came, and we had an enjoyable day. Of course, I know spending the day with me was not as enjoyable to them as if they had spent it with one of the other sisters or brothers, due to the incompatibility of our personalities, but we all made the best of it. I have always been and will always be the "sixth finger" of the family. I've made peace with that fact now. Having more or less severed myself from the other five fingers, figuratively speaking, the life I live here in New Britain, except for the thorn of welfare, is adequately satisfying.

I finally decided on turkey and stuffing for dinner. Turnip greens, cheese and macaroni, casserole, mashed potatoes, gravy, cranberry sauce, corn bread, rolls, cake, jello, and iced tea and soda completed the menu. Donna contributed the cheese and macaroni casserole and the cakes, so the dinner was pretty nice, for me, who would almost rather not eat than to cook. Somehow, I can bring neither interest nor creativity to cooking.

A competent hostess I'll never be though. The cooking, serving, etc., is a chore instead of a pleasure for me. I should have been born rich, or married rich, so I could have a cook to take care of affairs of this sort. Cleaning, ironing, sewing, etc., I love. Cooking I could live without forever. It's a nuisance that gets in the way of other more interesting things.

For Mother's Day, Donna gave me a nice cooking and serving set; Ricky gave me a card with three dollars in it; Candace gave me two white milk glass vases; Jeffrey gave me a sweet card that he made himself (I couldn't read the language that he wrote it in, but translated it to mean

Mommy, I love you); Alan gave me the $1.75 that he owed me; Melanie and Kenneth gave me an IOU for the future and their best regards.

I gave Donna a dress that I made for her. To the rest of them I gave my love and hopes and prayers for a good tomorrow for each of them.

So once again mothers throughout the land have been honored. In this day of women's liberation, when motherhood has been lowered in status and some see mothers as nothing but baby-making machines, those of us who feel that mothers are still something special, something of value to society, have had our day. Eternal black mother, with her own special woes and joys, has been honored. White mothers, with their own unique woes and joys, have been honored. Perhaps some yellow, red, and brown mothers have been honored. So we consign another Mother's Day to the grave where all the spent and used up days are forever buried.

Sincerely,
Richelene

5–16–73

Dear Self,

I knew it was too good to be true, and I had refrained from mentioning it for fear of tempting the gods. I had not had a seizure in two months. Last night the "demons" got hold of me again. My God, how I hate those episodes. You can imagine that blue funk I'm in this morning. Just when I was daring to almost dream the impossible dream again, the dream that perhaps I was on my way to being strong enough to take a full-time job and make a little progress.

What in heaven's name brings these episodes on? Stress, tension, or do the old brain waves just automatically go haywire every so often? All day Monday I had a terrible headache on the right side of my head. Yesterday, I was quite nervous, and last night when I went to bed there was a tautness and slight pain on the right side. So the right side must be where the obstruction or irregularity lies. I hope this is not the beginning of another series.

I had planned to check on an ad in the paper for a slip-cover sewer at a fabric store today. Now I'm so depressed and out of it that I don't feel like applying.

I went to Candace's school's spring concert last night. It was beautiful. The children, all sizes, colors, and shapes, performed so well and with such enthusiasm. One of their closing songs, *To Dream the Impossible Dream*, brought tears to my eyes (that song always does). How many other parents sat there with tear-dampened eyes? How many of us once dreamed what we, in our youth and naiveté, thought were realistic, easily obtainable dreams only to find that the impossible dream was couched inside? For many of us, how hard our dreams have died; how desperately some of us have held onto our dreams, to make the impossible dream come true.

Watching the children perform so harmoniously together on stage, one was tempted to once more dream that one day all God's children will live together harmoniously on the stage of the world, and no longer will we perform, pretend, as the children did, but live in honest harmony. "To dream the impossible dream, to bear the unbearable sorrow . . ." Lord, give me new strength and courage to run, to fight, to dream. . . .

Sincerely,
Richelene

5–17–73

Dear Self,

_____ is gone back to the Southland. Back to the homeland that she hopes will provide solace for the wounds that the land of broken promises and unfulfilled dreams, the North, inflicted upon her. She is a hurt and wounded spirit wandering.

Skeptic that I am, my head tells me that her bed will still be thorny. My heart tells me that with faith and courage, she will find the refuge that she has been seeking. Faith and courage she has in abundance, even at age fifty-two. Apparently she, too, is still daring to dream impossible dreams? I cannot say. I can only wish her the peace that passeth understanding. Then she can say, with Paul, "I have learned in whatever state I am, therewith to be content."

From my own lowly vantage point, I can see that trying to be content with one's lot in life is the passport to peace of mind, and contentment. It is a little bit of wisdom. By contentment, I don't mean complete passivity, not trying to better oneself or condition in the areas that need bettering. I mean simply trying to accept the things that we can't change, while striving (not straining) to change the things that we can. Many people look upon me as passive, without ambition. Maybe I am. But I see myself as an individual who has learned to accept my limitations and wait until such time as I can sensibly change such things as I can change.

The Welfare Department had to get one final lick into _____ . Yesterday was "check"day. They sent her the food stamp authorization, but no money. How cruel! She was really depending on that little money to help her in her move. For a family of three, it couldn't have been more than eighty or ninety dollars. I only got $114.00 and I have six children. For them to withhold that small amount from her was sheer, unadulterated cruelty. After all, they're rid of her now. They could have given her that little money as a "good riddance" gift. Welfare Department, they call it. So what if she's not from Connecticut? She's from the United States of America. As a citizen of this land of "liberty and justice for all" she is entitled to whatever benefits it offers, regardless of the state she's in or from. Life has buffeted her enough. Would the balm of those few measly dollars have broken the State of Connecticut? God bless them.

How heartless, how cruel the powers-that-be are to the weak, the dispossessed, the wretched of the earth. There's got to be a balancing of the scales someday, somehow.

There will be. President Nixon and the United States are reaping part of their whirlwind now. They will reap more. The strong cannot forever oppress the weak without reaping in due course.

God strengthen and keep you, _____, and grant you peace and rest.

Sincerely,
Richelene

5–18–73

Dear Self,

This week has been a rather sluggish one for me, physically, mentally, and spiritually. I still feel a little sad when I think of _____ moving back south. Perhaps it's because I've never experienced having someone move with which I felt a close kinship. She hadn't lived next door for quite a year, and we didn't visit each other much. The day she moved was the first and only time she had coffee in my house, but I liked her, and I felt she liked me. She was homey, comfortable. I could borrow a cup of sugar from her and she could borrow a bar of soap from me. Then again, perhaps the feeling of kinship sprang from our common problems, our sometimes flagging, but never dying will to overcome; our determination to fight fate—each in our own way.

Yesterday morning I went to pick up two small plants she left for me. They are two small plants fighting to live. They are a little droopy, still they are the only signs of life in that cold, empty apartment, suffocating in its loneliness. It was so quiet in there. As quiet as a tomb. It was so barren and lifeless whereas the day before there had been activity, laughter, music, life. There had been the hurts and heartaches there too, but there had been life, and hurts and heartaches are as much a part of life and living as laughter and joy. They are as necessary as the laughter and joy.

On the counter in the kitchen, a few lonely mementoes of the family, now departed, lingered in solitary silence. A partly used bottle of ketchup, a can of bacon drippings, a half full jar of spaghetti sauce, a little macaroni and spaghetti in their boxes, huddled together seeking to comfort each other. Just a few lonely tokens of food that were begrudgingly doled out by a state, a country, that covers its contempt for the weak, the afflicted, the aged, the poor with a thin cloak of charity that is not love. The powers-that-be are now stretching the fabric with which that cloak is woven, making it even thinner. It is becoming so thin that the wretched masses that hover under the cloak are chilled to the bone, to the soul. And through the transparent fabric, like looking through a veil, they catch glimpses of all the good things out there—fruit to be plucked by the strong, the rich, the powerful. Some of the wretched ones have endured the chill so long they are rigid, numb, and straining to see through the fabric has weakened their eyes.

·They no longer dare, nor have the will to dream, to hope. Others, angry in their despair, lash out in whatever way that seems appropriate to them. Cheating, fighting, stealing, prostituting their bodies and souls, burning up their own shoddy neighborhoods. Some move from city to city, state to state, always hoping to break out of that cloak of despair and hopelessness. The fabric is thin, transparent, but it is tough. Few of the old heads break out, except by extreme good fortune or exceptional skills or talents and perseverance. Good fortune I wish for _____.

Maybe I feel sad every time I think of _____ taking off to try to break out of the cloak of despair, because I know the same old bugaboos not only took off with her, but some await her there, and they will dog her tracks, relentlessly, like a pack of bloodhounds tracking a criminal, until she drops in final and total exhaustion. Only then will she find true rest and victory. I weep for people who are fighting life with such fragile weapons. I bleed for them.

What the heck! I'm probably just feeling sorry for myself and projecting my inner anger unto _____. So I'll get up from here and cook some ham hocks and collard greens and make a good old soul food dinner. Tomorrow might bring true soul food to me.

Until tomorrow,
Richelene

5–20–73

Dear Self,

This is my day of rest. It's 6:30 P.M. The day has been sunny, cloudy, sunny, and now it's raining. Except to prepare breakfast and get up to eat dinner, which Melanie prepared, I've been in bed all day—resting. I wonder if I'll ever be in a position to attend church with some regularity again. And I wonder if I can, having wandered away from certain fundamental aspects of the Baptist church. I wonder if I can ever again be honestly a part of organized religion? Can I ever again give proper and soulful attention to sermons preached by humans as fallible as I? I sing the songs that praise my Maker right here in the privacy of my home, and I pray the prayers that praise and thank him here in the privacy of my home. At times I even find myself wheedling Him for favors right here in the privacy of my own home. Am I less a human being, less a disciple, because my pathway has led me away from the organized church? I do believe in an Omnipotent Power that is above and in all creation, and I think I believe in an ongoingness of the spirit of man. But do I believe in a static heaven or hell in some mysterious far-off place, where the good will reap rewards and the evil will reap everlasting punishment? I don't think so. Am I a freethinker, a Christian, or merely one who harbors humanistic attitudes? I don't know. I might be a backslider and an infidel. That's what the church-going, dyed-in-the-wool Christians would call me. I don't know. All I know is that I feel deeply for the human condition.

I understand a little of it, and I desire, with all my heart, to better it some way. My offerings, at present are small, insignificant, but that is all I have to give. At least I try. I want to give more. Perhaps time and living will further teach me how to give, how to help, how to love.

The obstacles to right thinking and right living are so ever-present that it will take Herculean efforts for me to proceed to the pinnacle of goodness. Just last night, the devil reared his ugly head again. He wears so many faces. Last night his face was white.

Some friends and I went to a dance. The night was good. A big moon spread magic across the sky, and the land was cool, still. Fun, music, and laughter embraced us inside the hall. No wallflower, I, last night. I laughed a lot, flirted playfully a little bit, and danced a lot. And my friends did the same. It was nice, clean, refreshing. For a few hours we were young and gay, drinking in life, enjoying "soul food."

So where did the devil come in? On our way home, around three-thirty, we passed two police cars, one of the jerks eyed us as if we were criminals. _____ commented: "Look at them, just sitting there trying to think up some excuse for stopping us. Whenever they see a carload of blacks at this time of morning, they always try to find some excuse for stopping them." And so we rode on through the night, recapping the fun we'd had. Lo and behold! Suddenly there were flashing lights and sirens wailing in the night! _____ pulled over, and we all were dumbfounded, wondering what she had done wrong.

She is a very slow and cautious driver. The officer, young and no doubt seeking to prove his efficiency at some innocent person's expense, informed _____ that she had run through two red lights. Now, at that hour, the lights are all flashing red, and one only has to slow down, look both ways for oncoming traffic, then proceed. This she did. There was just no excusable reason for this "protector" to give _____ a $15 ticket. But, oh, he was so kind to us! Instead of giving her a ticket for running two lights, the greathearted spirit only ticketed her for one. How noble! A knight in shining armor! _____ related to him exactly what she had said to us a few minutes previously. Namely, that we were only stopped because we are black. He responded with this, "If you think I'm prejudiced you can contest it in court," bull. Of course it would be our word against his and his partner's, if she chose to contest the ticket. And, self, you know whose word they would take. "Land of the free . . . liberty and justice for all." A perfectly pleasant night spoiled by "liberty and justice for all."

But justice will come someday. And we will be free someday. It will be sweet for the innocent victims, but more bitter than bile for the oppressors. Justice will come.

Later, Self
Richelene

5–24–73

Dear Self,

I feel a little more alive today, after a good night's sleep, and I'm thoroughly ashamed of that little mono-logue of morosity that I inflicted on you yesterday. Still, in this morning's paper was a little sketch about being disgusted with life and its seemingly meager drippings of joy. If that columnist can write a bit of pessimistic poetry after all those flowery little dialogues about faith, hope, and optimism, I feel exonerated. It just reemphasizes once again, nobody wins them all.

Jeffrey and Melanie are home today with a virus of some sort, nothing big, just a little upchucking and lethargy. My own diagnosis is that getting up and getting out to school every morning is making them sick by now. This not-so-strange malaise usually strikes them down every year in the latter part of May. I'm getting so weary of dragging them all out of bed and prodding them out the door that I feel like upchucking it all myself. Alas, there is another whole month to go.

Tonight we go to our bowling banquet. I ordered a big juicy steak, my first steak dinner this year. So, self, you know I will savor each morsel, because unless I meet my magic man, I might not get another steak this year.

Today is Ricky's birthday. He's seventeen. Where did the years go? Just yesterday, it seems, he was a fat little baby, hugging my neck. Today, he's 6'2" and only comes near me when it's unavoidable in transit through the house. He's almost a man. What kind of man will he be? Will his character be as tall as his physical height? Will he be a feeling, caring, loving man? A good human being? I hope so. Oh, I hope so.

Well, self, I must go check on the cake I'm baking for Ricky.

Will get back to you later,
Richelene

5–25–73

Dear Self,

I had a good time at the banquet last night, though dressing up for a night out with the girls is not exactly my idea of a gala and exciting evening. Anyway, all the girls looked gorgeous in their long gowns, the food was nice, and we (my team) each got $10.00 back for ending up in next to last place. Of course, the teams that placed higher each got more money. I hadn't expected to get even that back, so it was a very nice surprise.

I never fail to get that old lonesome feeling when I'm in a crowd of females. As they sometimes comment, I just don't talk enough. The gift of gab will never be mine.

In mixed company, usually some man will talk to me, so I don't have to talk much, just listen. With a group of women, I just usually can't think of too much to say, or get the chance. If I do decide to try to hop in there when there's a pause for breath, I usually put my foot right in my mouth. So I come out better by keeping my trap clamped. Oh well, why belabor my "unmixability"?

Self, you know I said I wasn't writing any more letters to the editor. Woe is me! I did it again. I just can't seem to cure myself of my chronic letter-writis. This time I was moved to write because of a profile in the Sunday magazine on one of our local black celebrities. The article was excellent, outlining his struggles to overcome the obstacles of race, poverty, etc., and finally arrive at his goal in life. But then he blundered by stating that he was "part white, yellow, red, and black—a one man United Nations." It gives me the heebie-jeebies whenever I hear black people making the above statement. What is the point in giving a rundown on all the colors one is made up of?

Is one a better human being, a more elite member of the human race because one's ancestry is spotted rather than plain black? When you break the parts down, how do you designate the colors? Is the soul black? Is the personality white? Is the mind yellow? Is the character red? As I see it, one is either a good human being (or trying to be), or one is not. At least that's the way it should be. A multitude of problems in human relations could be solved if people could just forget color altogether and classify themselves as human beings. This could lead to a lot of good. I didn't word my letter this way, but in essence it said the same thing. After mailing it, I hoped that they wouldn't publish it, but they did. Now I feel uncomfortably conspicuous again.

I just couldn't help myself. Part this, part that, part the other. . . . Sometimes my children ask me what we're "part of." Being light complexioned, it's obvious enough that some white blood diluted the black somewhere along the way. My grandmother was half Indian, but of what consequence is it? Certainly it is of not enough consequence to point to with pride. Most people labeled black in this country are diluted. Should we be proud that our female ancestors were brought to this country as slaves and were raped, used and abused by white men that denied their humanity and saw them as nothing but "bodies" to be used sexually?

Just the other day, Candace came in from school asking me to tell her what we were mixed "with." "_____ said that her mother was part Blackfoot Indian." "Tell me something so I can tell here what we're part of," she said. Now listen, self. The little girl that told Candace that is ver-r-r-y dark, and her hair is nappier than mine. If she is part Indian, she never should have told it. That Indian must have had more than black feet.

I tell my children that they're "part" nothing. They're human beings, and yet I can understand why some of our people feel compelled to highlight the other than black strains of their ancestry. Black has been denigrated so much, to someone insecure as to his worth as a human being, someone with a poor sense of self, accentuating the fact that he is not completely black elevates his self-esteem. I'm not judging people who do this. I only wish they could truly see that black is beautiful if one is a beautiful human being. White is beautiful if one is a beautiful human being. Ditto for red, yellow, brown, or whatever. Most of all, being human, in the true sense of the word, is beautiful.

I hope to instill the value of being a human being in my children, not being part of this, that, and the other or even plain black. If I can do this, then I will have been successful as a human being; if not, I will have tried.

Sincerely,
Richelene

5-28-73

Dear Self,

What a miserable, miserable, and depressing day. Not just the weather; not just the dull monotony of the every-day routine. I feel like a leaf drifting on the wind; a blob of nothing marking time on the face of the earth until some giant hand erases me clean, leaving not even a little smudge to show that I had been here, that I had lived and suffered here.

What must I do to put some real meaning in my life? Where do I find a few spoonfuls of sweetness to sweeten this cup of bitterness? I felt good, vital when I was working across the street, interacting with people on a scale that satisfied me. Will I ever in this world be blessed to find a self-sustaining job doing work that is fulfilling? Why did that little job, like everything else good for me, have to be spoiled and evaporate into thin air so soon? Will I ever in this world be able to empty this cup of gall and fill it with sweetness? Pessimistic me.

I began the summer bowling league today. My partner said, in response to several low-key statements I made, "Don't be so pessimistic. I don't like to be with pessimistic people." I told her that we would have to part company then, because these days pessimism is my name. This too shall pass—I hope. I wish I could pretend, as in former days, that I'm still bubbling over with optimism for the future and everything is hunky-dory, but it was not pretense then. I really and truly believed that, like Job, my suffering would yield good fruit in the end, blotting out the bad times, but the future is here, and the bad times just keep right on rolling. It's getting harder and harder to put on my happy face. Most of the time these days, I look and act as drab as I feel.

Maybe a good night's sleep will chase the gloom away and redo my personality, so I'm hopping into bed, like now.

Later,
Richelene

5–29–73

Dear Self,

All this rainy, spirit-dampening weather is getting to be too much. Oh, to see a sunshiny day once more. Will we ever, will we ever?

The holiday was nice. Sunday the family gathered at Donna's house for a cook-in since we couldn't cook out due to the weather. We feasted on hot dogs, potato salad, chicken, baked beans, deviled eggs, corn on the cob, and for dessert—cake. Everyone chipped in, so there was plenty of food for all.

Yesterday I spent most of the day in bed, in lieu of Sunday. Not only was it my substitute day of rest, it was also a day of recuperation. I hate to bug you so much about my hypochondria, self, so as much as possible, I try to suffer in silence these days. Since I didn't feel well enough to do too much else, I read John O. Killen's *Black Man's Burden.* That's a hot piece of literature, self. Brother Killen gets down to the nitty-gritty and tells it like it is, not like the white man wants to hear it. When I read it before, I must have been scanning or reading with my eyes instead of my mind and soul. This time what the man said penetrated all the way into my guts and had me egging him on! "Preach, brother, preach!" Spread the gospel about our plight in the land of the free and the home of the brave. I was really thrilled to see that at least one black person other than me has a good word to say for the original

Uncle Tom, of *Uncle Tom's Cabin*. My contention that he has not deserved the vilification heaped on him by blacks was reinforced by brother Killen. Mr. Killen really sounds like a man after my own heart, or should I say Reverend Killen? That brother can preach to your natural soul. I must go to the library and look up some of his other writings and read them. I picked up the paperback edition of *Black Man's Burden* at a little bookery out in Plainville where you can get loads of used and otherwise damaged books for little money.

Miraculously, I felt better late yesterday evening and ventured into the "dungeon!" (cellar) and ironed quite a bit. The children go back to school today. It's a real chore getting them out these days. The fights over the bathroom; the sweeping or knocking them out of bed with the broom; the calls from the principal about Alan's tardiness; Jeffrey's daily announcements that he's going to be a Head Start dropout; the trying to stretch socks and school clothes the last mile of the way, all this is taking its toll on dear old Mom. And dear old Mom is just a mean old ogre trying to make life miserable for everyone, in her children's eyes. Again, this is why mothers get gray.

Oh, no! Ricky just announced that he lost his bus card, the free transportation for high school students. Kenny lost his a couple of months ago and couldn't get another. Now I'm going to be giving carfare to two more? Anything to upset you and use up whatever little change you have! Give me strength. A lady on TV yesterday said that she had four children, and four was just too many. Anything over two is just too many. On this note I will close. My urge to write suddenly disappeared.

Later,
Richelene

P.S. I was reading the paper this morning, and something in the column Family Doctor set me off. I just had to write him a letter, so I'll share it with you, self.

Dear Dr. Van Dellen,

You may be well qualified and informed as a doctor of medicine, but you are woefully ignorant regarding a segment of society that you referred to in your column of May 29, 1973. Your statement, "In some segments of society, early pregnancy is welcome and often encouraged because it means additional money. Some of the girls do very well financially, especially when they have two or three children by age twenty." This smacks of prejudice and outdated thinking. Evidently you have neither been a relief recipient, nor lived among them.

In fact, I am now a relief recipient, and I can tell you that in my experience, I have not seen the encouragement of early pregnancy to add to the family coffer that you glibly speak of. I see welfare mothers struggling to survive on subsistence allotments and striving to induce values in their daughters that will keep them from getting pregnant and traveling the same rough road that we're traveling. I see mothers hoping, praying, and prodding their children to stay in school and get a diploma or training that will enable them to progress beyond the life that we've fallen heir to, usually through no fault of our own. I see fifteen-year-old girls who sipped from the cup of life too soon, for various reasons, marrying the fathers of their children and making every possible effort to keep them from adding them to the "relief" rolls. My own, now eighteen, is among them. I see those not so happy or well-motivated, who might have two or three children by twenty, unhappily scrounging along on their meager "relief" allowances, and not living high on the hog "doing very well financially." I see mothers on welfare, of several children begging to have their tubes tied so they will not have more children, because they do not feel that additional children will enhance their lives financially or otherwise. I see a segment of society limping along on the welfare crutch because they have to for one reason or another.

If at some time in the past, young girls or families in "my" segment of society did look upon producing babies to put on welfare rolls as a good living (I've never bought that theory), that time is certainly past. If, indeed, it were true, society contributed to its making, and was obliged to take care of them.

I do not know how old you are, but certainly your unfounded knowledge of the segment of society of which you wrote has remained static, and, if you care enough to, you should update it. But then most of the people who make statements of the caliber of yours prefer to cling to their preconceived (and very wrong) notions about "my" segment of society and never bother to seek out the truth.

Now you're probably saying, "If you're so smart and intelligent, how come you're on welfare and not working?" I'm an epileptic mother of seven children (which I did not expressedly produce for welfare income). I do work part time, from time to time, as I feel well enough to. In time, I hope to be self-sustaining. I look disgustingly healthy, and most people are not aware of my little "thorn." To them, I'm just one of those lazy freeloaders that do not want to work because I have it so good on welfare.

It is a great loss to all of us that more people do not take the time and interest to learn the facts about "relief" people instead of perpetuating myths. Now that my anger at your blatantly false statement has been purged by this letter, I'll forgive you. You knew not of what you spoke, but you would do well to stick to counseling people on medical problems. A sociologist you are not.

I'm mailing it too, self. Not to the editor, but to the good doctor himself. More and more, I feel I have to speak up and set some of these people straight who are always downgrading and maligning unfortunate people on the basis of hearsay or myths. And I'm always willing and ready to take on the consequences.

Talk to you later,
Richelene

5–31–73

Dear Self,

Another month is breathing its death rattles today, and what a month it was. The Watergate scandal brought into the open; floods and tornadoes wreaked untold suffering and hardship in many areas; "peace with honor" in Viet Nam continuously peppered with bullets; a black man became mayor of Los Angeles, one of the largest cities in the United States; the governor of Connecticut announces a surplus of millions of dollars in the state's coffer, while some segments of the state suffer untold poverty; and Richelene Mitchell was compared to Shirley Chisholm. Wow!

It's raining again. Some little voice inside me begged me not to take yesterday's sunshine for granted, and to go the store, buy detergent and get my wash out on the line, but I ignored the little voice, to my regret. Now I've got a hamper full of dirty clothes, no detergent, and an eminent trip to the shopping center in the rain. I don't feel the need of that purging, cleansing trip to the store in the rain today.

Self, I received the most humbling little note in the mail yesterday. I've received nice little notes, responding to the things I've written before (and one not so nice), but this one really put a lump in my throat. A gentleman who read my last offering to the editor wrote his admiration of my courage for speaking out as I did. I had expected some "putting down" for my "arrogance." I still do. But to receive such a warm and intelligent (downright classy) kudo made me feel that perhaps the intent of my letter was rightly interpreted by some. And, for him to say "if there could be more Richelene Mitchells and Shirley Chisholms and Justina McDonalds, our problems would be the fewer and our world somewhat the better" made me feel very humble and very grateful. Humble, because something I said caused someone to think of me in the same league with Shirley Chisholm (unfortunately I don't know who Justina McDonald is); grateful, because everything I've ever written or ever will write is meant to contribute to enlightenment and understanding between people, and maybe, someday, love.

(Jeffrey is home today. He just relieved me of my pencil so he could write something. I knew what it would be L-O-V-E. It is one of the few words that he can spell, write, and recognize, and he is forever handing me little papers with L-O-V-E written on them.)

If I have lit a few small candles of understanding, I'm grateful. Even when I've written in anger, the anger was born of the suppression of truth; the dissemination of lies; the perpetuation of harmful myths; or the denial of an individual's or a people's humanity and dignity. If I hurt anyone, it was with what I hoped was helpful truth (as I see it) and not from maliciousness. When one is hurt by helpful truth, after the hurt and anger subsides, I believe, in time, one emerges a somewhat better human being—if one cares to be better.

Self, do I sound too high-flown or rarefied to be in such a low place in life? I don't mean to, I honestly don't. I merely express myself in the way that comes most natural to me. Whenever I try to "tone down" my writings, I feel that I'm being untrue to myself and assuming that my readers are less intelligent than I. Isn't it better to do one's own thing, assuming that one's readers are intelligent enough to grasp what one is saying than to "write down"? Dictionaries are marvelous inventions for looking up words one doesn't understand. I've learned an awful lot that way.

Anyway, getting back to the "fan" letter. I suppose I should drop him a few lines of thanks. In the past, I haven't responded to my little "fan or pan" letters, and maybe this was wrong. If people, who might lead busier lives than I, care enough to write, the least I can do is respond back.

Must get going now,
Richelene

6–4–73

Dear Self,

We're into June and life is moving along at about the same pace and the same weather pattern. Yesterday it was gloriously sunshiny, today raining; the same little aggravations. The children just ate breakfast and returned to bed. So I'll have to get the broom and sweep them out again; the same routine. This morning I have to go get the "check" cashed and replenish the refrigerator with hot dogs, hamburger, chicken wings (someday we just might fly away) and chicken gizzards; the same old aches and pains—my belligerent back is still hurting. Same, same, same. But I'll pause a moment and count my blessings. It could be excitingly worse. I know.

Would you believe I went to church yesterday? No kidding, self, I really did!

_____ invited me to go with her. She attends a Methodist church that is predominately white. The service was nice, brief, sedate, quiet, and, for me, sterile. Having been brought up in that good old soul-stirring, hand-clapping, foot-patting, body-shouting, "make-a-joyful-noise-unto-the-Lord" religion, no other satisfies me. The minister's sermon was lucid and dignified, but devoid of feeling. Even most blacks today look askance at "joyful noise" services and prefer a somber, dignified service. To each his own. For me, an emotional, spirit-filled service is better. One where I can join in singing those good old gospel songs that nourished the souls of my parents, my parents' parents, and back on down the line:

> Amazing grace, how sweet the sound
>   that saved a wretch like me.
> I once was lost but now I'm found
>   was blind but now I see!

The slow mournful refrain on songs like that and:

> Precious Lord, take my hand
>   lead me on, let me stand
> I am tired, I am weak, I am worn . . .

After singing such a song, one goes home feeling that the Precious Lord is holding one's hand, and He will not only help one to stand, in the face of all the obstacles of life, but He will impart new strength. I could go on and on calling to mind the good old spirituals and gospel songs that give my soul ease:

> Must I be carried to the sky,
>   on flowery beds of ease;
> While others fought to win the prize,
>   and sailed through stormy seas.

Yes, self, these are the songs that lift and inspire a weary traveler like me. Songs sung with feeling, with tears, sometimes with shouting. These are my people's songs. Songs that brought us through oppression, lynchings, castrations, man's most blatant inhumanity to man, you name it, these songs of praise, courage, and hope have been balm for our wounded bodies and spirits. If some of our people think of these songs with shame and prefer to move away from them and into a church whose members seemingly sing with their lips and not their hearts, this is their privilege and their right. I'm sure we're all still trying to worship the same God in the way that suits us best. But, as for me, when I go to church, I want life, vitality:

> I'm so glad Jesus lifted me!
> I'm so glad Jesus lifted me!
> I'm so glad Jesus lifted me!
> Singing glory hallelujah . . .
> Jesus lifted me!

A rousing, hand-clapping rendition of "Jesus Lifted Me" is food for the soul. Harriet Tubman must have sung this song as she traveled her underground railroad and delivered slaves to freedom. Frederick Douglass, dignified man that he was, must surely have sung it as he charted a course for freeing his people. No doubt Dr. Martin Luther King sang it as he whiled away the time in jail or while facing the venom of Bull Connors in Alabama. I bet old Adam Clayton Powell, dashing devil, even sang it sometimes.

But more than the sterility of the service yesterday, I found myself sitting there among that sea of white faces analyzing the people: That white blonde over there, wouldn't she pull up and move if I bought a house next door to her? That distinguished looking gentleman there, the one in the fine gray suit, mightn't he have been thrilled to take me into some dark place for some good old "nigger" stuff when I was a little younger? That nice looking dark haired young man, he's a policeman, the one that shot and killed fifteen-year-old Miguel just before Christmas. Look at all the bland white faces, some of which gave me a perfunctory smile. How many of them would invite me into their homes, along with their white friends? How many of them see me as a human being when they look at me? Don't they just see a black woman? And because they have diminished my humanity, when I look at them I see white people, capable of much cruelty, evil, and inhumanness, not human beings. Do they take the God they're worshipping here today home with them, or do they leave Him here in this cool, beautiful structure, to be picked up again next Sunday? In the movie *Sounder*, one of the characters jokingly said God told him it had taken Him 200 years to get into a little white church in Louisiana. Has He finally made it into this church? Or is he still standing at the door knocking? Questions, questions . . . a little spinning wheel of unanswerable questions spinning, spinning round and round in my mind. So I won't go to their church again. I'll go to ours so I can forget troubles and vain questions by getting into the service. Singing, clapping, making a joyful noise unto the Lord, where I can be a participator, not a spectator.

_____ and another of my friends are members there. They find the services satisfying. Religion is such a personal and private aspect of life. They enjoy sedate services, and this is their right. I enjoy emotional, soulful services, and that is my right. We are still friends.

Anyway I had my service when I got home. *Black Is*, a television program, had a black minister and choir from New Jersey on. They satisfied my soul, and when the program ended, I said, Amen.

So it's Monday morning again. Time to get back to the chores. Gotta go now.

Sincerely,
Richelene

6–5–73

Dear Self,

What a beautiful day today! The sun is kissing each new green leaf on the trees lining the mountains across the way; trees responding to the kiss of the sun and the soft breeze with a gentle sway. The faintest breeze is sifting softly through the screens like nectar through a sieve. Morning sounds of children getting ready for school without too many arguments or complaints. Cars starting up as people begin the journey to their place of work, a work that brings them quiet satisfaction or endless boredom. And I feel like writing; like singing; like laughing; like working; like loving the whole world!

Strangely at times like this it seems a sacrilege to write of sad, unhappy things. This is a day to be savored: a day to be thankful to our Maker; to be kind to our loved ones; to be tolerant of our enemies; to think on the things that make life good. So I will leave you on this promising note, self.

Happy day,
Richelene

P.S. I just mopped the kitchen and living room. While I'm waiting for them to dry, I will chat with you for a few minutes, self.

Mr. _____, the principal at Alan's school, just called again. Alan was tardy as usual. I don't know why the principal keeps calling me about it. It seems that he should know if I could get Alan to school on time, I would. Alan is fourteen now. I can't get inside him and make him over. Maybe he's just one of those individuals that just can't get the old motor moving in the morning. I've tried everything I can think of to speed him up, to no avail. His father was one of those perennially late individuals. It used to kill me the way he'd wait until it was time to be at work or any other place before he'd begin to get ready to go. So what can I do now about the genes that my children were bequeathed? If his father was still living with us, people would say Alan is falling into a habit like his. As it is, Alan has not been exposed to his father enough for him to acquire any of his habits, so how do you explain all the similarities between them except by accepting the fact that he inherited them? I will always maintain that inheritance plays a greater role in the shaping of one's personality than environment. I see it accented every day right before my very eyes. Since I can't go back and choose a different father for Alan, all I can do is work with the qualities he has, to the best of my knowledge, and hope for the best.

I've considered taking him to the Child Guidance Clinic, but decided against it. When Donna was his age, and I was having disciplinary problems with her, I took her there once. My hope was that a trained counselor would support me in my efforts to make her see that she was trying to live too fast. Instead, he more or less pooh-poohed my fears and stated that she was more or less a typical adolescent for today's world. Maybe. But mascara, eye shadow, long earrings, too short and too tight skirts and staying out all hours was not my idea of a typical fourteen-year-old girl. I felt that if the counselor had just talked to her and tried to make her see that this behavior was not good for a young girl her age, she might have listened to someone like him, whereas she wouldn't listen to me. But I got no support for my position. So the typical teenager got pregnant at fifteen and married at sixteen. Naturally my feelings for the Child Guidance Clinic are not good.

Alan also has more than typical teenage problems, and I know it, but to whom do I turn for help and support?

With the principal taking the position that I could motivate and change him if I really tried, and the possibilities
of the Child Guidance Clinic pooh-poohing me again, I
see no alternative but to let him drift along until he perhaps finds himself. His appearance is outrageous, shabby
pants, shirts, and badly combed hair. He goes out to play
football and loses or tears up his shirts. Am I supposed to
keep buying him things to lose or tear up when I can't afford to? Frankly, I feel like giving up on him. As the old
folks used to say, "Just leave him in the hands of the
Lord." I had to do that with Donna, and she now seems
fairly stable. Self, does it sound like I don't love my children and want the best for them? I do, God knows I do.
But sometimes this load seems too heavy for one frail pair
of shoulders to bear. In order to survive I have to tune it
all out and just let some chips fall where they may.

If only the principal could accept Alan as he is, make
slight allowances and stop calling me. I've already told
him to suspend him, if he feels that will help.

Can you begin to understand why I'm sometimes pessimistic and cynical, self? Didn't I begin this day on a
happy and loving note? Did I overtly invite the sour note
to creep in? I did not, but it never fails.

Happy day anyway,
Richelene

6–8–73

Dear Self,

Today is going to be a scorcher! It's now 7:50 A.M., and
already the heat and humidity are making the air thick and
oppressive, but it is beautiful. How sweet it is to see the
sun spreading golden rays over the earth, brightening the

land, brightening our spirits like the light of love shining from the face of a dear one. The poet in me is coming out again this morning, however badly. But back to reality!

Yesterday morning one of the housing officials brought a lady and her little son to look at the apartment next door. And, self, she was Caucasian. How I hoped and prayed that a black or Puerto Rican would move in there. This is just too close for black and white to peacefully co-exist. I'm just not in the mood to get back into that constant hostility, aggravation bag again. It's been so harmonious, so free of conflict since all the whites moved out of this unit, especially the ones on both sides of me. Self, you know I can get along with anyone on the face of this earth if they're fairly reasonable, fairly intelligent, and fairly tolerant. I'm not perfect, and I don't expect perfection in others. If a person will meet me just almost halfway, I can accept and treat them as I desire to be treated. But my experience in living next door to whites on a day-to-day basis is that it just doesn't work that way.

This family might well turn out to be an exception to the rule. I hope so, how I hope so. I'm keeping my fingers crossed that she won't like the place. At this point in time, as they say in the Watergate Hearings, I won't take the subtle and not-so-subtle expressions of racism that I've endured in the past. The first time the lady starts harping to me about little trifles involving the children and calling the police for little nothings that the children do, I'll just have to tell her that if she doesn't like living next to blacks she should move someplace where she'll be happier because it's far easier for her to find a place to move to than it is for me.

And don't say I'm being pessimistic, self. It's realism. I'd like nothing better than for her to prove me wrong. It would be soul food for her to prove that whites and blacks can live next door to each other in harmony. Then I would have more hope for the future of our country, hope for the future of man.

I went to Bingo with a friend last night. I didn't win a thing, of course. Games of chance are not my forte. I wasn't blessed with the kind of luck that's conducive to good fortune but I'll gladly compete for any prize on the basis of skill, within my abilities. Even if I know there are competitors better than me, I feel I have a chance if I give it my best. This probably contradicts my philosophy of fatalism in some way, but I don't think so. I believe that people are born with certain talents, capacities, or potentials. One can't work with what he wasn't born with, but one can work to develop and hone to a fine point the talents, abilities, or potentials they are born with, and then put them to use in the game of life or use them as weapons to fight the war of life—however one wants to label this brief sojourn on earth. Be all that as it may, it will probably be a long time before I go to Bingo again. I much prefer to spend the few dollars that I can squeeze out for myself on bowling, on a good book, on a canvas and a few paints, on a remnant of cloth, or on a good jazz or gospel record, if I'm ever able to afford a record player.

With food prices continuing to spiral, pretty soon I'll probably have to give up all the little activities that enhance life for me and make it at least livable. The best things in life are free (so they say), but it sure takes money to enjoy even a few of the second best things. I've never cared to settle for second best, but in this case the second best combined with the best could make a joyful whole.

Good day to you, self,
Richelene

6–10–73

Dear Self,

It's Sunday morning. I just got up and prepared break-fast and ironed a dress for Candy to wear to church. She is going with her girlfriend. I promised my next door neighbor that I was going to church with her today, but can't make it. I'm really ashamed to tell you why, self, but I will.

I went with some friends and my daughter and son-in-law to a dance last night. I really wasn't in the mood for going, but went along anyway. I had a lousy time; made no startling discoveries; gained no new insights; observed nothing to titillate the sensibilities and was anxious to get home.

But, self, I had already decided that after this year, I would attend no more dances unescorted, except under rare circumstances. To me, there's something infinitely pathetic about older women attending a dance unescorted. They sit at their tables, smiling brightly, chattering gaily, hoping that some man, any man, will ask them to dance. The men saunter by their tables, looking them over, looking past them to the younger women, unless a fairly well-preserved or gullible one catches their eye. Sometimes soon, sometimes later (much later), some bleary-eyed man will invite them, the lucky ones, to dance. They think by the blaring absence of an escort, they have license to squeeze too tight or take other liberties. Often, much younger men will be attentive. They often are gigolos, looking for older women who will pay for their company, or give them a place to stay, rent-free. Some of the women, desperately lonely, fall prey to the blandishments of these men. They know that these are of no substance, but in their loneliness, feel that the form of a man is better than no man at all. Even the older women that are there for simple amusement and fun are suspect. After all, what are you out for if not looking for a man? Any man! And, if in fact, a respectable woman is actively searching for that "right" man, it's highly unlikely that she will find him at a public dance hall. But loneliness is a bitter enemy, and so many of the older women will go on attending dances. Maybe next time a new crowd will be there, and "he" will be among them. For many, so what if "he" isn't there. I'll take whatever is there home with me to warm my cold bed for a night, and maybe he will like me and come to live with me.

So you see, self, I will not allow myself to join that sad procession. It's a fact that I'll never find my "right" man at a public dance. In fact, I'm almost convinced that I won't find "him" period. And you know what, self? The thought doesn't depress me as it once did. Now I feel that if the Good Lord will just grant me a large enough portion of health and strength so that I can find and hold a good job and provide for my own, I'll be reasonably content. Is that asking so terribly much?

Since I'm not going to church today, I will go back to bed now and read the paper.

Happy Sabbath, self,
Richelene

P.S. History just repeated itself. This morning, Jeffrey's two little white friends came up and asked if Jeffrey could go to the beach with them. I cautiously told them to go home and ask their mother first. In no time they were back, gleefully announcing that she said they could take him with them. With some trepidation, I got Jeffrey ready and they traipsed off happily. Jeffrey just returned, in tears. His friends just left for the beach—without him. Just as I knew they would. But it was better for me to let him learn this lesson in "interracial friendships" himself. If I had simply said he couldn't go, he would have screamed for hours. As it is, he is quietly disappointed and sad. This exact incident happened with Melanie and one of her little white friends a few summers back. So tell me, self, how can I change my attitudes and erase my antipathy toward whites when they continuously feed the fires?

Is it worth even continuing to try? This is life, as it is. Life as some of us, who once dared to dream, would like it to be is a whole different ball game. Life where children could grow up seeing children of different races and colors only as children; life where adults could allow their children to grow up free of racial hang-ups; life where all adults see each other as only human beings. Seemingly this is still much too large an order for most of us. So be it.

6–15–73

Dear Self,

This is the halfway mark of June, the halfway mark of the year, and I'm not halfway rid of my little hostilities and antipathies toward the "Master Race." But I'm trying, self, honestly I am. And I don't seem to be terribly much closer to being the human being that I'd like to be. But perhaps these cleansing dialogues with you, self, these airings of the bits and pieces of life that shape my attitudes, will eventually yield good fruit. Things always fall into place so strangely and unexpectedly for me. Who knows? Maybe by the close of this little journal, the close of the year, the pieces will fit together and form a whole, a beautiful whole. I just might emerge into the person that I'd like to be.

For over a month I've been trying to read *The Sunlight Dialogues,* but to me it's a wearying book, one I have to strain to read. There are some good insights in it, but I can't really get into it the way I like to immerse myself when I read. I took some shirts into Ricky's room (pig sty) and stumbled onto Norman Vincent Peale's *The Power of Positive*

Thinking. Imagine a seventeen-year-old boy reading that! Anyway, I took the book into my room and began reading it. It seems that I read it years ago, or maybe it was just articles by Dr. Peale in *Reader's Digest*. Anyway, I've read to about page 30. It's marvelous. Many of his thoughts and prescriptions for a fulfilling life jibe with mine. Maybe it's because we were both nurtured on the teachings of Christ. Now I must go back and see how the list of blessings I wrote down earlier in the year jibes with the list he suggests we make when feeling that life holds nothing good for us.

Self, to you I might sound terribly pessimistic at times, but those are merely examinations of the realities of my life in an honest unsugar-coated way. Deep down inside, I am the eternal optimist, hope does spring eternal.

Take a mundane thing like my bowling. All winter I bowled lousy, for the most part. But at the end of the season, I made up my mind that I would never finish next to last place again, even if I had to almost single-handedly win the games. And you know what? So far, this summer it's working. Yesterday I bowled a 211 game, and a 523 series. So far, we've won twelve games, lost four. The only reason we lost those four was because my partner was late picking me up, and we forfeited the first game by not getting there on time. Behind that, I was too disgusted to bowl, so we threw away the other three games. This is just an analogy to let you know how I feel about this game of life, self. I'm going to win! I won't finish in last place. Circumstances might cause me to lose a few rounds, from time to time, but I'm going to win! I wasn't put on this earth to crawl in the dust forever. I wasn't born to lose. When the pieces are all together, self, I will emerge a winner!

What else can I say? That's it, baby!

To you, to us, self,
Richelene

6–16–73

Dear Self,

Not much to talk about today. I did write a reply to a reply that I got from my "fan." After thinking about the contents of the letter, I decided against mailing it. See how well I'm progressing? After all, how much do I really accomplish by forever inflicting my opinions on others, and asking vain and foolish questions. So I'm a half-baked welfare philosopher and thinker of sorts—so what? Bertrand Russell, great thinker and philosopher that he was, admitted just before he died that his whole life's work had been in vain. By that I interpret his statement to mean that the world is still full of evil, hatred, misunderstanding, and pain. Evidently he felt that with all his philosophizing, etc., he had not made a dent in the world for the better. Those of us who probe for truth and dream beautiful dreams of enlightening others and fostering understanding through the written word are incurable optimists. But sooner or later reality hits us, reality being that the world will remain the same.

I'm keeping the letter, self. Why? I don't know, but I'll share it with you. _____ could no more answer all the questions that I put to him about the "white condition" than I could answer many questions that he might ask me about the "black condition." Really, I think the letter was just a projection of my yearning to talk to someone on a different level. Even conversations on "deep" subjects could easily bog down and get boring. So I'll just continue to discuss these things with you, self. Who knows? I just might meet a kindred spirit someday. Actually, I'm not too keen on face-to-face confrontation with a "kindred spirit" anyway. It would be more satisfying just to be able to write long letters and receive long letters to read over and over and savor. I really must be some kind of nut, but it takes all kinds.

I think I'll go to St. James Baptist Church tomorrow and get my spiritual strength renewed on some good old Baptist meetin'.

Until next time,
Richelene

Here's the letter, self.

686 Osgood Avenue
New Britain, Conn. 06053

June 16, 1973

Mr. DeWolfe,

Life is funny, isn't it? Reading your first note to me, I had no intent of responding to it. Many times I've received little "fan" or "pan" letters from people who've read letters of mine that were published, but I put them aside in silent appreciation. Then it began to dawn on me that perhaps it was discourteous not to thank the people who took time to drop me a note when they included their address.

In your case, I have to admit that my motive in responding to your note was less than selfless. Something about the way you expressed yourself piqued my interest. Now please don't get queasy! I'm not trying to get an ongoing correspondence started with you, to bore you with a barrage of words. But this one letter, just this one, had to be written.

I'm not particularly well read, and I'm not familiar with Jill Johnson or her works, but if she is for human liberation, she must be a person worth listening to. I'm sorry I wasn't able to catch her lecture and also have the pleasure of saying hello to you. Thanks for mentioning it and also for the fill-in on Justina McDonald.

Your statement about our need to solve some of our solvable problems instead of further studying and debating them hit me where I live and breathe and have my being. But for that gigantic little word—IF. It's such a tiny word but so pregnant with possibilities.

By your style of writing, Mr. DeWolfe, I gather that you are a man of great intelligence, depth, and sensitivity. You are also a white man, by your own admission. I have long yearned to come into contact with a white person with whom I could have a meaningful dialogue, just once. I've known many whites, some as friends, but there was always superficiality there, an inability for either of us to relate to each other honestly. Don't you agree that many of our seemingly unsolvable problems are due to a lack of honest communication between the races? Don't we need to begin at last to have honest dialogue about the roots of racism before we can truly begin to solve some of our problems?

By now you're probably beginning to think me a little crazy. Maybe I am. I'm crazy enough to want the world to be a better place for all God's children, crazy enough to know that it could be better if all of us tried a little harder to love. But that's a big order. So why pick on you for this little "honest" dialogue? You've revealed to me a measure of your intellect and humanity and, as presumptuous as my writing you might be, I believe you are a person of enough depth to understand and respond to this letter honestly. Also, I vaguely suspect that you might be afflicted with "writes," just as I am, and are not adverse to reading and thinking on anything of interest to you, so you will tolerate my impudence. Just as David of biblical fame slew the giant, Goliath, with a small, well-aimed slingshot, you, David, could lay to rest a few of the giant questions that plague me with a few well-aimed words. Would you? Since we have never met, face to face, and there is no fragile friendship to be slaughtered, would you please acquiesce my longing to know a few facts about the white condition? God knows the black condition has been studied, debated, hashed, and rehashed enough.

A couple of years ago I had a friend, a man whose skin was as white as the proverbial alabaster and whose eyes were like twin sapphires, if you'll pardon the cliché; he was technically labeled negro or black. I often jokingly suggested to him that he should "fade" into the white world for a year or so and study the white condition, firsthand, for me, so I could write a book about it. If John Griffin and others can blacken themselves in order to study the black condition, firsthand, and write books about the experience, is it so wrong for some of us to want to know what makes white folk tick? The cause of the black condition should be readily apparent to all thinking people; to what do we attribute the white condition? How did they "get that way"?

Can you tell me why whites, as a whole, have such an inherent hate and scorn for black people? Is it fear, as some say, that makes the white race determined to keep blacks oppressed? If so, fear of what? Why many well-qualified blacks are disqualified for certain jobs by their race only? I honestly can't understand it. Do you know the reason that whites withdraw their children from associations with ours after they reach a certain age? Is it fear of romance and marriage between the races? Why is it so much easier for the average white to accept and like a docile, buffoonish, or even ignorant black than one who asserts his humanity, his intelligence, and his right to be here? Is it because their notion of superiority is threatened by the latter? On what basis is the notion of white superiority formed? Why do most whites flee as if the plague were upon them when a nice black family moves next door to them? Is power the basis of suppression and/or oppression of blacks? Why does the white race, which calls itself the most civilized, blithely dehumanize every darker race with which it comes in contact, in the name of civilization? Do you think the day will come when a Thomas Bradley will be the mayor of a Los Angeles instead of the black mayor?

You, Mr. DeWolfe, having lived in a white skin, in a white world, for forty-three years, can give me some of the answers to these questions. I, being on a collision course with forty, having survived in a skin labeled black, in a black world, would dearly love some straight answers at this stage in my life. To me, the time seems past for glossing over issues with evasions, half-truths, subtleties and nice-sounding platitudes. If we could strip away our shields and pretensions and reveal ourselves in our common humanity, we might begin to like each other as human beings and eventually to love.

Thanks for your assistance in my quest for truth and understanding.

Sincerely,
Richelene Mitchell

6–17–73

Dear Self,

Today's *Hartford Courant* carried a letter to the editor from a sociologist who rebutted the statement that Dr. Van Dellen made on May 29th about fifteen-year-old girls being encouraged to have babies so the family will have more welfare money. Her feelings about his statement were essentially the same as mine, which made me think maybe I'm not so crazy after all. The *Courant* forwarded her letter to the good doctor and published his reply along with her letter. In his reply he acknowledged that he could not give an exact reference as to his source of that bit of misinformation but stated: "At any rate I've heard this said on television and also said by a speaker at a meeting dealing with unwed mothers less than eighteen years of age." His source of information still seems a little hackneyed to me. He further attempted to support his original statement by the following quote from a letter from a Welfare Coalition group in Illinois: "Insofar as early pregnancy is welcome and often encouraged, it is because it has become a fad among certain groups of teenage girls and by no means all such groups, even in the ghetto. The girls who subscribe to the fad do so for psychological reasons or reasons of social pressure, and in some cases because of gross misinformation, such as the amount of money welfare pays."

Sorry, doctor, I still can't buy your statement no matter how hard you try to squirm out of it. Get with it and inform yourself correctly or stick with medicine.

Self, I've just given up trying not to write letters, except to myself. I'm incurably afflicted with letter-writis. So all I can do is try to keep it in check better by Herculean efforts like yesterday's. So, I dashed off a quick thank you to the lady whose letter appeared in today's *Courant*, and included a copy of my letter to the good doctor. Apparently she is a real human being, and her support is gratifying beyond words. But I suspect that even she cannot speak for welfare recipients as well as one who is actually there. So I shared my little thoughts and insights with her. My vantage point might be a little better, unless she is a former welfare child.

I wonder if the *Courant* really forwarded my letter to Dr. Van Dellen. I wonder what his reaction was, if they did.

It will be interesting to see if _____ responds to the letter I wrote her, and interesting to see what her response will be. She might just think I'm a smart-assed so-and-so who needs to stop writing letters and get into some nonpaying office or factory job. Will see what develops.

Good day, self,
Richelene

6–19–73

Dear Self,

Another week begins. I finished over half of *The Power of Positive Thinking* and I'm determined to put the principles and exercises contained therein into practice. My little "realistic" or "pessimistic" self keeps chiding me, telling me that it couldn't possibly be as simple as that to change my life for the better. After all, haven't I always basically followed those precepts? One thing really stands out to me though. He states that we usually get what we want if we apply positive thoughts. That really could be the key to my seeming inability to move, to progress beyond my present state. Have I ever really known, with true conviction, what I really want in this life? As I discussed with you before, of all the things I wanted to be as I grew up, I could never narrow the field down to just one thing that I absolutely wanted to be beyond a shadow of a doubt. When I got married I didn't know for sure if I wanted a husband or to be married, but I drifted into it because it seemed the thing to do. I didn't really want seven children, but somehow they got here. I didn't really want to reconcile with my husband when I came here to New Britain, but it seemed the best thing to do then. Now, as I look back, my whole life has been a steady procession of doing things that I didn't really want to do. When I got pregnant with Jeffrey, I didn't really want to marry Norman, but I would have if I could have got my divorce right then. But I couldn't, and thus was spared another situation that would have produced unhappiness for all concerned. So I have been more or less drifting along with the tide, like a ship without an anchor—in spite of my belief that everything would ultimately fall into place in its own time. I'm living neither a hot nor cold life, just lukewarm in my endeavors.

Still, always in the deep recesses of my soul, I felt that the Almighty hand was guiding me, holding mine, leading in the pathways that He would have me go. Now, maybe I've arrived at the point where He would have me steer my own ship, beside me at the helm. Maybe I'm almost at that point. There are still things that I think I want, but am not completely convinced of.

1. I think I want a husband; the children are now at the stage where they do not really need a father; not the form of a husband; not an oppressor; not a manipulator or a boss; not a bed partner or a dictator; a husband. But I'm not really sure that I want one.
2. I think I want to get off welfare, but has my courage been restored to the extent that I can get out there again with the confidence that I had before? I'm admittedly fearful now. Fearful that my health will collapse again; fearful that I'll be even lonelier among all those women now; fearful that I'm even more unfit for blending in with the crowd now than before because my perceptions and sensibilities have been heightened; fearful of dissatisfaction and boredom.

So what do I really want?

1. I really want a job that requires a personality such as mine; one where it would be an asset rather than a liability.
2. I really want to be able to pay my way, and my family's way until such time as they can pay their own, and not be burdened with the knowledge that we are drains on society.

So I will begin to think positively on these two things, admittedly it's going to be hard for me to clear out all the negative thoughts about my overall condition. But with God all things are possible.

Sincerely,
Richelene

6–19–73

Dear Self,

I have a few random tidbits for you.

You wouldn't believe the strange bedfellows that inhabit my night stand: *Muhammad Speaks*, Muslim newspaper; *Awake*, the Jehovah's Witnesses' booklet; *Mysterious Worlds*, a book about the occult; *The Power of Positive Thinking*; and the *New Testament*. Now don't get panicky! I'm not trying to assimilate all those different beliefs; nor am I trying to reconcile them. They all merely make interesting reading.

I just finished *The Power of Positive Thinking*. It sounds convincing and powerful beyond words. Now if I can just stop being so "realistic" (labeled pessimistic in *The Power of Positive Thinking*) and apply the guidelines outlined, I'll be all set for the duration. It's going to be hard, but I shall try with all my being. Childlike faith! I had it once before the storms of life assailed and shattered it. Can I regain it? Can the pieces be truly glued back together? I'm willing to try. Lord, I do believe; help my unbelief!

I read a news story in yesterday's *Courant* where a pregnant woman was told in advance that she had placenta previa, so proper arrangements were made for her medical care. I wonder if the same would have been done for me, when I was afflicted with that malady, if I had been a paying "customer" instead of a black beggar. Oh well, all's well that ends well. The police emergency wagon got me to the hospital in time, thank God for policemen that morning, and Jeffrey and mother are doing fine.

Donna has been suffering from constant headaches and dizzy spells for over a month. It could be a side effect of the pill or a number of other things but, being me, I suspect she has neurological problems. Besides, having known her all my life, and knowing her inheritance, I would like for her to have a complete neurological examination. I called the clinic to see about it. The social worker advised me to have her doctor check her and if he refers her they'll examine her. I hope she goes ahead and sees her doctor. If there is a neurological problem it will be much better for her to begin getting treatment now than to suffer needlessly throughout the years.

Kenny, Donna's baby, broke a very cherished candy dish of mine. My sainted white friend (that I spoke about earlier this year) gave it to me. Of course, it upset me greatly, but *The Power of Positive Thinking* softened the blow. I'm trying hard to grow into a better acceptance of the daily disruptions caused by my two premature grandchildren. This has not been easy. Just when I thought things were kind of shaping up where all those kinds of problems were behind me, I am presented with two premature grandchildren. Will I continue to try to accept this continuation of "baby problems" more gracefully? Time will tell.

Shirley Chisholm will be in Hartford for a luncheon Saturday. I would dearly love to go and hear her speak. But my two "running buddies" are both occupied this coming weekend. One is going to New Jersey for a friend's wedding; the other is attending her club's picnic. I'd go alone if it weren't for the fact that I'd have to make two trips to Hartford, one to pick up the ticket, and one to attend the luncheon. I can't afford two trips and a $4.00 ticket. I'm sick, sick, sick, of being poor!

Gotta go bowling now,
Later, Richelene

6–21–73

Dear Self,

The first day of summer entered on cue. Hot, muggy, super hair-napping. This morning I washed my hair and simply brushed it up into a braid. I'm sick of looking like a frizzy-headed hen. So for the most part, this will be my hairdo for this summer. After all, I'm not trying to be glamorous and impress anyone. As long as it's clean and neat, that's all that matters. At least if a gentlemen shows interest in me now it will be for the real me and not because of some facade of glamour.

Yesterday, the letter that I wrote to the sociologist who rebutted Dr. Van Dellen's article came back. The address was insufficient. So I tore it up and threw it into the waste basket. In yesterday's column by the doctor, he took certain ecologists to task for disseminating information without knowing the facts. Look who's talking!

_____ called the other day. I told him I was reading *The Power of Positive Thinking*. He said he'd like to read it when I finished. Yesterday he came by for the book. We chatted for a while. While he was here _____ called. I was really surprised to hear from him again. But I'll never see him socially again. He is definitely not my type. Too many of his ways are similar to my ex-husband's. Dominating! Obstinate! Unreasonable! And, I suspect, capable of violence. I don't need that.

_____ is nice. But he's unable to hold a full-time job because of nervous disabilities. Who knows, if he really reads that book and takes it to heart, perhaps a change for the better will be wrought in his life. I hope and pray so. After he reads it, _____ has requested that I pass it on to her. I'm trying to talk my daughter into reading it, but she says she has no need of it, she's already positive enough. Good for her.

I had forgotten that I ordered *Enthusiasm Really Makes a Difference*, by Dr. Peale. It came today. I'm looking forward to reading it, but I'm canceling my membership in the Book-of-the-Month Club. I had hoped to acquire some books by black writers at discount prices. So far they haven't listed even one. I will write them explaining my reason for canceling.

I just walked over to the shopping center with Donna. She bought reams of cloth for me to sew her a new wardrobe. I'm not really enthused over sitting in a hot house doing all that sewing. But she is so ragged that I'll do it. It's going to take a lot of positive thinking on my part for me to work up any enthusiasm over this project. Anyway I might as well get started. No use procrastinating.

Later,
Richelene

6–23–73

Hi Self,

It's me again. School is out; blessing or curse? It's nine o'clock in the morning. Melanie just went to bowl in her league; the rest of the "nerve-wreckers" are in bed; and now I can sit here for a few peaceful moments and chat with you, self. If I hope to be able to thresh out the daily happenings with you, for the rest of the summer, I'll have to do it before the wrecking crew arises each morning.

It's a mournful day dawning, seemingly. The skies are dark, pouting, petulant, ready to weep. I'm supposed to go to a picnic with _____ this afternoon, weather permitting. Her club, composed of New Britain's black elite, is having their annual outing. Lowly little me doesn't exactly feel up to mingling with the elite today—so maybe the rain will save me. More and more, it's getting to be an effort for me to forego my reading and get out and mix and mingle. I keep working at it because I know it's not especially good to become too detached and isolated. Bowling is the only social activity for which I have any enthusiasm at this time. Maybe it's satisfying to me because there's activity and an awful lot of talking is not necessary. Lately, I've been playing volleyball (over the clothesline) with my children and the neighbors' children almost every evening. So what if it looks silly to some super sophisticated, jaded adults, it's good exercise and it's fun.

I got two pantsuits and a pair of pants made for Donna. I also made a play outfit for Candace and one for yours truly. Not bad. I will make two or three more outfits for Donna, then I'm going on strike. She has to learn to sew for herself since she is apparently going to be poor for a little while yet.

Alan shaved his head yesterday, and he looks like he's ready for a lobotomy. He needs one. He's been bugging me for over a year to either let him braid his hair or shave it off, since it's too hot in the summer. Seeing black boys and men walking around with braids gives me acute "disgustivitis," so I settled for the lesser of the two evils and allowed him to have his head shaved. And he does indeed look as strange as he must be. Oh well, he's mine, though sometimes I'd like to deny it. Now I'm afraid Ricky will follow suit. He and Alan definitely have a meeting of the minds, a rapport.

Kenny is the odd man out. Alan and Ricky are working in the tobacco fields, beginning Monday. Kenny feels himself above working tobacco and says he is not going to. Yet he requires more money, getting to band practice, etc., than the other boys. I told him if he doesn't go to the tobacco fields until something more to his liking opens up, I'm not going to give him one dime all summer. But can I stick to that? Won't I be afraid he might consider some illegal ways of getting money if I don't supply him with spending change? And won't I feel that perhaps I'm letting him down by not subsidizing his efforts to be a musician? I know that all people are not cut out for every type of work, but I still say he could stand tobacco for a few weeks. This is why mothers gray!

_____ came by last night. We chatted for a while and played a game of rummy—poor guy. He's so lonely. There must be a nice lady somewhere who could appreciate him for what he is, and sympathize with his weaknesses. How I hope and pray that he finds her soon. So why can't I be that "nice" lady? There are too many dimensions to my situation for it to work. Maybe I haven't progressed sufficiently to be able to give to the extent that would be needed. But he's so adrift, so in need of love and affection. I definitely think he should read *The Power of Positive Thinking* and sincerely apply it. There's still room for hope that he can make something better of his life. Lift it to a higher place. God help him.

There are so many things that need to be done around here until it makes me dizzy. The living room needs painting again; the floor needs sanding and refinishing; the cellar needs a good cleaning up and painting; the whole house needs a revamp. Last summer I painted every room in the house except for the boys' room (that foreign country is a complete wasteland). Now everything is beginning to look drab and dingy and dirty again. Wish I could move into a place where everything is cleaned and fresh and nice to begin with. Oh well, maybe the painting and cleaning mood will strike me soon. Every so often I still get the urge to throw away every piece of junk in the living room—I feel it coming on again. The fact that a truck just drove up and deposited new furniture next door (new neighbors are moving in, and my prayer was answered—they're black) isn't doing anything to dissolve the urge.

_____ just called to see if I'm going to the picnic. If the skies clear up I'll go. Otherwise, I can't see any point in forcing myself out on a drab day like today, even for good food.

I must leave you now, self, for chores and positive thinking.

Sincerely,
Richelene

6–25–73

Dear Self,

Another Monday morning is here. It's time to shop for the usual supply of chicken wings, etc. Frankly speaking, at this stage, I could almost become a willing vegetarian. Thinking of those poor animals being slaughtered that we might live never was appealing to me. Now that I have, of necessity, been restricted to an almost meatless diet for so many years, the idea is actually growing inside me.

Yesterday was nice. My next door neighbor and I had a cookout in the backyard together. I supplied the chicken wings, of course, and the potato salad. She supplied ribs, hot dogs, and pies. Admittedly, it was a very imbalanced affair, food wise, but the scales will balance better some day. After we ate, we went with the children to the park and played tennis. The weather was ideal, cool breezes deliciously filtering through the trees and blending with the warmth of

the sun. We played until dark. Admittedly our tennis playing leaves a lot to be desired, but it was a good day.

School is out, and all the children are bumping around
today tying up loose ends. Alan got up at five to go to
work on tobacco, but the bus didn't come. Apparently, the
fields aren't ready to harvest yet. Hope all of them soon
get started to work, not only for the financial aspects of
it, but for the benefit of my nervous system.

I had a minor episode of my affliction last night. I feel
out of it today, but must keep moving. Like Old Man
River, I must keep rolling along. On this note I will leave
you for now, self.

Adios,
Richelene

P.S. _____ called this afternoon. He says he's returning *The Power of Positive Thinking* for the present, because he doesn't have time to read it right now. And he's
not working? Tch! Tch! That's life. Sometimes the ones
who could perhaps benefit most from certain philoso
phies pass them up. But that's what makes the world go
round: diversity of opinions, religions, philosophies, etc.
Anyway who am I to say that he needs a new perspective
on life? Maybe he's perfectly content with his life as it is
even though it appears in need of much uplift to me. My
humble opinion, however, is that it would do quite a lot
of people good to read *The Power of Positive Thinking*.

6–27–73

Dear Self,

As usual when the children are all home, my poor brain
gets in such a state of confusion that I'm not able to think
clearly and articulate the daily happenings to you. My

inspiration for writing takes wings and fades into the din like a beautiful sunset fading into the night. But here I am anyway. I can't peter out in the middle of the year, since I still have six more months to correspond with you, self.

It's about that time of the month, and I'm having trouble getting to sleep. Last night after returning from bowling, I finished reading *Enthusiasm Makes the Difference*, and self, it's just as powerful and inspiring as *The Power of Positive Thinking*. I'm tempted to write Dr. Peale a letter expressing my admiration and gratitude, but am not sure if I will or not. Those two books have so clearly brought into focus my deficiencies in positive thinking, in faith, in functioning on the level that I should be functioning. I'm working hard at cleansing my mind of all those old bugaboos of fear, doubt and "realism" (pessimism) that I've allowed to seep in and crowd out the positive elements. I see now how I've rendered impotent my basic faith in God, in myself, in my fellow man, and the ultimate good of life. Even though a little core of faith has always remained, I've been too cynical to really assert that faith. I've grown too "realistic" to cultivate the seeds of faith that were planted in my childhood and make them blossom and produce the fruit that it is capable of producing. Now I'm going to nurture it, water it with the cool, clear flow of positive thinking. I shall cultivate these seeds with enthusiasm and allow my basic belief in God to fertilize them; and a good harvest is on the horizon.

Back to bowling. As I told you, self, I'm out to win now. Last week I bowled a 547 series; and this week I bowled a 570. My average has gone up from 135 to about 170. How's that for positive thinking? This week we moved up to third place. Look out, world, we're on our way!

Talk to you later,
Richelene

P.S. It's now about 6:30 A.M. Alan just returned home again. Again his attempt to work on tobacco proved futile. Either they missed the bus, or the bus didn't come today as it's quite cloudy. I'm not getting upset, at least he's trying to work.

6–29–73

Dear Self,

Rain, rain, go away! It's been raining off and on for three days now. Let there be sunshine! Alan finally got to the tobacco fields yesterday. Perseverance does pay off. But, agony of agonies, he returned home dripping so much dirt and mud that I wonder if the few dollars he earned was worth it. They work for slave wages, $1.45 an hour. Last year it was $1.30. That's a sin and a shame. Oh well, at least he's doing something constructive to occupy his time, and will be able to buy his school clothes.

Kenny and Ricky begin their job with the Neighborhood Youth Corps Monday, so things are shaping up very nicely. But oh how sweet it will be when they are all old enough to get real jobs and fend for themselves.

_____ is taking a course toward her master's at Central Connecticut State College this summer. I'm virtually frothing at the mouth with frustration because I can't enter academia or something intellectually stimulating at this time. They're studying Black America. She is the only black in a class of approximately forty-five. The professor is black. He assigned *Manchild in the Promised Land,* among other books about the black condition, for them to read. I read that book, and it's a profound commentary on coming of age in the north. She said that yesterday a very articulate and learned Black

Muslim lectured. According to her, he was almost too hot to handle and the "intellectual white liberals" were really thrown into a tizzy. I bet! Those Muslims can say a whole lot that white America does not want to hear. I agree that many of their theories are quite extreme and farfetched, but there is also a lot of truth and good in their ideology. Anyway, I just enjoy listening to all kinds of ideas and thoughts when they are well presented. How I wish yours truly could have heard him! Oh, well, my day is fast approaching. I've been bound up in this welfare bag for almost eight long, weary, frustrating, despairing, hungry, ragged, humiliating demoralizing years. It's time to break out, and I will!

_____ is taking an Afro-American dance class this summer. She teaches dance and plans to incorporate some of these techniques into her classes. Sounds stimulating! So what am I doing? Climbing the walls from doors slamming, babies crying, teenagers arguing and messing up the house—mine and everyone else's (so it seems). This is my last summer of this kind of flack. Next year my time and energy will be channeled into more productive and less nerve-wracking use. I promise you that, self.

Please, stop raining! The chair covers and rugs are so dirty until I can hardly stand it. It's shattering my nerves. Not that it takes that much this morning. Last night the wacky old brain had a field day. Instead of snap-crackle-pop, it went swoosh! Actually, self, I'm laughing to keep from crying. Like St. Paul, I beseech the good Lord once again to remove this thorn from me. But if it's His will that it remain, I ask only for the grace to continue to bear it.

Must move on now before I sink into that self-pitying mood . . .

Later,
Richelene

6–30–73

Six months of 1973 have gone by the board, and what an amalgamation of days has expired. One hundred and eighty one days of living, learning, growing, successes, failures, pain, anger, happiness, tears, laughter, sorrow, fun, and boredom. Six months of trying to assemble the assorted thoughts, emotions, and feelings that make up Richelene into a workable whole. Am I any closer to my goal than when I began my dialogues with you, self? I believe I am.

But there are still so many little loose ends that must be tied together by life; so many more threads of love and understanding must be woven into the fabric of my being; so many ragged places that must be patched. But I'm on my way. That I will never reach perfection, I'm certain. But as long as I have the will to aim in that direction, I can't be too far off target.

Lately I've been reading, reading, reading, everything I can lay hold of. It's as if I can't read fast enough to drink in all the wonderful worlds of thoughts and knowledge that were denied me for so many years, while the children were younger. Still I haven't read any of the classics, any of the truly great works from the past. Keats, Chaucer, Aristotle, Plato, names like those are just names to me. Perhaps I haven't grown to that plane yet, but somehow I prefer to read more recent writings. No doubt the writings of the above are as relevant to today as the books that I do read, but I haven't developed an interest in reading them yet. Would you believe I have the complete works of Shakespeare and can't bring myself to read them? I think I'll make that my next reading project, to read the works of Shakespeare.

I'm beginning to find myself dreaming again. What if I were to apply at some institution of higher learning and ask if I could perhaps take a test and write a dissertation on my years of struggle as a welfare recipient? It seems that I read something of that nature somewhere; certain people of potential can apply practical experience as credits toward a degree. Instead of having the professional sociologists debate and study me, I've debated and studied myself. My view from "down under" would be so much more valid than theirs. Oh well! Let me dream awhile.

I really came down to discuss my anger at Melanie with you, self. This girl is almost a straight A student, and she has opted to attend a trade school, and no amount of reasoning on my part will influence her to stay in regular high school and take courses that will prepare her for college. I could just grab the little silly goose and shake her until . . . What with all the loans, scholarships floating around to assist poor students these days! What's wrong with these kids? How do you motivate them to progress beyond the life they have now? How do you instill in them the desire to be something, to want to do great things with their lives? Why can't they see that a good education will more nearly assure them of a good life in this society? Apparently the guidance counselors do nothing to try to sway the black children toward higher education, even the bright students. It just reinforces what Jonathan Kozol says in *Death at an Early Age*, and what I've always known. The majority of these white teachers don't give a damn about the ultimate outcome of black students, unless they happen to be special pets, and I mean special, special.

That my little nitwit doesn't have enough common sense herself to want to strive for high goals is infuriating to me. Dear God, please breathe onto her brain and stimulate it to better logic. It's such a tragedy for a good mind like hers to stultify and die when our world so desperately needs to utilize its brain power to the fullest extent. I'll keep talking to her, and maybe, with your help, I'll get through to her.

Sincerely,
Richelene

7–2–73

Dear Self,

I just threw the rugs in the washer, even though it's cloudy again. Can't stand the dirt and grime another minute—though for all the good it will do, I might as well have left them and the slipcovers dirty. I'm running a genuine nursery this summer, or so it seems.

Donna and Steve took off for a two weeks' vacation—and the babies are here. How I managed to let it happen, I don't quite know. Maybe I was thinking back on how desperately I used to wish that someone would relieve me for a few days when mine were babies. But no one ever did. So I know how great the need is for a little let-up from it all once in a while.

Later today _____'s two will be here. Melanie is keeping them every afternoon while she is taking a course at CCSC. Confusion will reign supreme. I just might take off myself and leave it with them. Oh, well, I'll endure this summer. But I promise you self, this is the last summer that I'll allow myself to be snowed under like this.

Think I'll move on. Lying there in bed, I was greatly inspired to get up before the noise erupts. Now that I'm downstairs, reality has knocked all thoughts of beauty and wisdom out of my head.

Later,
Richelene

7–3–73

Dear Self,

It's early in the morning, 5:46 A.M.; I feel awake, alert, and refreshed after a good night's sleep. And I need it! There will be one more baby; the one Donna had been keeping for a friend was added to my nursery shortly after I chatted with you yesterday.

By 6:00 P.M. yesterday I was a grouchy mess. Tired, completely broken-down, and yelling at the kids. And yet it's not as bad as I'd thought it would be. In a way I'm enjoying my little grands. This is the first time I've really allowed myself—or really felt up to it—to really get close to them and enjoy them as miniature people. Kenny is at that really sweet toddler stage, in everything and into everything. Steven is a little past the meddling stage and plays with Jeffrey. So all in all, I think I will survive until the "honeymooners" return.

I just noticed the little plants that _____ gave me are greener, more alive. Is _____ striving, gaining new life and happier days wherever she is now? Has she found the comfort and solace that she sought for her weary spirit? Will the south be kinder to her this time and allow her the peace of mind that she deserves? I hope so.

Kenny just woke up and is raising the roof. Thus ends my time of introspection and contemplation for today.

Until later,
Richelene

7–4–73

Dear Self,

Today, the Red, White, and Blue is waving high over the land of the free and the home of the brave—Independence Day. Have a real cutie for you, self. As of July 1st we paupers were to get a $4.00 per month increase in our food stamps. That in itself is cute enough considering the rise in food prices. But listen to this: My food stamp allotment was raised four dollars, and I have to pay three dollars more for them. In view of the fact that I'm not receiving one dollar more in my budget—what is the gain? I always had to spend up to fifteen dollars above the food stamp allotment anyway so I cannot see any sense in it, can you, self? Wonder why they went through the trouble of processing the papers?

But positive thinking me shouldn't say things like that, should I? Be thankful for small, even invisible blessings, right? The Welfare Department does such preposterous things for us "beneficiaries" that it never ceases to amaze me.

Also: At the check-out counter at the supermarket yesterday, the girl said to me: "I thought by now you would have hit the lottery and be off food-stamps." Interpretation: "How come you're not working and off welfare by now?"

Also, yesterday the welfare department called and informed me that they have another address on my ex-husband (in Michigan) and for me to go back to Hartford on the 16th and take out another nonsupport warrant. That will lead to another futile trip, and another few dollars wasted on bus fare. Lord, if you deliver me out of this mire of deprivation and debasement, I will trust and never doubt again.

Happy Fourth of July to you, self,
Richelene

7–6–73

Dear Self,

Pandemonium, pandemonium! How else can I describe this week? Children fighting, babies screaming, teenagers clunking in and out of the refrigerator, empty doors slamming, clothes, clothes, and more clothes to wash, front door screen that I just paid for yesterday demolished. How can I get profound and erudite with you, self, in times like this?

Later!
Richelene

7–9–73

Dear Self,

Whew! The vacationers returned yesterday, the babies have gone home, and all I can say is whew! Is something basically wrong with me that I'm so relieved to be free of my week of "baby-sitting"? What about all the stories I read of welfare grandmothers welcoming babies into the fold, the more the better, and happily raising their grandchildren? I must be some kind of weirdo, and a tired weirdo at that. Right now I feel as if I could live happily henceforth if I never saw another human being less than eighteen years of age—in my house that is. This being swamped with babies and children has just about got me down now. I need a vacation! HELP!

Later,
Richelene

7–10–73

Dear Self,

Summer is here full force! Heat and humidity, sweat soaking everyone like a blanket dripping scalding water. And believe me we are withering on the vine! It's too hot to think—my brain is melting.

Tonight is bowling night again. My partner is in the hospital, and I don't know how I'm going to get to the alley tonight. I'll see how things go. Just when we had worked our way up to second place, and I held high series (570) and second high game (208).

How can I keep thinking positive? _____ asked me to type her term paper for her, so I think I'll ask her to give me a ride to the bowling alley as an exchange favor. Bet the response will be much slower than my response to her request. It never fails. Had I been in her place, supposedly a close friend, I would have offered her a ride under the circumstances. But that's life for me—people don't hesitate to ask favors of me, but reciprocation seems to come harder. Anyway we'll see how my proposition strikes her and I'll report back to you later, self.

Until later,
Richelene

7–11–73

Dear Self:

I didn't propose my exchange of favors to _____. Perhaps it's a disadvantageous quirk of my nature, but I find it very hard to accept anything that is not done for me freely and with good will.

Last week when I first learned of eminent hospitalization I broadly hinted to _____ that I would need a ride to the Alley.

She brushed my hint aside by stating her need to get to bed early and all the reading she had to do in connection with the course she's taking. Day before yesterday when she broadly hinted that she'd like someone to type her paper, I immediately volunteered to do it since I knew she was really asking me to do it. Since I did volunteer, my favor to her would have been null and void had I turned it into a bargaining session of favors.

I've always felt that if one does not give freely, without strings attached, the giving loses its essence. So I typed the paper, about five pages. At first I felt resentful. Though I suppose she feels that bowling just isn't that important, my time is as valuable to me, in my own way, as hers is to her. But thinking on my own philosophy of giving, the resentment faded. By the time she came to pick up the paper and her children, positive thinking had me in a normal and free state of mind. But, self, will I hesitate the next time she asks a favor of me, as she surely will do, or will I be able to toss this additional experience in human relationships into the wastebasket of unusable scraps and render it void until the next favor she asks of me? Only time will tell. Still, it always hurts a little to know that those we consider closest to us won't bend a little and sacrifice a little of themselves or their time to render favors to those who've shown their friendship or concern by being helpful to them in little ways.

Little incidents like this often make me wonder if it's worth it to continue to try to love. It really must be true that the world is made up of two kinds of people—the takers and the givers. I suppose the givers always manage to attract the takers—and the takers always have their antennas out for the givers. But it all balances out in the end, I'm sure.

As I always say, all's well that ends well. My next door neighbor heard me and gave me a ride. Would you believe I bowled a 98 game and a 109 game! Whatever happened? I guess it was because I really needed my partner for moral support. Of course I lost all three games. Just wait until next week!

Richelene

7–13–73

Dear Self,

_____ brought the new *Ebony* magazine over. There is a new feature in it, *Speaking Out*. So you know

what happened? Yes, self, yesterday I submitted a manu-
script to the column. This is really not a column where
they solicit readers' opinions—they select the people that
they want presented. But you know me, self; I can be
quite audacious at times. My subject matter and opinion
were quite controversial, but I'm thinking positive. They
will accept it for publication. Of course, if they do, it will
bring a lot of vituperation down on me from the black
community, the hue and cry of UNCLE TOM! But I stand
ever ready to take the consequences of my actions when
I feel they are right. I merely speak the truth, as I see it.
This presentation might just be a few years ahead of its
time, but I'm sharing it with you self. At least you will
understand and not spew venom on me:

RESPONSIBLE PARENTHOOD IS THE ANSWER

The current controversy over the involuntary sterilization
of two black adolescent girls in Alabama has various ram-
ifications in all its aspects. If one is black, as I am, one is
naturally inclined to jump on the "Anti-Black-Genocide"
bandwagon.

If one is a human being, as I am, one is naturally inclined to jump on the "Sanctity-Of-Life" bandwagon. If
one is a mother, as I am, one is naturally inclined to jump
on the "Right-to-Motherhood" bandwagon. But if one is a
black mother who also happens to be a welfare recipient
and a feeling, thinking, caring individual, as I am, one is inclined to look past the bandwagons and look at the facts of
the case at its deeper levels—as painful as that might be, or
as offensive as it might be to the majority of black people.

In the July 13 issue of *Muhammad Speaks* we read:
"The Lonnie Relf family was living in a shack on the
lower Wetumpka Road when they were spotted by a

white newspaper reporter some two years ago." The paper further states that the family was subsequently moved into a six-room apartment in a housing project and given public assistance. Evidently this sequence of events improved the family's lot to a considerable degree, and some people did care enough to want to make life somewhat better for the Relf family, inasmuch as one's life can be bettered under the current welfare bureaucracy.

Certainly no one has the right to play God and coldly and dispassionately decree who shall or who shall not propagate. But God did give many of us the ability to reason and make hard decisions, in the interest of our fellow man if they are incompetent to make their own decisions, even if they turn out to be unpopular ones. If the two girls were retarded, as stated, sterilization seemed to be in the best interest of both the girls and society. I, who have lived among the dirt poor, the physically and emotionally disadvantaged, the wretched of the earth, agree with the Montgomery Community Action Family Planning Centers that retarded girls have no right to bring children into the world to suffer as they have suffered.

How could they exercise their option to have or not have children if their ability to reason was seriously impaired? What kind of life could they have offered a child or children? Would they have been equipped to offer them love, stability, a good education—or would they have offered them only a trip into the "welfare" world?

We, as black people, too often think in terms of quantity rather than quality. Our ultimate outcome in this "land of the free and home of the brave" will be determined by the quality of life that we bequeath to our children rather than by the quantity of children that we bequeath to life. Now is as good a time as any to begin to stop emphasizing "black-power" and "brawn-power" and emphasize "brain-power."

Quality of life supersedes quantity, regardless of race, creed, or color. It is no accident that the poor, who can least afford children—in any sense—are the most prolific. Many of them, being below par intellectually, think with their genitals. The result is more children to further complicate the lives of the entire family, more complications to perpetuate the status quo. This applies to most of the truly poor—black and white.

I am not a sociologist by virtue of any degree of higher learning, but I am a sociologist by virtue of living and learning in the school of hard knocks, in the school of life as it is in my socio-economic group, and this is a real education. All around me I see sad examples of children propagated in abundance by the lesser endowed. Many of them have nothing to give to the world or to life but their presence—and in many cases, this is given reluctantly. I bleed for their innocence, their vulnerability, their lack of a good genetic inheritance that will better equip them to fight in this hard world and win. I flinch inside when I see their helplessness in the face of the forces that shape their lives. I see them passing on the same inherent weaknesses and its built-in suffering—unnecessarily.

Healthy reproductive organs are probably the best endowment many of them receive and they use these to perpetuate their problems. Our jails, reform schools, prisons, and mental institutions are overflowing with suffering humanity of weak endowment. Since we have come into enough wisdom and knowledge to see where the roots of much of this suffering began is it so wrong to try to stem the tide?

Any healthy set of reproductive organs can come together and produce children, but can the body, spirit and emotions that house the organs give the child proper love, nurturing, care, and education? History has proved over and over again that only the strong survive. Safety might be found in numbers, but strength is found in strong minds, emotions, intellect, and inner workings. When the facts clearly indicate that child-bearing—at all—would be an injustice to a female or society, is it a greater sin to make child-bearing impossible than to allow innocent victims to come into this world to suffer? By some quirk of nature a retarded person might produce whole productive offspring, but the odds against it are too intricate to go into in this brief essay.

Both observation and living have brought me to my present attitude—be it right or wrong. In today's world even those with the best of genetic inheritance do children no great favor by producing in large numbers, regardless of race, creed or color.

I have seven children, a fact that cannot now be changed. But far from rendering me impotent to speak out for birth control, by whatever means that seems most feasible for the individual, this fact validates my right to speak. I know the disadvantages of producing more children than one can economically, physically, emotionally, or educationally give one's best to. I've tasted the fruit of seed sown irresponsibly, something so prevalent among black men. I've both seen and suffered the despair of those caught in the "welfare-web."

No doubt I will be labeled an "Uncle Tom" by my black sisters and brothers for taking the stance that I do. I seriously wonder how many of you who yell "Uncle Tom!"—have actually read Harriet Beecher Stowe's *Uncle Tom's Cabin*? Uncle Tom, a black man who would choose to be beaten to death by the white man rather than betray black women, was beautiful to me. Call me Aunt Thomisa.

When all the controversy, pro and con, concerning the Relf case has died down, all of us would do well to strive to instill in our children the virtues of responsible parenthood and limited procreation, that only children who are truly wanted and can be given the advantages of life, rather than existence, should be brought into this world. That to have babies only as an extension of one's self is a sin. Only then can the quality of life begin to improve for everyone. We, as black people, must begin to recognize that responsible parenthood is the answer to many of our problems.

This is slightly different from the version I submitted to *Ebony*, but in essence it is the same. I truly believe everything I stated.

7–16–73

Dear Self,

Mission accomplished! I went to court this morning to swear out another futile nonsupport warrant against the man I made the grievous mistake of carrying out, or entering into, a legal baby-producing contract with. He'll take to his heels again. Always running, always hiding; running and hiding to keep from putting a little bread into the mouths of the seeds of his loins; running and hiding to keep from facing reality even after all these years. And his insides must be tormented; the sickness that's gnawing at his soul must be spreading the cancerous growth of his guilt and shame into an all-pervading stench. The odor must be enveloping his senses like an over-flowing cesspool. But will he allow the medicine of logic, reason, and reality to stop the metastasis of his sickness and to spell the malignity? Will he let all the light of the love that he so vociferously proclaimed for his children illuminate the dark depths of his soul and light the path of right? No. There was no love, only a will to possess, to manipulate, to bind and smother. A love that seeks to drain off all individuality, all personhood, all freedom, and when thwarted seeks only vengeance, can never attain that which it seeks, acceptance.

So run and hide. Wallow in your vengeance. I bet it ain't easy. But you are doomed to live with yourself.

Until later,
Richelene

7–19–73

Dear Self,

I had several incidentals to discuss with you this morning, but now they seem to have escaped me, in a clear sense. But here goes. Another little cutie: When the food stamp allotment came this time, I had to pay fifty cents more for the same amount of stamps. Wonder what they're trying to accomplish? Is this subtle harassment to prod me into going to work?

Guess what, self? I quit my Tuesday night bowling league. The "Great White Ones" did so many insidious, ugly little things, which were designed to thwart the one "black" team's progress into first place, until we decided not to contribute any more money to their cause. Understand, I didn't quit because I'm a poor loser, but because I can't stand unfairness and injustice in anything (strange statement, isn't it, considering that all black people have ever known is unfairness and injustice at the hands of the "Great White Ones"—for the most part).

In retrospect I realize that just "letting them have it" was not a noble course of action, but anger and resentment would have seriously hampered my game had I continued. Besides, all the fun had gone out of it. Fair and honest competition I welcome; dirty pool stinks, and I have to get away from the odor. So once again whitey and his deviousness have triumphed. God bless them.

Thinking once again on my resolve to try to overcome my prejudices, I feel so terribly helpless to make much progress when I'm continuously exposed to my antagonists. Now I see more clearly than ever why blacks in the South, as a whole, have a better sense of self and seem more secure.

They live in their own world, for the most part unexposed to the true nature of whites on a day-to-day basis. Their main intercourse with whites is economic. And good jobs have definitely opened up for blacks. Besides, there is a fairly good base of economic assets in black businesses there. This further enhances the stability and sense of worth of southern blacks. And they are thriving. Whatever faults one might still find with the South, there is no denying that many black people are materially and, seemingly, spiritually better off there. Of course the South is still no Utopia, but there is promise, a little glimmer of light. Here where we are in more intimate contact with whites, we are constantly exposed to their true feelings (veiled and unveiled), the living is harder—to my way of thinking. No wonder so many blacks are fleeing from the Promised Land back to the Land of Promise.

Just last week I read where the National Conference of the NAACP was threatening to dismember the Atlanta chapter because the Atlanta group is not pursuing busing and integration. I say bravo for the Atlanta group. They have good educations, good jobs, and good lives. What really have they to gain by just sitting beside a hostile white in school? Do the whites have some intangible something that is supposed to rub off on blacks and enhance their lives? I've often stated that, even here, if my children were assigned to be bused to some distant place just for the purpose of "integration," I'd resist it with every ounce of my being. If the Atlanta group gains more integration, they'll only gain more strife. Do they necessarily need that? To each his own. Let those blacks who prefer to live peacefully separately—as long as the quality of life is good, do so. Let those that feel that social intercourse with whites is the ultimate ideal pursue their ends, but don't try to intimidate all blacks as a means to that end.

On this note, I'll say good day to you, self.
Richelene

7–21–73

Dear Self,

The minute the ex-husband received notice of the new nonsupport warrant, he called me, as I knew he would. As blithely and matter-of-factly as if we had been in friendly communication all along, he asked if Melanie and Candy could spend a few weeks with him this summer. No mention of any financial settlement or anything relating to support. He then asked for Donna's address, which I refused to give him, as Donna lives so close to me. I'm sure he will find out where she lives, but he won't find out from anyone in this house if I can help it. He'd be dallying around a little too close for comfort.

He said he'd call back tonight to see if the girls want to spend time with him (they weren't home when he called). I've told them the answer must be no for many reasons, not the least of which is his emotional instability.

Will this poor creature just float around forever like a dark cloud chasing the sunshine?

What else can I say? Que sera!

Until later,
Richelene

7–23–73

Dear Self,

Another week begins. And I begin it feeling stronger, more normal physically than I've felt for some months. Dare I hope that this will be the beginning of a stretch of good health and vitality for me? How I could use such a stretch!

Candace goes to Fresh Air Camp today. Two weeks of fresh clean air and romping in nature's green garden. Two weeks of swimming, hiking, and drinking as much milk as she can hold—no rationed amount like at home. She's been to camp before, thanks to the generosity of some caring folk, and she loves it. So I know she'll have an enjoyable two weeks.

I watched the Miss Universe contest Saturday night. I correctly chose Miss Philippines as the winner. She was in a class all her own as far as beauty, poise, and elegance went. In short, she was heads above the other contestants in the outer facets of beauty. But as soon as she opened her mouth, she lost out with me. All she could talk of was money and materialistic things. The only one of the contestants who expressed a concern for humanity was Miss Israel. I immediately switched my allegiance to her. Miss Philippines won. I guess the judges were more preoccupied with the outside than the inside, which is normal. That's life.

As far as the black nations are concerned, they might as well stop sending contestants. No chance. Unless the judges decides it's time to be democratic one year.

Must go now and deliver Candy to the bus for camp.

Later,
Richelene

7–25–73

Dear Self,

I took Jeffrey to the circus last night. _____ had free tickets, so she gave some to us (also a ride). Jeff really had a royal ball! He was fascinated with the elephants with their massive bodies and musty hides; the tigers and lions, baring deadly fangs and roaring at their trainer (tormentor?); the bears, dancing and cavorting; the monkeys acting like natural humans. The white man is certainly a master trainer (tormentor?). With his whips and guns he has trained all manner of beasts—and darker humans. But on occasion the beasts and humans rise up against their trainer (tormentor). They stun him temporarily, and even occasionally exact the life of a few. But whip and guns always prevail.

It was a good outing, even if I didn't have any money as usual. Once again I'm thankful for such blessings as we receive. Jeff really enjoyed himself; Steven and Donna took their two; and the night was soft and gentle. Amen.

I shopped for groceries yesterday. Store-brand bacon was up from $1.09 lb. to $1.59 lb.; medium eggs were up from .77 to .93 per dozen; etc. Oh, Lord, how will your little children survive? How long, how far, and how high can all this go? But if He clothes the lilies of the field in beauty, nourishes the grass of the field and feeds the little sparrow, He will provide for children. O, ye of little faith, Richelene!

Good day, self,
Richelene

7–26–73

Dear Self,

I had a glorious day yesterday. Self, now I must confess something that I was ashamed to tell you before. At the beginning of summer I was bowling on two leagues, one on Tuesday night, and one on Wednesday morning. That was too much money to be spending on bowling, and I knew it. So I rationalized: I don't drink; I don't smoke; I don't eat candy or drink sodas, so, "Why not treat myself to bowling?" Still I felt finicky about the whole thing. Actually I did it so that if something happened and I had to give up one league, I'd still be bowling in a league. So if something did happen to disrupt the Tuesday night league I'd still be bowling on Wednesday morning. Anyway, to shorten a long story, we won three games yesterday, so we should be moving up again. We've been in and out of first place all season. Good, huh? We're determined to hang in there and get a trophy.

After bowling, Jeff and I went home with _____ and we spent the rest of the day together. She lives way out, and the air was cool and clean. It looks like God's country out there, leafy green trees swaying under blue skies, birds chattering happily as they play with each other, and quietness, blessed quietness. Jeff had a ball seeing her neighbor's horses, cows, and chickens and just romping around freely. It's really nice out there. _____'s family is the only black family in the immediate area. We went for a walk. I felt somewhat like a visitor in a foreign land as all those white faces surveyed us. We went for a long walk, greeted by "friendly" hellos.

In this seventh month of the year of my rebirth I have to finally admit that as much antipathy toward them remains as ever, and I suspect more wariness and suspicion, even paranoia from them. Is this wrong? No, self, I don't think so. It's just well nourished pre-sentiments. And they supplied the food for it abundantly and liberally. I'm still trying to overcome my anger at their ways though, self; I'm still trying.

All in all, it was a good day, a beautiful break from the daily routine. One little thing: every time I take break, when I return home a door screen is broken. This time it was the back door screen, another little bill. Must we always lose something for every little something we gain? I gained a good day and lost a door screen. Last night I had a most interesting and charming conversation. A young man (about twenty-three), whose wife and baby are away on vacation with his mother, called. He called for Melanie to corn-row his hair. It is a style which I abhor on men. But Melanie was at recreation, so somehow we started talking and it was a revelation. He is a beautiful, beautiful young man, corn-rows and all. I'm sure he was achingly lonely for his little family and just felt like talking.

The thing that struck me was his depth, his sensitivity, his seriousness about life at an age when so much youth is into the drug scene or just plain irresponsible. He seems to have such a firm grasp of life, such a keen sense of self. His head is together, and he knows where he's going. He's not just bumbling along without direction.

But he had a model, a guide. It was his grandfather. He spoke so lovingly of his little family and his plans to buy a home for them before age thirty. And he will too, I know it. And he talked with such pride of his admiration for and veneration of his grandfather, age ninety-seven. What a tribute he paid his grandfather. He admires him most among men, a black man who worked hard, loved God, loved and provided for his family (about eleven or twelve children), and now gets joy unlimited from just fishing. And he feels that if he follows in his grandfather's footsteps, he'll also have a long and fruitful life.

With love so evident I could feel it, he told me how he takes his cute little wife to church, and how their young love blossomed and grew into marriage, how it's still growing and enriching their lives. I believe every word of it too. I've observed them together and there's a goodness, a caring evident that can't be faked. How lucky they are to have found each other. How I hope that the Good Lord will continue to make their problems solvable ones, their blessings many, and nurture their happiness and love.

Will say good night to you now, self.

Sincerely,
Richclene

7–28–73

Dear Self,

I went to Hartford to the Bureau of Support the day before yesterday. It was another wild-goose chase. But I suppose they have to keep trying. Why, why, why do these men prefer to run and hide rather than face up to their responsibilities? They're sick, sick, sick.

_____ invited me to a party at her brother's house tonight. I don't think I'm going though. Why bother? I already know who'll be there and I know just about the kind of time I'll have. And so I think I'll stay home and read or watch TV. Most likely I'll read. I have a new *Reader's Digest* to explore.

I can't seem to get the old brain ticking this morning, self, so maybe I'll get back to you later today if something worth talking about comes up.

Later,
Richelene

7–29–73

Dear Self,

Guess what? I almost lost all my little intimate conversations with you! Believe me, self, I was almost there for a while. Know what happened? Donna brought a Shop-Rite bag of groceries down here and set them on my table where I was typing. By a coincidence, I keep my writing materials and daily journal in a Shop-Rite bag. So when she left she picked up the wrong bag.

I figured she had picked up the wrong bag when I got up to put away my work and discovered a bag full of groceries. Naturally I was frantic. As high as food is I should have been thrilled to discover a bag full of groceries instead of a bag full of meanderings of the mind. But I wasn't. I rushed up to her house, but my bag was nowhere in sight, nor was she. So what happened? She had taken my bag, thinking she was returning some things to the store. Much to the salesperson's amusement and Donna's chagrin she pulled out my notebook.

Being on her way to work—she works from 6 to 10 at Bradlee's—she took my precious revelations to work with her. I finally came back into possession of them at eleven o'clock last night. What a scare—seven months of meditations, introspection, laughter, tears, hopes, dreams, anger, and assorted bits of life almost lost forever!

My big hope now is that no one peeked in the bag. I'd die. How embarrassing it would be.

Good day, self,
Richelene

8–1–73

Dear Self,

July just sailed away, and August sailed in. I meant to assess the month of July and what it brought and taught me, but I got so caught up in making kitchen curtains I couldn't tear myself away. So now the curtains are finished and hung, and they are pretty. They're cheerful and homey, downright "down-homey." I found a steal—two yards of material for a dollar. It's a print with pretty pink flowers, a cut watermelon, carrots, mushrooms, strawberries, a basket of vegetables, a basket of fruit, and assorted other goodies. Doesn't that sound yummy, self? With food prices the way they are we might just have to feast on the visual delights of the curtains from time to time.

And guess what? Yesterday I received a notice from the housing authority that my rent is going up $10 more the first of September. Groan-n-n-n! What are they trying to do to us? Is there no pity? Is there no compassion for the poor? Is there no one to care whether we survive or not?

Be of good cheer. If God is for you, who can be against you. If God clothes the lilies of the field—in a way I feel guilty for even complaining. I saw a TV documentary about the plight of the migrant farm workers Sunday evening. My God, my God! What a deplorable way for human beings to have to exist. What an abomination! What a disgrace! What a cancer in the heart of a country that shoots billions of dollars into space! For what? And these are the people who are harvesting the food President Nixon eats. The food that all of us eat. And this one farmer had the audacity to stand there and say with a straight face, "They love this life. They wouldn't have it any other way."

Has he ever looked into the eyes of any of his workers (slaves)? Has he seen the emptiness and despair mirrored there? Even the eyes of the children were dead. The only signs of life I saw were when the interviewer asked several of the children what they want to be when they grow up. There was genuine sparkle and hope on the face of one pretty black girl when she answered: "A teacher." But the chances of her realizing her dream are so remote it sickens the soul. Why couldn't I be in a position to rescue at least that one bright hope from almost certain death? Why doesn't somebody that is in a position to do so care enough to grab her and run before the monster on her trail grabs and devours her? Before that sweet bud of promise is strangled by weeds? It's so sad, so sad. Now I know I'm really not so bad off.

I have a busy day ahead: bowling this morning; Jeffrey to the doctor for his school physical this afternoon; shopping (the cupboards are bare); plus all the other little odds and ends that fill my "leisurely" days. So I'd better get breakfast started. I'm learning to tolerate breakfast without even a slice of bacon.

Bye now,
Richelene

8–3–73

Hi Self,

My kitchen curtains greeted me cheerfully this morning. I feasted on fresh fruit and vegetables before partaking of an inflation deflated breakfast. I suppose my enjoyment of the delights of my curtains is like the voyeur's vicarious enjoyment when looking at pornographic pictures or watching other people's sexual activities. Now I won't be so quick to judge such people. We can be taught in so many ways to be more compassionate human beings. Imagine being taught by kitchen curtains!

I just read an article in the new *Reader's Digest* that's really going to cramp my style. This article says we should not use big words when we write, in order to be more effective. Now let me go back to the above paragraph and see where I went wrong: partaking, inflation, deflated, vicarious, voyeur's, pornographic, activities. Seven mistakes! Now how could I have worded the paragraph differently?

My kitchen curtains greeted me cheerfully this morning. I ate fresh fruit and vegetables before eating a skimpy breakfast brought on by high prices. I suppose my enjoyment of the delights of my curtains is like the sex pervert's substitute enjoyment when looking at dirty pictures or watching other people's scx acts.

Is that more "elegant" as the author says our writing would be if we expressed ourselves more succinctly (oops! I did it again). It's going to be rough going for a dyed-in-the-wool polysyballic maniac like myself to get away from my beloved big words. Do I really have to? Someday I'll tell you about my love affair with the dictionary, self.

But for now, bye,
Richelene

8–5–73

Dear Self,

I had a gorgeous night's sleep last night and feel deliciously refreshcd and alive this morning. Was up at 7:15 A.M.—and this on a Sunday! Today Melanie and Candy will embark on their long-awaited vacation. Two weeks in New Jersey with Steve's sisters and parents. The "getting ready" yesterday was just too much. Flurrying around washing and ironing and mending and packing and talking, talking, talking about all the wonderful things they'll do. They'll go to Coney Island; they'll visit the Empire State Building; they'll see the Statue of Liberty; they'll cavort at Palisades Park; they'll go to shops and parties; they'll go swimming, glorious youth.

Mom needs a vacation like flowers need sunshine; like the river needs water; like winter needs springtime;

like Dick Tracy needs danger. So who gets the vacation? The kiddies! So what? They're only young once. There're so many things I'd like to do for them to make their childhood happy, to give them good memories, but I can't. This is one little thing I can do, even if it is pinching the heck out of me financially, so I'm doing it. They're happy. My day will come yet.

Bon voyage, sweethearts!
Richelene

8–6–73

Dear Self,

Melanie called from New Jersey last night. They made it with no mishaps or misadventures. Frankly, I was a little queasy about those two little girls being alone in that big bus station in New York. But they came through admirably. Now the good times begin for them. _____ called yesterday evening. She just got back from Puerto Rico and the Virgin Islands. She was amazed at the beauty of Puerto Rico and at how well the people, apparently, are going. She was awestruck at the nice housing and the lack of slums there.

All this made her wonder how the Puerto Ricans can endure the living conditions they encounter here. I suspect most of the ones that migrate here are from the more depressed areas, which tourists don't see, and their living conditions here are an improvement over what they leave behind. Pretty much as the rural southern blacks who migrate north, hoping for a better land. Maybe someday I'll be able to see some of this big awesome world.

_____ invited me to attend church with her next Sunday, and, self, I was too big a coward to tell her my true reason for not caring to attend her church any more—

the mostly white church I told you about earlier. So I hemmed and hawed around it.

I just threw out an old chair that I rehabilitated several times. The final collapse was inevitable. That chair has persevered. From Georgia to Connecticut it stood by me. When its springs began to go and I doctored it with old spreads and drapes to hold up the cushion, it stood there. When its upholstery began to wear thin and I put slipcovers on it, it stood there. When the slipcovers faded with age and I dyed them and put them back on, it stood there. When the springs began to sound like juke box music playing loudly whenever anyone sat on it, it stood there. When I got ashamed of it (How could I?) and removed it to the basement, it carried on. When I brought it back to the living room and made a new cover for it and put more filling under the cushion, it kept trying. At last, the final collapse was inevitable. As with all things, age finally took its toll. That faithful old chair was just too weary and beat to hold up any longer. Thinking back on all the years of service we got from it and how faithfully it struggled under the assault of assorted "behinds" I feel cold and callous saying I threw it out.

So I feel awful saying we laid it to rest at last. It looks so lonely and forlorn, like an old mare put out to pasture—sitting out there waiting to be carted away to the dump. May you rest in peace, faithful friend.

Sincerely,
Richelene

8–7–73

Dear Self,

I finally made it to the doctor. The pain in my back still isn't fully explained, but at least he didn't tell me it's probably psychosomatic (a diagnosis without any really diagnostic procedures like X-rays, etc.). I'm grateful for that, even though he probably was saying it to himself. The mouth of my uterus is infected (cysts) so he cauterized it. It isn't the most pleasant sensation in the world. I have small fibroids, and he says if my periods keep "messing around" for two weeks as it has the last couple of months, he'll have to give me a DNC. Women and their problems! At least I don't have cancer, as I feared. So much for that.

The doctor asked me if my tubes were tied, and I told him no. I told him I asked the doctors at the clinic to tie them when Jeffrey was born and they wouldn't because of some far-fetched technicality about the husband having to sign, etc., etc. Now this doctor tells me that he would have tied them if he had been taking care of me. See. I only went to the clinic because I felt so badly about having a baby on welfare and wanted to do the whole thing as economically as possible. It still hurts when I think of it.

Still, I have to admit that the moral aspects of having my tubes tied when I didn't even have a husband gave me a lot of conflicting feelings. On the one hand, being normal and sexually alive, I know I would have relations if a suitable partner came into the picture. On the other hand, having one's tubes tied while single seems like an open declaration of permissiveness. I have to admit that certain religious conflicts also were involved. It can be a real mess when religious and moral standards that you've set for yourself run head-on into reality.

All this is to say that I didn't really press having my tubes tied at that time because the different factions of my inner beliefs were at war. Even now, I sometimes wonder if it's so much my sense of morality as my fear of pregnancy that keeps me walking a chalk line. Oh, well, since no likely prospects seem on the immediate horizon

(I still run into unlikely ones) the contraceptive problem is one of my lesser concerns.

Have to get my prescriptions filled.

Bye now,
Richelene

8–9–73

Dear Self,

What a day! I bowled this morning and lost all four games. Our team really took a plunge in the standings. I took Jeff to the hospital for a thyroid scan this afternoon. He has this lump under his chin; it's been there since he was about a year old, and so I thought it would be good to check it out while he's having his pre-school physical.

On our way home, we splurged on a small sausage pizza and soda. By the way self, my bad back hurt so badly today, and I'm so tired of hurting and dragging until I went into a first-class depression this afternoon. Going to the doctors, the hospital for Jeffrey's tests, having the prescriptions filled, Kenneth, Alan and I had our eyes checked last Saturday—all of this contributed the biggest part to my present depression. Every single time we have to go for medical treatment or services, I go into a depression. Usually, it's all I can do to keep from breaking down (even typing this, the tears are welling up) right in the doctors' offices. Every time I have to pull out that "welfare" card to pay for services rendered us, I die a little. And knowing that the doctors don't delight in servicing us charity cases doesn't help any.

Sometimes I wonder which is worse, sitting for hours at the charity clinic at Grady hospital in Atlanta or going to private doctors here who really don't want to be bothered with us. It seems I've been in this "charity" bag all my life. Anyway, it all hung out this afternoon when I got home, and I cried until my soul was satisfied. Just as I was into it really good _____ called and said she was on her way over. So I had to dry up real fast and try to look normal and happy by the time she got here. I don't know if I succeeded or not, but we had a nice visit anyway. I felt somewhat better after she left.

As if our minds were thinking together a welfare recipient had a letter to the editor in today's paper lamenting the lack of humaneness on the part of many doctors where welfare recipients are concerned. As she said, "We're human beings who hurt and bleed and get sick just like anyone else. We want to feel well and live too—even if for no other reason than to see our children safely launched into life. Why must we be made to feel so worthless, so expendable?" Oh, well, in man's scheme of things, we are worthless and expendable. Oh, Lord, how long?

Good night,
Richelene

P.S. I think I'm going to cry some more.

8–10–73

Dear Self,

Dear, dear, dear! What a life! What a world! Last week Ricky got his driver's license. So he was on pins to get a car. Yesterday he saw an ad in the paper, a 1961 Comet for fifty dollars. So he went over and put ten dollars down, my last ten dollars. Today when he got his check, he paid the rest. I was skeptical about the whole thing, but since he was so full of enthusiasm and supposedly the car was in good running condition, I decided to keep my pessimism (realism) to myself this one time. Beside, I was more than a little proud that at last one of my boys had grown up enough to try to better the family's condition to a certain extent. You know how desperately we've needed transportation for eight years.

So today, self, we scraped up $6.50 for the temporary plates and went to claim his car. When I saw it I was a little disappointed at the appearance of it—but what can you expect for fifty dollars? If it ran good, so what? It was a standard shift car, which Ricky didn't know how to drive, so the lady agreed to drive the car near our house to a school parking lot and show him how to operate it. No sooner had we got into the parking lot than the brakes gave out completely! How lucky we were that we weren't on the street!

The thing that really set me off, once I started thinking about the whole thing, was that this was an elderly white lady that sold him this hunk of junk. If I had a brand new car, as she has, plus another car (her husband's) in good condition, I would have given that old heap to anyone that wanted it, much less put it off on an innocent young boy just trying his wings. How can people be so money hungry—even in these trying times? You'd think a lady of that age with her life behind her and aware of the struggles that younger people, especially blacks have, would have had more compassion and humaneness than to grab at the almighty dollar to that extent. Sure, self, I know many old people are catching heck just like the rest of us, but I just don't believe that lady and her husband could be quite so bad off.

Anyway, I called her and asked if Ricky could have his money back since this was a total loss, a total disaster. She agreed to give him his money back since, according to her, "She didn't want to have it on her conscience." I was almost disappointed that she agreed to return his money so gracefully. I was getting ready to write her some gospel according to Richelene, and according to the Christ that she must profess to follow since she said she is a member of Trinity Methodist Church. The same church that my friend attends (the one I told you about earlier).

This world is in a sad, sad condition, self. People who have everything are so selfish, so money-hungry. Since I was denied the chance to preach to the lady, I'm pouring it all out to you, self. I know as well as anyone that it takes money to live, but must everyone always be out for a buck? Always out for self? Can't anyone share their blessings, do nice and kind little things sometimes, even to total strangers, just for the purpose of feeling good inside and pleasing one's maker? Must we always expect and demand some return for everything we do? Can't we sometimes do things for the "least of our brothers" as unto the Christ that so many of us profess to love and follow? It never ceases to amaze me how some of the most verbal "Christian" people in the world can act so completely contrary to Christ's teachings. I'm far from perfect, but anything I have that I don't need or can't use I gladly give to anyone that wants it or can use it. Oh, well, why belabor the whole thing. At least the lady has a conscience. And she did give Ricky a dollar to put some gas in the car. She's probably a nice person; maybe she really did desperately need fifty dollars as desperately as we need a car.

We'll ride in a Rolls-Royces one day, self. Just wait and see.

Richelene

8–12–73

Dear Self,

I had another of those "days of days" yesterday. Got up early and did a few household chores—as many as my bedeviled back would allow—then went grocery shopping.

Just before I left for shopping, I noticed two white men going next door. They took the young black man (about twenty-two or twenty-three years old) that lives there with them. This big, beautiful looking boy has problems (drugs, I think) that have made him nothing but a magnificent looking empty shell. He has a beautiful singing voice, and I don't know him well enough to know what other wasted potential is dying with him. But it's so sad.

Anyway, his white girlfriend was over there at the time, so she took his sister's baby, which he was baby-sitting for, with her. No sooner had I gotten home and put away my groceries than she pops up and asks me to keep the baby until his mother got home from work. I did. So there I was, chasing after an active one-year-old until almost six o'clock! No sooner was I relieved of him than Donna pops up with her two for me to watch until Steve got home (she works at night). So I was stuck with two active babies until eight o'clock. By then I was almost screaming. Between my nerves, my aching back, and my psychological block against coping with babies after having coped with my seven, I was a wreck by the time Steve picked them up.

I told him they'd have to get one of the neighborhood girls to watch them every evening until Melanie comes home. Mean old Grandma! Now I'm the villain again. Sorry about that. As I told you before, self, I've long since learned that if I don't take care of myself, no one will. I'm almost used up now, so it seems. It's definitely up to me to preserve what's left for the duration. I still say if Donna and Steve hadn't forced grandmotherhood on me prematurely (in duplicate, at that!), I would no doubt have been in a better position to enjoy it and play the part.

I'm still in over my head just trying to cope with all these over-grown children here at home. They drain me.

And as far as babies go, if I still wanted the work, responsibilities, and headaches and joys of babies, I could still be having them myself. As much as I basically love children, at this stage I only want to "kitchy-koo" at babies and keep going. That's all I'm physically, emotionally, or psychologically capable of doing right now.

As much as it would hurt me, if something happened that I had to take Donna's babies right at this time, I would be forced by circumstances to let them go to foster homes until the pieces of my dilapidated self are better mended.

Until later,
Richelene

P.S. Had a seizure last night. Whether the physical and emotional strain of the past several days brought it on or it was just that time again I don't know. One thing I do know: I function more normally when things are going at a pretty even pace, with no undue physical or emotional strain.

8–13–73

Dear Self,

August is approaching the half-way mark, and the lessons of life continue to be assigned to me from life's open book. I'm drinking them in like a thirsty man at a fountain. Man's inhumanity to man, his greed, his corruption, and small glimpses of his inherent goodness—all these lessons have been emphasized in abundance this year. But beneath the problems of life, there is promise. Promise that the quality of life can be improved when man taps his inherent goodness more. Beyond the hazards of living there is hope. And hope is the life spring, the living water that lubricates the axles of life, the ever-flowing stream that washes away yesterday's disappointments and disillusions and allows a new flow of dreams to replace the worn and tattered ones. Life is good and worth living!

Melanie and Candy returned home from their vacation last night. Their brief holiday from home delivered all it promised: trip to Atlantic City, an outing in New York, movies, a dance, and just fun, in general. These memories should hold them for a while.

Now Mom needs a few good times to add to her memory bank. She just plain and simply needs a change of pace—a vacation!

We'll see what develops.

Sincerely,
Richelene

8–16–73

Dear Self,

Instead of getting closer to that much needed vacation I seem to be getting farther away from it. Now I have two more children to enliven my already too lively days. Steve's two sisters are here to spend a few days with Melanie and Candy. They're nice, lovely girls and no trouble at all but right now is such a bad time for company. My physical, emotional, and economical resources are at an all-time low ebb. But what can I say? Melanie and Candy visited them at a particularly bad time for their mother—she was sick the whole week they were there. In fact, she's had an operation today. So it goes . . .

Today is "check day." This day won't enhance my recent procession of "emotionally bankrupt days." First the shame of cashing the check; next the embarrassment of standing in the food stamp line; then the downright panic of shopping for groceries for nine people when I only have money enough to shop for three or four at the most. But, "We are more than conquerors through Christ who strengthens us."

Keep the faith, baby,
Richelene

P.S. I got through the ordeal of check cashing, groceries, etc. I was standing at the meat counter, my head spinning trying to figure out a menu for nine that included at least a taste of meat when I said to the person behind me: "How can I figure out a way to feed nine people?" A well-dressed white gentleman offered this sage comment: "You can't." And how prophetic he was. Nevertheless, I down-heartedly made my way through the store and ended up with a shopping cart full of tidbits, which, if I pray hard enough, I might be able to stretch for a week. On this dismal note I bid you good night, self. (Visions of sirloin steak will probably dance through my head, or I might have nightmares.)

8–18–73

Dear Self,

You won't believe this, you really won't! I think I'm going on a vacation today, a real live vacation! Can you believe that my poor shattered, tattered, battered, overwrought nerves just might get a brief chance to mend?

If my ornery old back doesn't start acting up before 3:20 P.M. today, I'm taking the bus to Kalamazoo, Michigan, courtesy of Norman. He's such a nice man. Too bad circumstances won't allow us to merge in matrimony. Oh, well, that's life.

Right now I'm just grateful for the chance to escape for a brief respite from the routine.

Bon voyage,
Richelene

8–20–73

Dear Self,

I made the trip to Kalamazoo, and what a trip! I've always said I'd rather travel close to the ground than high in the sky. But, self, I think I just changed my mind. We missed the express bus from New York to Detroit so we took the next bus. What bedlam changing buses among a Saturday night horde of weary travelers.

But first, let me tell you about the little "fleecing" I got in the bus terminal in New York. My bag was like lead. Not wanting to aggravate my sensitive back, I was very grateful when a seedy looking teenager asked to carry my suit-case to the gate. Being at about gate four and having to walk all the way to gate thirty-eight, it was a Godsend to have someone carrying my bag. So-o-o we got there and I handed the "nice young fella" a dollar. "That will be three dollars and fifty cents plus a fifty cent service charge," he politely informed me. I was stunned, but forked the money over, as one never knows what to expect from a "nice young fella" in New York. So I got took. This will never happen again (not that particular little scheme anyway).

Then the trip proceeded. The bus was full of complaining menopausal and older women, mostly black, and most probably too poor to be traveling at all—just like me. But poor people get tired and weary of the hassle just to survive and have to get away from it all once in a while too.

The scenery was nice. Miles and miles of green trees blended into occasional monuments to man's progress, the cities. Fields of corn told us that food is still going on tables—even if scarcer and harder to come by. In Albion, Michigan, I got a swift glimpse of what looked like brotherhood in action, from my passing vantage point, rows of houses, nicely kept with pretty flowers decorating the yards which were inhabited by people of different races. At one house black people lounged in a shady yard; at another, what looked like Spanish people lolled on a quiet Sunday afternoon; and then a white man sat among the most abundant splashes of flowers I've ever seen. On down the line, as the bus rolled along, I took in the apparent peacefulness and harmony. It looked so much like America should be, human beings living together with no thought of race or color. Such a beautiful picture!

And we finally made it to Kalamazoo! Left New Britain at 6:00 P.M.; arrived in Kalamazoo at 9:00 P.M. the following day. That's a lot of riding the bus, enough to start me flying.

But now, self, I'm so sad, so sad. I'm crying on the inside, but of course, I must weep silently. I can't let Norman see my utter despair. Despair you say? Incredible! Here I am on that desperately needed respite from washing, ironing, cooking, fussing, fighting, noise, clutter, and aggravation, and I'm crying my poor heart out. Why? How can say it? Where do I begin?

Self, I'm here in my house. This is the house that Norman bought for us when I got pregnant with Jeffrey. This is the first time I've seen it, the first time I've been in my house, and, self, I love it. It's not a not a mansion—just an old house, but beautiful on the inside. There are eight rooms, room enough for all of us. Eight nice clean beautiful rooms, with character. My house is not in a ritzy section. In fact it's in a neighborhood peopled by the lower class blacks, the common people. Welfare recipients live on either side, but at least they're living in houses, not projects, where there is no privacy. My house is set among the people I love, identify with, empathize with, sympathize with, and care about. These are the "soul folk"—the gut-feeling, open, laughing, soul-crying, hopeful, hopeless, hard-drinking, love-making, knee-praying, loud, cussing, fast-dancing people that give something to life. And if life returns less to them than they give it, they say, "Kiss my ass!" and go right on trying to live.

How do I know all this about people that I've never even met, in a town I'm just passing through, while my heart weeps to stay? These are the universal soul folks, baby. They're universal. I've known them in Carver Homes in Atlanta; talked with them on Sixth Street in Berkeley; gone to church with them in San Diego; laughed with them in New Britain; prayed with them on Victory Street in Hartford; took a drink with them in Willimantic, CT; cried with them in Philly. Yes, self, I know them, and I love them. But through it all I've remained me, Richelene.

But back to my house; in back there is green grass, big trees and lots of room, room enough for a big vegetable garden, room for the children to have a basketball hoop. Room to live, to breathe, to grow, and I can see myself fixing the place up. Making curtains, reupholstering the dining room chairs, maybe one day buying new furniture for this beautiful living room, blue or gold crushed velvet. I see tall clear vases on either side of the rich mahogany room divider, and maybe I'll even sneak one or two pieces of my original artwork onto the walls! My house will really express me. I see a happy family living in this house. A home headed by a loving, gentle father instead of a tired, drained mother-father. I hear music coming from the stereo and children dancing the bump. I can feel life and laughter lighting up all these rooms. My house is alive, but its soul is dead. We could revive its spirit with love and bring out all its potential.

I see one room made into a work room for me, where I can sew and paint and write and type. I can do all the little creative things that give substance to my life. There's just so much beautiful, glorious room here! There is such comfort, such promise that could be brought to fruition with love and care. I'm dying on the inside because this is my house, but apparently I can never call it my home. It's a house that's crying out for life and vitality and love. It needs me, but apparently I can never answer that need. It's a house that wants to enclose children in its empty arms, wants to shelter them and watch them grow, but apparently I can never give it mine. It's a house that is lonely and cold and would welcome companionship and warmth, but apparently we can never give it ours.

You see, self, Norman doesn't love Jeffrey and me enough to dare take a chance on our being a family. Yet I can understand his reluctance to take on my six appendages (even though one is his); I'm getting reluctant under the load myself. I can understand his getting cold feet after the enormity of what he was asking for at the beginning of our relationship sank in. But why couldn't he have the courage to give it a try now? The boys are big enough to work part time now, and they'll soon be moving out. I can work now that Jeffrey will be in school. Maybe here I could even start a business at home, sewing or a little boutique. The possibilities for us to have a better life here are unlimited. But the love Norman professes is not love. Love that bypasses the pain and seeks only the pleasure is not love.

So, self, this trip was made not only for rest, but for a total and final assessment of the situation between Norman and me. I've summed it all up now and will close this chapter of my life. I suppose Jeffrey will still talk about his "daddy" and wish for him as he has so constantly these past few months.

I don't quite know how or why he came into such an acute awareness of and longing for his daddy, but he did. Maybe it was seeing his little friends' fathers. It hurts. Oh how it hurts to hear him almost daily talking about his daddy—the daddy that doesn't care enough to be with him and watch him grow. Norman is a decent man, but apparently he is not a man of deep sensitivity and warmth. Then again it might just be that whatever he felt for me, or thought he felt for me is dead. That happens, and that's life.

Having purged myself of my hurt with you, self, I'll put it all out of my mind and get on about the business of enjoying my holiday. This weekend, I'll pack my little suitcase and Jeffrey and me will move on back down the line, back to New Britain, back to the projects, and welfare, and despair. And Norman will still be here rambling around in this big, cold house that is not a home. Together we could have made it a beautiful home. But that's life, baby, that's life.

On with the show,
Richelene

P.S. Rereading this, self, I noticed I didn't say if I love Norman, or not. I really believe I do. Even if it's not total love that I feel for him now, the feeling I have could blossom into something beautiful if it were in the right climate. Since it apparently is not to be, the seeds of promise must fall into fertile soil and die. So be it.

8–22–73

Dear Self,

Just lying here in the bed—in my house that will never be a home, thinking; Why has life been such a series of complications and contradictions for me? Such a maze of hopes gone astray and unfulfilled promises? Is it because I haven't tried hard enough to bring my dreams to fruition? All the things I dream of in life seem like that elusive rabbit I chased in my childhood—always just one step ahead of me. Why do I come so close to the things I want in life and then have helplessly watch them slip away? Here this house that was built for me, even before I was born, is at my fingertips. I can touch it, feel it, and even sleep in it for a few brief moments, yet in a few days it will be gone from me forever.

And that man in the next room, that big, slow, silent, shy, comfortable man I could love as a husband—he will slip away from me forever in a few days. I will let him slip away because I know for sure now that he doesn't really love me. Life is so strange. At the beginning I was sure he loved me, but I didn't love him. Now I'm sure I could love him, but he doesn't love me. Yet I somehow get the feeling that he feels if he hangs on tentatively until all my children are gone, then he, Jeff, and I can get together. No way, baby, no way! If he's not man enough to help me bear my burdens in the heat of the day, we will not relax together in the cool of the evening.

Having threshed all this out with you, self, I'll take Jeff to Battle Creek this afternoon to meet his grandmother (Norman's mother), and tomorrow I think I'll head home to the kiddies.

> Mission accomplished,
> Richelene

8–27–73

Dear Self,

Home again with the kiddies—Home where I belong. The brief refresher was good and sweet. I'm grateful for the rest, but this is where I belong. After that first burst of what-ever-you-want-to-call-it at Norman's house (and it is Norman's house—not mine), I realized that house could never in essence be mine. It's too delicate, too cool, too unused to life and love, as my family practices it. It's like a fine old antique piece of furniture, beautiful to look at but not utilitarian. Like a well preserved old movie actress whose thin veneer of makeup over aged beauty will crack and reveal a sad and lonely old woman.

My family could never live in that house, I mean really live. My children are lively, active boys and girls, not perfectly programmed robots. Only robots could exist in that house—children who creep docilely about, not touching the rich mahogany woodwork, not running up and down those beautifully appointed stairs, not bumping into those walls whose makeup is already cracking.

But Norman can live there. He's quiet and slow, and much of the essence of life seems missing from him. So he and his house can co-exist well together. After my tears washed away my sugar-coated vision, I saw clearly that Norman's house is dead beyond resurrection. It's a well-embalmed beautiful corpse. Whatever soul it might have once had is long departed. And no children's laughter, music, joy, or sorrow, or love can penetrate it and bring it back to life. Maybe, if Norman's lucky, he can find a quiet, slow and dead little woman to complement him and his house. And maybe they can be happy there. I hope so.

I know now whatever Norman and I had between us, it was not complete. Maybe it was partly my make-up, partly his. One thing I know for certain now: Norman is not the man I need: we're not on the same wavelengths where it counts—in the soul. I like to dare, to question life. To look beyond the status quo and give it a few jolts, in my own way. Norman is conventional, content to go to work, eat and drink, live and die without ever questioning the wherefores and wherewithal's of it all. I like to reach outside myself, stretch myself a little, and try to see if I can't make the way a little smoother for all God's children, in my own way. Norman is wound up in a tight little knot inside himself, and there's no room for anyone else, not even his own little son.

But someday I'll find my man and my house. My man and my house will have soul and warmth and will respond to the liveliness and vitality that we offer. My man and my house will be strong and tough, yet soft and loving. Together we will find the last of life for which the first was made. I got to get going now. Back to the old routine, but this morning I can face it with far more grace than a week ago.

Sincerely,
Richelene

8–29–73

Dear Self,

I have never been angrier in my life than I was today. We bowled our last competition in the summer league, won all four games and ended up just a 1/2 game out of first place. Why was I so angry? The powers-that-be in the league decided to only give first place trophies this year, so for all our hard work we got nothing but a few cupcakes and sandwiches.

As usual, a bit of sneaky manipulation went on near the end, to try to make sure we blacks didn't end up on top. What really rankled me was that every previous year I've bowled in summer leagues they gave at least a second place trophy. Last year, they gave third place trophies. So what if they would've had to get small ones, they should have given the top three teams something to show for it. It's only right and fair. This morning I was so full of hate for white people that it frightened me. I, who was going to try so hard to overcome my prejudices this year and love them. I had to pray really hard for my thoughts and emotions to get back into perspective.

Why, why, are they so dirty, so determined to be on top, even in something as mundane as a little two-bit bowling league? If we're supposed to accept losing gracefully why can't they ever do it, in anything? I can accept losing gracefully when I lose fair and square, but when people will go to all lengths to try to block and undermine you, how can I suppress my anger and indignation and accept whatever is delivered to me gracefully?

When I asked one girl why they only gave first place trophies this year, and this was done without the voting or knowledge of all the teams, she exploded, "What do you expect for $2.25 a week? Look at all this food!" Her white fat ass and quite a few of the others could have done without all those cupcakes and sandwiches. The money could have been better spent or returned to the bowlers in proportion to the place they finished in as in previous years. You can bet your life if any of the favored teams, the teams that usually finish at the top, had repeated their feat this year, they would have gotten trophies. And, self, you know I'm not trophy-crazy or money-crazy, but I am crazy when it comes to unfairness and injustice.

We never, ever bowled one easy team in the league, the secretary manipulated to give us a tougher team in order to try to block us. White folks! Please, dear God, help me to keep trying to co-exist peacefully with these denizens of evil called white folks. It's getting harder by the day. Please don't let me start hating at this stage of my life when I'm more acutely aware of the need for love than ever in this cruel, cruel world. I want to love everyone, but folks won't let you. Please help me to keep trying.

Sincerely,
Richelene

9–5–73

Dear Self,

The first day of school, whew and hallelujah! I can really get my poor self together.

I remember the joyous first days of school when the children were small. How happy I was braiding hair and fixing ribbons in it; dressing the girls in cute little dresses, lovingly made for them. The boys prancing proudly about in new $2.98 shoes and pants; then the camera would start clicking and I'd capture a small memento of that first-day-of-school rapture. Those were the happy days when having a house full of children didn't seem all that bad. Now all the joy of first-day-of-school is gone, and in its place there is only relief. Why did the sweetness go so swiftly?

This morning the boys are clunking about in $20 high heeled shoes, $20 pants and $15 shirts (they bought them with their own earnings). The girls are grumbling, "I don't got nothing to wear; I don't got no shoes," even though I made them new dresses and the closet floor is lined with shoes and I refused to buy new ones for them. But maybe, just maybe, I can recapture a little bit of the joy when I dress Jeff for his first day of kindergarten this morning. I hope so . . . I hope so. . . .

Until later,
Richelene

P.S. Self, I meant to tell you—I spent Labor Day weekend in Toronto, Canada. And it was glorious, you hear me?

Glorious! We left Friday night, the West Indian Social Club sponsored a bus trip. They go there every year to play cricket against a Toronto team.

Self, those West Indians are a beautiful, life-filled, spontaneous people. They know how to have fun, how to forget their everyday cares and celebrate life. The bus literally rocked with music and laughter all the way there and all the way back.

In between, in Toronto, we ate, drank, and were merry for two tingling, refreshing days. I got high, self, high on life as it could be, high on luxurious air-conditioned comfort and relaxation (even though I only took one drink the whole weekend).

Now, self, I'll fill you in on some of the little light moments. As usual, the male animal being what he is, several "romantic" overtures came to _____, my roommate, and me. Men, bless them! One came right out and asked me to spend the night in his room Saturday night after the dance. His friend was to spend the night with _____. Now how could they think that we'd be receptive to a weekend of bedding down with men we hardly knew? Maybe they thought that away from home we'd shed our morals, like a butterfly shedding its cocoon, and emerge free as the wind. Fun and games are fine, but fortunately, or unfortunately? _____ and I just aren't the type to play to that extent.

But we really had fun foiling our "pursuers'" little ego trips. After the dance, we went right to bed. The phone rang umpteen times, but we didn't answer it. The next morning at breakfast, we demurely offered an excuse of "being dead to the world" after the dance. After the banquet Sunday night, two handsome gentlemen knocked on our door just as we were preparing for bed. Imagine their shock when I appeared at the door not as a svelte glamour girl, but as an old fogy all done up in hair rollers. There was unmistakable shock registered on the gentleman's face, whether it was from surprise or disappointment. I'll never know. But I'll never forget that look, and he'll probably never forget how ugly I looked. Thanks for the attention anyway, fellas. We love you. Kiss! Our weekend would have been dull if you had ignored us completely. Men are definitely necessary, in one sense or another.

All in all, self, it was a delightful weekend. But like a drunkard facing reality after a binge, I plunged head-on into reality the minute I returned. Before I could get to sleep good, we got home around two, and the phone rang for Steve at 5:30! Reality hit me over the head, and it hurt. Being awakened for someone to go up to Donna's and give them a message at that hour, and hard on the heels of my sweet interlude, sent me reeling back into the everyday nitty-gritty that is life for me. Having to be at the bank at nine o'clock for food stamps didn't help matters any either. By the time I finished shopping for groceries I was in a first-rate depression. I'm not kidding. I actually spent every spare private moment I could find crying. The contrast was just too much, I guess; one minute freedom and laughter—the next minute aggravation and scrounging again . . . Anyway the memories of this past weekend will hold me together for a while.

Guess what? Just before I left for Michigan, I wrote a letter of support for Senator Weicker to the editor—in response to a letter criticizing the senator as a "pompous oaf, a clod," etc. I try not to write letters to the editor, self, but sometimes I still can't help myself. It was published and evidently someone sent a copy of my letter to the senator. Yesterday, I received a personal letter, signed by the senator, thanking me for writing my letter! Isn't that something? To think the senator took time out to personally write me a little letter—a little nobody like me. Isn't that something?

Guess I'll get going now. The weather is slightly cooler; it's been "punishingly" hot and humid, and I feel something akin to vitality creeping into my bones. (Please weary old self, come to life completely so you can propel me into a job and off welfare. Please, please, please. . . .)

Naturally, I took a few minutes out to meditate and contemplate life and my puny little existence. Those two days gave me an all too fleeting peek at the good life—a tiny taste of what the wealthy take for granted and grow bored with. Just think, self, I had to scrimp, scrape, and squeeze to the nth degree to take that $60 trip, and feel guilty for doing it in the process. After all, there are so many ways I could have spent that $60 right here at home for necessary things. And yet there are people in this world, right here in the United States, who leave $60 tips, and that little week-end, which was heaven to me, would have been a drop of snot off their nostrils. It's just not fair! I want some of that "good life" too, now! This minute smidgen on my taste buds has whetted my appetite for something better than this dreary existence I'm trapped in. Why should the balance of my good days be spent scrimping and worrying and crying—and grabbing gratefully at scraps? I deserve a full helping of laughter and joy and living. I'll have it too, self, you just wait and see—I'll have it! I've paid my dues in excess; now life better deliver something to me! And I'll not settle for microscopic drops and tidbits anymore. I want it all! To heck with poverty vows!

> Later Self,
> Richelene

9–6–73

Dear Self,

I joined a winter bowling league last night after all. I so enjoy bowling in a league that it's hard for me to give it up because of dirty maneuvers. So we shall see what we shall see this time. Our team consists of three blacks and two whites. If the whites can keep their prejudices in check I can certainly do the same. One thing I might as well accept, to get away from racial conflict (or any kind of conflict) I'd have to go out of this world. Since I'm not quite ready for that yet, I'll keep trying to love them.

Anyway, we won all three games, which will put us in bad graces from the beginning. I was hot last night, I bowled a 527 series.

Self, I was supposed to go to the clinic in Hartford yesterday but didn't make it. I will go next week. This afternoon I go to the welfare department for my periodic review. That's some social work isn't it self, we'll see? Oh well.

Later,
Richelene

Later: Review accomplished. This time I saw a lady social worker. The last few times it was a man. My lady was very friendly. She profusely complimented me on my pant suit, made out of $1.50 worth of on-sale denim. And she talked longingly of getting out of social work and into something else, but she can't find anything that pays enough.

Oh yes! "Don't forget you have to register for work when Jeff gets in school all day."

"Oh, yes, I know." End of social work for the next six months.

9–7–73

Dear Self,

Here I am again—smack dab in the middle of a fresh dilemma. All of a sudden daughter #1 jumps up and decides she's going back to school to complete high school, and then on to nursing school. Beautiful! But who is expected to get trapped in the house with two overactive, scrapping little boys? You guessed it. Me.

Now monstrous old me must decide whether, as a good mother and granny, I can bear it or not. If I do, even though my back has had me dragging all year, I'm beautiful and big-hearted. If I don't, I'm just a selfish, cold, heartless, lazy old ogre.

Self, what would you recommend? Do I have an obligation to sacrifice my time and such energy as I can rake, scrape and pray up for this daughter of mine that couldn't wait to get into what she's into? The daughter who, at fourteen, screamed at me to leave her alone and let her make her own mistakes? The daughter who told me she hated this house and couldn't wait to get away from it, and yet proceeded to settle right in my lap with her two babies? Do I have a moral obligation to stretch myself this far when this child, disguised as a woman, could have gone on to school unencumbered? Must I, on principle, allow myself to be further encumbered just at a time when a ray of light seemed to be dawning on the horizon for me? Am I being punitive or uncaring because of feel it's her responsibility to stay home and take care of her own children now that she has them? She's only 18. In four years Kenny will be in school. She's got ample time to pursue her ambitions.

The plain truth is this girl is sick of being tied down at home with two babies and wants the freedom she gave up prematurely. And I want the freedom I feel I'm entitled to now. I feel for her, but I'm just not able to chase after those two little rascals every day. I'm just a tired, weary, aching almost-forty-year-old woman who, frankly, has had it with raising children for now. Love them, yes, but physically, psychologically and emotionally unable to bear the constant responsibility of caring for them at this stage. I gave my best, my all, to my seven. If it wasn't good enough, at least I tried. Now I'm drained. Depleted. What more can I say?

Sincerely,
Richelene

9–9–73

Today was one of nature's masterpieces. She painted this day perfect. The day was sun-splashed, yet it has sloughed off the oppressive heat of the past two weeks, replacing sweat and discomfort with a warm, zingy glow—that special tingle that only autumn manufactures sifted softly through the air and settled all over me. It felt good to be alive, and I fairly floated to the shopping center. Fall's magic chased away my little worries of this morning like sunshine chasing rain.

Now maybe I can sum up August, when the sweltering heat of the sun and the heat of my anger melded one day, and joyous happy times balanced the scales the next. All in all August reemphasized to me that the good and the bad always go hand in hand, or follow each other as night follows day.

Fall always makes me feel alive, but nostalgic. Tonight is cool, soothing. I feel good but a little misty. The long hot summer is past and the mellow glow of autumn reminds us that these precious days will all too soon fade into the cold, cold winter. Wicked old winter will swallow these delicious days like a guppy eating its young. And we'll shiver in the cold, but for now, and as long as they last, I'll revel in these days that are finer than wine.

Later,
Richelene

9–10–73

Dear Self,

Monday morning! Monday morning! The kids are off to gather knowledge, and I'm here with a sniffly nose doing the usual. What a zesty, zingy, singy sun-sparkled day! On days like this I feel like I could walk to the ends of the earth, but I won't. I'll amble over to the shopping center and get myself a depression in the grocery store.

Saturday night two of my girlfriends and me went to the club to hear the band Kenny plays in. I guess I told you Kenny plays guitar in a band. They're really good. Really good! The music was swinging, but we weren't. We didn't get asked to dance even once . . . sob. . . .

Where have all the old men gone?

Gone chasing young skirts, all and one,

When will they ever learn . . .

I did see a couple of my old ex-swains, but they chose not to see me. It's really funny how men that have not succeeded in bedding down certain women seem to take it as a personal affront and the woman becomes persona non grata, but that's life too, I guess. Well, self, lemme get going.

Until later,
Richelene

9–11–73

Dear Self,

Would you believe I got through grocery shopping yesterday without plunging into a depression? Maybe it was because I ran into two of my "soul mates" on the way to the store and we had a brief communion before I waged the battle of the cash register.

_____, a friend who is also fighting the good fight to deliver her four children to adulthood, as a mother-father, was one of the "souls" I ran into. But, self, she had good news to talk about. She thinks she and her husband are going to reconcile. She sees a great change for the better in him and believes they can make a go of marriage now. Isn't that wonderful? That bit of inspiring news made my day.

While we were standing there talking, a casualty of the Nixon administration's War on Poor People, whom we both know, stopped to chat. He's white and worked as a clerk-typist for OEO for five or six years—until the present administration decided to zap the OEO. Now he wanders about, lost, unable to find another job. You see, self, he suffered a nervous breakdown some years ago, and OEO was his best hope of being self-sufficient. So who was the first to go when the changes were made this year? You guessed it, the one that should have been the last to go. People who could easily find employment in private industry are still working for OEO, while my little friend walks the street. How many more in these United States, put to pasture by the Nixon administration, are walking the streets lost, hopeless, and gone back on welfare? "These are they . . ."

Talk to you later,
Richelene

9–13–73

Dear Self,

Oh, self, I hardly know where to begin, Self. White Power has triumphed again. Would you believe I'm out of my bowling league already? Late yesterday evening, bowl-

ing night, _____ called and told me the secretary of
the league called her and said our other black partner
couldn't bowl in the league. You see, self, this is a scratch
league, and the by-laws do not allow anyone with an average under a 130 to bowl in it. Since _____ finished the
summer scratch league with a 131 average, we thought
she qualified. In fact, her average was only 127 when she
went into the summer scratch league, but they by-passed
the by-laws and let her bowl with me.

In fact, one girl in the summer scratch league had a
125 average. Now suddenly they decide to stick to the letter of the by-laws. They said the summer league doesn't
count. As I understood it, any sanctioned league counts.
So we went out there anyway, trying to get a better understanding of why suddenly _____ couldn't bowl in the
league. The secretary finger-pointingly insisted they had
to go by the by-laws, and that was that.

But, self, I believe the true picture is this: I told you last
week we bowled like a house on fire and won all three games.
_____ had a 166 series, which was hot for a 127 bowler.
So the powers-that-be got shaky and started envisioning the
big money and prestige floating away from the Chosen Ones
to a team, supposedly weak, predominately black. They had
to think of some way to break up the team now, so they dug
back into the records and discovered that _____ ended
the winter league last year with a 127 average, and that's the
one that counts. I believe with all my heart that if _____
had bowled lousy last week and we had lost all or some of
those games, they would have considered us no threat and
let _____ stay in. Understand, self, she paid her sanc-
tioning fee last week and was a sanctioned member. Yet they
blithely kicked her out with no compunctions. She was
stunned into almost a state of shock.

What are these specimens of humanity called white
folks? Have they no true humanity?

Is power-and-money the all-encompassing passion that governs their lives in everything? One would think a humane group would've said, "Oh, well, since she's been sanctioned into the league, we might as well let her stay." But no, just as one of the big powers said to me a couple of years ago when I said I'd like to keep our team together even though our averages put us at a disadvantage, "Just wait till you see the money going the other way . . ."

Lord, Lord, money truly must be at the root of all evil! For the few dollars involved in a little shit-ass bowling league, they'd sell their soul to the devil (and make me lose my religion)?!! It's time for me to get out! So I walked out with _____ never to darken the doors of that den of iniquity again.

Strangely, I don't even feel a great anger, just a dull hurt; my beloved bowling, that I found so much enjoyment in at one time, has turned into a blob of gook in my hands. I suppose my anger and indignation have been exhausted over the past months of dealing with "them." They're truly rid of me now. And God bless 'em. Still, I keep trying to figure out how they (the pale-faced ones) can be so heartless, so devoid of human instincts when it comes to maintaining the status quo—in everything. And yet why should I wonder at their casualness in tossing _____ out of the league (they had already replaced her with one of their "own" last night) when they have extinguished a race (the Indians); oppressed a race (us); and snuff out lives (ours and anyone's that seemingly pose a threat to their exalted position), with the same casualness . . .

It's a funny thing; yesterday morning the song "Open Mine Eyes, Illuminate Me," a song I learned and sang in a little one-room schoolhouse in Georgia, was on my mind, in my soul. The TV is out of order, and the radio wasn't on. The grandkiddies hadn't converged on me, and the house was quiet, blessedly quiet. There was a stillness, a sweet solitude that reverberated loudly in my soul's ear. And then, from the stillness, that song came upon me, and I began singing it and couldn't stop as I went about my household chores:

> Open mine eyes that I may see,
>   glimpses of truth thou hast for me.
> Place in my hand the wonderful key
>   that shall unclasp and set me free. . . . .
> Silently now I wait for thee
>   ready, my God, thy will to see
> Open mine eyes, illuminate me,
>   Spirit Divine!

Were last night's glimpses of truth the ones the Divine Spirit was seeking to reveal to me? The truth that the white race is so deeply steeped in money and power-lust that there is no length to which it will not go in its sickness? That this race's collective soul is so sick it just might be beyond redemption unless it lets the healing power of love into its fold, and soon?

Now I think of all the letters I've written, publicly and privately, trying to touch a chord of humaneness, trying to build bridges of understanding and love, but how can a violinist strike beautiful chords if a string is broken or missing? How can a pianist play beautiful music on a piano that's badly out of tune? Maybe, just maybe, someday, somehow the strings will be mended and the piano will be tuned by the Master Tuner. Then maybe all of God's children will strike beautiful chords together. But how long will it take, Lord, how long . . .

Sincerely,
Richelene

9–14–73

Dear Self,

The dilemma I talked to you about a few days ago is resolved. Donna decided to forgo furthering her education for now and stay home with her little sons. The right decision in my, perhaps biased, opinion.

I took Jeff to the barber shop yesterday and ran into an opening for a "sugar daddy."

I let the opening close (what kind of fool am I?). An affair with somebody else's husband is not for me, as I've told you before.

But, self, I have a confession to make. Once, seven years ago, I did allow myself to become involved in a liaison with a married man. He was older, urbane, sophisticated, a well-to-do professional man. I met him when I was a broken little wreck washed onto the debris of a storm-annihilated marriage. I was lost, alone, vulnerable. My path crossed this man's at that mixed-up time in my life, and he offered me friendship, comfort, solace for the raw and open wounds that covered my battered self.

He seemed like a refuge from the storms I'd so recently been caught up in. Like a safe and restful harbor beaconing me from a stormy sea. But he wasn't. He was a storm center. The storms of fear and fury and hopelessness of my marriage were replaced by the storms of guilt and deception and ugliness. No thinking, intelligent, principled woman can enter and sustain an illicit relationship without fighting a terrible war with her true self. And her baser instincts will never win the war over her true self. She might win a few victories, but she will lose the war, every time.

Oh sure, self, this man was generous with his money, and he would have been even more so if I had allowed him to be. But my tortured self would let me accept no more from him than would make things just a little better financially for my family. That way, I felt less debased, less like a one-man call girl—for that is exactly what I was, self, a one-man call girl. When the pressures of his profession, his life, bore down, he used me as a "relaxant," a diversion from the everyday routine. And I hated him for using me that way; hated myself for allowing myself to be used. Sure, we spoke of love. It was proper and fitting to speak of love. The words "I love you" made a pseudo-cover for a relationship built on nothing more than sex, convenience, and diversion. There was no mutual respect, no real caring, no love—how could there be? And there was no joy, no celebration of our sensuality (for me anyway).

I didn't even really like the man once I got to know him. For all his exalted position in black society, to me he was merely an exploiter, a coolly dispassionate, atheistic run-of-the-mill man. He knew the war I was waging with myself, knew that I was caught up in something beyond my scope; and he delighted in making light of my moral and religious hang-ups.

After a few months of sneaking and hiding and tormenting myself over the ugliness of it all, the affair fizzed out, ran its course, with no pain on either side. Later he made a couple of attempts to resurrect our little "love affair," but there was nothing to resurrect.

And so it ended, my first and last affair with a married man. Then Norman came along, a true oasis of quiet . . . until the storms came. . . .

That one experience was enough to teach me that I wasn't cut out to play with "sugar daddies." I have to admit I've been sorely tempted since then, but all I have to do is think back on that one futile attempt to be something I was never meant to be. And I keep right on steppin'. Financially poorer, yes, but richly at peace with myself. And that's where it's at!

For now,
Richelene

9–15–73

Dear Self,

I know I must bore you with my continuous complaints, etc., about bowling. They say, true love never runs smooth, and bowling and I are having our storms.

_____ just called and asked if I wouldn't reconsider and come back to the team. And you know how sorely tempted I am to say yes, self. It's so terribly hard for me to give up this game. I've been hurting since last Wednesday night. Of course I knew at the time I was only hurting myself by quitting. But the jungle atmosphere had got to be too much for me.

Yes, self, if I really do give up my league bowling, just what recreation or diversion from the everyday routine do I have to look forward to? Life is blah enough these days. Without bowling I'd have no meaningful change of pace. What to do . . . what to do. . . .

This love affair of mine with bowling is almost like a man-woman relationship; we have our fights, yet I can't seem to live without bowling, and I can't live with it. But, oh, breaking up is so hard to do. . . .

Knowing there is no perfection in life, should I just close my eyes and go on back? Can I ever feel the same, or must I just pretend the spontaneous pleasure is there that I once felt? Can I truly give my best on this predominately white team, or should I go back and just go for self? Aim for the high average; the high game; the high series. How can I bowl on a team if my team spirit is gone? Should I just go ahead and try to forget and forgive and do what I enjoy in spite of the ugliness? Can I? The long cold winter looks pretty bleak with nothing to look forward to each week. . . . I think I'll sleep on it.

Good night,
Richelene

9–17–73

Dear Self,

I have some scrumptious news for you—simply scrumptious! You just won't believe it. Listen here, self: This morning I got up at 6:15, prepared breakfast for the tribe, and got them all out of the house on time. Even Alan got out on time, and that's an accomplishment. Then I brought the dirty clothes down, the first time my aching, belligerent back has allowed such a feat in months, and put a load in. Then I ironed a little. Then I cleaned the stove. Then I defrosted the refrigerator. Then I washed down all the contact in the kitchen. Then I mopped the floor and I am now waiting for another load of wash to finish so I can hang it out. And miracle of miracles! Not a peep out of my back. Isn't that something? Dare I hope. . . .

But, Dear Self, now I must talk softly and sadly with you for a little while. Today at one o'clock an eighteen-year-old black youth that I knew will be buried. Self, it's so sad . . . so sad . . . he seemed like such a promising young man. And now he's gone—forever. Just when life should be beginning for him, it ended. He had had some problems in school and the community in his early teens. Then he started going to the Muslim Temple and a great change for the better came over him.

He sold the Muslim paper, *Muhammad Speaks*, quietly and politely, often leaving us a free copy when I didn't have a quarter. And he went back to school and graduated this year. Then he got a job.

The last time I saw him, he had come to our home to give Donna, Steve, and I a ride to the Temple. I wanted to go just to see what the meetings were like, to get a closer view of their philosophy—not to join. Self, admittedly I'm in sympathy with many of the concepts of their ideology, but I could never worship Muhammad as my God.

Anyway, that Sunday he came to pick us up, but Donna and Steve were still in bed, so I didn't go. I looked out the window as he walked back to his car. How nice and clean he looked in his burgundy dress jacket and checked flared trousers. How proudly he walked. He looked like a man—big, tall, and strong, and he walked like a man—placing his footsteps firmly, as if he knew where he was going. In the Muslims he thought he had found the key to unlock the door to his true black manhood. And maybe he had. Yet maybe he hadn't. Maybe later in life he would have found that Elijah Muhammad was not God's messenger and he had been misled. Maybe he would have found that he could not find his true manhood couched in an ideology but only by searching out the deep recesses of himself and coming to grips with life as a human being—not as a black Muslim, nor even as a black man could he find his true place in life—only as a human being.

But he had made a good beginning—from whatever the source the seeds were sown. And I admired his struggle to grow into a man. Now he's gone; so suddenly, choked to death on beans and rice. Rich people choke to death on steak; poor people choke to death on beans and rice, but they all go to the same place. . . .

Divine Spirit, grant him peaceful rest.

Sincerely,
Richelene

9–18–73

Dear Self,

Br-r-r it's chilly in here! I just turned the oven on for a bit of heat. I was talking to _____ the one black girl that works in the Housing Authority office yesterday. She said the Housing Authority has received no bids for a contract on oil to supply heat this winter. So God only knows how long babies will be walking around with runny noses, and we'll be shivering. Oh, well, the little bit of heat I get here amounts to almost no heat anyway—so what's the difference to my family.

Self, I finally made my decision about going back to the league. I'm not. This is one of the most painful decisions I've ever had to make. But, like a marriage gone sour beyond repair, bowling has gone sour, too sour for any little droplets of sweetness to make it the same—for me. And I must divorce myself from it in spite of the pain. Maybe sometime in the future I will join another league at a different alley. But next time, like entering a second marriage, I'll know more of the pitfalls and will enter with a more realistic attitude. For now I leave it with the "warriorettes," the "blood letters." Something will turn up to put a little diversion back into my life. . . .

In today's paper I read where the head of the food stamp program in Connecticut says 40,000 Connecticut households are issued stamps at an average cost of $57 with which they can buy $116 worth of food. Wonder why I only get $90 worth (bi-monthly) for $66.50? Oh, well, maybe they want us welfare recipients to hurry up and starve to death. Anyway, I think I'll pen a polite query to the director and try to get an explanation.

I honestly don't understand how they arrive at their estimations and am curious about it.

Got to go now,
Richelene

9–19–73

Dear Self,

I didn't write the letter I was tempted to write yesterday, but guess what I just did? Dare I tell you? Yes, I guess I will since it's a secret between just you and me. I just wrote a query letter to Stein and Day Publishers, asking if they would read a sample of my letters, and hopefully publish them as a book. Oh, my goodness! It's sinking in now, that's a lot of nerve, isn't it? I really must think I'm a writer. But, self, I really and truly believe I have a message for the world that needs, is begging, to be heard.

Me and thousands of other kooks. Oh, self, I'm so queasy now. Just suppose they really do agree to read a sampling, and publish them? Wouldn't that be something? Unreal! Would I have the courage to have them published under my real name or would I use a pseudonym? Do I really and truly want to lay myself bare before the world? Or am I just on another of my wild tangents of impossible dreams?

So what! At least I still dare to dream, to hope. Nothing ventured, nothing gained. Anyway, it will be interesting to see if I get a response.

Until later,
Richelene

9–20–73

Dear Self,

It's good to be alive! This morning I'm running up and down the stairs. Did you hear me, self? Running! Somebody up there has had pity on my back. Thanks.

All morning I've been humming the "Candy Man" song. I got into it so heavy as I was making the kids sandwiches until a chorus of hums and whistles suddenly settled in my ears. It must have been contagious. Everybody in the house was singing, humming, and whistling "Candy Man." Maybe we struck a little chord of love and felt like mixing it up this morning. For quite a while now it's seemed like precious little love was being mixed up in this house.

Feeling good sure makes a big difference. Even the fact that Donna succeeded in "trapping" me with the babies a few hours a day doesn't seem so bad now. She is going to work early this week—anything to get out of the house and away from the constant patter of little feet, and chatter of little mouths, and smatter of little hands.

Our little tête-à-têtes are awfully short these days, aren't they, self? But I'll have more time to rap with you next week, I hope. I'm sorry.

Sincerely,
Richelene

P.S. I meant to tell you. Melanie decided not to go to trade school after all. I'm keeping my fingers crossed. It looks like she's growing into a little common sense. Isn't that good news?

9–21–73

Dear Self,

Last night Mrs. _____ called. The State NAACP convention is having its annual conference in New Britain this year, the end of October. The New Britain group is also having its annual banquet that weekend. Julian Bond is speaking!

Anyway, Mrs. _____ asked me if I'd serve as a hostess at some of the affairs. Now self, you know my talents do not lie in the direction of public hostessing, etc.

(not even private hostessing). Mrs. _____ knows it too, and she also knows the elite and I don't make a good blend. They don't feel at ease with me, and I don't feel at ease with them, and it's just a no-no.

Wonder why she even bothered to call on me? Whatever impelled them to decide to utilize the welfare scribe of Osgood Avenue? I can't quite figure it out.

I do intend to go to the banquet and hear Mr. Bond talk. I'm afraid that's the best contribution I can make.

Talk to you later,
Richelene

9–23–73

Dear Self,

I took the kids (Jeff and Candy) skating last night. The last time I took them, I ventured onto the floor and made some sad attempts at skating. I only fell once.

Last night I dared not press my luck with BB (belligerent back) so I sat it out. But it's really hard for me to be just a spectator at any sport. I like to get in there and do my thing.

It was kind of fun watching the kids' valiant efforts to pick themselves up and try again. You'd never guess the "kid" that stole my attention and my heart? It was one lone "kid" who was anywhere from fifty to sixty years old. This "kid" put the youngsters to shame. Round and round he floated circling the rink, graceful, keeping perfect time with the music. When the tempo of the music turned snappy he snapped to it with fast little dance steps; when it was slow and sweet, he glided around making soft turns and sways. Self, this "kid" knocked me out! He was just too much.

Now I actually know what people mean when they say they get "goose pimples" when something truly beautiful makes contact with the senses. This bald-headed white senior citizen, yet so young, was beautiful. He wore peace and serenity like a crown.

When the skating ended, he packed his skates in their bag and stepped jauntily out into the night. He thumbed his nose at the years, had his fun, and left feeling alive and happy. Each turn around the floor he stated boldly, "Sing no sad songs for me; I'm off into a beautiful sunset." And he was.

Self, my puny little descriptive powers are impotent to let you know my true feelings about that lovely, lovely episode, but I had to try to share it with you. It was just too much. I truly gazed upon that man with the same awe with which I gaze upon beautiful sunsets.

There were a couple of incidents that made me sad. But I'll push them way back. My "sunset kid" so lifted my spirits that I'll forget the sad little things.

Richelene

9–24–73

Dear Self,

You're not going to believe this, but it's true: I went to church yesterday! And you're talking about some meeting. Self, we got down and had some revival meeting. The place was rockin' and I don't mean from Rock 'N' Roll. It was rocking from Jesus, rocking for Jesus. My people took their burdens to the Lord and left them there yesterday. We sang them out, cried them out, laughed them out, clapped them out, and shouted them out! We let them all hang out! Jubilation! Jubilation!

Was I surprised to see a little pianist with inch-long false eyelashes, and loads of hairpieces; a swinging organist; and the drummer that played with the band Kenny plays with. They made beautiful music for Jesus while the choir sang for Jesus. And it was a hallelujah chorus indeed. They made a joyful noise unto the Lord.

The preacher outdid himself in admonishing us to change our sinful ways (and I'm not being facetious). He preached until his soul was on fire, and the sweat like drops of blood ran down his face. "What came ye out to see?" He asked us. "What did you come to church for this morning? Was it because you had no place else to go? Was it from force of habit? Was it to criticize? Was it to socialize with your friends? Was it to get dressed up?"

Reverend, brother, I came out to get my cup replenished with the cleansing joy and spirit that only a good-old-down-home type church meeting can give me. And I got it replenished. Indeed, I did. My cup runneth over. . . .

And now to face the new week. . . .

Sincerely,
Richelene

P.S. Self, I just thought of something. Do you suppose the white folks and the "upper class" black folks can go to church and sedately worship their God because they have no burdens? Do money, position, and/or power erase all your burdens? But if people have consciences they must have burdens. The little old lady who sold Ricky that hunk-of-junk said she had a conscience. I guess those people can fly to Jamaica or Hawaii or Miami and leave their burdens there. Or they can go to Lord and Taylors and buy an Ann Fogerty dress, or go to a health spa and relax, or go somewhere and get their faces and behinds lifted, or take a tour of Europe, or cry all the way to the bank and deposit their money. There are just so many ways and places where they can leave their burdens. So they can go to church unencumbered by burdens. But I wonder if their God is really pleased with a people that can manage so well without coming unto Him with their burdens? I wonder if their joy is really complete?

9–25–73

Dear Self,

. . . bring me your sad, your lonely, your depressed . . . bring your problems to 626 Osgood Avenue (or call) . . . and I will lend you my ear. . . . And so they come! Last night at 1:30 A.M. I was roused out of a sound sleep by a relentlessly shrill phone. It was _____. From almost a thousand miles away he calls! All because he couldn't get to sleep and needed to talk to someone. Well, he said he needed to talk to me. My, my, my! It's good to be needed, but did I need to be needed at 1:30 A.M.? So what time did I get back to sleep? 4:30 A.M. And I had to get up at 6:00 A.M.! Oh, well, I said I wanted to be used in the service of the Divine Spirit. If this is one of the ways he chooses to use me, I won't complain. "For as much as ye did it unto the least of your brethren . . ."

That _____! Will the guy ever get his head together and decide what direction he wants his life to take? Why can't he take stock of himself and say, "Listen here, _____, you're supposed to be a man. Now grow up and start acting like a man."

Yet he's still drifting like the changing sands, but the changes don't seem to be for the better. He says the doctor has taken him off booze because of a kidney infection. But I can't imagine my friend existing without his beloved bottle. He must be waging a terrible battle. God, give him the desire and the strength to overcome his weaknesses and that terrible bottle.

But he says he doesn't want to give it up. He says he isn't an alcoholic and that he can handle his liquor and his life. Maybe he can handle his liquor, but he doesn't seem to be handling his life terribly well. Drifting, drifting. One job after another, one woman after another . . .

I wish I could tell him plainly to take his burdens to the Lord and everything will work out a whole lot better for him. But he, like most lost drifting people, doesn't want to hear that. Don't preach to me! I've tried to steer him in that direction before but he says he doesn't need it. Religion is not his bag. One thing's for sure, the bag he is in sure doesn't seem to be too cool.

I could lend him my ear and my shoulder to cry on for the next umpteen years, but he'll never be at peace until he looks inside himself honestly and makes peace with himself and his Maker.

Got to go now,
Richelene

LATER: I dashed downtown to my favorite shoe store before I went shopping for groceries this morning. It's my favorite shoe store because it's the only one in town where I can get decent shoes for the girls and Jeffrey at a reasonable price. By reasonable I mean cheap. I got Candace a good-looking pair of $8.95 shoes for $5.00 (on sale).

By now the salesman knows me and my "treasure-hunting" ways. So this morning, self, he confided to me that he is raising his two little children, age three and five, alone. His wife walked off and left them flat over a year ago. It just proves all over again: troubles and heartaches are no respecter of persons. Then I confided to him that I am trying to raise seven children by myself, so we had tête-à-tête about our lot in life for a few minutes. We both are still optimistic about meeting that "special someone." He smilingly offered that he goes to Parents Without Partners meetings and affairs. Saturday night he has a blind date. Maybe she'll be the "someone special." I hope so. I know it's beginning to sound monotonous, my always wishing and praying for happiness for others. But, self, I just can't help it. I've known unhappiness. And I feel everybody deserves a fair share of happiness, especially some people.

Anyway, we both agreed that life is better as is than raising children in a bad home full of confusion and unhappiness. And we both agreed we'll make it—as long as we keep smiling. But how long can we keep smiling? I don't know. Aw, shucks! Sure we can keep smiling, just take one day at a time—wallow in yesterday's troubles, and don't borrow trouble from tomorrow. Right, self?

Bye now,
Richelene

P.S. My salesman happens to be a human being with white skin (in case you're interested).

9–26–73

Dear Self,

What can I say? _____ called again last night at 12:30 A.M. and talked until 3:30 A.M.! My friend must be really lonely and or depressed. How much ear-lending can a person do? How much good does it really do? A little insight, compassion and understanding I might have, but I'm no psychiatrist.

I could flatter myself and say _____ is lonely for me, but I know better. The guy is just mixed-up and depressed and I'm probably the only person he knows who would stand being awakened and having their whole night shot.

A couple of years ago we had what passed for a romance, but it wasn't. We were just two lonely people that needed affection and companionship, and found it, to a certain extent, in each other for a while. We had some pleasant times together, going to dinner, movies, playing cards with friends, and dancing. But there were too many conflicts for it to grow into anything beautiful: his love of himself and the bottle; his instability and selfishness (last night he finally admitted his selfishness); his always wanting to take and reluctance to give.

And me? I do indeed like myself, but I'm not in love with myself to the exclusion of others; contradictory and changeable I am, but I am stable in the ways that count; and I have learned to give. At least I try.

He still jokingly says he thinks he and I could get along living together. I still say we couldn't. Maybe he takes my understanding ways and compassion as weaknesses he could exploit, because I went along with certain things that most women wouldn't out of compassion for human frailty (and knowing I'm not perfect myself), he might have taken that for compatibility. Maybe he really knows I'm strong in many ways, and since he is a weak man, he thinks he could use me for a leaning post. I admit he needs one.

But it can't be me, except for lending him an occasional shoulder to cry on. I can't take on any more "little boys" to raise. I know everybody has to cry on somebody, and I can't hold it against him, but I couldn't sit down and rock a grown man in my arms forever—legally or otherwise. He gave me his address and insisted that I write him sometimes. I will. But they might not be the kind of letters he's hoping for. When I take a pen or pencil in my hand I never know what might come out. But write him I will.

Have a little story in connection with last night's call to tell you later, self. Right now I have to stop, the grandbabies just swarmed in.

Later,
Richelene

THE OTHER LITTLE STORY

LATER: I was supposed to go to Hartford this morning to take the Post Office Clerk examination. I had to be there at 8:30 A.M. sharp, which meant I would've had to get up at 5:30 A.M. in order to make connections on the buses and get there on time. But after not having the heart to tell _____ to stop talking last night, and finally deciding to see just how long he'd talk, I just couldn't get up at 5:30 A.M.

But as things turned out, it happened for the best. Donna came down here crying, with a migraine headache. So I kept the kiddies while she went to the Emergency Room at the hospital for some medication. I'd fibbed on the Post Office application anyway. I answered no to the question: Do you suffer from epilepsy or back trouble? You most definitely need a strong back for that job.

Seven years ago I took that examination and passed it. A white lady and I were called in and were to be the first women in the New Britain Post Office. They showed us around, the work we'd be doing, etc. The work included lifting heavy boxes and unloading trucks. After the man explained the hours and the work, I knew I couldn't handle it with the children being so young then.

Now they're (most of them) well able to get themselves out in the morning, and I feel much stronger and more confident. And I'd lift boxes, unload trucks, or dig ditches just to be able to earn enough to tell welfare to go to hell. I'm going to call and see if I can take the examination another day.

9–29–73

Dear Self,

This world is mad, crazy, and sad. A twenty-three-year-old white youth I know shot himself to death last night. Life had become intolerable for him so soon? My God, my God! Didn't he know there was strength for the journey? He had only to call on it. Wasn't there anyone to tell him that life is worth living? However, abundant life could only be found in Christ Jesus?

I could have told him. I used to talk with him occasionally, but he never asked me. I knew he was another lost and drifting young wayfarer, but I never tried to show him the way. He probably wouldn't have listened. Youth thinks it can find its own answers in drugs, in bottles, in fast living.

His sister was a close friend of Donna's. She somehow got caught up in the drug culture. For several years she was drifting. But a couple of weeks ago she came by to see me. And she seemed rejuvenated, had her head together. She said she's enrolled in college and is looking forward to a good future. Oh, this mish-mash called life! Just when she seemed to have found herself, her brother got utterly lost.

Oh, the agony their poor mother-father has had to endure! Yes, she's one of us, a mother-father who's done her best to rear her children alone. God comfort her in her sorrow.

Peace, lost young traveler with the guileless smile.

Sincerely,
Richelene

10–1–73

Dear Self,

October just sneaked up on me, quietly, serenely. The sun is glorifying the land this Monday morning, and the air is cool, soothing to the spirit. It really was a long time from May to September, but the long hot summer finally melted like butter on crisp brown toast, and September was mellow—happy-sad, bittersweet September.

September sang its swan song on a melancholy note. Maybe it always does, I just never noticed it before. Norman called yesterday and we communicated (not talked). Once again he reemphasized his myriad excuses (reasons he calls them) for us not having been able to get together after all these years, seven of them, self, seven years. He's just been in too big a bind financially. I'll buy that. But there were ways of getting around that, even if it had meant my children would've still had to get "welfare" help. Once again he says: "Next year I'll have my bills down." Well, self, I told him exactly what I thought about the whole thing. "Next year" just doesn't come in some cases.

I still say Norman's a basically good man. Maybe that's why I've been so reluctant to really let him go. I just haven't found the quietness, peace and comfort with any other man that I've found with him. And maybe that's exactly why it was so impossible for us to get together, a big helping of such bliss just wasn't meant for this world. Then again maybe I've just been seeing with my mind what my heart so wanted to see, sweetness, quietness, beauty in a man-woman relationship. Maybe it was all just an illusion.

Anyway, I'm really and truly stepping out of the picture now, self. He said, "Wait until next year"; but too

many "next years" have passed. So this is it, self. Finis!
I'll share the letter I wrote to him last night with you:

Dear Norman,

Just lying here in bed this lonely Sunday afternoon
thinking about you, about us, about our conversation
today. You asked me to write you, but now that I've
started writing, what else is there to say? How many times
have we gone over all the pros and cons of our situation
these past six or seven years and come up with nothing?

You said something about "people not being willing to
wait." I agree that patience is a virtue. But just how long is
a person supposed to wait? Life isn't waiting for us. Let's
face it once and for all, Norman, you just didn't really care
enough for me to want to share my problems and help me
raise my children. I guess it was a little farfetched of me to
think I could find that kind of love in this day and age.
That kind went out of style a few years ago. These days
the "easy" kind of love is in style, the kind that skirts
around the hard times and grabs the pleasure.

I'm truly sorry things turned out this way. It just
seemed that you and I had so much potential for happiness.
Then again maybe it was just a little "pipedream," one of
several I've indulged in over the past few years, because I've
had so little happiness. Anyway I got Jeff out of the whole
deal, and he's pretty special, so it wasn't a total loss.

So go ahead, Norman, and find your happiness in your
own way. I'm stepping out of the picture for good now. Life
is just too short to keep trying to hold onto lost causes, to
keep hoping for that "next year" that never comes.

God knows best. I feel confident that as I close this
door he'll open a better one for me, and for you too.

So take care,
Richelene

10–4–73

Dear Self,

Busy, busy, busy! I took Candy to Newington Children's Hospital for her scoliosis check-up. The doctor says it's getting worse, so I have to take her back in three months instead of six months this time. He says these things usually take a spurt for the worse when girls reach Candy's age (eleven), and she might have to wear a brace or cast for a while.

The day was Indian Summer Supreme, so the trip to Newington on the bus and the walk up the hill to the hospital were tonic for the soul. But when I take her back in January it will be a whole new ball game. Oh, well, can't win 'em all.

Yesterday, Kenny, Ricky, and Alan were featured in a whole column in the *Herald*. They held the unique distinction of being the first three brothers to play with the New Britain High football team. Besides, they're pretty good players. Of course, they're beside themselves with pride. Just imagine their pictures and a whole column devoted to them in the paper! I'm a little proud myself—after all, I did contribute something. I contributed them, didn't I? Right on! This is a great boost for their self-esteem. And when I think of all the troubles and heartaches this game has cost Ricky, I'm doubly happy for them. I must drop the sports editor a note of thanks for the day brightener.

I bought paint to paint the living room after I came home from Newington. I'm painting it brown. Hope it's not too dark. I will begin painting first thing tomorrow morning, BB (belligerent back) permitting.

Bye now,
Richelene

10–5–73

Dear Self,

BB wouldn't let me begin painting today so I'll do it when I can. I could let Ricky paint, but I'd rather do it myself than clean up the mess after him. Maybe that's the wrong attitude, but I just can't stand to clean up messes behind other people! Since I didn't feel like painting today, I took advantage of the opportunity to write a letter that was burning in my soul.

This week, Dr. Louise Bates Ames devoted her columns to "helpful" advice for black parents. What a travesty! She merely subtly reinforced the standard myths that "all blacks hate themselves and want to be white; hate their kinky hair, etc., ad nauseam." She recommended the book *The Black Child: A Parent's Guide. How to Overcome the Problems of Raising a Child in a White World* and she took some pretty denigrating quotes from the book out of context.

As I see it, she offered no solutions to the problems of raising children in a white world; she merely set down a concoction of shit that is passé, and we didn't need to hear. So I had to write and set her straight. White folks! Why don't they tell it like it is sometimes, namely the race problem begins and ends in the white psyche and heart? That they started the whole problem, and once they cleanse themselves of their sins of superiority and supremacy, everything will fall into perspective? Oh, self, they make me so sick!

Until later,
Richelene

10–10–73

Dear Self,

I've really neglected you shamefully these past few days. But I've been so busy painting. I'm finished now and everything looks pretty nice. We still have to paint the cellar though.

Nothing of much interest happened these last few days anyway, self, so there isn't much to bring you up to date on.

Oh, yes! I got a reply from Stein and Day yesterday. They're not interested in publishing my "world-shaking" memoirs and pearls of wisdom. They'll be sorry when some other publisher snaps them up and makes a mint! So what? I'll keep sharing my experiences and feelings with you, self. If the world refuses to hear me, it's their loss and your gain.

Crazy, crazy!

Later Dear Self,
Richelene

10–11–73

Dear Self,

It's me again, in a rush, as usual these days. I had two interesting phone calls last night. One was from a former beau who got married a couple of years ago. Guess the novelty of his child-bride is wearing off, and he feels a need for diversion. "Sorry, dear. I'm not being yours or anyone else's plaything, least of all yours. You could have had me for your very own. But no! I had too many little 'appendages.' You weren't almost about to take on the responsibility of helping me raise my children. You got what you wanted, a real prize package, young chick with a good job and only one child. Now enjoy, enjoy, enjoy! But leave me alone!"

Looking at it from a different viewpoint, if I were a different kind of person I probably would grab the opportunity to show that "young chick" that we "old hens" have the flavor that makes the best dressing, that an experienced woman is like fine wine—better with age. But I'm not a different kind of person. I'm me. And I've got sense enough to know I wouldn't be proving anything. I'd only be lending myself to a mutual ego trip, signifying nothing. No way, baby, no way!

The other call was from _____. He claims he didn't get my letter. I believe he did. He just didn't want to discuss its contents. I didn't either. Maybe I was a little too rough on the poor guy. I just can't help from trying to shock him into being a man, if he's ever going to be one.

Anyway, he said he broke his left ankle (stepped in a hole); then broke his right toe shortly afterwards. That guy catches almost as much heck as I do. In fact I think he needs someone to watch over him worse than I do. It's just too bad that I'm not quite "human" enough to adopt him for my very own. Last night he jokingly said he was coming back to Connecticut and live with me. I replied, "I don't need another little boy," and he got very insulted. Oh, well, what you gonna do?

Last night I wrote a cute little poem for a neighbor girl for her English class.

Talk to you later,
Richelene

10–15–73

Dear Self,

Off we go into another week. Washing the dishes this morning, the view from the kitchen window momentarily intoxicated me. Yellow and gold, orange and red, burgundy and brown sun-splashed trees beckoned to me from the mini-mountains across the way. But I cannot answer the call because fences on either side of the highway keep me from indulging my yearning to inspect all that beauty close up. And it saddens me. It saddens me so that I don't have the transportation or means to get out somewhere where nature usually paints masterpieces of perfection like the Mohawk Trail in Massachusetts, even just a ride out into the country around here or taking a leisurely hike through the woods would be tonic. And I'm saddened more because in a very few days all that glorious color and splendor and pungent bitter-sweetness will be gone, leaf by leaf, and all I've had were a few meager glimpses. A pretty tree here and there as I walked to the store, this morning's view from the kitchen window, brief glimpses of beauty, bits and pieces—scraps. Is this to be my portion in life always?

All year I've been telling myself and anyone that will listen, "Wait until next year. Next year it's going to all fall into place and life is going to open up for me, for the Mitchell family." Hope, the substance of things hoped for, the evidence of things not seen. No, that's faith. Faith, hope, and charity, the recipe for a successful life, but the greatest of these is charity. Love, do I truly have these necessary ingredients in my life? Hope—yes, I have hope. Faith—I have faith. Charity—puny and insignificant though my expressions might be, self, I have charity. Not enough, no, but it is there. And if I could only stop the world's darts from penetrating so deeply, and stop rubbing my wounds, I know I could be a vessel full of charity. I will keep trying to be what I should be.

Ricky is home from school this morning. He got his left shoulder dislocated in Saturday's football game. Three or four weeks ago his mouth was smashed, but he won't give football up. I've accepted it now and look at it this way: Just suppose his obsession was for drugs or liquor or stealing or sex or some other thing that would keep him at the police station instead of the hospital. Wouldn't I prefer being called about football injuries to being called about any of the above offenses? Yes. So his obsession with football brings him pain and possible disfiguration—it's only himself he's hurting (and me). If his obsession was for any of the other things I mentioned, he'd be hurting other people as well, and so I've finally accepted the facts. It's better that he get rid of his hostilities, aggressions, etc.; through the socially acceptable medium of football. God, in his wisdom, does know best.

Time is slipping away, self, so I must run now.

Later,
Richelene

P.S. Got a reply from Dr. Louise Bates Ames today. She's disappointed that I didn't find her columns addressed to blacks helpful but said she'd like to use excerpts from my "interesting" letter in her column soon. Self, doesn't that kind of prove once more that I've got something to say that needs hearing? I'm sure she being white didn't like much of what I said. But, in fairness, she probably had to admit there was some truth and a viewpoint worth sharing in the letter.

10–21–73

Dear Self,

I guess you think I've given up my little communications with you. I haven't. For one thing everything has been dreadfully uneventful the last few days. For another, I've been feeling so doggone lousy. BB has me dragging again. Today is beautiful. It's Sunday, a warm October Sunday. Instead of being somewhere basking in nature's glory, absorbing soul food, here I am lying in bed feeling sorry for myself. It's been so-o-o long since I've been com-

pletely free of pain, except for an occasional day or so . . .
Oh, well, so what? Why should I waste pity on myself
when our government seems to be fast falling apart at the
seams and Israel and Egypt seem bent on wiping each
other off the face of the earth. Problems, problems. Man is
such an evil, ornery, mean, greedy, unsatisfied creature!
Will we ever learn to love, to live and let live?

The other day some one wrote that no one ever wrote
a poem about October. That's not true, of course, but this
particular October is more beautifully gorgeously scintil-
lating that I think I'll write a poem about it. Don't laugh:

October

Warm sun sifting through a sieve of tingling air,
Cooling breeze wafting through
    fast changing trees.
And suddenly yellow and gold and burnished red,
    color our awakening eyes.
Leaves made tired by summer's heat flutter
    open to behold
    beauty stroked gently by nature's brush.
A masterpiece!
Now hearts keep time with autumn's song,
    bittersweet melancholy voices
    taunting summer, teasing winter,
    lulling senses into sweet reverie soon to be broken
    by icy fingers.
We will not weep for what is yet to be.
Now the golden days embrace us, whisper softly
Come close to me,
    cling to me,
    savor me . . .
I am October.

How's that for poetry, self?

While I was beleaguered by BB these past few days I read E. Frederic Morrow's *Way Down South Up North*, a beautiful tribute to his parents. Their determination that their children would not occupy the niche in life cut out for them by the white man was something to read about! And indeed their five children did rise above their prescribed roles in life. But in the epilogue Mr. Morrow admitted per se that although he had sat with kings and mingled with the mighty, he had still been seen by the whites he mingled with as "a superior nigger" and not just an American. And even now he sees total acceptance of black people in America as a "someday, someday" probability. I see it as an almost "no way, no way" fact.

Sure, self, there will always be blacks that are above the norm in intelligence, talent, etc., who will reach the mountain top and get a glimpse of the promised land, but they'll still be "superior black men or women" or "superniggers" in the eyes of white America.

And it will be a long, long time—if ever—before they can walk in the promised land as free human beings unencumbered by the burdens of the white man's bigotry.

I tried to read George Jackson's *Blood in My Eye*, but got nowhere. It's just not my speed. Maybe it's because I'm so thoroughly convinced that only a revolution in the hearts and souls and minds of white people can bring about the sweeping changes needed to free us. As long as whites are imprisoned in their walls of hate and bigotry, they'll keep us imprisoned in the ghettoes.

But if they ever break free, then their eyes will be opened and they will be able to see that all of God's children must be free or no one is free. If! Who, Lord, can break down those walls and penetrate the hearts of the white masses? Will you raise up someone to do the job?

One man's victory (Mr. Morrow's) is inspiring to read about, self, but the plight of the masses is not changed.

That's where the war is, and it ain't almost won! It will never be won unless that revolution takes place in the white folks' hearts. Someday, someday? Or no way, no way?

Sincerely,
Richelene

10–25–73

Dear Self,

Teeth-gnashing time again! Lost transportation cards calling for money for bus fare to school, refrigerator sounding like the Russians are coming calling for money I don't have to buy another dilapidated hunk of junk, oldest daughter mad at me because I admonished her to think before she speaks . . .

Good times hurry up and get here before I flip my poor, harangued lid! I can't even think—that *%!©!! old refrigerator is making so much noise. And it's giving me a headache. And there's no way I can get it out of here before next Thursday, "Check Day," and just barely and by the skin of my teeth then. Oh Lord, how long!?

One small ray of hope: Today I received my rating from the Post Office Examination I took on the fifth of this month, 77.5. I passed it. Please, Dear God (I hate to beg like this), please, please let the Post Office call me and give me a job. It's my only hope of being able to support my family without still having to depend on "welfare." Please, please don't let them think that just because I'm forty years old, and a woman at that, I can't handle the job. Maybe I can't, but how will they know (or I) unless I'm given the chance to try? Please, Lord, put it in the Postmaster's heart to give me a chance at the job. That's all I'm asking for), all I'm begging for, just a chance!

This eternal scraping, scrounging, and humiliation of "welfare" has been my lot too long now, Lord. I deserve something better now. I've earned something better. You know it, and I know it too, Lord. I'm crying now, Lord. Have pity on me and wipe away my tears by letting me get this job and once again lift my family out of this quagmire of helplessness and despair. Let me once again know the fulfillment and satisfaction of knowing the roof over our heads and the food in our mouths is paid for by the labor of my own hands. Let me walk proud and free once more, unburdened by the weight of ill-begotten "charity." Give me the strength to set an example of self-sufficiency for my children once more. Not self-sufficiency without you, Lord, but the independence that only you can give. Thank you. Amen.

Sincerely,
Richelene

10–27–73

Dear Self,

I'm feeling down, down, down. I'm sick, sick, sick of this dreary dead-end existence. I'm sick, sick, sick of being stuck here in this junk-filled house with no outlet, no money, no nothing. Sewing machine out of order; TV out of order; refrigerator out of order; stove just making it; winter coming up with its necessities; and no money in sight to repair, or replace, or buy anything! I'm sick to my soul of scraping, squeezing, and scrounging.

I just made up my mind about something, self. I'm going to look for a job. A full-time job, and if I find something, I'm saving the money to buy some kind of jalopy to get around in—Welfare Department be damned! They can arrest me or whatever they want to do in the interest of my "welfare." I cannot and will not take this God-forsaken rut I'm in any longer.

Just suppose the Post Office does give me a job; how would I get to work? The buses aren't running at the hour I'd have to go to work, and I wouldn't be able to afford a taxi every morning. Just how does this "Welfare" Department propose for us to raise ourselves up by our bootstraps when we're squashed down on every turn? You go out and work part time and they take part of that and then raise your price for food stamps again, so you profit practically nothing, in addition to neglecting your home and children.

Where is the help, the justice of it? Unjust laws, not in accordance with the laws of God, were made to be broken, and these "welfare" laws that keep us groveling in the dirt are unjust. They strip us of our dignity, our humanity, our very life, and doom us to an existence void of any life.

Is being unable to take my family to church, to McDonald's, skating, bowling, for a ride in the country, to football games, to a drive-in movie—is this living? No, it's existing—barely. But this is what the world wants those unable to pay their way, for whatever reasons, to do. Exist. To them, we have no right to live. I say I have a right to live. I've existed for much too long. And now, dammit! I'm mad! I'm going to do what I have to do, and I'm willing to take the consequences.

Later,
Richelene

P.S. If President Nixon can spend $125,000 of the taxpayer's money for a swimming pool, I sure ought to be able to buy a four- or five-hundred-dollar used car if I work and earn the money, and an old second-hand refrigerator.

10–31–73

Dear Self,

The last of October, and it's a downer—rainy, cloudy, and mournful. And I'm mournful too. Wonder when something will happen to renew my physical, emotional, and spiritual strength? It better happen soon, or I might be sunk. This was to be my year, the year when things were going to begin to spiral upward. Admittedly, things haven't gotten any worse—there's no farther down to go—but there are only two months left in this year. My miracle better hurry up and happen because I'm giving up after this year. You hear me, self!

I'm giving up if things don't change for the better by the end of 1973. If life doesn't begin for me at forty, I refuse to fight a futile battle any longer. I will give up all hope, and when hope is gone, we die for sure.

How many years can one go on hoping for that bright tomorrow? How many dark nights of the soul can one endure when daybreak never comes? How many blows can one take without crumbling finally? I figure I've fought a pretty good fight, self. Still I see no real signs of victory. Every time I think I see brief flickers of light, just over the horizon, they are obliterated by darkness. How many more hills can I climb and how many more valleys can I plod through without becoming utterly exhausted? I'm close to the point of utter exhaustion now. Once I thought I could be like Job, "Wait until my change shall come." Well, doggonit! My change just might almost be here, but it seems it will only be the "change of life!" What will that profit me but a bit of release from monthly discomfort?

Oh, well, enough of self-pity for today. Tomorrow is "check" day. We'll be able to eat again for a few days. Be thankful, girl!

Bye self,
Richelene

11–1–73

Dear Self,

"Check" Day! Trying to stretch $10 for the last two weeks sure depleted me emotionally.

We just made it—except there was nothing for breakfast this morning, the first time the kids ever had to go to school without breakfast (Lord, deliver us from Nixon). I hope this isn't the beginning of a trend. Oh, well, now they'll have something to reflect on when they grow up and are financially successful. The experience might even give them a little character.

It sure didn't do anything to improve my character. In fact, the experience is driving me faster to criminal activity. We will not sink that low again. Tomorrow I'm going job hunting. If I find something, I intend to deliberately and willfully defraud the "welfare" department, for the welfare of my family. And I could care less about being arrested. In fact, being arrested for a good cause should be an interesting experience.

Will keep you informed of the developments, self.

Sincerely,
Richelene

11–2–73

Dear Self,

This, the second day of November, I, Richelene Mitchell, am coming out of the depression of a week or so. Maybe the good dinner we had yesterday did it. Cheese and macaroni, pork chops, cabbage, corn bread, and banana pie. It's been ages, self, since we had pork chops. Yesterday I "splurged," and bought one pork chop each, and one extra for grabs, enough sausage and steak to fill our cavities, bananas, oranges, donuts, real chicken (not gizzards or wings) and a few other "extras." Of course, it shot my food budget. The bill was $58 instead of the allotted $45.00. But just think what it would have been if we each had two pork chops and a real piece of steak? Oh well, if I get some work, we'll manage to eat until "check" day again. It was certainly nice tasting meat again.

_____ called again last night. Would you believe he's trying to make me believe he "loves" me, and always did? It never ceases to be amazing how we distort that poor, precious little word—love. How, self, can that person even fix his mouth to say such a thing when he never did a thing to indicate real love. He never asked if the children or I needed anything; never asked if there was anything he could do to help; never once evinced any real concern for my total well being; never once took the boys to a football game or other outing; never once inquired as to whether we had enough to eat; never once . . . Why go on? Suffice it to say he never had anything but his own interests at heart. "Welfare" was supposed to take care of our interests.

And he's egotistical enough to think I loved him (or still love him). What basis would I have for loving him? Would his good looks and "charming" personality be the basis in his mind? Not for me, baby. You've got to come from farther than the exterior for this jaded heart to link up with yours. Granted, I've got enough charity (agape love) to keep from telling him what I really think of him. I feel he's suffering enough just trying to live with himself, and I won't pour salt on his wounds. But love? That person would have to be regenerated and born again completely before I could love him with a man-woman love. I've given him some suggestions as to how he could make himself and his life more lovable, livable and attractive, but I seriously question his ability or motivation for truly trying to alter his insides. He still he keeps coming back for more, so maybe he really does want to improve.

Gotta run now,
Richelene

LATER: Here I am again, self. Back from my half-hearted job hunt. First I went to Manpower, the temporary agency. I worked for them several years ago. The last job they sent me to, I quit after the first day (as a matter of fact, I quit most of the jobs they sent me to after the first day). I almost died of boredom. I sat there all day and did nothing but cover the phone, typed one item, and watched the clocks: and prayed for five o'clock. But if they call me, self, this time I'll die trying to stick the jobs out because we so desperately need the money. The truth is, my record with them is so spotty, they might not call me at all.

Next I checked with another agency about temporary work. The interviewer wanted to know why I didn't want a full-time job. I couldn't tell her, of course. How do you tell them you don't want their little chicken-shit boring schoolgirl jobs when you are a woman, a mother-father, the sole support of a family of seven? How can you tell them you refuse to work an honest week's work and not begin to clear enough to support your family and still have to hang your head in shame and cash a "welfare" check? How can you tell them you feel every mother-father that must work to support her family should make enough to support them whether she's a dishwasher or a teacher? How can you tell them you'd rather suffer the demoralization of total dependence on "welfare" and nurture and guide your children at home than be a half-worker, a half-"mother-father" that can give your best to neither role, until such time as you can throw the "welfare" crutch away completely? How can you tell them you feel it's morally wrong for a mother-father who knows how to work and is willing to work her fingers to the bone, to exhaust herself and stagnate her brain in jobs that require almost no brains, because the jobs she qualifies for are rarely given to black women? And if the "Equal Opportunity Employers" already have their token quota of blacks in good jobs, the job seeker is out.

But I don't need to tell you all this. You see "something" in my eyes, written on my face, but you don't quite know what it is. I'll tell you. It's cynicism, bitterness, hostility, pain, and I don't really want to be out there among you any more. I can't stand the pseudo-friendliness or the cold indifference. I can't stand the friendly little ethnic jokes, the curiosity over my hair, the cattiness.

So since this little "something" settled in my eyes, a reflection of what's in my soul, I can't openly smile and talk and joke with you and act like we're just all human beings. You don't want that. You want me to act slightly niggerish so you can feel more white. You put this "something" in my soul, in my eyes, and now I'm messed up. I won't blame you for all of it, but you contributed much to my being the "mess" I am now. This soul has been wounded too much, and these eyes seen too much now, and they don't like much of what they see. So what am I to do? I can't put blinders on. I wish to God I could!

Once, I was such a sweet, nice, acceptable little nigger. I had only to walk in a place, flash my brightest smile, open my "sweet" mouth, and the job was mine. When I was eighteen, I walked into a VA Hospital and they "accepted" me (the personnel manager's words) as a secretary. Less than a year later, he offered me a better job; they would "accept" me in Physical Medicine Rehabilitation, he said. They merely hired the white girls, but the blacks had to be "accepted." Since then, I have been "accepted" in other white collar jobs because I was so "acceptable" a nigger. But the years have diminished my "acceptability," dimmed the smile and made "bitter" the mouth.

When I look at you behind your desk, I don't want to smile. I want to cry. And when I open my "bitter" mouth, I want to tell you some truth, but I try to manufacture a few weak smiles and mumble a few inanities to make you think I really want your little nothing jobs. You know I don't. You sense my disinterest. You know I'm hoping you won't call me. So you probably won't.

In the meantime I'll keep praying for the Post Office job, a job where if I work like a man to support a family like a man, I'll get paid like a man. For that I could endure monotony, boredom, stagnation, or whatever I must endure. The sum total would be security, independence, respectability, life.

11-3–73

Dear Self,

If I don't plunge over the brink soon, I don't know why not! Or maybe I have already and just don't know it. Last night was one more revelation—of what? Pain? Hopelessness? Or one more opportunity to draw on His strength? Despair?

Where do I begin? I agreed to baby-sit for the grand kiddies while Donna and Steve went to the college to see WAR, a rock group, last night. Imagine my shock when little Steven came out of his bedroom, his eczema badly infected and running a temperature, and not a drop of his medicine in the house. Now just yesterday, my addle-brained daughter bought a new rug, pictures for the wall, and they paid $12.00 for tickets for the concert. Yet they couldn't spend $4.60 on medicine for that baby. Lord, help those two nitwits who're caught up in responsibility beyond their mental or intellectual scope. And just how much can I do, self? How much do I have left over to give of myself or any other thing, after coping—somehow, with these six here in the house?

Anyway Steve gave little Steven a hasty kiss as he sat in my lap crying, and was off to see WAR. See what I mean about "love"? They both would probably swear by all that's holy that they "love" those two babies! Yet they could ignore little Steven's obvious suffering and run off to play, a twenty-five year-old "child" and an eighteen-year-old "child" off to play, parents in name only.

It's so sad. Donna is such a re-run of her father until it breaks my heart. So irresponsible in the ways that really count; she would take "money" that was needed for shoes for the kids, or the rent, or other necessities and blithely take the kids to an amusement park or spend the money for some other trivial thing. As for Steve, he contributed two children to the world that he didn't have presence of mind enough to love, and his constant refrain was "I love you, I love my kids." Yet how can I judge him and Donna. Maybe some people just don't have the inborn talent for loving, just as some people have no inborn talent for cooking, for singing, for art or whatever.

Maybe Steve inherited his inability to love responsibly from the father who deserted him when he was six months old. The pressing thing now is can they be taught to love responsibly? Can one who has no inborn talent for singing be taught to sing? Or one who hasn't the gift for painting beautiful pictures, can he be taught to paint like one who is naturally gifted? No. One might make a lot of noise and think he's singing, while he has no talent. The listener would say, "Cut out that noise!" One who thinks he can produce art might only be dabbing paint on a canvas. The observer would say "Ugh! That's horrible!" Yet and still, if the person trying to sing hears music in his own soul, or the painter sees beautiful images on his canvas, can anyone else say that he's not singing or making art? So I guess they do love their children in their own way (Donna and Steve). They just don't have the talent for responsible loving. After all is said and done, I guess we all try to love in the best way we know how, to the best of our ability. If only they just don't add any more babies.

After they left last night, I gave Melanie money to run over to the drug store, a long night walk she shouldn't have had to make, to get some medicine. When she wasn't back in an hour and I couldn't stand little Steven's misery any longer, I called a police cruiser and took him to the emergency room at the hospital. This pointed up once again how desperately we need a car. Of course, the doctor there chewed me out because cases like Steven's should be continuously followed by their own doctor and are not cases for the emergency room. I know that. But what else could I do? Where else could I have taken him to try to get some relief for him? He grudgingly gave little Stevie a shot and informed me that, barring a miracle, the poor little guy might suffer like this until he's in his teens.

So now, in addition to the miracle I'm already working on, I've got to start praying for another miracle. Lord, you heard my tears mingling with that poor little baby's last night. As I rocked him in my arms, you know I felt his pain as acutely as he did. And it's not right for a little fella like him to have to suffer so. It tears me apart to see him crying, "My leg hurts," and scratching until he's bleeding and raw. And you know his mother and father are too wrapped up in themselves to really care for him as they should, too unconcerned to really comprehend his suffering. And, Lord, I'm just too tired and belabored to take him over completely. If I could, Lord, you know I would. I'd take him and love him and watch over him the way he needs to be loved and watched. He's suffered so long. His two little years have been spent suffering. So now I'm placing the matter in your loving hands. Touch him, Lord. Heal him. Make him whole and happy like all little boys should be. Amen.

Sincerely,
Richelene

P.S. I got the money I spent on Steven's medicine, and for a taxi home, back from Steve and Donna. Not because I need it that desperately, but to try to teach them some responsibility. And they're a little peeved at me because I took little Steven to the hospital and made another bill for them. And listen to this self, after being medicated, little Steven's legs are so much better today you wouldn't believe it. But do you know what that hopelessly demented girl said to me? "That medicine doesn't do any good. He's still scratching. Even Jo Ann (Steve's sister who is a nurse) said the medicine doesn't help." Trying to convince that child of something she doesn't want to be convinced of is like arguing with a brick wall. So I didn't try, even though she sees the evidence with her own eyes. I've decided that I'll buy some of his medicine and keep it here. Then I'll check him every day, and the first signs I see of a flare-up, I'll start right in medicating him. I've always known that the medicine works real fast, but even though I've told them a thousand times they should keep his medicine in the house as steadfastly as they keep food in the house, it hasn't penetrated. So I'll just have to do it myself. But I'm not really counting on the medicine, self. I'm counting on the miracle. He's going to get well, just wait and see.

11–5–73

Dear Self,

   Yesterday was another of those blah-stuck-in-the-house Sundays, at least until late evening. Then _____ called and said she and her daughter were coming over to visit with Donna and me for a while.

   I hastily ran a comb through my hair, threw on some clothes and went up to Donna's. The four of us spent three very pleasant hours playing Bid Whist. Our daughters won three games and we won two. I'm really glad they beat us, or Donna would have exhibited her "Sore Loser's Complex," and it's not pretty to see. It would have spoiled the whole evening. For a while there it seemed _____ and I would never get good hands, and we lost the first three games. I told them we'd just have to play all night, because nobody was going home until we won at least one game. So our luck changed, and we won the next two games. Who knows, we might have won more, but it was time for _____ and her daughter to go home.

   This fits in with my determination about life now. I know I told you I was giving up if the "big event" doesn't happen by the end of this year, self, but you know better than that. Just as I was determined we were going to win some games last night, I'm determined not to travel all the way through life losing. And mark my words, self, I'll not depart this earth until I win. I'm going to overcome all these "unlucky hands" that fate dealt out to me. All these years of hoping, praying, agonizing, are not going down the drain like so much sewage. Just as I sit down at my sewing machine and make beautiful garments out of marked-down remnants, I'm going to make something beautiful out of the remnants of my life. I won't go down without fighting. I'm going to win!

Later,
Richelene

11–7–73

Dear Self,

I don't think I told you about the birthdays, November 4, 5, 6, and 7th. That's right! Kenny, November 4th; Alan, November 5th; Melanie, November 6th; and Candy, November 7th! Isn't that something, self? We really lined 'em up, eh, self? So we've been having birthdays in this house for the past few days. Today is the last one until November 17th, mine. Then that momentous number will come up for me—forty! I'm looking forward to it with great expectations in view of what is supposed to happen. Life, you know, begins at forty.

I tried to get all of the kids a little something for their birthdays. Now, I'm you-know-what—flat broke. Self, I made Candy the cutest fake fur midi-coat. It's cranberry, trimmed with navy. It has a hood, a belt, and navy fur around the cuffs and hem. Really warm looking, and actually warm, I hope. I gave Kenny twenty dollars for sneakers and a haircut. Alan got some socks and a pink shirt (which he said he wanted, but will never wear. It's too decent looking for his taste); I bought some double knit material for Melanie, to make a pant suit in her sewing class at school. And, in addition to the coat, Candace is having a slumber party Friday night.

She and some of her friends painted the cellar, in preparation, and you just wouldn't believe the mess they made! Now I'll have to buy some paint and paint the floor and stairway to cover the mess they made. Lord, give me strength!

Oh, self, I'm so-o-o disgusted. I could be working today, if I had a car. Manpower called yesterday with a job for me, but it wasn't on a bus line, so I couldn't take it. I could just cry. As bad as we need the money! Damn, damn, damn, damn, damn!

Oh, well, since I couldn't take that one I hope they won't call again before the weekend. This will give me a chance to try to undo the damage in the cellar to a certain extent, and do some more sewing. The truth is I'm getting sick of having to sew. Absolute necessity is causing me to sew more and enjoy it less. Someday . . .

Must run now, got to walk over to the shopping center for the paint and my supermarket depression.

Later,
Richelene

11–10–73

Dear Self,

My second miracle seems no closer than the first. Stevie is so sick, so swollen, so utterly down with his allergy that it's heartbreaking to see. What in the world is causing this? How I wish I knew what to do to help him. What to avoid to keep him from such distress?

Anyway, Donna and Steve are taking him to the doctor again this morning. The doctor says he might have to hospitalize him. I hope so. Then maybe they'll find out what he's allergic to and we can steer him clear of those things in the future.

Everybody, including the doctor at the hospital last week, has been asking me why I don't just take him over. Now I know I have to. Maybe he won't fare any better with me, but at least I'll watch him closely and try to head off such suffering as he's enduring now. It just breaks my heart to see that poor little fella in the condition he's in. I must try harder to help him.

Just when Jeff is at a stage where it's beginning to look like I can soon cast welfare off, this little child, my grandson, needs me at home to watch over him. Oh, well, it'll all work out. It's got to!

Later,
Richelene

11–12–73

Dear Self:

Last night, _____ called and asked me to go out with her. I knew it was because she was mad at her husband and needed to talk, so I went. Besides, I wanted a few more slices of life to share with you these last few days of 1973. So-o-o we went to the Elk's Club in Hartford. A little hole in the wall swarming with different varieties of life as it is in the ghetto. Dear self, it was a replay of the same old sad song. Women out in groups looking for that "right" man, or a diversion, or a break from the monotony of a dull, lonely, manless existence, and the usual contingent of down-and-out men, or diversion seekers, looking for a woman they could use for the night, or for as long as they need them.

Enter a tall, coffee-and-cream complexioned man, extremely handsome. His expensive beige knit suit fits him like a department store mannequin. On his arm is draped a black soft-looking, maybe cashmere coat. Beige patent leather shoes complete his ensemble. He ambles by, eying the crop of females. His bleary brown eyes soon light on me and he extends his hand for me to dance. I accept. He keeps me on the floor for several long numbers, talking persuasively, setting me up, he thinks. Finally I insist on returning to my seat. He seats himself beside me, his charm going full force. I turn to talk to _____. Sensing his plan for the evening is not going to pan out, he gets up, leaves, and dances several times with seedy-looking characters. I decide not to dance any more and sit there observing the crowd. The women, young and older, writhe and shake in time with the music. I feel increasingly out of place and foolish sitting there, nursing my whiskey sour.

Finally, the too loud band winds down, and the revelers file out into the night. The women, some talking a little too loudly and laughing a little too forcefully, go back to the demands of their lives. Some to face that new week of stretching a few welfare dollars, trying to barely sustain their families; some to dead-end jobs that barely sustain too many children; some back to a husband or lover, more albatross around their necks than husband or lover; some, the desperate ones, possessively hanging onto the arms of men they picked up. Some of the men go back to the streets to loiter, no longer daring to hope for that call from some factory tomorrow morning; some not even caring any more; some make their way back home to take out their still unabated frustrations on an innocent wife and/or children; some, the lucky ones, to the warm beds and arms of the desperate, searching women. All the men and the women have broken the rusty, languid chains of their dreary existence for just a little while. And their burden seems a little lighter, more tolerable. And so they go home. Wherever home may be.

Sitting in the car, _____ and I talked. At least she talked, and I listened.

After all, what can you say to a young wife coming into maturity and suddenly growing into the realization that she is tired, gut-weary of shouldering the burden of an alcoholic husband? What can you advise her even though you faced the crisis of your own unsalvageable marriage at just about her exact age and decided it was more important to salvage what could be salvaged—your children and your sanity (such as was left) than to try to hold together the unrepairable scraps of a legal contract? How can you suggest that she should do the same when you know the soul-splitting

392 ■ DEAR SELF: A YEAR IN THE LIFE OF A WELFARE MOTHER

pain that is inflicted on both parties when one has to take such action? What can you say to her when she sees first-hand the sad spectacle of women alone, lonely, searching for an elusive something most of them will never find? Can you in good conscience encourage her to join that unhappy throng? On the other hand, can you encourage her to try to ride it out and risk damaging her children or herself beyond repair? Do you tell her about the lonely nights, the empty days of a manless existence? Or do you let her in on the re-wards, the peace of mind, the freedom to be yourself, the room to grow, the quiet environment for your children? What can you tell her of the prospects for finding a better man out there when you've looked over and examined a fair share of the crop of "eligible" men and found most of them woefully lacking for a woman who is searching for security, solidity, stability, a shoulder to lean on?

Ah life! How long, how hard, how fruitless the search for strength, for substance . . .

My God! How _____ echoed my own now-dying yearnings of past years: "I'm tired of making excuses, of holding up this man. I want somebody I can lean on for a change!" This is the universal cry of the black woman, ex-cept for the star-kissed few. Of course _____ has to make her own decision. I hope and pray she'll make the right one.

Most of all, I hope and pray her husband will find the strength to forsake that eternal life-wrecker, alcohol. I hope and pray he'll evolve into the shoulder she can lean on for a change and spare her that futile search . . .

Self, I can honestly and with equanimity state I'm no longer searching. If there's a man somewhere in this world just for me, our paths will cross at the appointed time. I'll still go out with the girls from time to time, but it will be strictly for diversion. I'm not looking for any man. There's a peculiar peace now where there was despair. I wish for _____ and for all my groping, searching sisters, that peace. I pray for the time when more of our men will be solid and strong. I pray that our society will allow them to be. Not so much so we can lean on them, but so that it will be unnecessary for them to lean on us.

Sincerely,
Richelene

11–14–73

Dear Self,

Three more days to go to the big four oh (40). . . . Today, I lay in bed for a while after I got the kids off to school. Little cyclones of thoughts whirled through my mind, whirling dervishes of still unanswered questions, pieces that still float at random without fitting together. I am me, for better or for worse, but now what do I do with me? In what direction do I aim me? Do I sit tight and wait for that big Post Office job or do I get on out there and take one of the schoolgirl jobs. Well, what do you know! The phone just rang. It was Career Girl calling offering me a part-time job at New Britain General Hospital from one to five every afternoon for a couple of months. I guess I'll try it and see what develops. Wow! I'll just have time to take a quick bath and get there. Gotta run!

Later,
Richelene

11–15–73

Dear Self,

Here we go again, the usual routine. . . . I'm not going back to that job. Oh, self, what's the matter with me? Is there any hope I'll ever be able to get back out there and work for a living? Or have I just really gotten lazy, limping along on this welfare crutch? Have my "self-sufficiency" muscles atrophied?

I'm so disgusted with myself. Here's the story: The job was as a receptionist, typist, with lots of phone work. Okay. You know I can't stand messing around with phones. Okay. The typewriter was one of the newer electric ones. Okay. You know how hard it is to sit down, cold, to an electric typewriter when you're used to pounding a manual. So the whole afternoon was one big tension producing mess for me. I actually feel they should make me pay them for messing up all that letterhead and carbon.

I hate to be such a quitter, self, so all night I wrestled with: Should I go on back and try to get used to it? Is it actually worth it? Four hours a day at $2.25 per hour comes to $45.00 a week, before deductions. I ask you, self, is that worth the aggravation to my nerves, the running up that long hill to the hospital, and getting arrested finally? Does it really make sense? If it were full time, and I was clearing close to a hundred dollars a week, maybe I could save enough to get a car and a few things for the house before they arrested me for unreported income, but at this little job, I'd have to work almost three weeks before I could save a hundred dollars. By then someone would have reported me to the "welfare" department, I'd be arrested, and it would all be for nothing. Like a thief getting put in jail for stealing $3.00.

And who should I see first thing after work but an old "friend" of mine who caused me a great deal of distress when Jeffrey was born. She reported to me that another "friend" had spread a rumor that Jeffrey was fathered by a man who I had taken away from his wife, etc. etc. The other "friend" said the "friend" that reported to me actually started the rumor. Be that as it may, the old "friend" just might have taken it upon herself to see if I was report-

ing my working at the hospital to the "welfare" department. Oh, well, maybe I should just sit tight and wait for
the Post Office to call me (Lord, give them a little nudge,
please) and better our condition in the right way.

Sincerely,
Richelene

P.S. I came to work after all. So I'm one of the little fish
who will get caught for nibbling on the worms, while the
big fish that eat us little fish swim free. It's 2:40 P.M. and
I'm already out of things to do, except answer the phone.
I'm praying hard and keeping my fingers crossed that
these phones and I will come to a workable truce, because
I think I'm going to try to stick it out until Christmas, or
until I get arrested, whichever comes first.

11–16–73

Dear Self,

The school nurse just called. Alan isn't feeling well and
is coming home. She mentioned his record of tardiness and
wants me to try to get him out mornings on time. I told her
I try mightily to get him out on time, but success is minimal. So he'll perhaps go through life being one of those
perennially late persons. What can I do about it? Once
more I reemphasize I can't get inside him and make him
over, nor can I recycle him and get a speedier edition. I can
only work with what's there to the best of my ability. It's
sad that he has these inherent weaknesses, but that's life.
Lately he's been singing a little ditty: "I love my
mother, she brought me in this world." Whether this is his
original creation or a real song, I don't know, but it saddens
me when I hear him singing it. Why? Because, self, I know

I didn't do him any great favor by bringing him into this world, especially, in view of his inheritance. Now, more and more, I find myself hating his father for thrusting all these poor innocents into the world, and I hate myself for having been the weakling I was and allowing it to happen.

But what's done is done. Now I can only pray for strength and guidance to do the best I can to shape and mold them in spite of certain liabilities. If they fail to be strong enough to make it, I only hope I'll be strong enough to help them along in the ways they need help. Just as Alan says, "I brought them in this world," and if the world fails them, I only hope I don't. I'm all they have. And they're all I have.

Sincerely,
Richelene

P.S. Me again. At work bored. Will I be able to stick it out until Christmas, or until I get arrested? The kids are all telling me it's not worth it. Jeffrey says I should wait until he's twenty before I get arrested so he can have the money to get me out of jail. Besides, he says he'll be upset and cry if I go to jail now.

Am I really committed enough to my protest to withstand the embarrassment of being arrested? Or am I now trying to rationalize and quit this job because I'm so bored?

I was reading some articles in a psychiatric journal earlier this afternoon (incidentally, I'm working for the heads of Psychiatry, Surgery, and several other services). I can see by the information in these articles that I really am a mental case. Of course, I've always known it, but I can cope pretty well, and I'm not dangerous to myself or others, so why turn myself in? Yet, anyway.

I almost didn't make it to work today. The mailman was late, and I had to wait so I could get the "check" and the food stamps before the banks closed. He finally came, and I made it to work, fifteen minutes late. I hate to be late. Well it's almost that time, so I'll wrap it up and get home to the kiddies.

11–17–73

Dear Self,

Today I am forty. Four decades ago, I, Richelene, came onto the stage of life. They say I entered squalling lustily, wet and red. "What shall we name her?" My mother asked my five-year-old sister. "She looks like a bip to me," the little girl said. And so they called me Bip throughout my childhood, though my Aunt, sensing that I was part and parcel of Richmond and Lurlene, announced that I should be named Richelene.

Today Bip, the child, departs for good. And, Richelene, the woman, emerges full-blown. Life begins today for a woman, a natural woman, birthed through forty years of pain and travail. Today, I know there are no bit players on this stage of life. Everyone is a star! How do I assess these four decades in which I've starred on this vast stage of life? Can I evaluate the process of growth in words? Let me try:

THE FIRST TEN YEARS

These were the happy years. The tender tine spent in affinity with nature, in tune with the universe. On a little farm in Georgia, I wandered through green pastures and romped through woods of pine trees and honeysuckles reveling in nature's splendor.

Here I saw firsthand the miracles of births, the creation of new and growing things, from pigs to cotton. I was a participant in these miracles, sowing seeds in freshly ploughed earth, and then watching the little sprouts shoot up from the ground and grow into food or rent. I remember travailing with my mother when my little brother made his entrance in the next room. Of course, I was too young to really appreciate the miracle of being so close to all this new life, but even then the essence of it all gave a vast dimension to my life.

These ten years I was free, dreaming high-blown dreams, feeling all life was mine to capture and embrace. Nothing was impossible. I would grow up and reach whatever star I put my hand to! Being poor, black, and southern, how did I get that way? I mean how could I dare to think the world was mine? I don't know, except that I had a good and gentle mother and father who watched in love, pride, and dignity, and gave their children a sense of worth, and so the unbound years of learning, growing, and dreaming passed.

THE SECOND TEN YEARS

Life began unfolding some of its more profound questions in this decade, questions for which I groped for answers. Now it was time to begin working, and I shelled peas and snapped beans in the white folks' kitchens and washed and ironed their clothes and cared for their babies. It was time for me to start thinking on life, to look to some of the whys and wherefores, to seek religion. I'd heard of God, heard that He was real, but where would I find him? And so I opened the book of life, the Bible, and sought to find the risen Savior. "I am the Way, the Truth and the Life," He told me in His book, and I believed this with every essence of my young being. If I walked in His way, believed His truth, I would find life, abundant life. I accepted Him, and vowed to forever walk in His way. I asked no questions, I simply accepted Him.

During this decade I was transplanted from the gentle quiet of shady green pastures onto the grimy ghetto streets of South Philadelphia, and the transformation shocked my sheltered nature. So suddenly my sensitive ears were assaulted by crude language that made me cringe inside, and I saw a poverty much worse than any I had endured on the little sharecropper's farm in Georgia.

At least we had a richness of spirit, but here there was a spiritual poverty, spiritual death, that masqueraded as sophistication and gaiety. It was here that I first learned of the sad spectacle of mothers alone drawing a welfare check, and jumping from one sorry lover to another, adding more innocent lives to suffer. It saddened me.

And, one of the paradoxes of life, it was in the City of Brotherly Love that I truly became acquainted with bigotry and prejudice. How strange that the South, which spawned the inhumanity and indignities heaped on the black race, had spared me the realization that my race was a handicap. Thrust into the world of whites at school in the North, I first found out that the world was not mine. It was the white man's. I was merely an interloper, competing in a world where the deck was stacked on the side of whiteness. But I finished high school in the City of Brotherly Love, then moved to the Land of Lakes, Michigan, and worked. Here I allowed boys into my sphere of life for the first time and blundered into matrimony.

THE THIRD TEN YEARS

Ah, that third decade! This was the tumultuous, almost indescribably mixed-up time.

Babies, fighting, hopelessness, fear, fury, pain, hate, and love. I'd best not disturb the memories of those years.

These were the truly anguishing years, years pregnant with pain, yet promising a birth of better days. Promise always lurks behind pain. So I lived on the promise behind the pain of that third decade.

THE FOURTH TEN YEARS

These were the key years. Now I was truly free to grow, to unwind, and to mature. The albatross of an unworkable marriage was cast off at the beginning of this decade, and a herculean weight was lifted. In comparison, the load of six children seemed like a lightweight blanket, good for warmth. But now the spectacle of mothers on welfare in Philly came back to haunt me. I cried long and hard, dried my tears and got on with the business of becoming a welfare mother.

At least it would be a roof over my children's heads and a little food in their mouths until I could do better. Best of all, I'd be able to keep them together and nurture them in peace, free of the distorting conflicts that made life a travesty for us all. For that I was grateful. During this decade, I felt the faith I'd held, like a precious jewel, slipping away from me. Like a thief in the night, time was robbing me of my most precious possession. Without faith, faith in God and faith in tomorrow, how could I endure the storms? How could I face the todays that buffeted me without mercy? Where was God? Did He really know I was here and care about my struggles? Why didn't He do something to make things better? Yes, this was the decade when questions that faded into a dark void without answers almost made me think that God was dead, as people were beginning to say. But I did endure that fourth decade, and by that very endurance I knew that He still lived and cared. I drew on His strength daily. It was sufficient. And now I see glimpses of a restful shore, small rays of sunshine are flashing through the windows of my world. The better day is dawning!

The children are growing up now, and I've grown right along with them. I watched me grow as I watched them grow. Our simultaneous growth has been liberally laced with threads of pain and happiness. Now one has flown the nest, and soon another will be ready to try his wings. I can't predict what the outcomes of their lives will be, but I hope their wings will be strong enough to take them high, and I pray that abundant life will be theirs. The process of my own growth has been an experience: Many times I've had to look inside myself and examine all the pieces that make up me. Some pieces were good, some bad. The bad and un-usable pieces I've tried to sort out and throw away. Through trial and error, I think I've learned the secret of how to love, how to live, how to give. A little understanding combined with a lot of tolerance and much compassion seems to be the way. Having learned this and trying to practice it daily, I think I've emerged into a human being.

A little bit of the dreamer will always lurk inside me, and a child-like spirit will always keep me young and wondering and growing. But today I become a woman in totality; today I am forty.

Sincerely,
Richelene

11–18–73

Dear Self,

"When I was child, I spoke as a child, acted as a child. Today, I am a woman, and have put away childish things" (paraphrase of Proverbs). Today I am a woman, and so last night, self, I went out with some of my friends and celebrated my fortieth birthday. I started to wear a black dress, but then I thought, black is for funerals, for mourning. I'm not in mourning, I'm getting ready to celebrate the beginning of life! So I wore a red dress, a color that signified life, vitality, warmth (and a little bit of devilment because I felt a little "devilish" last night). And the girl in the red dress had a lively, fun-filled time. She danced, flirted, and laughed the night away.

But then the girl came home, took off the red dress, and with it put away childish things like flirting. The season is past for that. I'm no longer a "girl" needing the attention and flattery of men of no substance. I won't even bore you with a replay of last night, self. It was the usual. Suffice it to say I've had the little season of girlish flirtations and "fun" that should have been out of my system years ago, but which I denied myself. But then it seems I always do things backwards, or the events in my life seem to conspire in an unorthodox manner. Anyway the over-age teenager is gone for good now.

The fun occasions out with the girls will be rare now. Last night I put away the pretensions of gaiety, the smiling in the faces of men who mean nothing to me and to whom I mean nothing, the laborious dancing. Henceforth, self, I will just be me. The serious, introspective me.

Sincerely,
Richelene

P.S. Donna and Steve invited me for dinner yesterday to celebrate the big four oh. And what a nice dinner it was: steak with onion gravy, mashed potatoes, green beans, corn, hot rolls, and cake for dessert. Evidently Donna didn't inherit either my dislike or non-talent for cooking. The dinner was delicious.

And they gave me the cutest sweater set: Off-white with brown and orange stripes and little dots, warm colors that I love. They also presented me with a beautiful bouquet of yellow chrysanthemums, real live flowers. They're so fresh and pretty now. In a few days they will be withered and gone. All life is like that . . .

Anyway, I'm off into those frightful forties now. Strange, but I don't feel frightened.

I feel terribly grateful. The four or five gray hairs I counted and the little lines around my eyes are testimonials of many beautiful days that have shaped and molded me into a human being (I hope). I actually feel more confident and unafraid than I've ever felt. Now I think I'm ready to seize the promise of yesterday, to move in positive directions that will lead to real fulfillment.

Until later,
Richie

11–20–73

Dear Self,

I'm pooped! You wouldn't believe yesterday. I got up at 6:15 A.M., got breakfast ready, got the kids off, cut out and made a pantsuit for Melanie, did four loads of wash and hung them out, got a call to come to work an hour early, which I did, got off from work and scooted to Newbrite Plaza and bought material to make Candy a pantsuit, which she claimed she absolutely had to have to wear to a Thanksgiving pageant tomorrow morning. I made it, then fell into bed.

I had a restless over-tired night and an "episode." I got up at 6:15 A.M. tired and out of it and started thinking I couldn't possibly make it to work today. I will though. I'm going to get going on a more productive path now if it kills me. I've got to. The time is past for rationalizing and lollygagging.

Yesterday, the girl I work with asked if I'd like to work at the hospital full time.

She says if something opens up, she'd be happy to put in a good word for me. If something is offered me after I complete this assignment, I will try it. The start to self-sufficiency must be made somewhere. Let's face it, other than the Post Office, there is nowhere I'll get the salary I need, and I can't stagnate on welfare forever. So-o-o I guess I'll have to be realistic and readjust my thinking on the subject of working. I still say I'm not cut out for secretarial work though. I don't have the personality for it.

Self, I guess, I won't have too much time to wax poetic and philosophical with you these days. But I'll share with you as I can.

Sincerely,
Richelene

11–22–73

Dear Self,

Thanksgiving Day. The morning dawned gray and damp. But the clouds lifted and now the day is bright and warm. The sun is kissing us intimately for perhaps the last time before the chill of winter days sets in. All the children are at a football game, some playing, some observing. I'm here getting the turkey ready, and all the trimmings. Little Stevie and Kenny are keeping me company.

Now seems a good time to think on my blessings and thank the Good Lord. So I am. Thanks, Lord, for all the blessings of life, as it is, for me and mine. And give everyone, everywhere, a goodly portion of health, happiness and love.

Sincerely,
Richelene

(AT WORK)
11–23–73

Dear Self,

One of the girls in the office just told me about an open-ing for a secretary in the Mental Health Clinic. How about that? If they did hire me there, I'd really be getting close to home. About six years ago I went to the Mental Health Clinic for one session. At the time I was still terribly mixed up and unhappy over finding myself on welfare, and saw no way to get off. So I wanted to learn how to live with it as comfortably as possible until such time as I could do bet-ter. After one session that seemed rather boring and point-less, with me unable to really verbalize my fears and feelings, I decided to try to work out my problems on my own counsel. And I've succeeded to a workable degree.

I wonder if they still have my records there, or if Mr. Accetullo (who I'd be working for) would remember me? If he did would he be reluctant to accept me, a self-confessed neurotic, and a black one at that?!! Of course, personnel might not select me for the job, but if they did, I do think I'd feel a little queasy for a while.

I honestly think I'd enjoy working over there among kindred spirits. At least I can empathize with the people who come there seeking help. And maybe I could give them a little comfort and warmth that someone less sensitive to their problems and needs might not be able to give. In a very small way I could contribute something while earning a liv-ing. My first job out of high school was at a veterans' men-tal health facility. I learned a lot there, and was also able to give a little something. This could be the job for me.

Until later,
Richelene

11–25–73

Dear Self,

I was just thinking about the energy crisis as it effects my immediate family. It doesn't. It feels pretty good after all to know we won't have to give up anything. We won't have to give up Sunday driving; we won't have to cut down on electrical appliances; and we won't have to lower our heat (it can't get any lower unless it's cut completely off), so things do work out for the best. Just think how hard it would be if we had had the opportunity to get used to cars, nice TVs, stereos, good heat, etc., over the years.

It's Monday morning again. I'm up to my old tricks, washing and all that jazz. I will go into work a little early so I can check on the job in the Mental Health Clinic. The girl that told me about the job and thinks I'm so well-qualified for it (good skills, personality, etc.) is young and liberal. Maybe it hasn't occurred to her that they might not "accept" a black secretary over there, but it has occurred to me. I'm too well acquainted with the wiles and ways of white folk, even in this day and age, to take for granted they'd give me this job just became I'm qualified for it. Anyway it's worth a try.

Self, I'd just about made up my mind to tell the "welfare" department about this little job, but I just can't. We need the money too desperately. My food stamps are long gone, there's no food in the house, and a whole week before "check" day. It's just impossible to feed these kids, and we're eating routine, nitty-gritty stuff, barely, not luxury items. It would be more of a sin for me to turn this little money in and let my kids go hungry than for me to break these "welfare" laws. Things will just have to take their natural course.

Well, self, I've gotta run. Will rap with you more when I have a chance.

Richie

AT WORK

P.S. I spoke to Lois in personnel about the job in the Mental Health Clinic. Evidently nothing is going to come of it because of the clause in the temporary employment contract, she says. The clause: The client agrees not to hire temporary employees within ninety days of completion of assignment. Of course, I knew the customer can buy the employee's contract if they really want them. And, of course I knew I don't really want that job any more than they want me. Secretarial work just isn't my thing. I sure wish I'd hurry up and find my thing, but secretarial work isn't it. Maybe the Post Office will send me a letter soon.

Nothing to do here this afternoon, and I'm you-know-what and ready to split! Home chores are much more enticing to me than sitting around watching the clock move slowly, slowly, slowly. But I get more respect and admiration for doing this. Life!

I called a dermatologist this morning before I came to work about removing two large moles, one from my chin and one from my chest. The one on my chest is like a cluster of grapes, and lately I've been having pain in that area. Anyway, the doctor doesn't take state patients unless they can pay the fee at the time the service is rendered. The secretary said it could cost up to $60. So I'll have to wait until I can save $60 for said removal. One more reason to not report this little money I'm making. God, it hurts to be poor!

Until later,
Richelene

11–27–73

Dear Self,

I didn't make it to work today. Thinking back on yesterday's boredom, I just couldn't force myself to make the effort today. What's to become of me? Anyway, the afternoon will be put to good use. I'll walk over to the shopping center in the rain and cash my little check and buy some food. By carefully manipulating and miracle-working, I should be able to make $24 last for food and carfare for Alan until next Monday. My God! My God! How I need a genuine miracle in my life! How I wish the tides would turn and a shower of good things would swoosh down on us so I could have a reprieve from this constant hassle of trying to stretch no money so many ways.

A little moment of sweetness and light greeted me this morning. Upon awakening and reluctantly facing the mirror, my reflection showed me all done up in a yellow ribbon! While I slept last night, Jeffrey took it upon himself to prettify me. He had combed my hair up and tied a yellow ribbon around it. He's too much! "Tie a yellow ribbon 'round the old oak tree . . ."

Richelene

P.S. Me again. Back from the store. The first installment on our car just went into bags for our stomach, in entirety. It's just so hopelessly impossible. I feel like giving up. When I called in to tell the girl I wouldn't be in to work today, she said it was awfully slow anyway. I knew that. And for the life of me I can't see why it's so much more "acceptable" to this society for a woman to sit around in do-nothing jobs away from home than it is for her to stay home and attend to her business of making a home for her children, even if she is on welfare, if that is her desire. I remember when Candace was around a year old. I was working full time, and she and all the children were going to nurseries. Candy screamed her little heart out each day as she boarded the bus that took her to the nursery. And I, with a heavy heart, went to a job where sometimes the supervisor had to scat around in other departments looking for work for us to do. It seemed so wrong, it used to just kill me. They didn't even particularly need me at that job, and my children desperately needed me at home. Yet because of foolish pride, and society's disfavor of mothers who stayed home "on the state," I watched my baby tearfully go to be cared for by who? I didn't know. The kids don't particularly need me at home now, but I never have and apparently never will fit in that workaday world out there, and I'm happier and feel that I'm still contributing something by staying at home. Oh, well, that's just my own biased way of looking at things, because I always feel so alone, so lonely in these offices peopled by women who "fit in." Maybe I'll find someplace to work where I'll "fit in" yet. I've got to keep hoping. Anyway, I'll probably go on back to work tomorrow.

11–29–73

Dear Self,

I saw a really moving and penetrating movie on TV last night. We shook, and jiggled, and knocked the TV until it decided it would be easier to show a picture than to endure all that assault and battery. The movie was *Lisa Bright and Dark*, a story about a young girl caught in the throes of mental illness; her pleas for help fell on the deaf ears of parents too proud to heed the cry. It so poignantly pointed out one of life's ironies: The wealthy, who can well afford whatever help their children need, when faced with emotional or mental illness are often reluctant to accept reality and get that help when it's right at their fingertips. For the poor, like me, even when we recognize problems in our children that we're realistic enough to want to arrest, if possible, before they progress to serious proportions, help is hard to come by. Sometimes it is beyond our reach.

But pretty Lisa did finally got the help she cried out for after a series of manifestations of her illness, like setting a fire in a young man's car; attacking her girlfriend, and finally leaping through a glass door. It was a sad story, but one with a message.

Sincerely,
Richelene

11–30–73

Dear Self,

The last day of November. Just one more month, thirty-one little days left for my prophesy of better days in 1973 to come true. 764 more puny little hours to move on to that goal of getting off welfare, to break out of this tight cloak of charity that is not love. That's such a little bit of time . . .

I'm so disgusted with myself for quitting that little job at the hospital. At least I could have tried to hang in there until Christmas. And I'm actually ashamed to tell people I've quit another job. Really, self, I'm almost tempted to lie to those that wouldn't know differently and say I'm still working. But I won't. Lies never accomplish anything except to weave a sometimes inextricable web. Yet I can't really tell them the truth of why I quit. They just wouldn't understand. After all, that was such a nice job working for the big doctors. That was a "prestige" job for a black woman, they say. "I'm certainly glad to see one of us sitting here for a change," said one woman I know.

And now I've let them down. Already several have tried to find out why I quit. I sputter around, then finally say the job was just too dull and slow. "What!" They're probably thinking. "All jobs are dull and slow at times. What makes you too good to keep a dull and slow job when thousands of other women are going to them every day?" If they can do it they have my deepest admiration. I wish I could. "Okay," they say, "What if you didn't have welfare to fall back on? You'd keep on going to a dull job everyday too."

And it's true. I'd keep on going until I began to fall apart at the seams like I did before. Only now the falling apart would come much more quickly. Then what? Who cares? Nobody! So why should I even try to explain my actions to people who could really care less. Except that they resent my being able to quit jobs and still eat (somehow) while they're still out there. And I can understand it. But I'm only trying to make it through this world in the best way I can, just as they are. The fact that I keep zigzagging from job to job is a grievous weakness, and I know it. But what can I do? If I ever found the right work, the right job, I'd stay there for the duration. I'm not lazy. I like to work, but I was not cut out to sit and decorate a desk every day.

Am I looking for too much perfection in everything? In a man, in a job, in marriage, in my children, in life? I've never thought of myself as a perfectionist, per se, but maybe I am. I've been accused of it many times. If I am, can I help it? I can't make myself over. I am what I am, good or bad.

Self, I was just thinking in the wee hours this morning. Thinking of the misery and despair the poor of the earth endure. I tried to project myself into a setting of great affluence to see if I'd be happy then. When I think of having anything and everything, materially, in this world that my heart might desire, it doesn't really appeal to me. As unhappy as I am now, at times, over my lot in life, all the riches in this world wouldn't satisfy me. I've been through too much now; seen too much pain and hopelessness. How could I be happy if I had everything knowing the masses of the world are suffering untold hardships and indignities? Having had this adventure through the world of the wretched of the earth, I'd never be content to wallow in riches. Not that I'll ever have the chance anyway, most likely.

But I do wonder sometimes how people who have everything this world offers can be happy when they know so many have nothing; they just exist until time erases them. I'd feel guilty as hell. For instance, I recently read where Isaac Hayes just bought another Rolls-Royce. Apparently he already had several Cadillacs and other cars. What for? Does he feel that his talents were given to him to make money and see how much of the world's goods he can accumulate? Does wallowing in material goods make him a man, an example for other poor black boys to follow? When I read that, I felt like writing him a letter. But I didn't. That's his thing. And it's his money. But it seems to me that those of us, especially blacks, who have been gifted with talents that place us on a higher plateau in life owe it to our brothers and sisters to throw out a lifeline, to help them up. Maybe Isaac Hayes is helping to ease the distress of some of his brothers and sisters. We just don't read about it. At least I haven't. I hope he is doing more than seeing how much material goods he can accumulate. Otherwise, he is prostituting his talents, his soul. "Freely ye have received; freely give."

Oh well, maybe the ones that have always had it all are too far removed from the despair of poverty to care. And the ones that pulled themselves up by their "own bootstraps" are too happy to have escaped to care about the ones still writhing at the bottom. There doesn't seem to be much "There-but-for-the-grace-of-God-go-I" sentiment these days. Maybe there never was. Maybe man was always selfish and greedy.

Maybe that's why a Watergate, an energy crisis, and much of the other tumult the world is in had to be. Maybe a balancing of the scales, maybe justice, is on the way.

Self, I'm not going to bore you with too much heaviness this morning. So I'll come to an abrupt end of this little dissertation.

Sincerely,
Richelene

P.S. Now I really feel foolish. I pulled another impulsive little number I shouldn't have. I might as well tell you about it, self.

In Sunday's *Hartford Courant,* there was an article about William Armstrong, who wrote *Sounder.* Seeing that he lives here in Connecticut, I got the bright idea to send him a "sample" of my writings (three letters) and have him give me an opinion on my chances of having it published. I also wanted him to tell me honestly if he thought I had talent as a writer. But he didn't. So that must mean my writing didn't impress him at all. He says he's a poor judge of others' writing. And he merely sends his books to one publisher after another until one likes it. I'm so embarrassed now, sending little chunks of my soul, my most private self, around in the mail. It's almost as if I'd stripped off all my clothes and went parading around naked. I guess I thought he'd say: "You're a genius! The find of the century! By all means send your year's reflections to my publisher. I'll recommend you!" How foolish of me. I know now I'd like to write for a living more than anything else. But that's a silly, farfetched dream that I'll just have to let die. I don't know how to write. Sure, this little daily exercise is a good, cleansing catharsis for me. But what makes me think anyone else would be interested? And interested enough to pay for the pieces of my soul, at that! How could I even want to parade my nakedness before the world?! After all, what is *Dear Self* good for except maybe a study in abnormal psychology? I'll keep sharing my thoughts and emotions with you, self, until the end of this year. Then I'll cease and desist indulging my little pipedreams and face reality.

Anyway, self, something good came of my impulsive little act. I got Mr. Armstrong's autograph. I'll keep and treasure it since I enjoyed his book *Sounder* so much. Also the movie. That's one way to get an autograph, right?

Something Cute: When I took the letters that Mr. Armstrong returned to me out of the envelope, a well-pressed ladybug fell out! Now I'm dreaming of the country and Georgia again.

12–1–73

Dear Self,

I've got it. I finally got it! I'm going to write a book. The title is *Flight from the Promised Land*. I've always known I had to write a book. But I've been flailing about, not knowing where to begin or how to do it. I know now baring my own personal soul before the world would be impossible. But I can transpose some of my own experiences and observations onto a fictional character. I've got her. Nevada Brown. It will be a story about a woman who finally tires of the deprivations and hypocrisies of the North, the Promised Land, and flees back to the Land of Promise, the South. Now all I have to do is work out a plot and start writing. I'm ready to begin. Look out world, here I come!

Later,
Richelene

12–3–73

Dear Self,

You just wouldn't believe the first two days of December. The softest, sweetest weather you ever dreamed of is ours to bask in. The sun is as bright as an Indian Summer's day, and almost as warm. And this morning the birds were frolicking as if they were intoxicated by spring's nectar. It's too much!

Today I began a new job. But this job is different. No dull office routine. It's a labor of love, a little bit of giving.

Sunday an acquaintance of mine called and asked if I would consider helping one of her friends out. This friend's eighty-five-year-old mother, a diabetic, had a stroke. The friend has to work every day and needs someone to prepare breakfast and lunch for her mother, and take her urine count. She needs someone to kind of watch over her in general. I agreed to give it a try. I've always kind of liked old folks and young children, and they've always seemed to like me. Besides here was an opportunity for me to kind of compensate, in a small way, for being a burden on society. Here was a small chance to pay a little bit of my debt and also placate my humanistic instincts a little.

But naturally the devil had to get in on the act. "You're the biggest fool," he said scornfully. "You're going to get up every morning and walk down there in the cold before eight o'clock and stay until three for $25.00 a week? You must be crazy. Those people are total strangers to you. You think they'd do a damn thing for you if the roles were reversed? What has anyone ever done for you, except try to do you in?" I pondered the devil's argument. It was logical, and there was a lot of truth in it. I'd have to leave the house before Jeff and Candace got off to school, and I'd be leaving all my work to do in the late evening. For the small amount of money involved, it certainly wouldn't be worth it.

I could go out there and get another office job and make more money. Besides, I'd be just as liable for arrest in this case as if I were making a hundred dollars a week. Like the Devil said, why bother? "You and your 'In as much as you do for the least of your brothers and sisters jazz,'" he continued in outrage. I just can't stomach people like you. Always letting people take advantage of you. You ain't got "a pot to pee in" in this world. Why are you always getting involved in other people's problems that you ain't going to get a damn thing out of, except maybe more trouble?" I tell you that old Devil had some excellent points. I considered calling the acquaintance back and telling her I wouldn't be able to do it.

Bright and early this morning I found myself sticking the little strip in the old Lady's urine and marking the count on her chart. It was negative. Good.

She's such a delightful old soul. The stroke didn't damage her thinking ability, and she's able to carry on a sensible and spirited conversation. I kind of enjoyed listening to her reminiscences, her forays into the long ago. Looking out at the bright sunshine, she was filled with nostalgia of bygone years when, down south, she sat outside in a corner by the chimney and drank in the warmth of the December sun on days like today. "And it seemed like that was the warmest, coziest place in the whole world," she mused, half to me, half to herself. I agreed. We used to do the same thing, as children, in Georgia. So it seems my dear old friend and I will have a good rapport. And in giving my small token of such as I have, much will be given to me, it seems.

Sincerely,
Richelene

12–4–73

Dear Self,

The weather is still unbelievable for December. I half expect to see roses blooming any day. What have we done to deserve this clemency, in view of the energy crisis?

Today my father went into the hospital to have a tumor removed. Mother wrote me. I feel so far removed from them, from the rest of the family that it's almost like hearing of a stranger's surgery. It's as if my little family and I are stranded out on an island all by ourselves. How did I ever get so estranged from them? How did the wall grow so high between us? Will we ever be able to breach that wall? I hope so. I hope so. . . . That's not a stranger going under the surgeon's knife. It's my father, a good and gentle Christian man. With the armor he has, I know he's not afraid, but I pray his anxiety will be soothed away and the surgery will be successful so many more good years will be his.

My time with my dear friend was good today. She spilled her urine sample at noon and couldn't muster up another one, and this upset her slightly. Other than that, she is a wonder, an indomitable spirit. She has given up six of her children to the grave, and now in the relentless grip of death and decay herself, she smiles in the enemy's face. Her toothless grin is contagious, her courage inspiring.

One would think an eighty-five-year-old woman who has endured untold hardships and survived a stroke would be cantankerous, grouchy, and mean. But she complains about nothing. Whatever one does for her, she accepts with thanks. She is sharp, spirited, alive, still wondering and curious about life. "Sometimes I wish I could trace my ancestors back," she said wistfully. "Find out where they came from, what part of Africa we sprang from. For all I know I might be a princess!" she laughed.

She is. In fact, she's a queen, a queen whose crown is a collection of years bejeweled with gems of laughter, tears, pain, sorrows, and happiness that she wears with great dignity. Imagine! Even in her twilight hours, she still feels her disenfranchisement, still wonders about her roots. What a cruel, cruel hoax was perpetrated upon the black race! Mother Africa, your stolen children long for you, cry for you! And my dear lady will take her yearnings into that dark, dark place of no return with her. She'll die lonely—an alien in a far country.

I still believe she'll smile in death's vile face to the very end. It has no power over one like her. She's made her peace. It's written in every line of her face, every movement of her body. Her victory is won. There'll be no sting. My lady is the personification of "soul." It oozes from every pore. As gentle as a lamb; she is as strong as a lioness—an indomitable spirit.

Until later,
Richelene

P.S. I'm going to paint her portrait. It will be amateurish, but I must try to capture that indomitable spirit before it departs. I don't care about the physical features—it's the "soul" I want to capture on canvas.

12–7–73

Dear Self,

This morning I want to rap with you a little bit about my Jeffrey. That little kid is too much! Last night I was lying in bed reading. Jeff usually grabs a book, Sesame Street or some other children's book, and reads along with me. Last night he picks up the Bible and says in all seriousness: "I guess I should learn to read the Bible first, huh Mom?" "That's right," I replied. Honestly I don't know how he comes up with these little gems.

Then to top it off: I haven't been sleeping well for about a month or so. So a few nights ago I put a new composition book on my night table. Then if I feel like writing while waiting for sleep to make it's belated arrival, I can reach for my composition book. On the cover are two lines: NAME / SUBJECT. This morning when I picked up the composition book, that little monkey had printed, LOVE, on the subject line. It's such an appropriate title for the little ramblings I fill the book with. Of course, I write hateful things at times, but underneath it all there's love. And I love that little Jeffrey!

Sincerely,
Richelene

12–18–73

Dear Self,

I guess you wonder why I haven't been letting you in on the happenings lately. I just haven't had the heart.

What can I say? Suffice it to say events have continued to conspire in such a way as to make me despair of encountering that miracle that 1973 promised me in glowing terms at the beginning of this year. Faith is at an all-time low ebb as of December 18, 1973; hope is almost dead, and charity is seriously questioning its existence.

So how do I get it together now? How do you manage without faith, hope, and charity? Should I go on and prepare to indulge in a brand new set of fantasies and delusions that will serve to uplift my sagging spirits throughout 1974, or must I finally and absolutely accept reality? Reality being life is just one big helping of shit served up on huge platters of trials and tears?

I could go into details of the past few days that brought me to my present state of mind: the illness of my father, and me with no money to go and visit him. The conking out of the washing machine, and me with no money to replace or repair it, and no way to get to the washerette. The snow and ice storm that will make it even harder for me to get groceries home. The painful knowledge that Christmas is here, and I have practically no money to buy the kids anything. The stupidity of my still giving of myself, my talents, and my time for people who don't give a damn about me and could care less about how I manage to work out my problems; it's been proved, but I won't bore you with the details, self. Why bother?

So thirteen days of 1973 remain. There's still time for a miracle, but I can't seem to muster up any more "hoping" strength. My stock and all my reserves are depleted.

I have learned a lot in 1973. But it seems I learned more of man's selfishness, his evilness, his greed, and his basic meanness than I did of his supposed basic goodness. There were small drippings of joy this year that I devoured like cool water from a fountain, but more often I was suffused with tears and gall. Sometimes during my reflections with you, self, I think I offered the theory that the drippings of joy we get are sweet enough to overpower the gall. But they aren't. The drippings are saccharine, a little sweet, but bitter to the aftertaste. The bitterness prevails.

Remember how I said that the things I've dreamed of and longed for most in life always seemed just one step ahead of me, like that little rabbit I chased through the fields and pastures of Georgia? Well, that little rabbit is still running, still one step ahead of me, maybe two.

And so, dear Self, in case I don't get back to you this year, Merry Christmas.

Sincerely,
Richelene

EPILOGUE

Our mother, Richelene Mitchell, passed away March 27, 1975, at New Britain General Hospital, in New Britain, Connecticut. Two days earlier, she had suffered a massive aneurysm. Perhaps that fatal affliction was connected to the "thorn in her flesh," the epilepsy that she battled so valiantly, and as far as we knew, so secretively, for the duration of her life.

At the time of her passing, she had not been blessed to see the actualization of her first miracle, her freedom from the humiliating and stultifying crutch of welfare. However, she did get to witness the transformation of our tenement apartment from "junksville" to a respectable, presentable habitat. By scrounging and stretching pennies into nickels, nickels into dimes, and dimes into quarters, she was able to finally purchase a new living room set: sofa, chairs, coffee and end tables. The very day everything was delivered and set in place and she was able to gaze upon the scene she had longed and worked so hard for, she suffered the aneurysm that would lead to her death.

Her other miracle would eventually be realized. Her little grandson, Steven, would outgrow his eczema. He would continue to grow physically, becoming a Division I college football player, and intellectually, obtaining a BA in psychology from Central Connecticut State University and an MS in Human Services from Springfield College. A licensed substance abuse counselor, he currently works with troubled youth in New Britain, Connecticut. Her other grandson, Kenneth, would not fare so well. A personable athletic prodigy, he would succumb to the debilitating combination of substance abuse, petty crime, and inadequate services that steal life from so many poor black youth.

As for her own children, we all have become productive members of society, and her prayer that none of us end up on welfare has been answered. Donna, the oldest, gave birth to another son, Anthony. She continued the maturation and stabilization that our mother noted in her writings. Learning profound lessons from both the school of hard knocks and a variety of technical and academic institutes, she would become a successful businesswoman.

As for myself, Ricky, I was blessed to complete a successful stint in the United States Air Force, obtain a master's degree in political science from Rutgers University, and having converted to Islam in 1977, eventually become one of only two Americans to graduate from the Abu Nur Islamic College in Damascus, Syria. During the better part of 1988 and 1989, I would serve as the director of workfare for the Hamden, Connecticut, Welfare Department, and I hope that I was able to perform my duties with the human touch my mother found lacking in so many of the welfare workers she was forced to interact with.

Kenneth, the guitarist, would enjoy a brief but successful music career, touring for a while with Junior Walker and the All Stars. A graduate of Aenon Bible College in Ohio, a respected Christian minister, and a licensed contractor, for over twenty years he has taught at a school for troubled youth in Kalamazoo, Michigan.

Alan, the tardy one, now a registered nurse, still has the ability to draw a laugh out of anyone, quicker than any comedian I've ever seen. Some people might view him as slightly eccentric; we have always viewed him as a nut. However, he is a lovable, charitable nut who will literally give the shirt off of his back to a needy person. He is also an accomplished martial artist, competing successfully in many tournaments before being sidelined by a bad back.

Melanie has worked in the field of human services dealing with a number of populations. She has also run a successful daycare and an online business, the Red Clay Spirit, celebrating our Georgia roots. She is the uncontested heir to our mother's singing ability, which is brilliantly displayed on the CD that is found at the end of this book. She is also a gifted writer, a fact the introduction to this volume adequately attests to.

Candy has always followed her own star, wherever it led to. She enjoyed a successful career as a super model and is a credible poetess. However, her greatest passion is working with autistic, mentally, and physically challenged individuals. She currently works at a group home in Indianapolis, Indiana.

And then there is Jeffrey, Jeff, the special one. Like so many young black male members of America's underclass coming of age in the 1980s, Jeff was influenced by the emerging hip-hop culture, its good, bad, and ugly. As a young, intelligent, charismatic, and talented DJ, Jeff was introduced to the glitter of night life at too young an age. Unlike many, he was blessed to receive a wake-up call before the call of the streets totally seduced him.

For Jeff, that wake-up call was the murder of his best friend, Clarence, who was shot in the head at point blank range as they walked shoulder to shoulder, departing from a night club on a cold New Britain street. Shortly thereafter, Jeff would join the Army. A veteran of the 1991 Gulf War, and a recent graduate of Pace University, he has enjoyed a successful career at Verizon, where he currently serves as a switch room technician.

Though one could certainly find a more accomplished group of siblings, we have not done badly for a collection of underclass urchins with all of the odds stacked against us. No alcoholics, no drug addicts, no one incarcerated, no one unemployed, and five of us stably married for more than twenty years. I can proudly say this is a testimony to the dedication, wisdom, perseverance, and sacrifices of our mother. Then she lived for us, and now, in unique but very perceivable ways, she lives in us.

As for our father, in our individual ways, we have all made our peace with him. For me that was an especially painful process. However, as our mother frequently remarked, "With God, all things are possible."

Like all books that deal with the intricacies of human relationships, this one has its fair share of secrets that we would prefer to remain hidden. However, these writings were meant to be shared, and their power is rooted in their brutal honesty. For our mother, the writing was cathartic, and for us children, and our father, the reading will prove the same, and in the cleansing there is healing. While we may feel that we have been laid bare before an oftentimes unforgiving, overly critical world, what our mother has courageously exposed of herself in these pages dwarfs any of our concerns in that regard.

For all of us, whoever we may be, our ability to contribute to the reformation of the world lies, in part, in our ability to be honest with ourselves, to see our faults and try to correct them, to understand our strengths and try to develop them, and to recognize our people and try to love them. In her brief, sometimes torturous life, against the daunting odds and challenges the reader is now familiar with, our mother, Richelene Mitchell, struggled to do just that. As a result of her efforts, all of our lives have been forever enriched.

Imam Zaid Shakir,
1–11–07